USBO

BIG SPOTTERS GUIDE TO NATURE

Internet links

There are lots of fun websites where you can find out more about nature. We have created links to some of the best sites on the Usborne Quicklinks Website. To visit these sites, go to www.usborne-quicklinks.com and enter the keywords "big spotters nature". Here are some of the things you can do on the internet:

- Keep an online nature diary
- Find out which flowers grow near your home
- Design a tree and find out how it would survive in different climates
- Identify mushrooms in an animated game
- Watch video clips of bee dances

Internet safety

The websites recommended in Usborne Quicklinks are regularly reviewed. However, the content of a website may change at any time and Usborne Publishing is not responsible for the content of websites other than its own. We recommend that children are supervised while on the internet.

Usborne Publishing is not responsible and does not accept liability for the availability or content of any website other than its own, or for any exposure to harmful, offensive, or inaccurate material which may appear on the Web.

USBORNE

BIG SPOTTER'S GUIDE TO NATURE

Christopher J. Humphries
Department of Botany, The Natural History Museum

Esmond Harris
Director of the Royal Forestry Society

Peter Holden
National Organizer of the Junior Section of the Royal Society for the Protection of Birds

Anthony Wootton
Richard Clarke
Alfred Leutscher

Illustrated by Hilary Burn, Annabel Milne, Peter Stebbing, Trevor Boyer, Phil Weare, Joyce Bee, Chris Shields

Consultants:
Richard Scott
Derek Patch, Director, Tree Advice Trust
Harry Pepper, Advisor, Tree Advice Trust
Dr Margaret Rostron

Contents

Bugs & insects

Mushrooms & fungi

Animals, tracks & signs

How to use this book

There are thousands of plants, animals and fungi in the British Isles and other parts of Europe. This book will help you identify some of the most common, and a few of the rarer ones too.

The guide is divided into six sections: flowers, trees, birds, insects, fungi and animals, tracks and signs.

Identification

Each different kind of plant, animal or fungus is called a species. All the species in this book have a picture and a description to help you to identify them. An example is shown below.

Keeping a record

Next to each picture and description is a small blank circle. Whenever you spot a new species, you can put a tick in the circle to remind you of what you have seen.

Useful words

On pages 360-367 there is a list of words that you may not have met. Look here if you read something you don't understand.

Name and description of species

➡ Scarlet pimpernel

Grows along the ground. Flowers close in bad weather. Black dots under the pointed, oval leaves. Cultivated land. 15cm tall. June-Aug.

Where to find species

Average size

When to see plant in flower

Circle to tick when you spot this species

➡ Flower descriptions

Most of the flowers that grow inland are arranged by colour, to make it easy for you to look them up. There are also separate pages where you can find out about some common plants that grow in water or by the seashore.

The last line of the descriptions tells you the months you usually see each plant in flower. The rest of the plant can often be seen at other times of the year.

To find out more about identifying flowers, turn to pages 20-26.

You can find out more about spotting trees on pages 27-37.

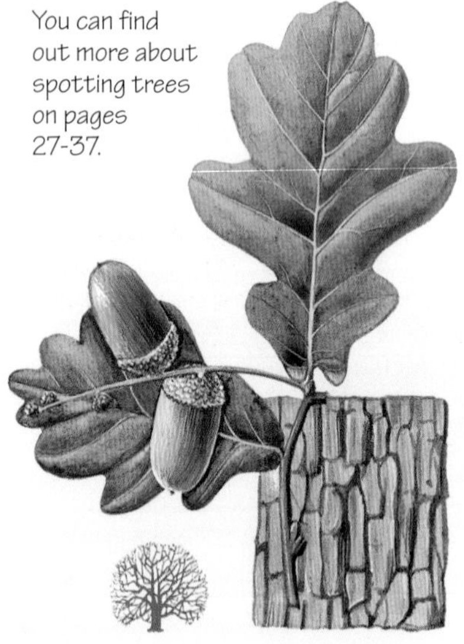

⬅ Tree descriptions

Next to each tree picture, you can see its bark, leaves and fruits and sometimes its flowers as well. A small picture next to some trees shows how they look when they lose all their leaves in winter.

Bird descriptions

You'll find similar birds grouped together, so for example, all the finches can be found on the same pages. Some descriptions have extra pictures to help you tell very similar species apart.

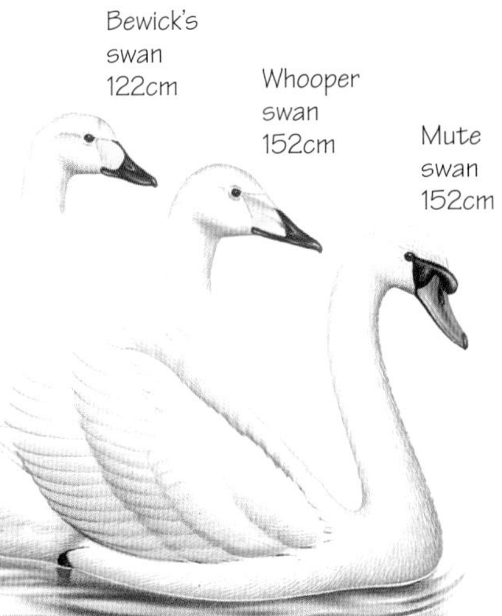

There is more information about looking at birds on pages 38-41.

Insect descriptions

With some birds and insects, the male ♂ and female ♀ look different. In this case, both sexes are illustrated and identified by their symbols. Most of the insects are shown much bigger then they really are. Look at the measurement to check their real size.

Small white

♂

♀

♂

♀

Turn to pages 42-45 to find out more about insects.

➡ Mushrooms & fungi descriptions

The fungi are grouped by their appearance so that when you spot one, it's easy to find in the guide. Many of them are illustrated with a cross-section so you can see how they look inside.

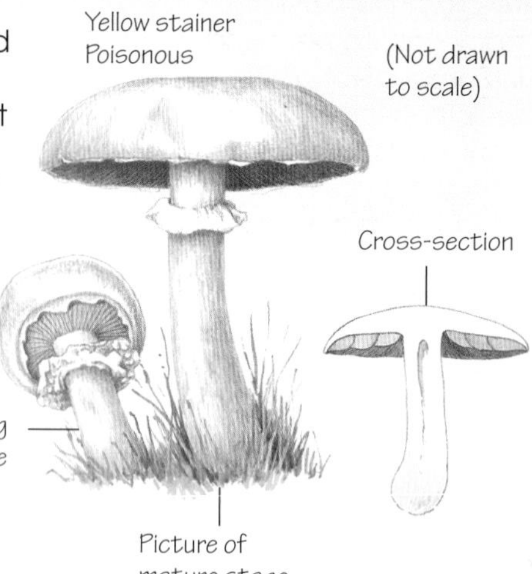

Turn to pages 46-49 to find out more about fungi.

⬅ Animal descriptions

Some mammals and birds have an outline of their track next to them. This will help you identify animals by their prints, even if they are no longer in sight.

An average size is given for each track. If the male and female of a species look different from one another, the symbols for male ♂ or female ♀ will be used to show you which is which.

Fallow deer

To find out more about spotting tracks, turn to pages 50-53.

What lives where

The species in this book can all be found in Europe. Not all the species that live in each country are in the book, and some are not found everywhere in Europe.

Some species are more common in one country than another. A few animals and plants will be very rare in the British Isles, but you can keep an eye out for them when you visit other European countries.

The green area on this map shows the countries covered by this book.

Scorecard

At the end of this book there is a scorecard, which gives you an idea of how common each species is. A common type scores 5 points, and a rare one is worth 25 points. If you like, you can add up your score after a day out spotting.

Some species may not be common where you live. Try to spot them if you go on holiday. Other species are rare in the wild.

Species (name)	Score	Date spotted
Barberry	15	26/01
Bark beetle	15	
Barnacle goose	15	20/05
Barn owl	20	
Bar-tailed godwit	15	
Bats-in-the-belfry	15	27/08

You can fill in the scorecard like this.

You could count rare species if you see them in a garden or on television.

When and where to spot

When to go spotting

The best time to go spotting is in spring and summer when plants are flowering and many animals are breeding.

Winter is also a good time for spotting birds, especially early in the morning and at dusk. It is also surprisingly easy to identify trees in winter, by looking at their leafless outlines and the way their branches are arranged.

A place to live

Animals, birds, insects, plants and fungi are almost everywhere, which makes spotting them a good hobby, no matter where you live. The places where plants and animals live are known as habitats. If you go away from home, you will be able to see new species when you visit new habitats.

Towns and cities

If you live in a town or a city there are plenty of places to go spotting. Try looking in parks, gardens, churchyards, playing fields, or see what you can find in waste places, and along canals and rivers.

In the country

The countryside contains a huge variety of habitats. Fields, hedgerows and woodland are particularly rich in things to spot. There are plenty of things to find in bleaker and wilder places such as moors, mountains, marshes and seashores, too. Lakes, ponds and streams are also home to a wide range of plants and animals.

Do not disturb

When you go out spotting be as quiet as possible. It is important not to frighten or disturb any of the wildlife you find. For example, it is illegal to disturb breeding birds, their nests or their eggs.

Make sure you don't touch any of the animals you are trying to identify, or pick any plants or fungi. It's better to leave them growing where everyone can enjoy them.

Spotting safely

- Always take a friend or an adult out spotting with you and make sure you tell someone else where you are going.
- Wear comfortable clothes and shoes, suitable for outdoors.
- Never go into water, even if it looks shallow.
- Don't use logs or stones as stepping-stones as they may move.

What to take spotting

It's useful to take the following things with you when you're out spotting:

- this book
- a notepad and a pencil, so that you can record your finds
- a tape measure or clear plastic ruler, to measure the things you find
- a magnifying glass, so you can examine individual flowers and insects
- a camera to take photos of things you see
- binoculars, if you have them, for birdwatching

Keeping records

It can be useful to keep notes of the things you spot, and you might even decide to make a nature diary. You could draw a picture of the species you have seen, make a cast of its tracks, and note down when and where you found it. Jot down how long or tall it is, as well as its colour, markings and anything else that takes your interest.

You can stick photos, maps, feathers and leaves into your nature diary.

Robin
Curlew feather
Jay sketch
29TH AUGUST 2011 IN THE GARDEN
WEATHER - SUNNY AND WINDY
BIRD
HOW MANY?
WHERE?
BLUE TIT
1
ON FEEDER
HERRING GULL
5
IN SKY
JAY
1
ON GROUND
OBSERVATIONS:
Saw jay picking up acorns from the ground. It ate about five and must have been stuffing them in the food pouch in its throat. It then flew off with one acorn still in its beak. It was probably going to bury the acorns in the ground as a food store for later.

Include the date.

Stick in sketches too.

Add observations.

Measuring plants and animals

The plants and animals in this book are not drawn to scale, but the average size of each species is given in the description beside it. The measurements are given in millimetres (mm), centimetres (cm) or metres (m). The pictures below show you how they are measured.

Birds and insects: total body length (including tail but not legs)

Butterflies, moths and dragonflies: distance across wingspan (W.S.)

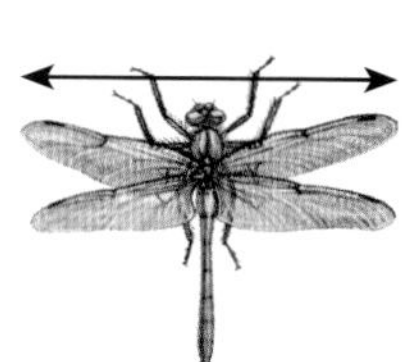

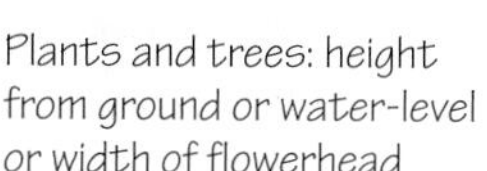

Plants and trees: height from ground or water-level or width of flowerhead

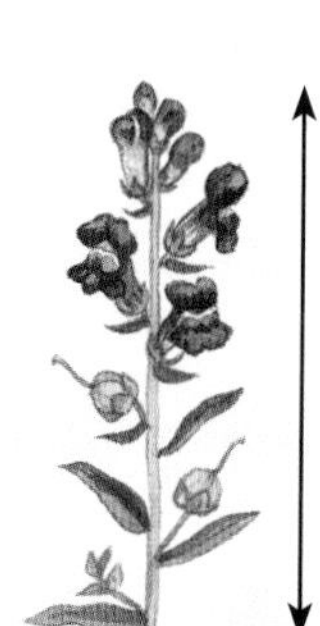

Some fungi and berries are deadly poisonous, and only experienced experts can be sure which these are. If you decide to measure a fungus, you should do so without touching it.

Mushrooms: height from ground and width of mushroom cap

Hoofed mammals: shoulder height in metres or centimetres

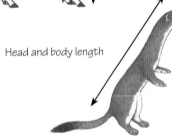

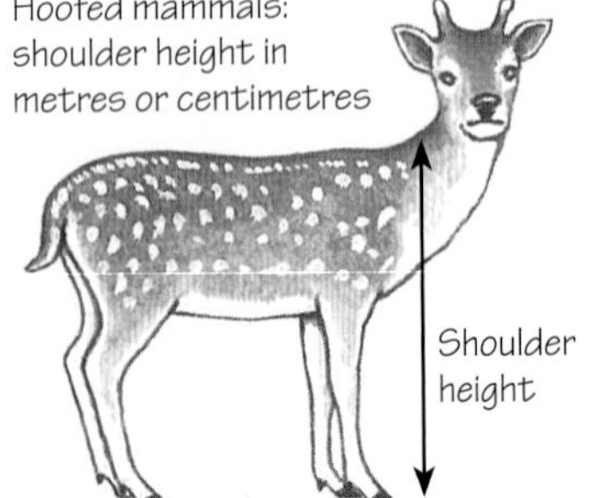

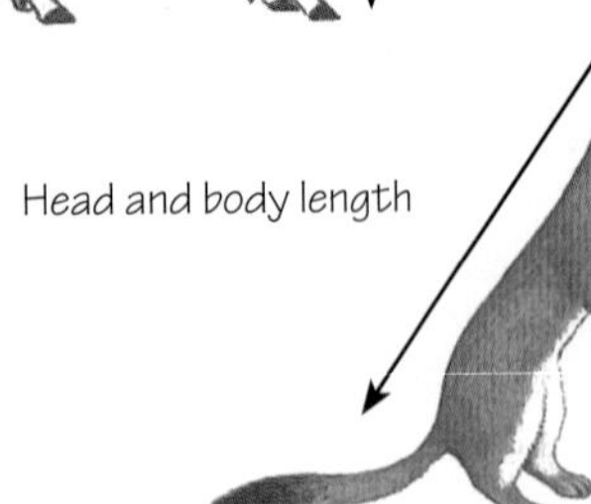

Other mammals: length of head and body, not including tail, in centimetres

Respecting nature

When out and about in the countryside, always remember to follow this code:

- Never light fires.
- Keep to the paths, and close gates behind you.
- Keep dogs under control.
- Don't damage hedges, fences, walls or signs.
- Look, don't touch: leave plants, animals and nests alone.
- Take your litter home with you.

Taking pictures

If you want to keep a record of tracks, plants and fungi you've seen, you can take a camera out spotting with you and photograph your finds. Here are a few tips on how to take a good picture:

• Keep the sun behind you and make sure your shadow doesn't fall across your subject as you're taking the photo.

• If there isn't much light you may need to use the camera's flash.

• If your subject is difficult to see amongst leaves or grass, place a piece of card behind it to make a plain background.

• If you don't have a ruler to measure the subject, you can photograph an object, such as a coin, next to it to show how big it is.

You could use your camera's zoom function to take close-up pictures of tiny things, like this garden spider on its web.

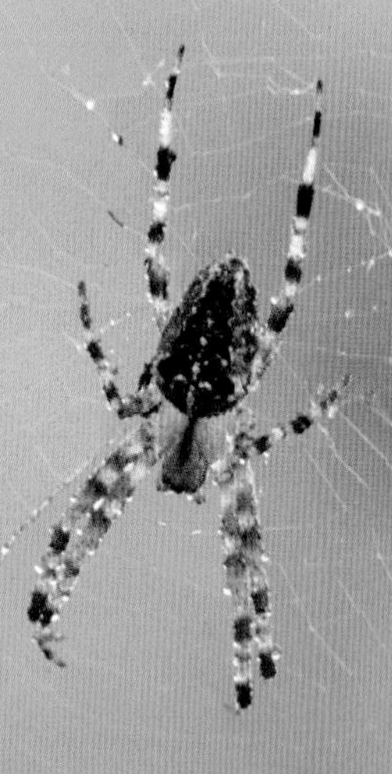

Making a spore print

Spore prints make an unusual and attractive addition to any nature diary. Experts often take a spore print to identify gilled cap fungi, because the spores are sometimes a different colour from the gills. You can try making your own spore print with mushrooms you've bought from a shop or market.

1. To make a spore print the cap will need to be mature and undamaged. Cut off the stem close to the cap.

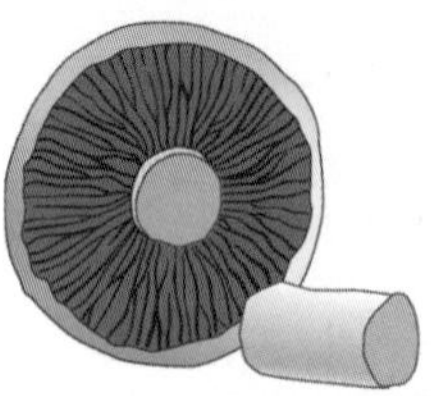

Fungus

2. Place the cap on a clean piece of paper, gills facing down. If the gills are dark, use white paper; if they are white, use black paper. Cover the cap with a bowl to protect it from draughts. Leave it overnight.

3. When you lift up the cap in the morning, a print will have been left by the spores that have fallen from the gills.

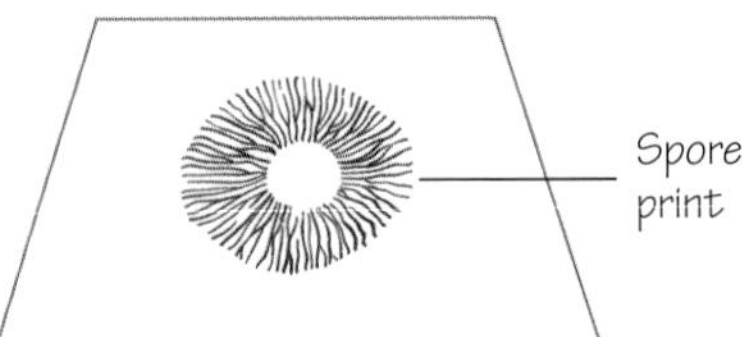

If you have a microscope, you can take a closer look at the spores. They are a different size and shape in every fungus. Here are a few of them:

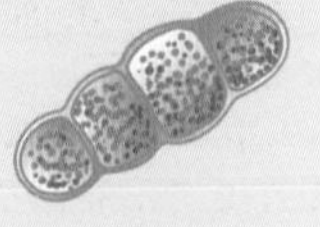
Cup fungus spore

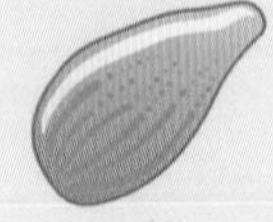
Boletus spore

Russula spore

Making casts

Instead of sketching animal footprints, you could try making a cast. While the footprints shown in this book are complete, the ones you find may have parts missing or be misshapen. So if you spot a perfect, deep print in firm ground, you can make a plaster cast of it to keep as a permanent record of your find.

To make a plaster cast you'll need:

- quick-drying plaster of Paris from a craft shop
- a strip of cardboard 30cm x 5cm
- lip balm
- a paper clip
- a container
- an old spoon
- water

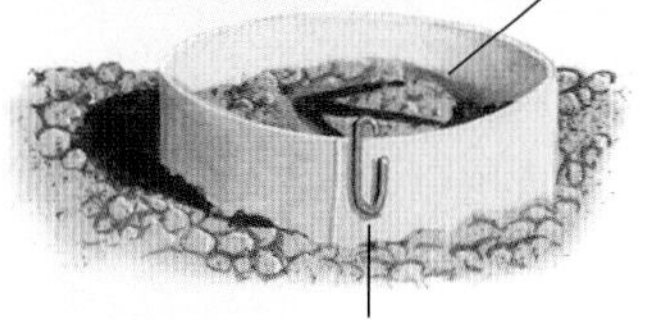

1. Smear lip balm on one side of the cardboard. Bend the cardboard around the print, clipping the ends together to form a ring.

2. Press the ring into the soil. Using the spoon, mix some plaster in the container, as directed on the packet, then pour it into the ring.

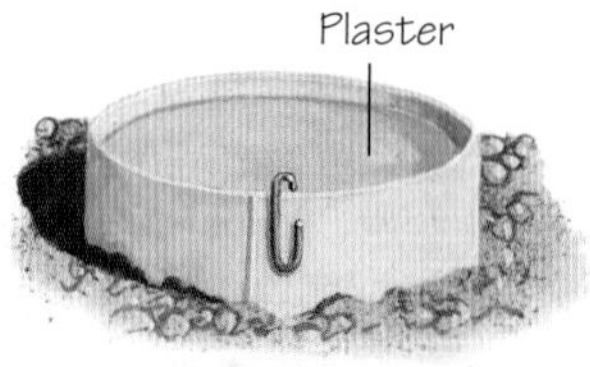

3. Leave it to set for about 20 minutes. Gently lift up the plaster cast.

Looking at flowers

These pictures show some different kinds of flowers, and explain some of the words that appear in the book. When you are examining a plant, look closely at the flowerhead to help you to identify it.

Some flowers have petals of even length and lots of stamens.

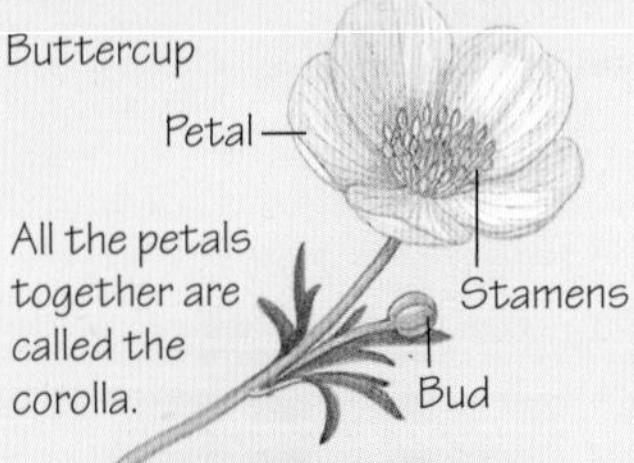

The petals of some flowers are joined together.

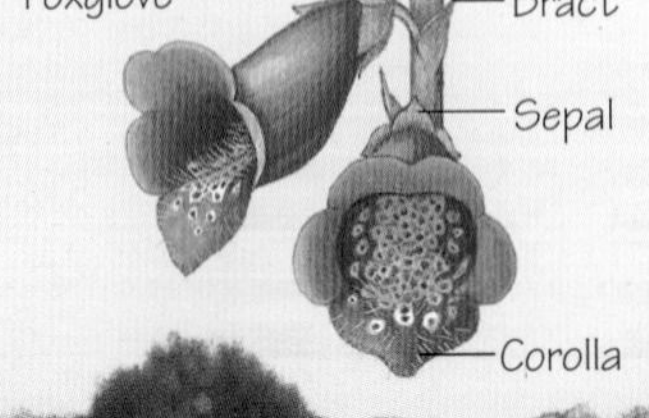

Some flowerheads are made up of clusters of tiny flowers.

Daisy

Centre is really lots of tiny flowers.

Some flowers have petals which form hoods and lips.

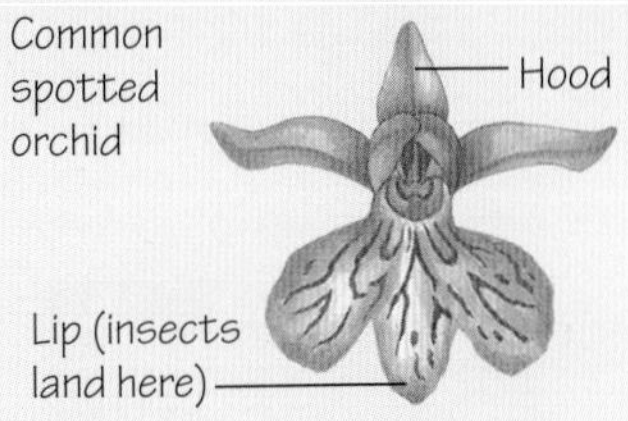

Toadflax

The petals of some flowers form a tube called a spur.

Spur (contains nectar which is drunk by bees)

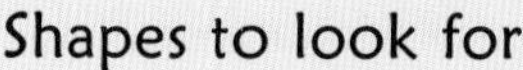

Shapes to look for

These pictures show some of the different ways that plants grow. Looking out for these shapes will help you to recognize different plants.

An "erect" plant grows straight up from the ground. "Runners" are stems that grow sideways along the ground, as though they are creeping. Some plants grow in thick mats or carpets close to the ground. These are called "mat-forming" plants.

An erect plant

Early purple orchid

A plant with runners

Creeping buttercup

A mat-forming plant

Stonecrop

Inside a flower

This is what the inside of a buttercup looks like. The stigma, style and ovary form the female part of the flower, or "carpel".

The stamens are the male parts. Pollen from the stamens is received by the stigma (this is called pollination). It causes seeds to grow inside the ovary.

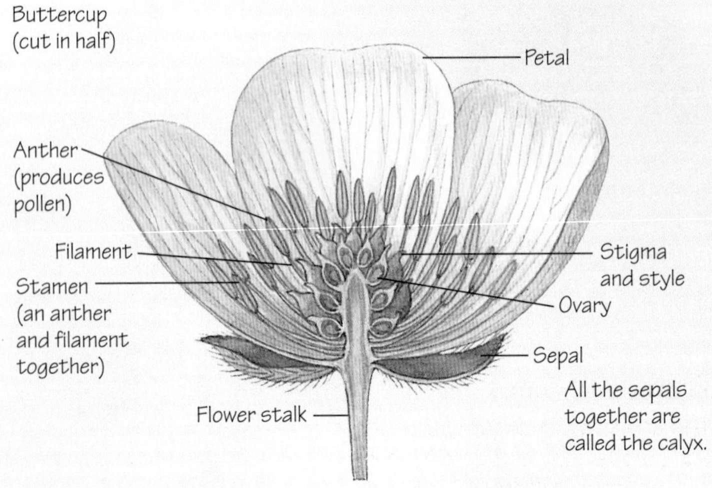

Some flowers can pollinate themselves and some are pollinated by wind. Other flowers need insects to spread their pollen. These flowers have special scents and markings to attract insects.

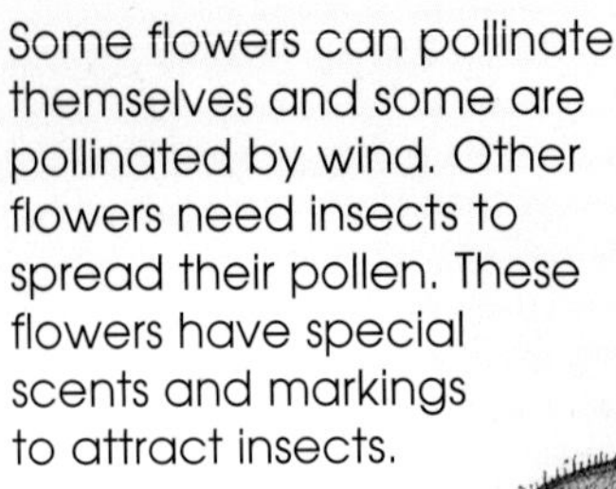

Pollen brushes onto the bee; when it visits another flower, the stigma will pick up this pollen from its body.

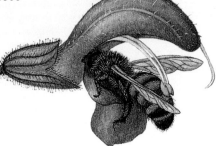

The scent and colour of this meadow clary flower have attracted a bee.

From flower to fruit

A flower helps a plant to produce seeds. Once a flower is pollinated, the seeds start to develop and the petals wither and fall off. The rest of the flower becomes a fruit containing seeds.

A bee pollinates the poppy flower.

The petals and stamens die.

The ovary swells and develops into a fruit.

Fruits and seeds

The seeds of a plant are usually surrounded by a fruit. Different plants have different-looking fruits, so you can recognize plants by their fruits. Here are two examples.

Remains of flower

Seed

Rosehip (fruit of dog rose) cut in half

Blackberry fruit (the seeds are inside)

Remains of flower

Leaves

Even if a plant is not in flower, you can recognize it from its leaves. There are many different leaf shapes.

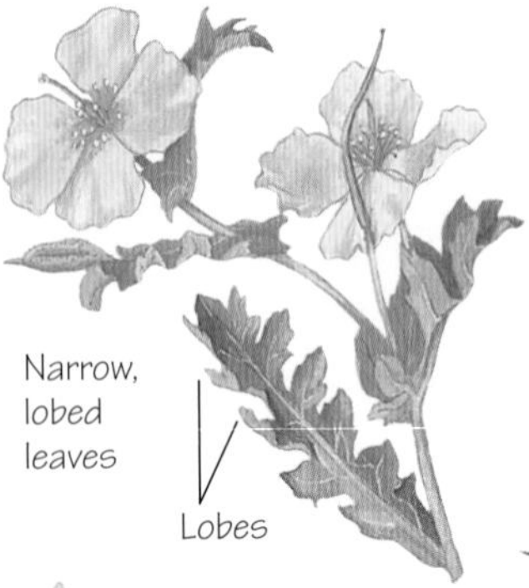

Narrow, lobed leaves

Lobes

Spiky leaves

Oval leaves

Toothed leaves

Heart-shaped leaves

Narrow, entire (i.e. not toothed or lobed) leaves

Lobed leaves

Leaves can also be arranged in different ways on the stem of a plant.

Protecting wild flowers

Be careful not to tread on young plants or to break their stems.

These flowers are all rare in the wild.

Corky-fruited water dropwort

Many wild plants that were once common are now rare, because people have picked and dug up so many. It is now against the law to dig up any wild plant by the roots, or to pick certain rare plants such as red helleborine. If you pick wild flowers, they will die. Leave them for others to enjoy. It is much better to draw or photograph flowers, so that you and other people can see them again.

Pasque flower

Cornflower

If you think you have found a rare plant, let your local nature conservation club know about it as soon as you can, so they can help protect it. You can get their address from your local library or look on the internet. There are links to some useful websites on the Usborne Quicklinks Website at www.usborne-quicklinks.com.

Looking at trees

This book will help you identify some of the trees of Britain and Europe. Not all the trees will be common in your area, but you may be able to find many of them in large gardens and parks.

What to look for

There are lots of clues to help you identify a tree – whatever the time of year.

In spring and summer, look at the leaves and flowers. In autumn, look out for fruits, and in winter examine twigs, buds, bark and tree shape.

Conifer or broadleaf?

The trees in this book are divided into two main groups: conifers and broadleaves.

Conifers have narrow, needle-like or scaly leaves, and their fruits are usuallly woody cones. Most conifers are evergreen, which means they keep their leaves in winter. Their shape is more regular than broadleaved trees.

Sitka spruce

Broadleaved trees have broad, flat leaves and seeds enclosed in fruits, such as nuts. Most are deciduous, which means they lose their leaves in autumn.

Sweet chestnut

Leaves

Leaves will often give you the biggest clue to the identity of a tree. Be careful, though, because some trees have very similar leaves. There are many different types of leaves. Here are some of the most common ones.

Simple leaves

A leaf that is in one piece is called a simple leaf. Simple leaves can be many shapes: round, oval, triangular, heart-shaped, or long and narrow. The edges are sometimes spiky (like holly) or toothed (slightly jagged). Some leaves have very wavy edges, called lobes.

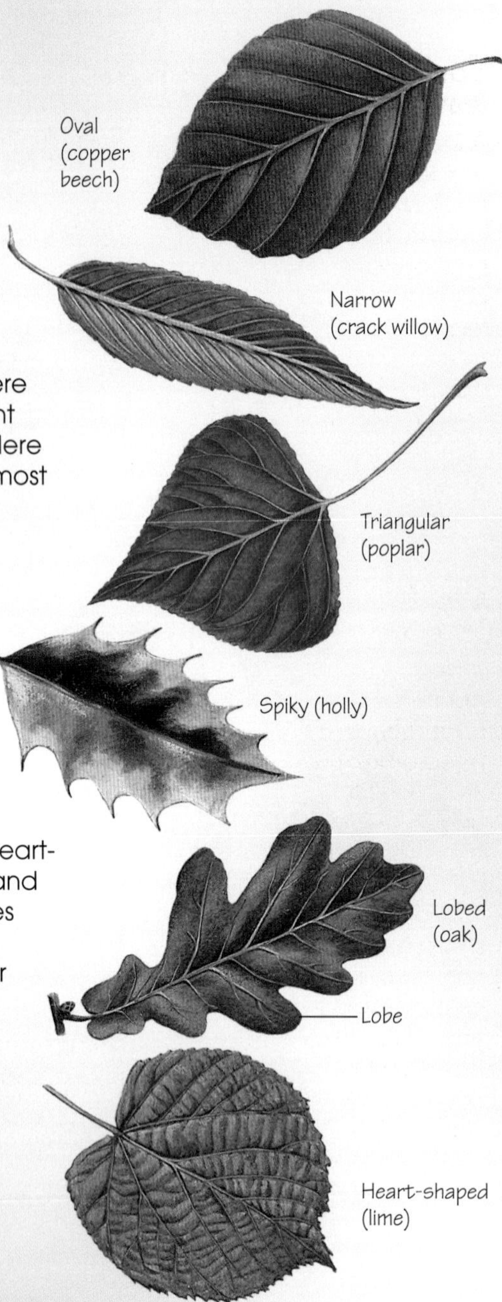

Compound leaves

A leaf that is made up of smaller leaves, or leaflets, is called a compound leaf.

Finger-like (horse chestnut)

Leaflets

Feather-like (common ash)

Conifer leaves

Many conifers have narrow, needle-like leaves – either single, in small bunches, or in clusters. They can be very sharp and spiky. Some conifers, such as cypresses, have tiny scale-like leaves, which overlap one another.

Bunch of needles (Atlas cedar)

Pair of long needles (Corsican pine)

Short single needles (Norway spruce)

Scale-like leaves covering twigs (Lawson cypress)

Flowers

All trees produce flowers that later develop into fruits, though some flowers are so small you can hardly see them. Most flowers have both male and female parts. A few species, such as holly, have male and female flowers on separate trees.

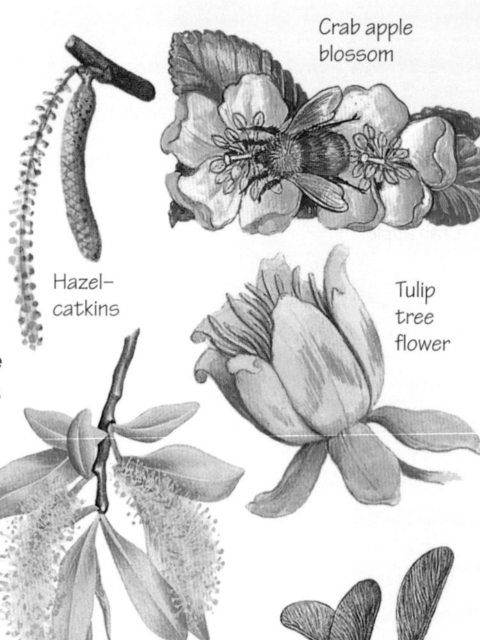

Fruits and seeds

Fruits contain the seeds that can grow into new trees. Broadleaved trees have many different kinds of fruits and seeds. Here are some of them.

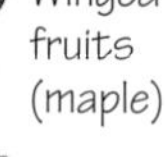

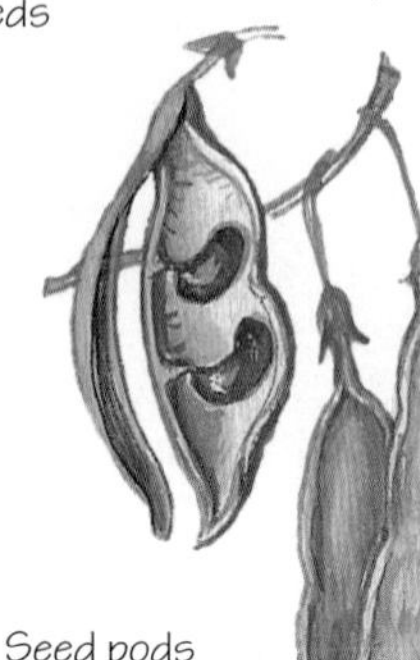

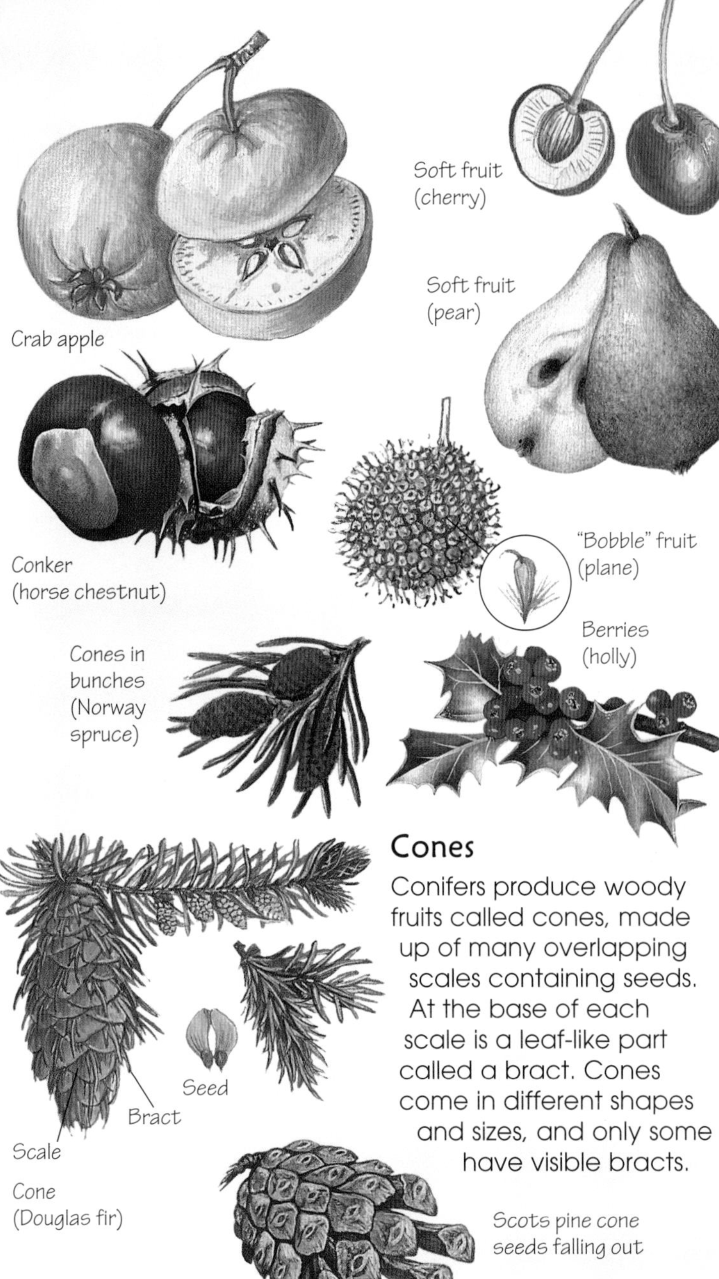

Cones

Conifers produce woody fruits called cones, made up of many overlapping scales containing seeds. At the base of each scale is a leaf-like part called a bract. Cones come in different shapes and sizes, and only some have visible bracts.

Finding the right tree

The trees in this book are divided into conifers and broadleaves, with more closely related trees, such as all the oaks, grouped together. If you spot a tree you can't identify, but you know what type of leaf it has, you can use this chart to help you match it up with a tree in this book. The numbers show where you'll find the illustration.

Broadleaves

Simple

Unlobed leaves

Lobed leaves

Compound

Leaves with a central stem

Finger-like

Conifers

Single needles

Needles grouped in 2s

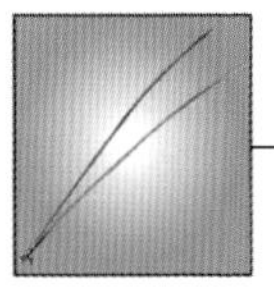

Needles grouped in 3s

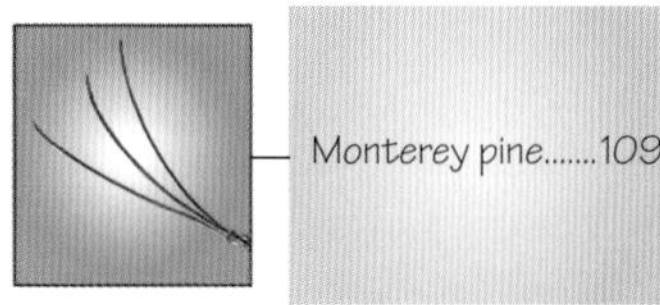

Needles grouped in 5s

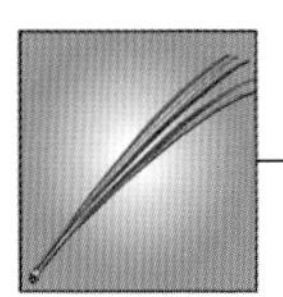

Needles in more than 5s - Evergreen

Needles in more than 5s - Deciduous

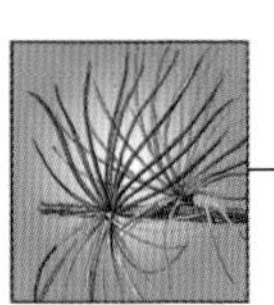

Other conifers

Scale-like leaves

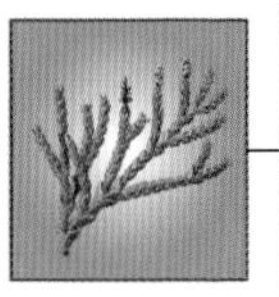

What else to look for?

Although the most obvious way to identify a tree is by its leaves, there are lots of other features to look out for too.

Tree shape

You can sometimes tell a tree by its shape, especially in winter when many trees are bare. The leafy top of a tree is called its crown, and each type of tree has its own particular crown shape. This comes from the arrangement of its branches.

Cone-shaped (Norway spruce)

Narrow crown (Lombardy poplar)

Broad crown (Oak)

Twigs

Look closely at the way the leaves are arranged on the twigs. On some trees, they grow opposite each other in matching pairs. On other trees, the leaves are single and alternate from one side of the twig to the other.

The leaves of a silver birch alternate from one side of the twig to the other.

The leaves of a horse chestnut grow opposite each other in pairs.

Bark

The outside of a tree is covered in a hard, tough layer of bark, which protects the tree from drying out and from damage by insects and other animals. The type of bark a tree has can give clues to its identity too.

Silver birch peels off in wispy strips that look like ribbons.

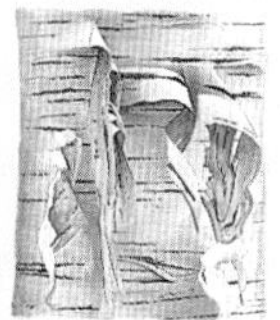

The bark of Scots pine flakes off in large pieces.

English oak has deep ridges and cracks.

Beech has smooth thin bark, which flakes off in tiny pieces.

On the right is a cross-section of a tree trunk, showing the different layers, or rings. Each year, the trunk thickens by growing a new layer.

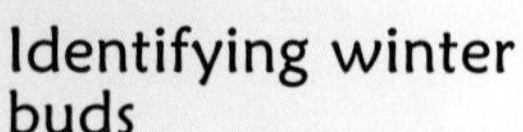

Identifying winter buds

Most broadleaved trees have no leaves in winter, but you can often identify them by their winter buds. These contain the beginnings of next year's shoot, leaves and flowers.

What shape is the twig? What colour are the buds, and are they pointed or rounded? Are they positioned in opposite pairs, or single and alternate? Is the bud covered with hairs or scales? If scales, how many are there? Is the bud sticky?

False acacia

Small buds with thorns at base, on grey, crooked, ribbed twigs

English elm

Pointed, hairy, chocolate-brown buds on stout twigs

Ash

Large, black opposite buds on silver-grey twigs

Turkey oak

Clusters of small, brown, whiskered, alternate buds

Common alder

Alternate, stalked purple buds, often with male catkins

White poplar

Small, orange-brown buds covered by white, felty hairs on green twigs

Sweet chestnut

Rounded, reddish-brown buds on knobbly, greenish-brown twigs

Common beech

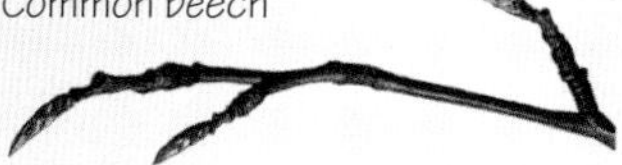

Long, pointed, copper-brown buds sticking out from brown twigs

London plane

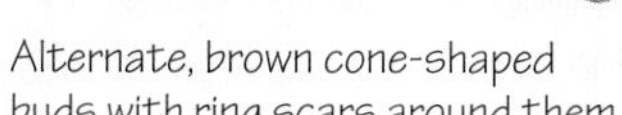

Alternate, brown cone-shaped buds with ring scars around them

Sycamore

Large green, opposite buds, with dark-edged scales on stout, light-brown twigs

Common walnut

Big, black, velvety triangle-shaped, alternate buds on thick, hollow twigs

Whitebeam

Downy, green, alternate buds on twigs without thorns

White willow

Slender buds enclosed in a single scale, close to pinkish, downy twigs

Common lime

Zigzag twig. Alternate, reddish buds with two scales

Wild cherry

Fat, shiny, red-brown buds grouped at the tips of light brown twigs

Looking at birds

When you are trying to identify a bird, ask yourself these questions: What size and shape is it? What colour is it? Does it have any special markings? Where does it live? How does it feed? How does it fly?

Remember that in some cases the males and females of a species look different from each other. In this book these symbols are used show which is which:

♂ = Male
♀ = Female

Be aware that some species have different plumages (feathers) in summer and winter.

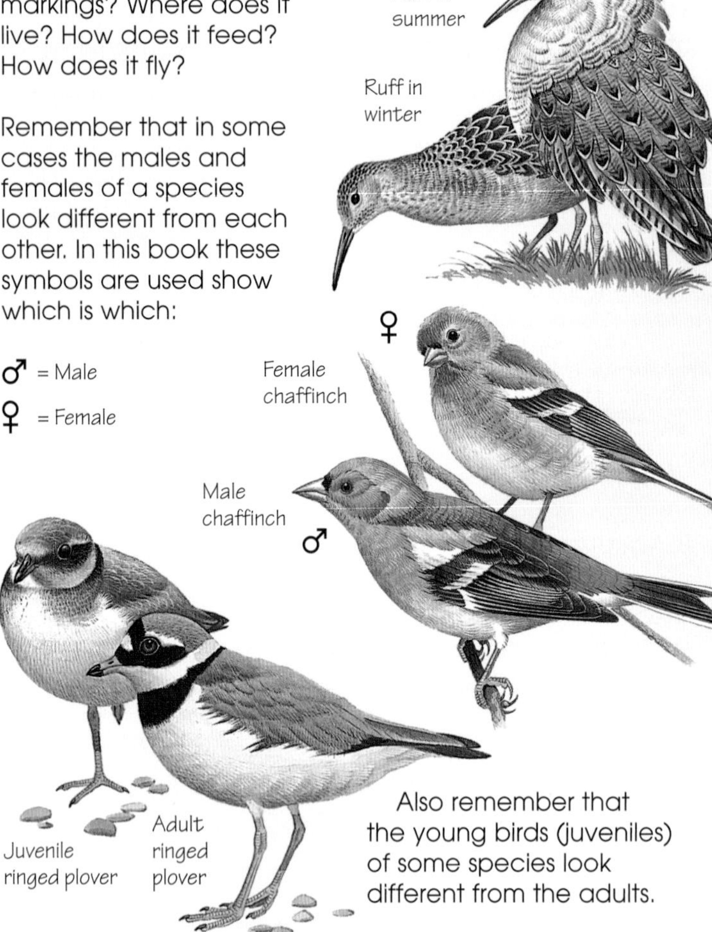

Also remember that the young birds (juveniles) of some species look different from the adults.

The parts of a bird

Although birds vary from species to species, they all have wings, feathers and a beak. To describe birds accurately, it's useful to know the names of some of their other parts too.

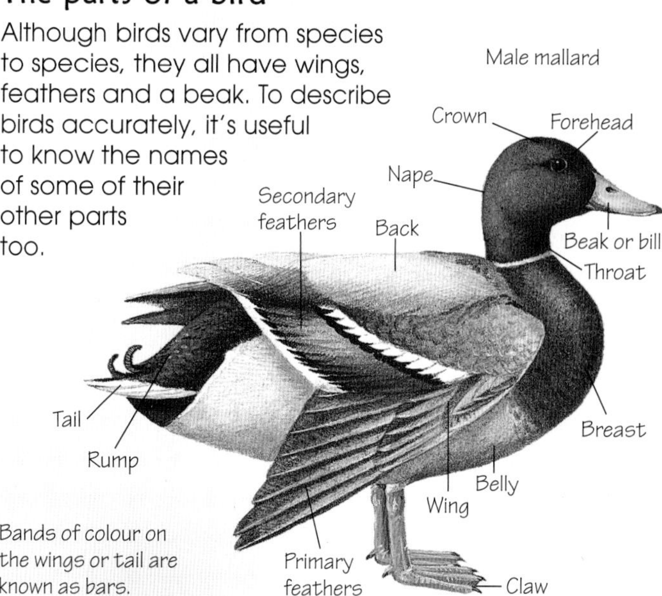

Bands of colour on the wings or tail are known as bars.

Binoculars

As you do more birdwatching, you will probably want to use binoculars. Visit a good shop and try out several pairs. The best sizes are 8x30 or 8x40 (never more than 10x50 or they will be too heavy).

Make sure your binoculars are light enough to carry around with you.

Migration

Migration is the making of regular journeys from one place to another and back again. Some birds migrate in spring and autumn. In Europe birds usually travel between a summer breeding area and a wintering area in Africa.

Why migrate?

Birds migrate in autumn when food, such as insects, becomes hard to find. It is food shortages rather than cold weather which cause migration.

Finding their way

Scientists don't fully understand how birds can navigate over such huge distances, but they have come up with a few theories. Some species might use a combination of these methods.

Some birds that migrate during the day might follow landmarks, such as mountains and islands. The position of the Moon and stars may help night-fliers to find their way. Research on pigeons suggests that they are guided by lines of magnetic forces from the centre of the Earth.

Returning home

The birds return in spring when food supplies have built up again. By doing so, the birds feed better and face less competition for food from other animals. If they travel northwards, they have more daylight in which to hunt and feed their young.

Irruptions

Irruptions are irregular journeys from the usual range. They are usually caused by changes in the food supply. Snowy owls, for instance, irrupt well to the south of their normal wintering range when their usual food sources are scarce.

Recording birds

Much of the information about migration comes from ringing schemes in which birds are caught and carefully fitted with metal leg rings by trained ringers. Each ring bears a unique number and address.

Finding and reporting ringed birds tells us a great deal about the age and movement of the birds. Wing tags bearing numbers or letters can be read with binoculars so that the birds don't need to be caught. Tracking individual birds on their flight paths is also possible if a small radio transmitter is attached to each bird.

Whooper swans setting out on their long flight from Iceland to the UK, where they will spend the winter

Looking at insects

All adult insects have six legs and their bodies have three distinct parts – a head, a thorax and an abdomen.

As you will see in this book, though, different kinds of insect look very different from each other. Bugs are just one kind of insect.

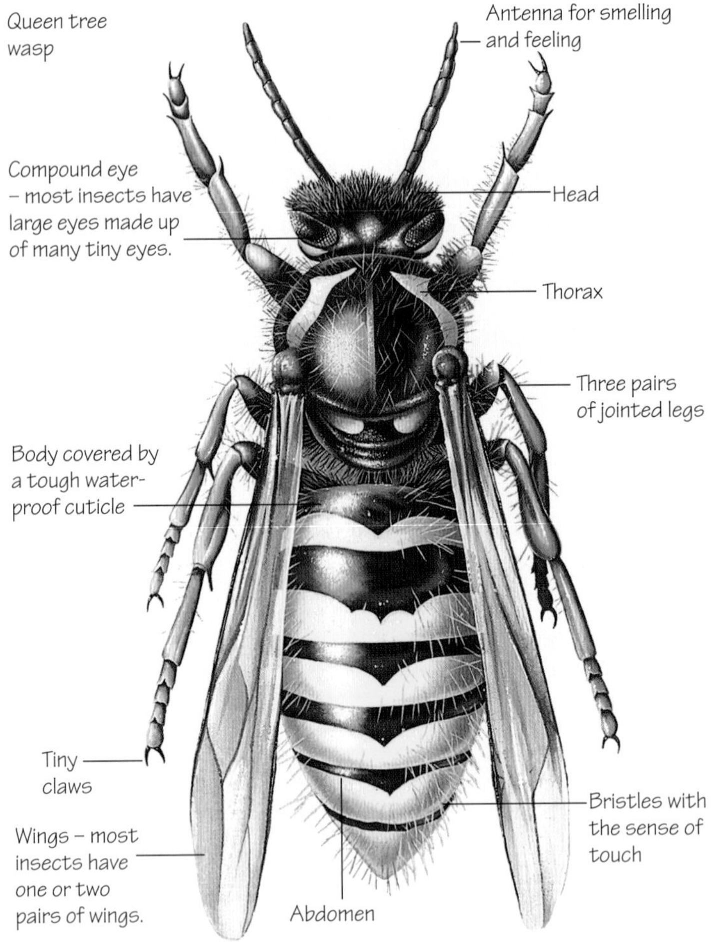

An insect's life cycle

Most insects hatch from eggs. After hatching, they go through different stages of growth before becoming adults.

The eggs of some insects, such as butterflies and beetles, pass through two more stages before becoming adults – a larva stage and a pupa stage.

These three pictures show a larva developing into a swallowtail butterfly.

1. The egg hatches into a larva known as a caterpillar.

2. The caterpillar becomes a pupa. Inside the pupa, the body of the caterpillar breaks down and becomes the body of the butterfly.

3. The pupa splits and an adult emerges.

Some insects, such as bugs and dragonflies, lay eggs that hatch into larvae called nymphs. Nymphs look like small adults. They shed their skin several times, each time growing bigger. This is called moulting. A nymph's wings start as tiny buds, which grow bigger each time it moults.

This grasshopper nymph looks very like an adult grasshopper, but it does not have wings.

Food and feeding

Insects feed on all kinds of animals and plants. Insects are carnivores (meat-eaters), herbivores (plant-eaters) or omnivores (meat- and plant-eaters). Some insects, known as parasites, actually live on or inside the bodies of other living animals.

Insect mouthparts

Insects use their mouthparts to suck up liquids, or to bite and chew solid food. Insects that suck have a hollow tube called a proboscis. Bees, butterflies and moths use a proboscis to suck nectar from flowers.

Bee

Proboscis

Butterflies have a coiled proboscis.

House-flies have suction pads at the end of their proboscises. Saliva passes into the pad and partly digests food before it is sucked into the fly's mouth.

House fly

Sucking pad

Some insects pierce plants and animals with a pointed tube called a rostrum.

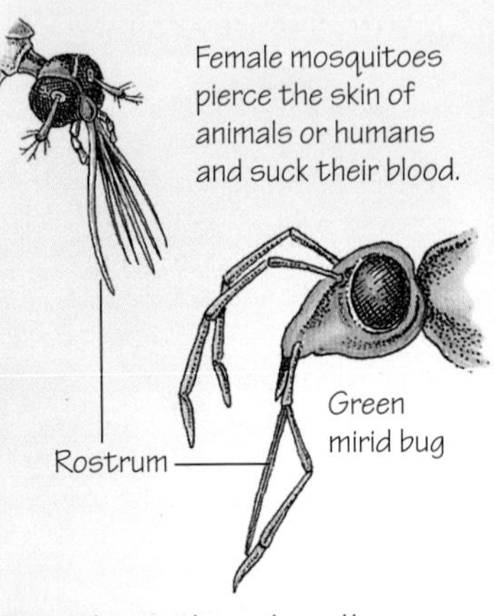

Female mosquitoes pierce the skin of animals or humans and suck their blood.

Insects, such as beetles, that bite and chew have strong jaws.

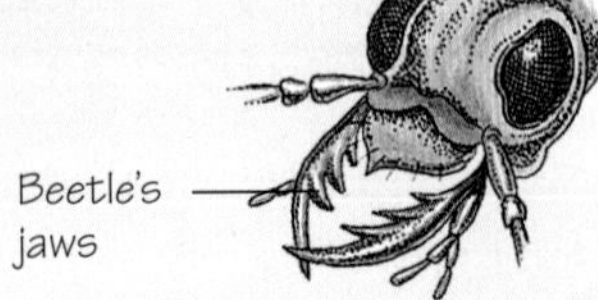

Self-defence

All insects are in constant danger of being eaten by other animals. Here are some of the ways they defend themselves.

Shock tactics

Some insects sting, bite, or produce nasty smells or poisons to shock their enemies and give them time to escape. Others try to look dangerous, or make sudden movements to frighten their enemies.

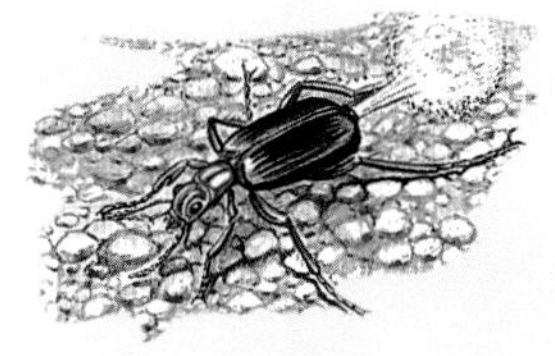

A bombardier beetle fires a puff of poisonous gas at its enemies.

Colour warning

Insects that taste unpleasant are often brightly coloured so that predators will avoid eating them. Some harmless insects protect themselves by copying the colours of bad-tasting or poisonous insects.

Camouflage

The colour of many insects makes them difficult for predators to spot.

The poplar hawk moth caterpillar is well-disguised by colours and markings which match the leaves it feeds on.

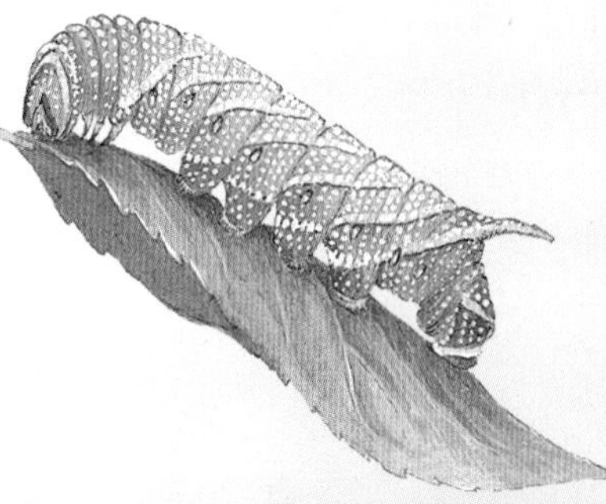

Shape can also be a camouflage. For example, stick insects and some caterpillars resemble twigs. Other insects can look like leaves, grass or seeds.

Stick insects look so like twigs they are hard to detect.

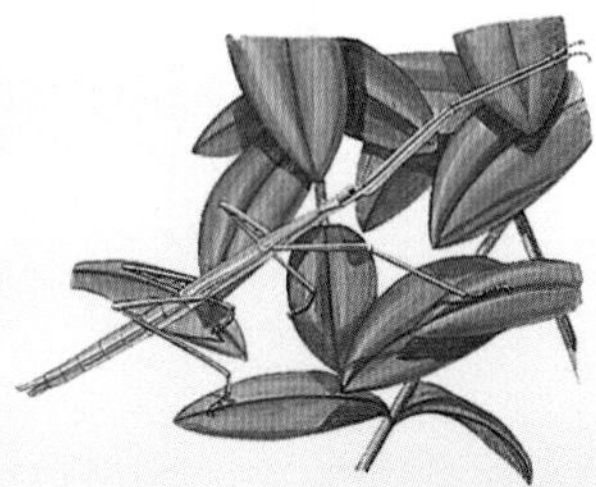

Looking at fungi

Although fungi often grow out of the ground, they are not plants. Fungi can't make their own food, but get it instead from plants and animals.

Spotting fungi

Most of a fungus lives underground as a mass of tiny threads called the mycelium. These live all year round, buried in the plant or animal matter on which the fungus feeds. The illustrations in this book are designed to help you spot the part of the fungus that grows above ground. Mycologists (fungus experts) call it a spore body as it produces thousands of dust-like spores from which new fungi can grow.

Where do they grow?

Fungi are found in damp woodland or grassland. Look for caps poking through dead leaves and long grass, or growing on trees and decaying wood.

Different names

Mycologists use the word "toadstool" as a general term for fungi with caps. "Mushroom" is often used to describe edible fungi, even though some fungi with "mushroom" in their names are, in fact, very poisonous.

Identifying cap fungi

Cap - What colour is it? Does it look smooth, scaly, sticky or dry? Is it ribbed?

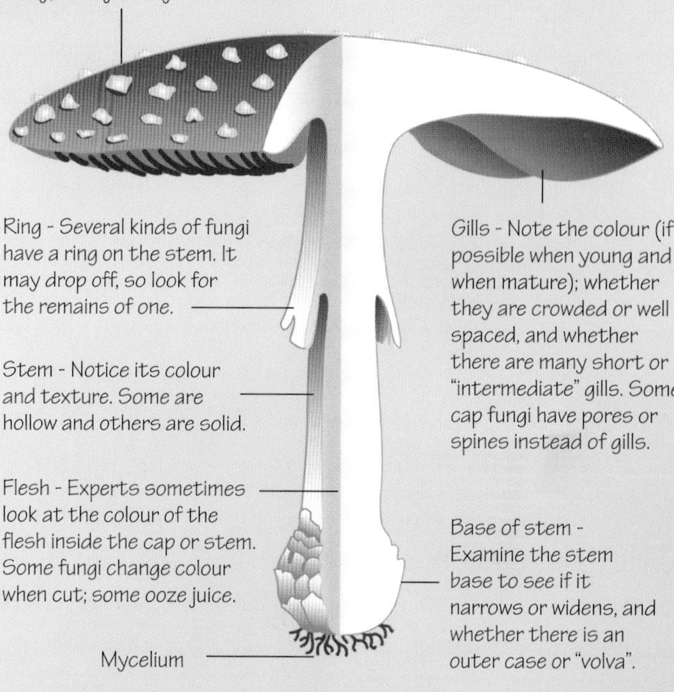

Ring - Several kinds of fungi have a ring on the stem. It may drop off, so look for the remains of one.
Stem - Notice its colour and texture. Some are hollow and others are solid.
Flesh - Experts sometimes look at the colour of the flesh inside the cap or stem. Some fungi change colour when cut; some ooze juice.
Mycelium
Gills - Note the colour (if possible when young and when mature); whether they are crowded or well spaced, and whether there are many short or "intermediate" gills. Some cap fungi have pores or spines instead of gills.
Base of stem - Examine the stem base to see if it narrows or widens, and whether there is an outer case or "volva".

These diagrams show the different ways that gills can be attached to the stems of cap fungi.

Gills attached to stem

Gills run down stem

Gills free from stem

Different types of fungi

Cap fungi with pores

These fungi all have pores on the underside of their cap. Pores are the openings to a mass of spongy tubes where the spores are made. *Pages 248-251*

Yellow-cracked bolete

Cap fungi with gills

Many fungi have thin gills that run from the edge of the cap towards the centre, a little like the spokes of a wheel. Their surface is lined with spores. *Pages 252-276*

Blusher

Cap fungi with spines

As their name suggests, the fungi on this page have spines underneath their cap. The spores are produced in these spines. *Page 277*

Wood hedgehog

Funnel-shaped fungi

The sides of these fungi's caps are turned upwards to form a hollow in the centre. The underside of the cap is wrinkled with thick folds. *Page 278*

Chanterelle

Bracket fungi

These fungi grow on trees (living wood), or stumps and logs (dead wood). Like cap fungi, their spores are in gills, pores or spines. *Pages 279-283*

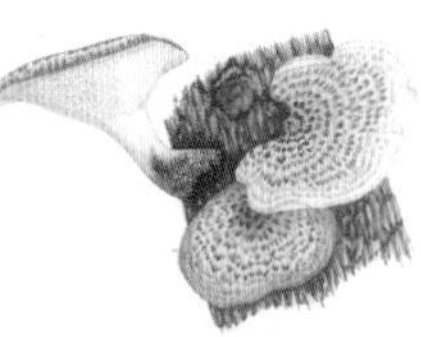

Dryad's saddle

Cup fungi

Cup fungi grow on logs, tree trunks or on the ground. Their spores are made inside the cup. *Pages 284-285*

Orange peel fungus

Puffballs

Puffballs are round or pear-shaped fungi. The spores develop inside the "ball". Ripe spores are scattered either through a small hole at the top, or cracks in the surface. *Pages 286-287*

Common puffball

Soot fungi

The spores of soot fungi are produced in tiny flask-shaped bodies buried in the surface. When the spores emerge they form a dark, dusty covering that looks like soot. *Page 288*

Dead man's finger

Jelly fungi

Many fungi have a jelly-like texture, especially when wet. Jelly fungi often have irregular shapes, and sometimes grow in clusters. *Page 289*

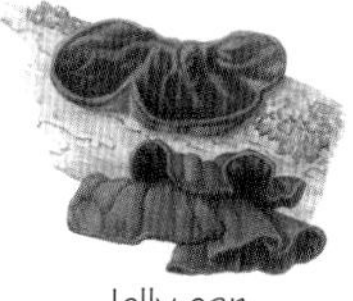
Jelly ear

Morels, stinkhorns

These fungi have pitted, spongy heads. Stinkhorn spores are in a dark, smelly slime that attracts flies, which then carry the spores away with them. *Pages 290-291*

Stinkhorn

Looking at tracks and trails

A track is an animal's footprint and a trail is a series of tracks made by a moving animal. Finding a trail can not only give you clues to the type of animal that made it, but also where it was going and how it was moving.

This is a fox trail. There's only a single line of footprints, showing that the fox was trotting along, placing its back feet in the prints made by its front feet.

Direction of travel

These prints belong to a running hare. As it ran, it leapt into the air, landing on its front feet first. Then, it put its back feet down a little way in front before leaping again.

A blackbird usually hops, but can break into a run if it senses danger. These tracks are paired, so you can tell that the blackbird that left them was hopping along calmly.

Wading birds, like this curlew, leave trails as they pace up and down muddy shores looking for food.

Spotting tips

- You can take this book with you to help identify animals and their tracks.
- Binoculars are a great way to spot birds and their nests in treetops.
- If you don't have a pair of binoculars, use the zoom function on a camera to see faraway animals.
- Many animals are easily startled and might not wait for you to identify them. So take lots of photographs in case you miss a rare spot.

Places to look

- On the lower rung of gates and fences for fur
- In muddy and sandy places for tracks
- Under trees and bushes for fruit and nuts
- On tree bark for peeling and scrape marks
- In grassy areas for paths made by animals
- In front of burrows for tracks

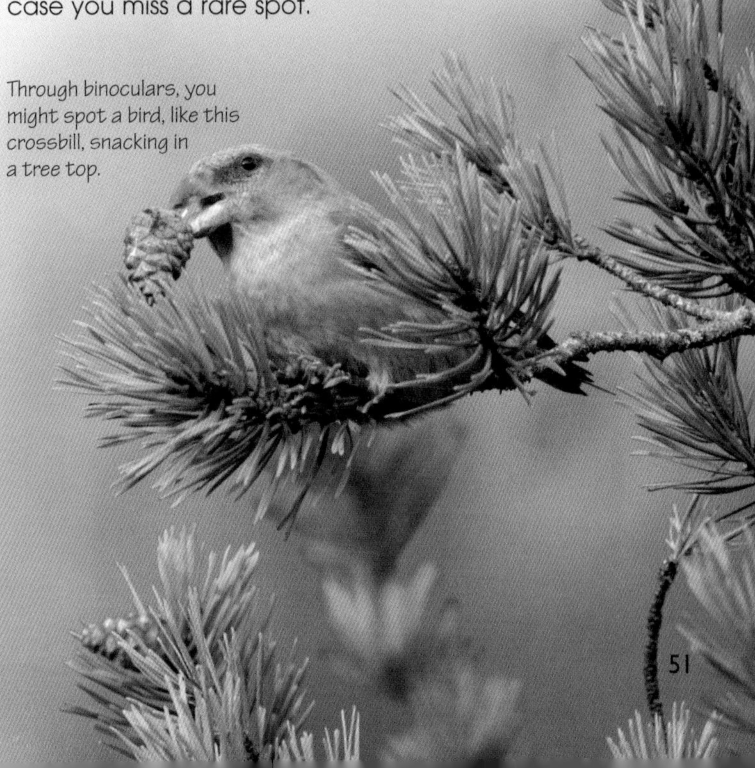

Through binoculars, you might spot a bird, like this crossbill, snacking in a tree top.

Different types of tracks

You can often identify animals by the size and shape of their tracks. The number of toes an animal has, or differences between its fore feet and hind feet are simple ways to discover which animals have passed by.

One-toed tracks

Mammals with one main toe per foot include horses and ponies. The front of the toe is protected by a thick, continuous nail called a hoof. Each hoof leaves a deep, circular track.

Exmoor pony

Two-toed tracks

Large grazing animals such as goats, cows and deer have cloven hoofs, where the hoof is split between two toes. Pigs and some deer may leave tracks with claw marks at the heel.

Domestic sheep

Three-toed tracks

Most birds have four toes: three in front and one at back. For ducks, gulls and some game birds, the back toe is often too small to leave a mark.

Mallard

Four-toed tracks

Cats, dogs and foxes have four toes per foot. Unlike dogs and foxes, cat tracks appear without claw marks. Fox tracks are dog-like, but spacing between toes is more compact.

Wild cat

Five-toed tracks

Bears, badgers and weasels have five toes. The hind foot of the bear leaves surprisingly human-like tracks.

Brown bear

Fore feet and hind feet

Many rodents and small animals have four toes on their fore feet and five on their hind feet. The tracks of rabbits and hares show long and powerful hind feet compared to short fore feet.

Rabbit

Webbed feet

Some animals and birds that live near water have a layer of skin between their toes that helps them to swim better. On tracks in this book, these webbed areas are shown in yellow.

Beaver

Drag marks

Seals are the only mammals in this book that make drag marks: trails made in mud and sand when seals drag themselves onto land.

Common seal

Tunnellers and fliers

Animals such as bats and moles rarely leave tracks behind. While bats spend most of their time flying above ground, moles spend most of their time digging beneath it.

Mole

Wild Flowers

Yellow flowers

Look for these flowers in damp places, such as ditches, marshes and water meadows.

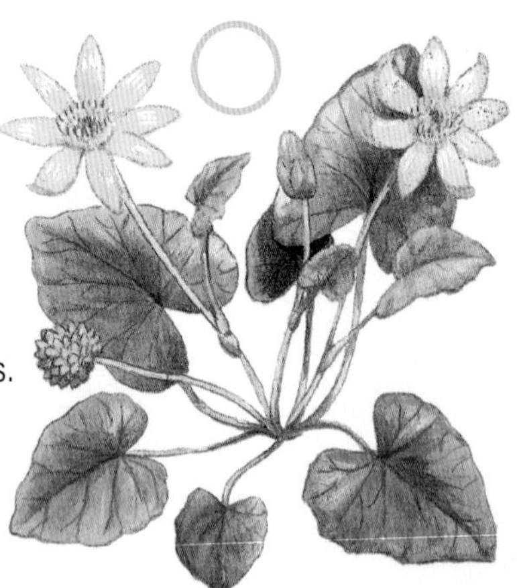

➡ Lesser celandine

A small, creeping plant with glossy, heart-shaped leaves. Shiny yellow flowers. Look in damp, shady woods and waysides. 7cm tall. March-May.

Each flower has four yellow sepals.

⬅ Alternate-leaved golden saxifrage

Small plant with round, toothed leaves and greenish-yellow flowers. Look in wet places. 7cm tall. April-July.

➡ Creeping buttercup

Look for the long runners near the ground. Hairy, deeply divided leaves. Shiny yellow flowers. Common weed of grassy places. May-Aug.

➡ Creeping Jenny

A creeping, mat-forming plant with shiny, oval leaves. Yellow flowers are 1.5-2.5cm across. In grassy places and under hedges. June-Aug.

➡ Cowslip

Easily recognized in April and May by the single clusters of nodding flowers. Rosette of leaves at base. Grows in meadows. 15cm tall.

Sepals

⬅ Common meadow rue

Tall, erect plant with dense clusters of flowers. Leaves have 3-4 lobes. Look in marshy fields and fens. Up to 80cm tall. July-Aug.

Yellow flowers

Look for these flowers in woods, hedgerows and heaths.

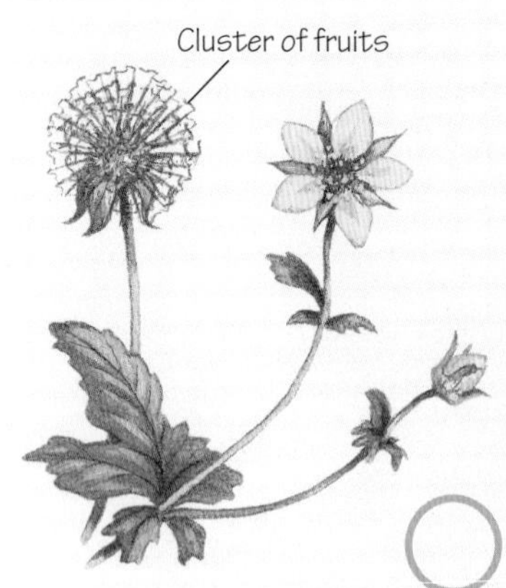

➡ Herb Bennet or wood avens

Fruits have hooks which catch on clothes and animals' fur. Woods, hedges and shady places. Up to 50cm tall. June-Aug.

⬅ Yellow pimpernel

Like creeping Jenny, but smaller, with more pointed leaves. Slender, trailing stems. The flowers close in dull weather. Woods and hedges. May-Sept.

Barberries can be used to make jam.

➡ Barberry

A shrub with spiny branches. Bees visit the drooping flowers. Look for the red berries. Hedges and scrubland. Up to 100cm tall. May-June.

⬅ Wood groundsel

Erect plant growing on heaths and sandy soil. The petals of the small flowers curl back. Narrow lobed leaves. 60cm tall. July-Sept.

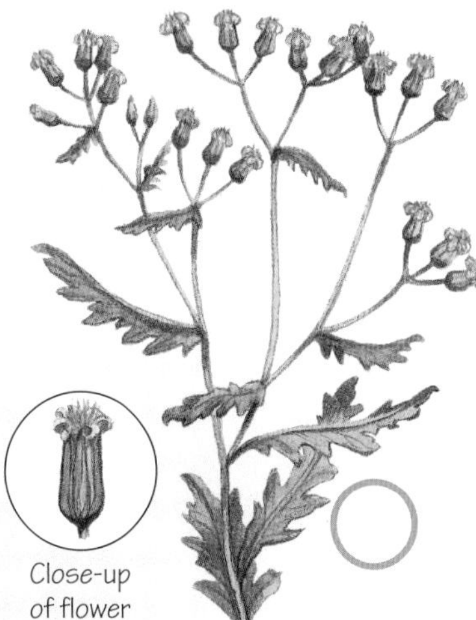

Whorl of flowers

➡ Yellow archangel

Also called weasel-snout. Look for the red-brown markings on the yellow petals. Opposite pairs of leaves. Common in woods. 40cm tall. May-June.

⬅ Primrose

Well-known spring flower, with hairy stems and rosette of large leaves. Often grows in patches. Woods, hedges and fields. 15cm tall. Dec-May.

Yellow flowers

Look for these flowers in open, grassy places, such as heaths and commons.

Furze

Also called gorse or whin. Dark green, spiny bush on heaths and commons. The bright yellow flowers smell like coconut. 100-200cm tall. March-June.

Close-up of flower

Bird's foot trefoil

Also called bacon and eggs because the yellow flowers are streaked with red. Look for this small, creeping plant on grassy banks and downs. May-June.

Creeping cinquefoil

Like silverweed, spreads close to the ground with long, rooting runners. Hedge banks and grassy places. May-Aug.

⬅ Common St. John's wort

Look for see-through dots on the narrow, oval leaves, and black dots on the petals and sepals. Damp, grassy places. 60cm tall. June-Sept.

➡ Woad

Look for the hanging pods on this tall, erect plant. The leaves were once boiled to make a blue dye. Waysides and dry places. 70cm tall. June-Sept.

Seed pod

Dandelion "clock"

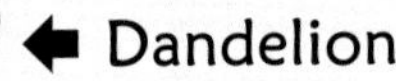

⬅ Dandelion

Common weed with rosette of toothed leaves. The flowers close at night. Look for the "clock" of downy white fruits. Waysides. 15cm tall. March-June.

Close-up of fruit

Yellow flowers

➡ Stonecrop

Also called wallpepper. Mat-forming plant with star-shaped flowers. The thick, fleshy leaves have a peppery taste. Dunes, shingle and walls. June-July.

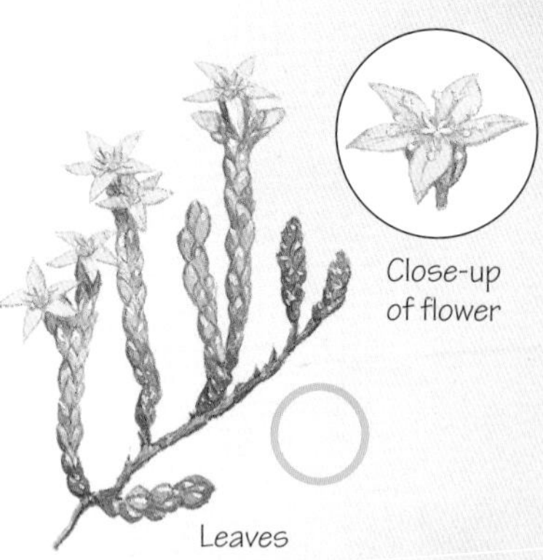

⬅ Purslane

A low, spreading plant with red stems. The fleshy, oval-shaped leaves are in opposite pairs. A weed of fields and waste places. May-Oct.

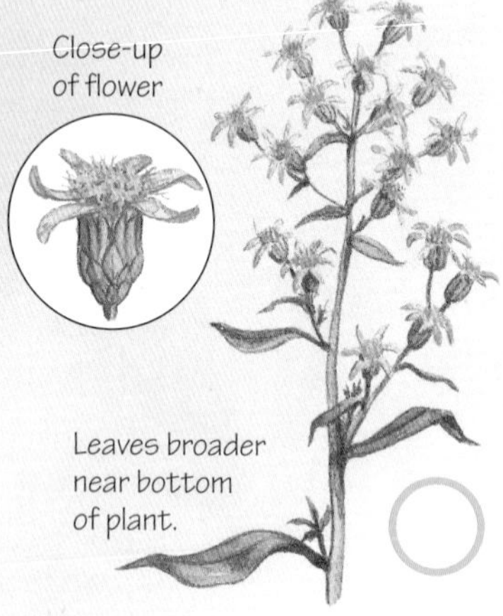

➡ Golden rod

Erect plant with flowers on thin spikes. Leaves are narrower and more pointed near top of plant. Woods, banks and cliffs. 40cm tall. July-Sept.

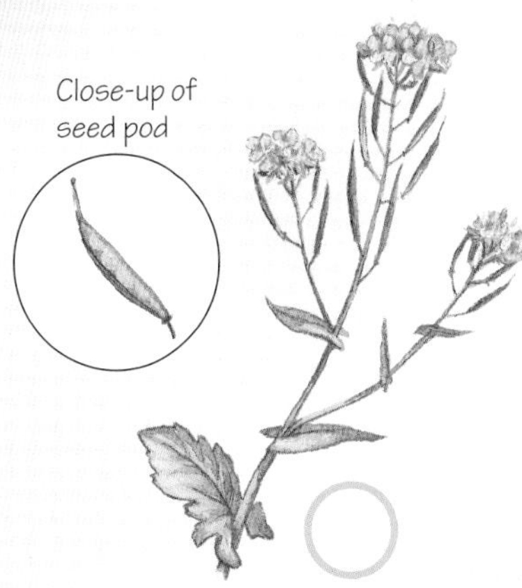

⬅ Rape

Common on roadsides, fields and motorways. Also grown as a crop. Dark blue-green leaves. Flowers grow in clusters and have four petals. Look for the long seed pods. Up to 100cm tall. May-July.

➡ Cypress spurge

Erect plant with many pale, needle-like leaves. Spray of yellowish flowers. Roadsides and grassy places. Rare in Britain. 40cm tall. May-Aug.

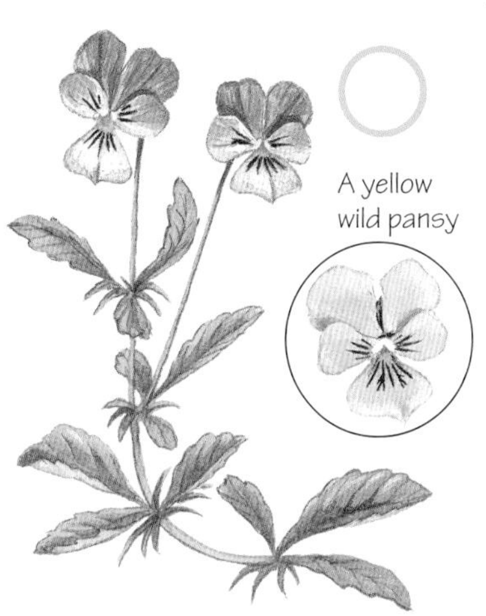

⬅ Wild pansy or heartsease

The flowers can be violet, yellow, or a mixture of both, or sometimes pink and white. Grassy places and cornfields. 15cm tall. April-Oct.

Blue flowers

⬅ Cornflower

Also called bluebottle. Erect plant with greyish, downy leaves and a blue flower head. Cornfields and waste places. 40cm tall. July-Aug. Rare.

➡ Larkspur

Slender plant with divided, feathery leaves. The flowers have a long spur. Cultivated land. 50cm tall. June-July.

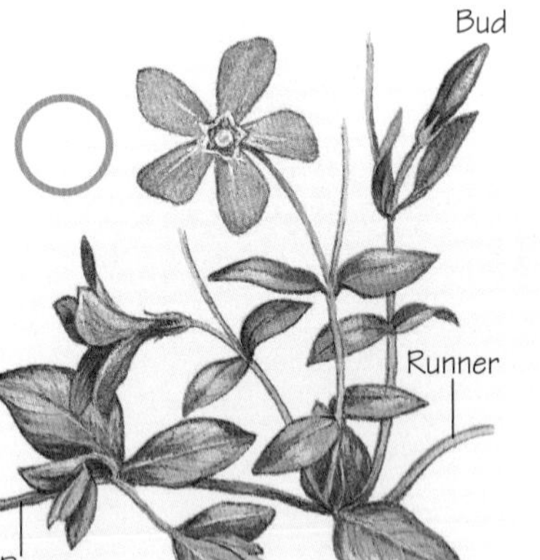

⬅ Lesser periwinkle

Creeps along the ground with long runners, making leafy carpets. Shiny, oval leaves. Woods and hedges. Flower stems up to 15cm tall. Feb-May.

➡ Viper's bugloss

Long, narrow leaves on rough, hairy stems. Erect or creeping. Pink buds become blue flowers. Waysides and sand dunes. 30cm tall. June-Sept.

Bud

Stamens

Sharp hairs on stem

⬅ Common forget-me-not

The curled stems of this hairy plant slowly straighten when it flowers. Flowers turn from pink to blue. Open places. 20cm tall. April-Oct.

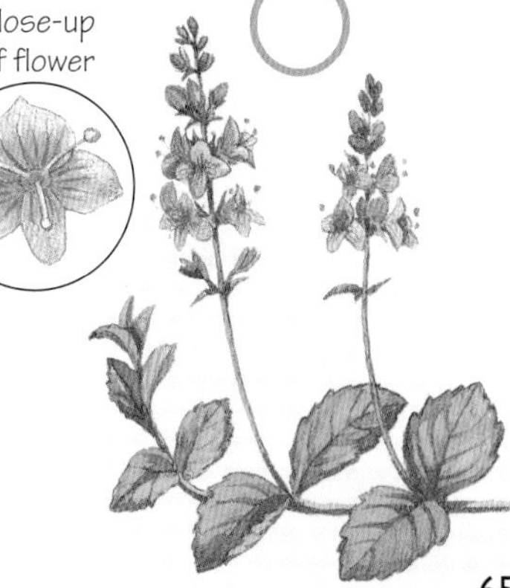

➡ Common speedwell

A hairy plant which forms large mats. Pinkish-blue flowers on erect spikes. Opposite, oval leaves. Grassy places and woods. 30cm tall. May-Aug.

Blue flowers

Look for these flowers in damp places.

Flower is shaped like a monk's hood.

➡ Common monkshood

Also called wolfsbane. Upright plant with spike of flowers at end of stem. Notice hood on flowers and the deeply-divided leaves. Near streams and in damp woods. 70cm tall. June-Sept.

➡ Brooklime

Creeping plant with erect, reddish stems. Shiny, oval leaves in opposite pairs. Used to be eaten in salads. Wet places. 30cm tall. May-Sept.

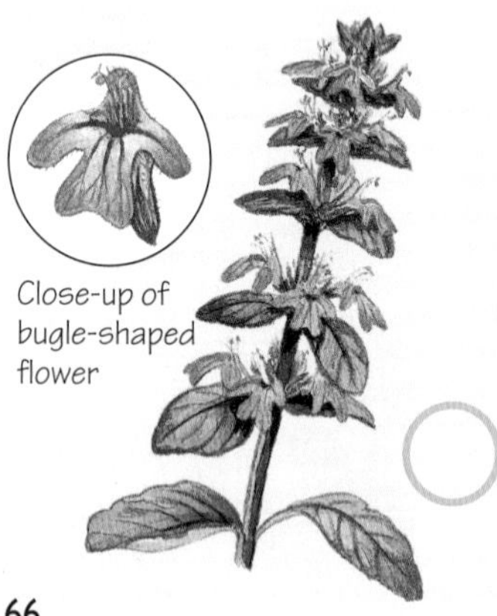

Close-up of bugle-shaped flower

⬅ Bugle

Creeping plant with erect flower spikes. Glossy leaves in opposite pairs. Stem is square and hairy on two sides. Leaves and stem are purplish. Forms carpets in damp woods. 20cm tall. May-June.

➡ Water forget-me-not

Grows in damp shady places next to still or running water. Blue flowers that may be pink at first. Flowers about 1cm across. June-Oct.

⬅ Meadow clary or meadow sage

Hairy stem with wrinkled leaves mostly at the base of the plant. Grassy places. 40cm tall. June-July.

➡ Bluebell

Also called wild hyacinth. Narrow, shiny leaves and clusters of nodding blue flowers. Forms thick carpets in woods. 30cm tall. April-May.

Pink flowers

Look for these flowers in woods or hedges.

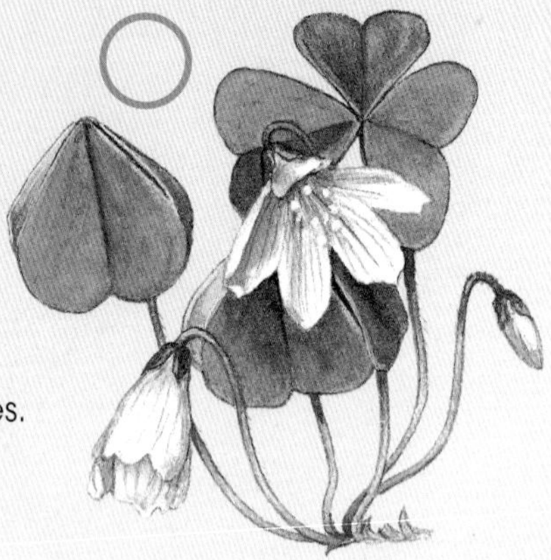

➡ Wood sorrel

A creeping, woodland plant with slender stems and rounded leaves. The white flowers have purplish veins. Woods and hedges. 10cm tall. April-May.

⬅ Red helleborine

Upright plant with pointed leaves and a fleshy stem. Rare plant, protected by law. Woods and shady places. Up to 40cm tall. May-June.

➡ Blackberry or bramble

Dense, woody plant that climbs up hedges. Sharp prickles on stems and under leaves. Berries are ripe and good to eat in autumn. June-Sept.

⬅ Bistort

Also called snakeweed. Forms patches. Leaves are narrow. Flowers in spikes. In meadows, often near water. 40cm tall. June-Oct.

➡ Greater bindweed

Look for the large, pink or white funnel-shaped flowers. Climbs walls and hedges in waste places. Leaves are shaped like arrowheads. 300cm high. July-Sept.

Bud

⬅ Dog rose

Scrambling creeper, up to 300cm tall, with thorny stems. Look for the red fruits, called rose hips, in autumn. Hedges and woods. June-July.

Rose hip (fruit)

Pink flowers

➡ Knotgrass

A weed that spreads in a thick mat or grows erect. Waste ground, fields and seashores. Stems can be 100cm long. July-Oct.

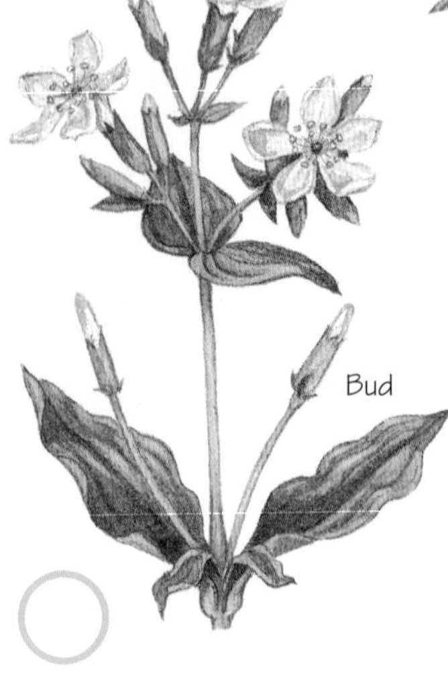

⬅ Soapwort

Erect plant with clusters of scented flowers. The broad, oval leaves were once used to make soap. Near rivers and streams. 40cm tall. Aug-Oct.

➡ Common fumitory

Creeping plant with much-divided, feathery leaves. Tiny flowers are tube-shaped and tipped with purple. Cultivated land. 30cm tall. May-Oct.

➡ Sand spurrey

Spreading, mat-forming plant with sticky, hairy stems. Narrow, grey-green leaves end in a stiff point. Sandy places. 10cm tall. May-Sept.

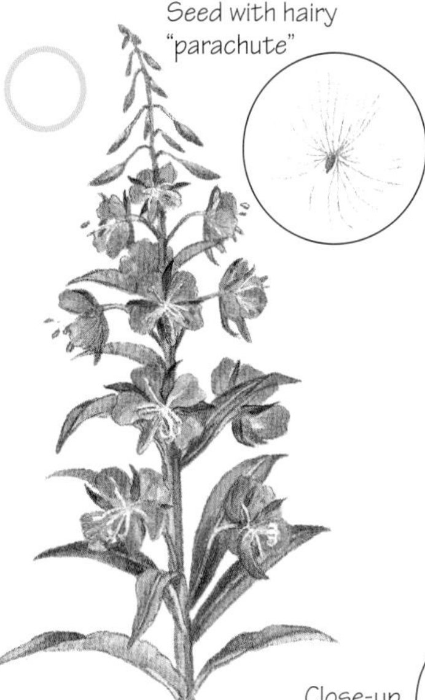

⬅ Rosebay willowherb

Also called fireweed. Tall, erect plant with spikes of pink flowers. Long, narrow leaves. Common on waste ground. 90cm tall. July-Sept.

➡ Herb Robert

Spreading plant with a strong smell. The flowers droop at night and in bad weather. Leaves are red in autumn. Woods and hedgebanks. 40cm tall. May-Sept.

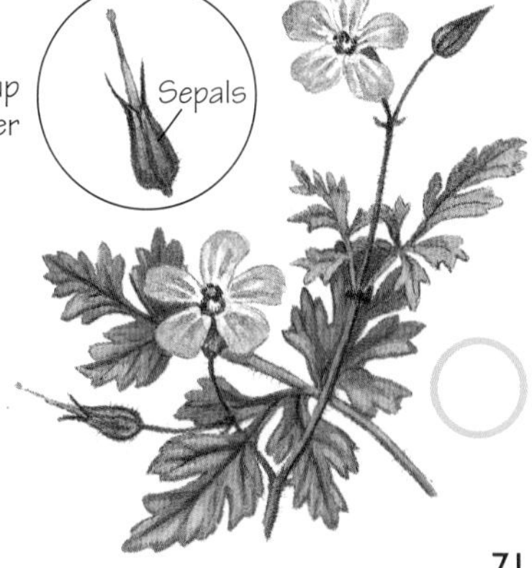

Pink flowers

Look for these flowers on heaths and moors.

Heather or ling

Shrubby plant with small, narrow leaves. Grows on heaths and moors. Leafy spikes of pink or white flowers. 20cm tall. July-Sept.

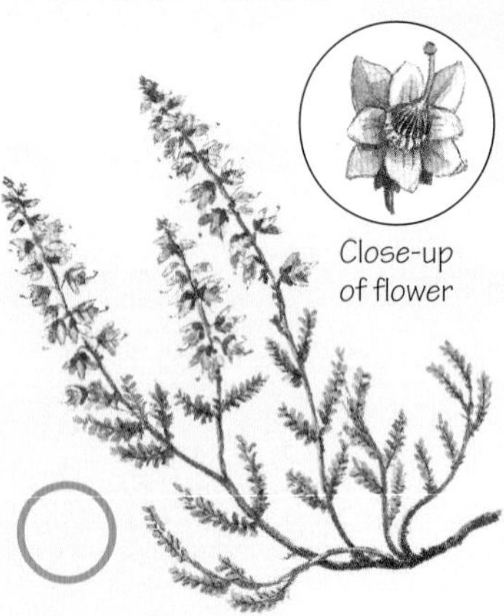

Close-up of flower

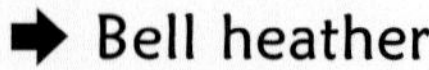

Bell heather

Like heather, but taller. Thin, needle-like leaves and clusters of bell-shaped, pink flowers. Dry heaths and moors. 30cm tall. July-Aug.

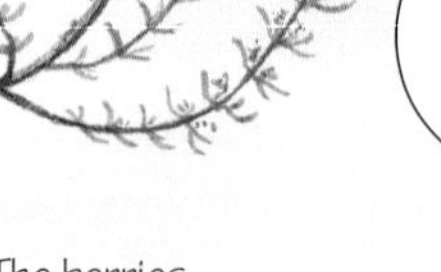

Close-up of flower

The berries are edible.

Bilberry

Small shrub with oval leaves. Drooping, bell-shaped, green-pink flowers. Heaths, moors and woods. 40cm tall. April-June.

Look for these flowers in dry, grassy places.

➡ Sorrel

Erect plant. Arrow-shaped leaves have backward-pointing lobes. Branched spikes of flowers. Leaves are eaten in salads. Pastures. 20-100cm tall. May-July

⬅ Sheep's sorrel

Smaller than sorrel. The lobes on the leaves point upwards. Dry places and heaths. 30cm tall. May-Aug.

➡ Common centaury

Erect plant with rosette of leaves at base and opposite leaves on stem. Flowers close at night. Grassland, dunes and woods. 50cm tall. June-Oct.

Pink flowers

➡ Ragged Robin

Flowers have ragged, pink petals. Erect plant with a forked stem and narrow, pointed leaves. Damp meadows, marshes and woods. 30-70cm tall. May-June.

Bract (a kind of small leaf near the flower)

Grooved stem

⬅ Knapweed or hard-head

Erect plant with brush-like, pink flowers growing from black bracts. Grassland and waysides. 40cm tall. June-Sept.

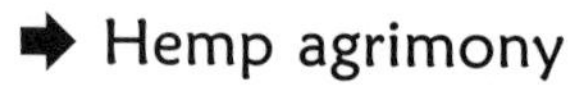

➡ Hemp agrimony

Tough, erect plant with downy stem. Grows in patches in damp places. Attracts butterflies. Up to 120cm tall. July-Sept.

Close-up of flower

Deptford pink

The clusters of bright pink flowers close in the afternoon. Pointed, opposite leaves. Very rare in Britain. Sandy places. 40cm tall. July-Aug.

Fruit

Blood-red geranium or bloody cranesbill

Bushy plant with erect or trailing stems. Deeply divided leaves are round and hairy. Hedgerows. 30cm tall. June-Aug.

Red campion

Erect plant with a hairy, sticky stem and pointed, oval leaves in opposite pairs. Woodland. 60cm tall. May-June.

Purple flowers

⬅ Early purple orchid

Erect plant with dark spots on the leaves. Smells like cats. Look for the hood and spur on the flowers. Woods and copses. Up to 60cm tall. June-Aug.

➡ Tufted vetch

Scrambling plant with clinging tendrils. Climbs up hedgerows. Look for the brown seed pods in late summer. Flowers 1cm across. June-Sept.

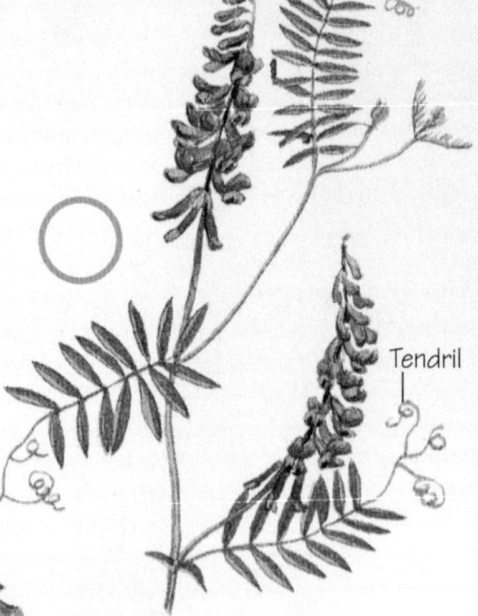

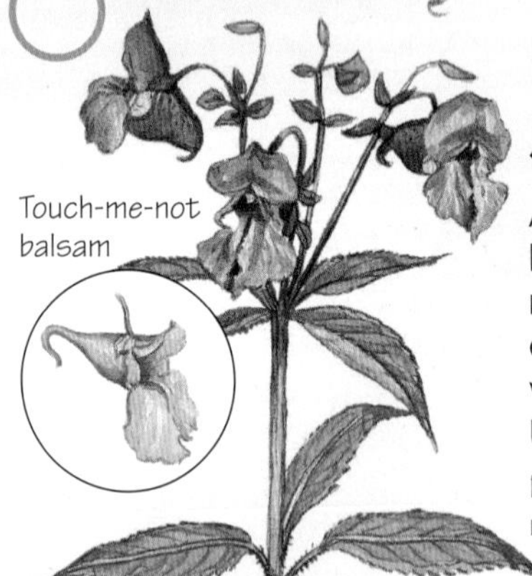

⬅ Policeman's helmet

Also called jumping Jack. Flowers look like open mouths. Ripe seed pods explode, scattering seeds when touched. Streams. Up to 200cm tall. July-Oct.

Policeman's helmet is closely related to touch-me-not balsam.

Look for these flowers in woods or hedgerows.

Bats-in-the-belfry

Erect, hairy plant with large, toothed leaves. Flowers on leafy spikes point upwards. Hedges, woods and shady places. 60cm tall. July-Sept.

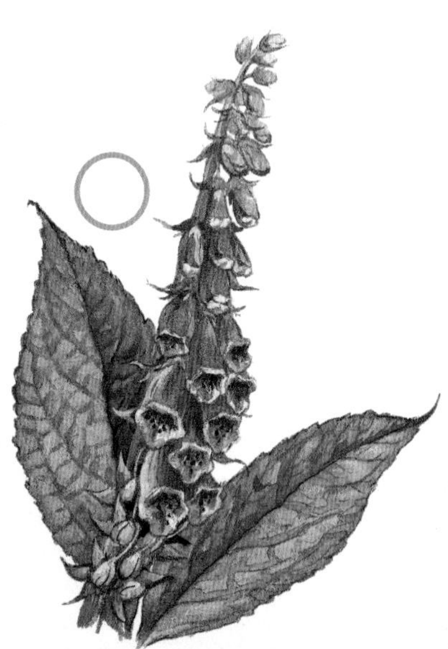

Foxglove

Erect plant with tall spike of tube-shaped flowers, drooping on one side of the stem. Large, oval leaves. Open woods. Up to 150cm tall. June-Sept.

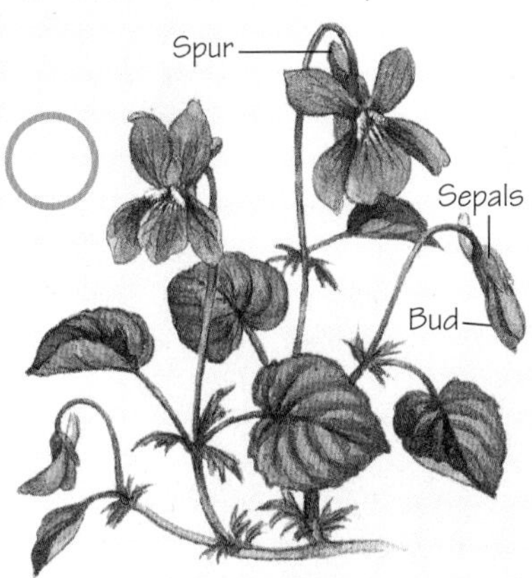

Common dog violet

Creeping plant with rosettes of heart-shaped leaves. Look for the pointed sepals and short spur on the flower. Woods. 10cm tall. April-June.

Purple flowers

Look in fields and other grassy places for these flowers.

➡ Pasque flower

Very rare in the wild, but grows in gardens. Hairy, feathery leaves. Purple or white flowers have yellow anthers. Dry, grassy places. 10cm tall. April-May.

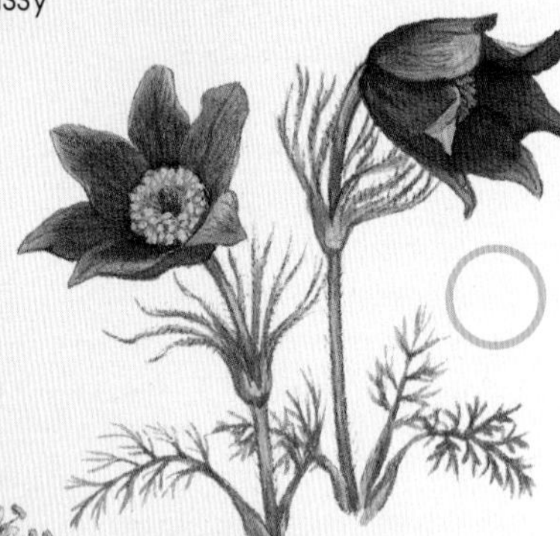

Devil's bit scabious

Field scabious

Field scabious is a similar species.

Lobed leaves

Entire leaves

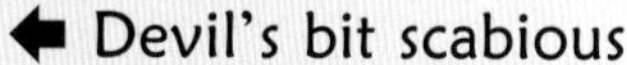

⬅ Devil's bit scabious

Erect plant with narrow, pointed leaves. Flowers are pale to dark purple. Round flower heads. Wet, grassy places. 15-30cm tall. June-Oct.

➡ Fritillary or snake's head

Drooping flowers are chequered with light and dark purple. Varies from white to dark purple. Damp meadows. 10cm tall. May.

You may see these flowers on old walls.

➡ Ivy-leaved toadflax

Weak, slender stalks trail on old walls. Look for the yellow lips on the mauve flowers. Flowers 1cm across. Shiny, ivy-shaped leaves. May-Sept.

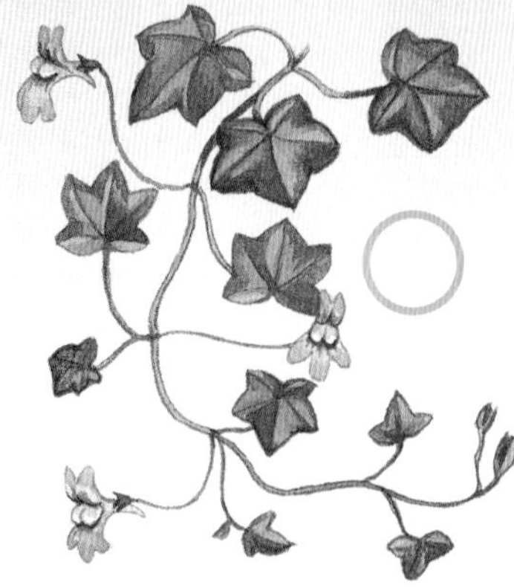

⬅ Houseleek

A rosette plant with thick, fleshy leaves. Dull red, spiky petals. Does not flower every year. Old walls and roofs. 30-60cm tall. June-July.

The stalk, with flowers, does not appear very often – usually you will see only the rosette.

Rosette of leaves

➡ Snapdragon

Erect plant with spike of flowers. Long, narrow leaves. Pouch-like flowers are yellow inside. Old walls, rocks and gardens. 40cm tall. June-Sept.

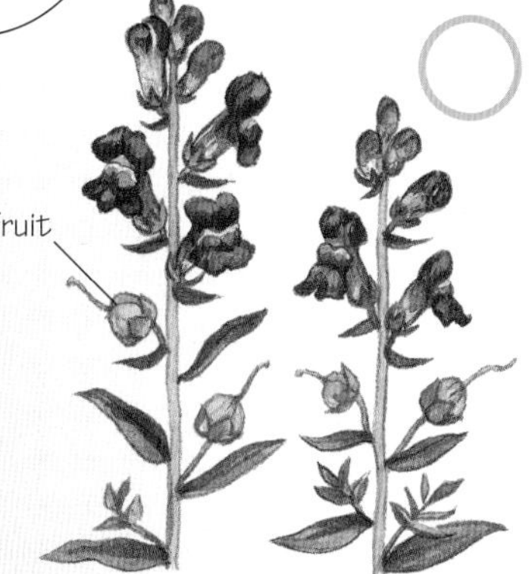

Red flowers

Look for these flowers on cultivated land.

➡ Scarlet pimpernel

Grows along the ground. Flowers close in bad weather. Black dots under the pointed, oval leaves. Cultivated land. 15cm tall. June-Aug.

Flowers may also be blue.

➡ Poppy

Erect plant with stiff hairs on stem. Soft, red flowers have dark centres. Round seed pod. Cornfields and waste ground. Up to 60cm tall. June-Aug.

Seed pod

Bud

⬅ Long-headed poppy

Like poppy, but flowers are paler and do not have dark centres. Pod is long and narrow. Cornfields and waste ground. Up to 45cm tall. June-Aug.

⬅ Pheasant's eye

Rare cornfield weed with finely divided, feathery leaves. The red flowers have black centres. 20cm tall. May-Sept.

Summer pheasant's eye (not in Britain) is a similar species.

➡ Sweet William

Tough, narrow leaves and flat flower cluster. Mountain pastures and cultivated land in Europe. Gardens only in Britain. 60cm tall. May-June.

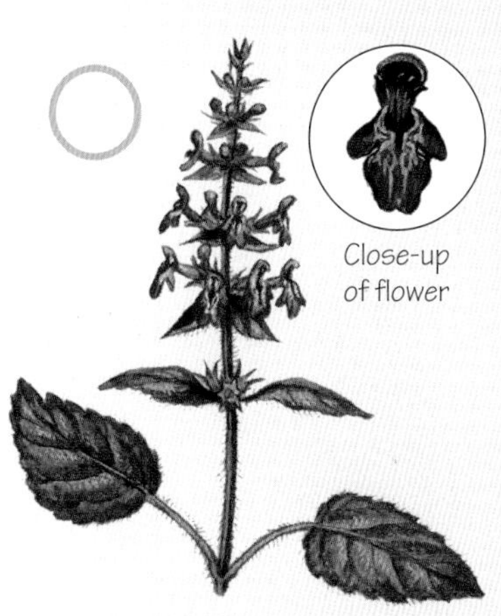

Close-up of flower

⬅ Wood woundwort

The leaves were once used to dress wounds. Spikes of dark red and white flowers in whorls. Smells strongly. Woods. 40cm tall. June-Aug.

White and green flowers

These flowers can be found in woodlands quite early in the year.

➡ Greater stitchwort

Look in woods and hedgerows for this slender, creeping plant. Grass-like leaves in opposite pairs. 15-60cm tall. April-June.

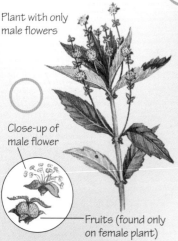

Plant with only male flowers

Close-up of male flower

Fruits (found only on female plant)

⬅ Dog's mercury

Downy plant with opposite, toothed leaves. Strong-smelling. Male flowers grow on separate plants from female flowers. Found in patches in woodlands. 15-20cm tall. Feb-April.

➡ Lily-of-the-valley

Grows in dry woods. Broad, dark green leaves and sweet-smelling flowers. Red berries in summer. Also a garden plant. 20cm tall. May-June.

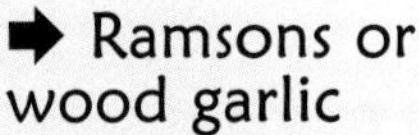

➡ Ramsons or wood garlic

Smells of garlic. Broad, bright green leaves grow from a bulb. Forms carpets in damp woods, often with bluebells. 10-25cm tall. April-June.

Notice the long veins that run from one end of the leaf to the other.

The large sepals look like petals.

⬅ Wood anemone

Also called Granny's nightcap. Forms carpets in woods. The flowers have pink-streaked sepals. 15cm tall. March-June.

➡ Snowdrop

Welcomed as the first flower of the new year. Dark green, narrow leaves. Nodding white flowers. Woods. 20cm tall. Jan-March.

White and green flowers

Look for these flowers in hedges or woods.

Seed pod

⬉ Jack-by-the-hedge or garlic mustard

Erect plant with heart-shaped, toothed leaves. Smells of garlic. Common in hedges. Up to 120cm tall. April-June.

➡ Wild strawberry

Small plant with long, arching runners and oval, toothed leaves in threes. Sweet, red fruits, covered with seeds. Woods and scrubland. April-July.

Fruits are smaller than garden strawberries.

Tendril

Pod

⬅ Wild pea

Very rare, scrambling plant with grey-green leaves. The seeds, or peas, are inside the pods. Climbs on thickets and hedges. Up to 250cm high. June-Aug.

Look for these flowers in hedges and waysides.

➡ White bryony

Climbs up hedges with spiral tendrils. The red berries appear in August and are poisonous. Large underground stems, called tubers. Up to 400cm tall. June.

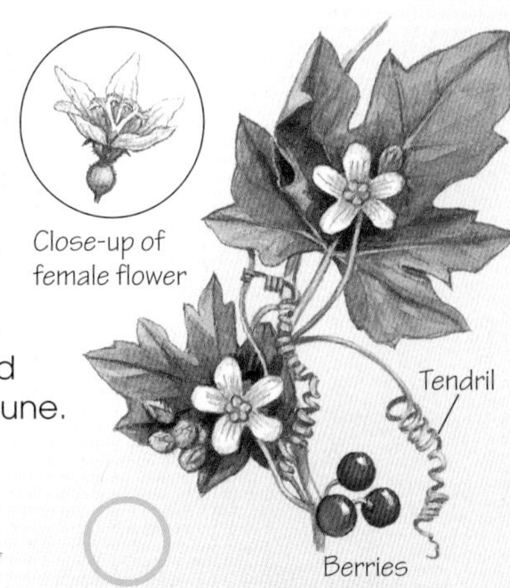

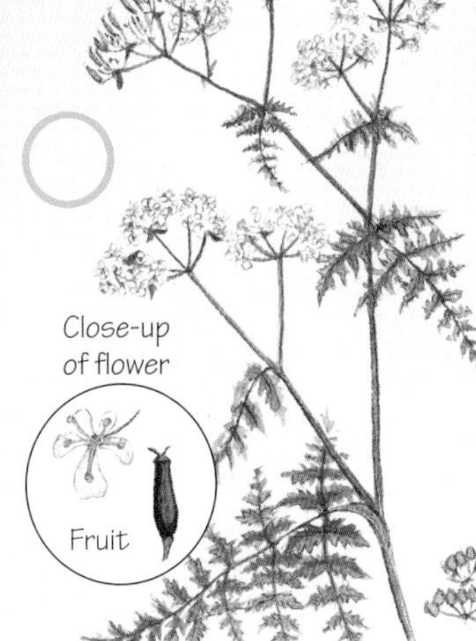

⬅ Cow parsley

Also called Lady's lace. Look for the ribbed stem, feathery leaves and white flower clusters. Hedge banks and ditches. Up to 100cm tall. May-June.

➡ Hedge parsley

Like cow parsley, but with a stiff, hairy stem. Look for the prickly, purple fruits. Cornfields and roadsides. 60cm tall. April-May

White and green flowers

Look for these flowers in fields and other grassy places.

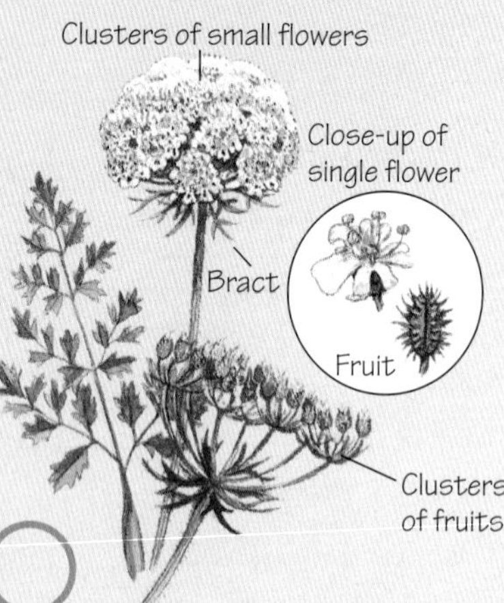

➡ Wild carrot

Dense clusters of white flowers with a purple flower in the centre. Erect, hairy stem with feathery leaves. Grassy places, often near coast. 60cm tall. July-Aug.

⬅ Hogweed or keck

Very stout, hairy plant with huge leaves on long stalks. Flowers are in clusters. Grassy places and open woods. Up to 100cm tall. June-Sept.

Close-up of single flower

➡ Corky-fruited water dropwort

Erect plant with large, much-divided, feathery leaves. Clusters of flowers. Meadows. 60cm tall. June-Aug.

White petals
are sometimes
tinged with pink.

⬅ Daisy

Small plant with rosette of leaves at base. Flowers close at night and in bad weather. Very common on garden lawns. 10cm tall. Jan-Oct.

➡ White or Dutch clover

Creeping plant, often grown for animal feed. Look for the white band on the three-lobed leaves. Attracts bees. 10-25cm tall. April-Aug.

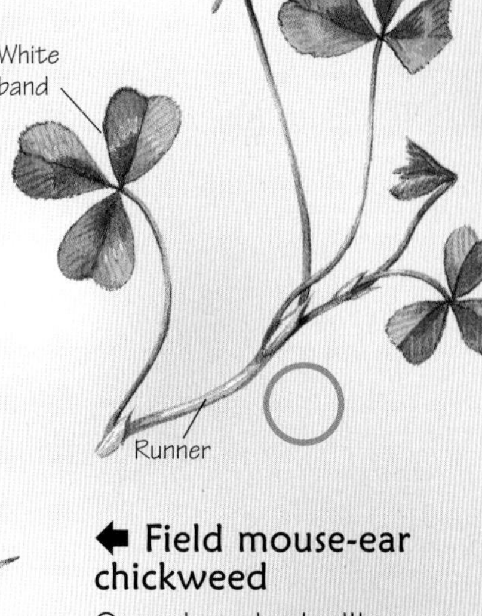
White
band
Runner

Look for the divided petals.

⬅ Field mouse-ear chickweed

Creeping plant with erect stems. Narrow, downy leaves. Grassy places.10cm tall. April-Aug.

White and green flowers

Look for these flowers on cultivated land, waste land and waysides.

Common orache

An erect weed with a stiff stem and toothed leaves, both dusty grey. Cultivated land or waste places. Up to 90cm tall. Aug-Sept.

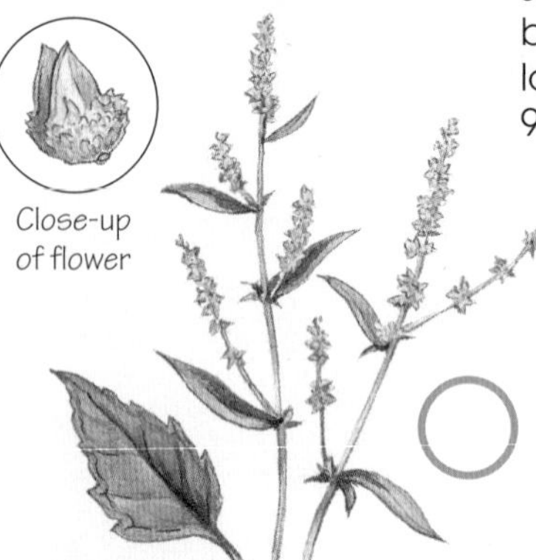

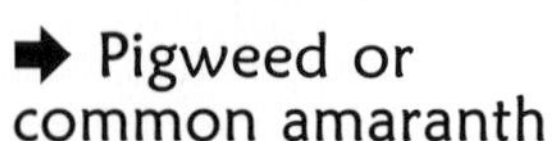

Pigweed or common amaranth

Erect, hairy plant with large, oval leaves. Large spikes of green, tufty flowers. Look for it on cultivated land. 50cm tall. July-Sept.

Close-up of flower

Nettle

The toothed leaves are covered with stinging hairs. Dangling green-brown flowers. Used to make beer and tea. Common. Up to 100cm tall. June-Aug.

➡ Good King Henry

An erect plant with arrow-shaped leaves and spikes of tiny, green flowers. Farmyards and roadsides. 30-50cm tall. May-July.

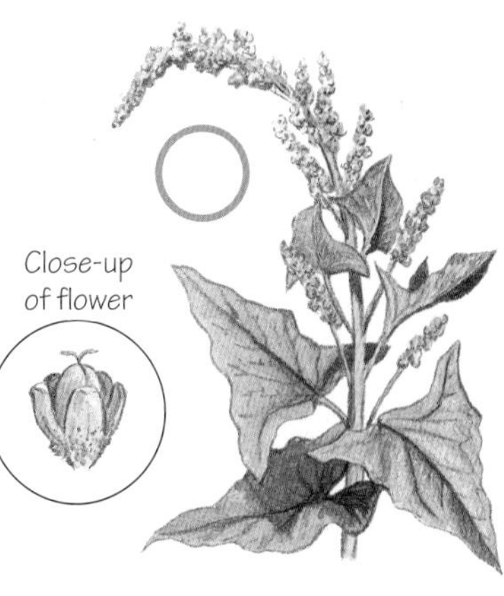

⬅ Shepherd's purse

Very common plant. The white flowers and heart-shaped seed pods can be seen all year round. Waysides and waste places. Up to 40cm tall.

➡ White dead-nettle

Looks like nettle, but the hairs do not sting. Flowers in whorls on the stem. Hedgerows and waste places. Up to 60cm tall. May-Dec.

White and green flowers

➡ Bladder campion

Oval leaves in opposite pairs. The sepals are joined together, forming a bladder. Grassy places and hedgerows. 30cm tall. June-Sept.

When flowering is over, fruit grows inside sepals (calyx).

Calyx is smaller than that of bladder campion.

⬅ White campion

The erect stems and the sepals are sticky and hairy. The white petals are divided. Look in hedgerows. Up to 100cm tall. May-June.

➡ Corn spurrey

Spindly plant with jointed, sticky stems. Narrow leaves in whorls around the stem. Weed of cornfields. 30cm tall. April-July.

Whorl of leaves

⬅ Chickweed

Mat-forming plant with stems that can grow up to 40cm tall. You can see the small flowers all year round. Common weed in fields and gardens.

➡ Black nightshade

Shrubby weed of cultivated ground. Shiny, oval leaves. Petals fold back to show yellow anthers. The berries are poisonous. 20cm tall. July-Sept.

Anthers

Berries

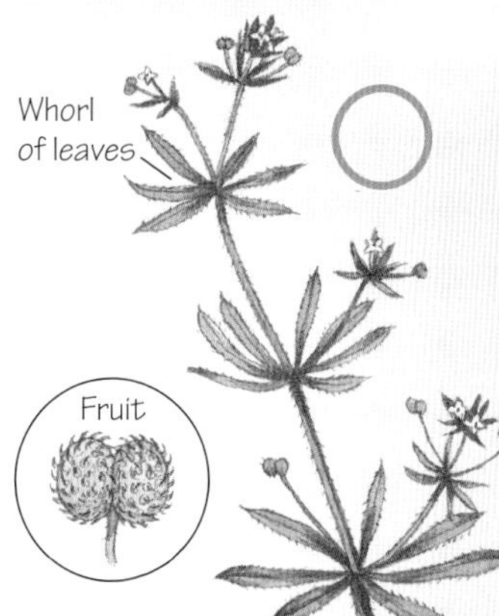

⬅ Goosegrass or common cleavers

Scrambling plant. The prickly stems stick to clothes and animal fur. Hedges. 60cm tall. June-Sept.

White and green flowers

Look for these flowers in grassy places, on waste or cultivated ground.

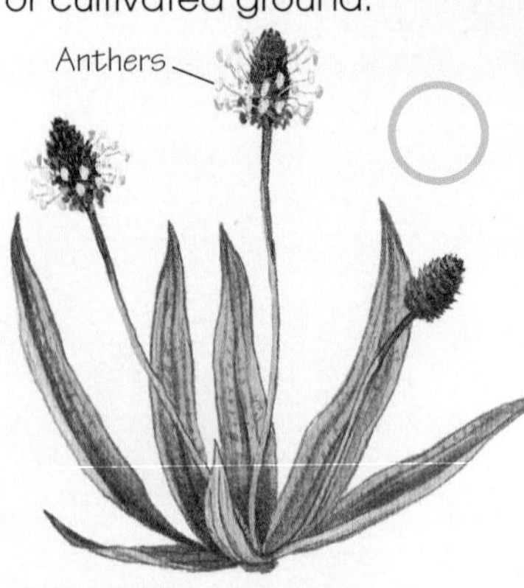

Ribwort plantain or cocks and hens

Tough plant with narrow, ribbed leaves. Green-brown spikes of flowers have white anthers. Common. 20cm tall. April-Aug.

Anthers are mauve at first, changing to yellow.

Anthers

Greater plantain or ratstail

Broad-ribbed leaves in a rosette close to the ground. All kinds of cultivated land. 15cm tall. May-Sept.

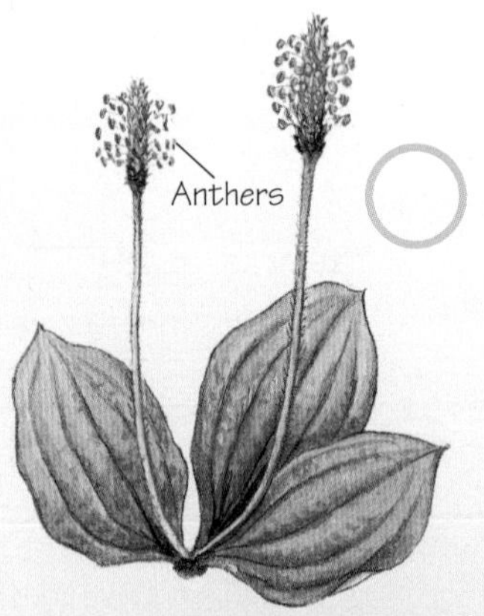

Hoary plantain

Rosette plant with oval, ribbed leaves. Fine hairs on stem. White flowers have purple anthers. Common in grassy places. 7-15cm tall. May-Aug.

Look for these flowers on grassy or waste ground.

⬅ Yarrow

Common plant with rough stem and feathery leaves. Flat-topped clusters of flowers. Smells sweet. Was once used to heal wounds. 40cm tall. June-Aug.

➡ Wild chamomile or scented mayweed

Erect plant with finely divided leaves. The petals fold back. Waste places everywhere. 15-40cm tall. June-July.

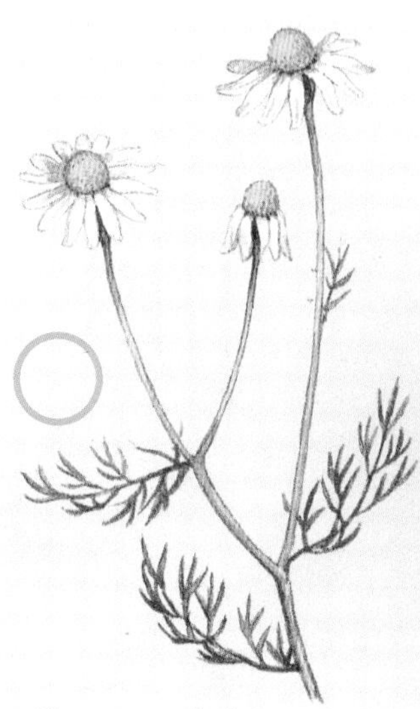

⬅ Ox-eye daisy or marguerite

Erect plant with rosette of toothed leaves and large, daisy-like flowers. Roadsides and grassy places. Up to 60cm tall. June-Aug.

White and green flowers

➡ Starry saxifrage

A rosette plant with shiny, fleshy, toothed leaves. Mountain rocks. 20cm tall. June-Aug.

➡ Meadow saxifrage

Downy, lobed leaves. Up to 40cm tall. Grassy places.

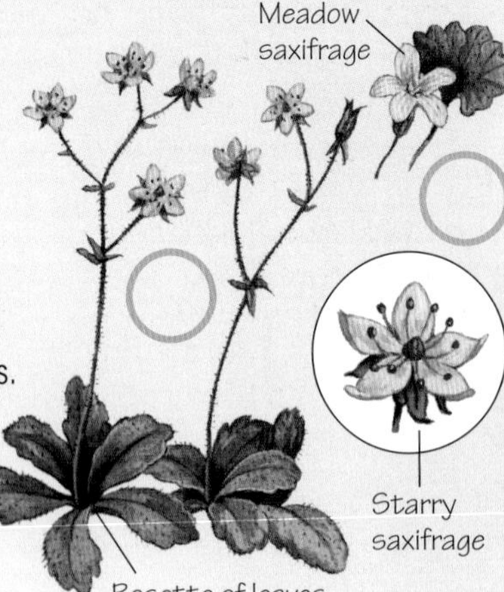

Seed pods

⬅ Alpine rock cress

Short, mat-forming plant with rosette of greyish-green leaves. Dense clusters of white flowers. Rocks on hills and mountains. April-June.

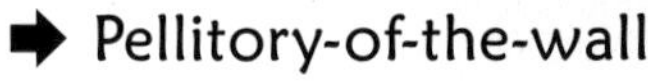

➡ Pellitory-of-the-wall

Plant with red stems and soft hairs. Tiny, stalkless green flowers. Cracks in rocks and walls, and hedgebanks. Up to 100cm tall. June-Oct.

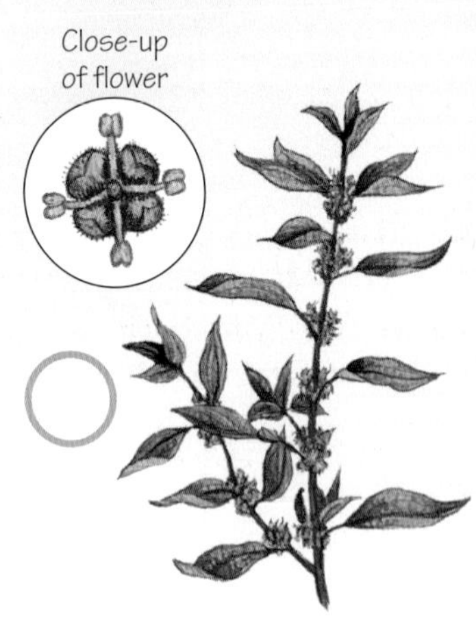

Freshwater flowers

These flowers can be found in or near fresh water, such as streams and ponds.

Undersides of leaves are silvery-grey.

➡ Meadowsweet

Clusters of sweet-smelling flowers. Grows in marshes, water meadows and also near ditches at the side of the road. Up to 80cm tall. May-Sept.

The flower stem is three-sided.

⬅ Triangular-stalked garlic or three-cornered leek

Smells of garlic. Drooping flowers. In damp hedges and waste places. 40cm tall. June-July.

Water surface
Underwater leaves are longer and thinner.

➡ Floating water plantain

Water plant with oval leaves and white flowers on the water surface. Look for it in canals and still water. Flowers 1-1.5cm across. May-Aug.

Freshwater flowers

➡ Water crowfoot

Water plant whose roots are anchored in the mud at the bottom of ponds and streams. Flowers (1-2cm across) cover the water surface. May-June.

These leaves are on the water surface.
Fine, underwater leaves

⬅ Water soldier

Under water except when it flowers. Long, saw-like leaves then show above the surface. Flowers 3-4cm across. Ponds, canals, ditches. June-Aug.

➡ Frogbit

Rises to the surface in spring, and spreads with long runners. Shiny, round leaves grow in tufts. Flowers 2cm across. Canals and ponds. July-Aug.

Bud
Runner

Floating-leaved plants

➡ Broad-leaved pondweed

Common in shallow pools of acid water. Oval floating leaves and thin, delicate underwater leaves. Spikes of green flowers. Up to 1m tall. June-Aug.

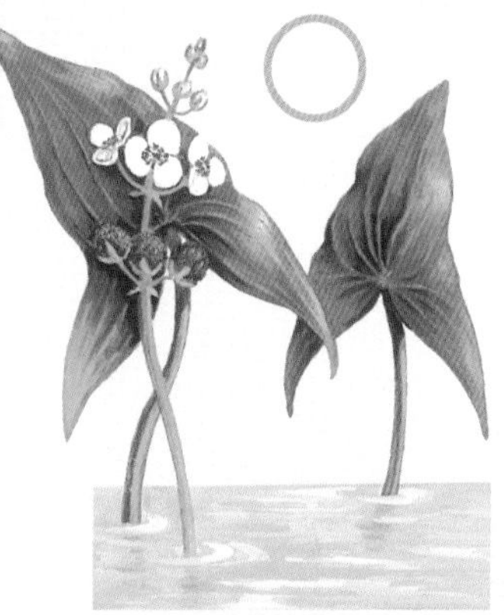

⬅ Arrowhead

Long, narrow underwater leaves grow in spring, followed by oval floating leaves and large upper leaves like arrowheads. In muddy water. Up to 1m tall. June-Aug.

➡ Yellow water-lily

Glossy floating leaves look like blunt, rounded arrowheads. Seedheads shaped like light bulbs. Yellow flowers about 7cm across. June-Aug.

➡ White water-lily

Flowers and leaves float on the surface of the water. White petals, sometimes tinged with pink. Flowers up to 20cm across. June-Aug.

Underwater plants

➡ Canadian pondweed

Introduced into Europe in about 1850. Grows fast and has choked many waterways. Leaves grow in threes on stem. Flowers are rare. Up to 3.5m long. June-Sept.

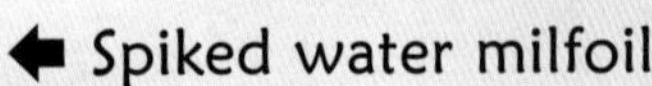

⬅ Spiked water milfoil

Very common in chalky, still water. Many small invertebrates shelter on the underwater leaves. Slender flower stem grows above water. Up to 3.5m long. June-July.

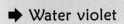

➡ Water violet

Long stem and feathery leaves are under water. Cluster of flowers rises up to 40cm above the water. Rare. Found in ditches, ponds and lakes. Mainly eastern Britain. May-June.

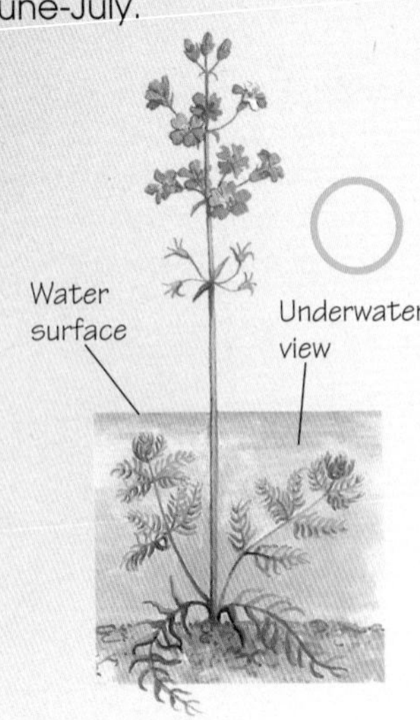

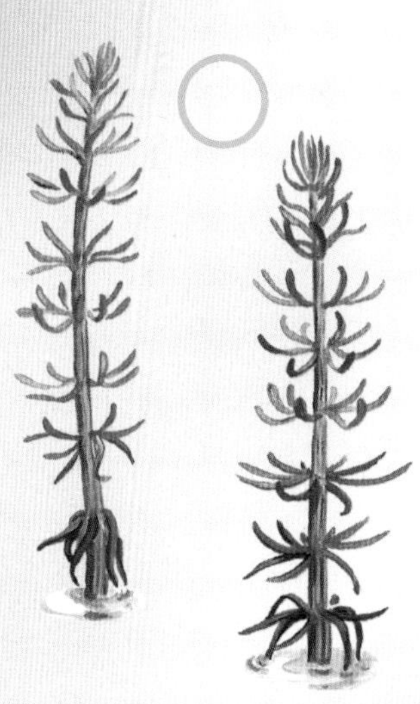

⬅ Mare's tail

Narrow leaves, grouped in whorls around stem. Tiny flowers appear at base of leaves. Grows partly submerged in still or slow-moving water. Up to 1m tall. June-July.

Star-shaped cluster of leaves

➡ Water starwort

This water weed is often seen in ditches, streams and ponds. Upper leaves float on the surface in star-shaped clusters. Very small flowers at base of the leaves. Up to 50cm long. May-Sept.

Tiny flowers

Anchored to the mud by colourless threads.

⬅ Stonewort

This plant does not have flowers. It is found in chalky or salty water. It is brittle and snaps easily. Eaten by ducks. Up to 20cm long.

Seashore flowers

➡ Thrift or sea pink (left)

Grows in thick, cushiony tufts on rocky cliffs. 15cm tall. March-Sept.

➡ Sea mayweed (right)

May be creeping or upright. Feathery leaves. Daisy-like flowers. Grows on cliffs. Up to 60cm tall. Can be seen in winter.

Thrift or sea pink   Sea mayweed

⬅ Sea campion

Common on cliffs and shingle beaches. Spreads to form cushions. 20cm tall. June-August.

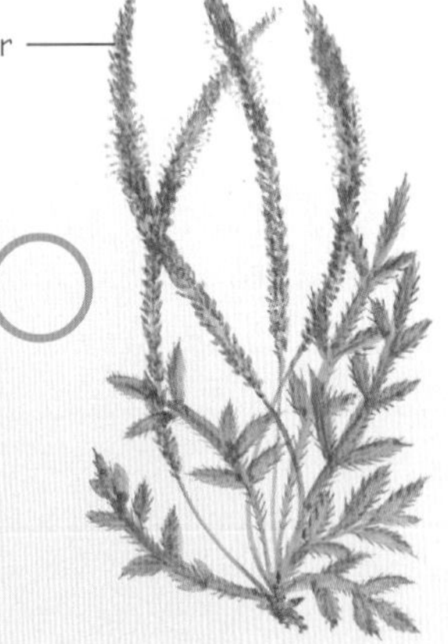

➡ Buckshorn plantain

Hairy leaves grow from a point close to the ground. Look on gravel near the sea. Spikes of flowers. 10cm tall. May-Oct.

➡ Annual seablite

May grow along the ground or upright. Fleshy leaves. On saltmarshes in areas of bare mud. 20cm tall.

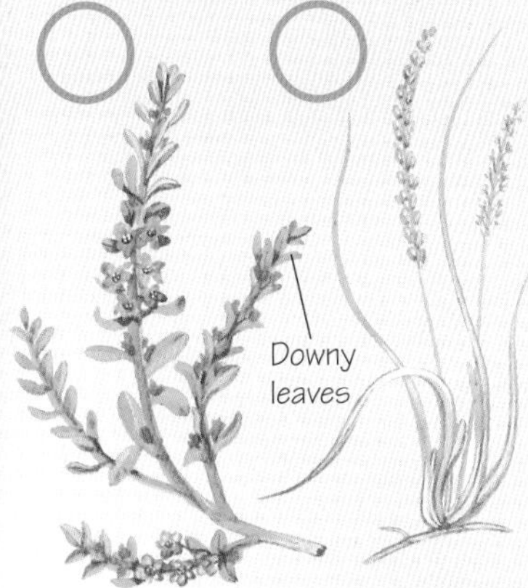

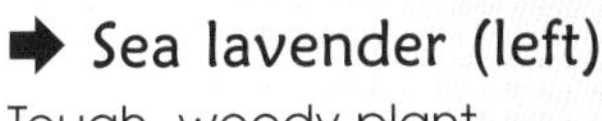

Sea milkwort Sea arrowgrass

⬅ Sea milkwort (left)

Creeping plant that spreads over grassy saltmarshes. June-August.

⬅ Sea arrowgrass (right)

Tough plant with flat, sharp leaves. Grassy saltmarshes. 15-50cm tall. May-Sept.

➡ Sea lavender (left)

Tough, woody plant with leaves in a clump near the ground. Muddy saltmarshes. Up to 40cm tall. July-Sept.

➡ Sea aster (right)

Flowers in late summer, with lilac or white petals. Saltmarshes. Up to 1m tall.

Sea lavender Sea aster

Seashore flowers

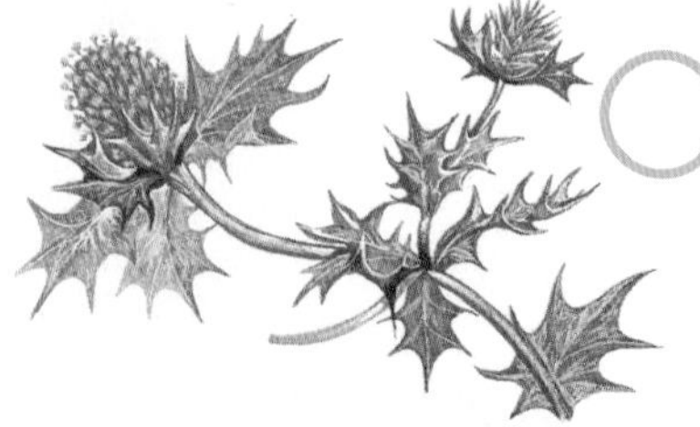

← Sea holly

Prickly plant with clusters of tiny flowers, which attract butterflies. Its thick leaves turn white in winter. Sand and shingle. Up to 50cm tall.

→ Sea wormwood (left)

Strong-smelling plant. Leaves are downy and greyish green. Grows above high tide level in estuaries. Up to 50cm tall.

→ Sea purslane (middle)

Grows on edges of deep channels in saltmarshes. 60cm tall. June-Oct.

→ Marram grass (right)

Common on sand dunes. Its long roots and leaves trap sand and stop it blowing away. Up to 1.2m tall. July-August.

Flower spike

Beware of sharp leaves.

Sea wormwood

Sea purslane

Marram grass

← Sea bindweed

Trailing plant with thick, shiny leaves. Can be seen on sand dunes and sometimes on shingle. June-Sept.

➡ Yellow horned poppy

Called horned because of the long, green pods which appear in summer. Shingle beaches. Up to 1m tall. June-Sept.

⬅ Sea kale

Grows in clumps on shingle. Broad, fleshy leaves have crinkly edges. Up to 1m tall. June-August.

➡ Golden samphire

Sturdy plant with shiny, fleshy leaves. Often grows in large clumps on saltmarshes, shingle and cliffs. Flowers in autumn. 60cm tall.

⬅ Sea sandwort

Common creeping plant on loose sand and shingle. Helps to stop sand drifting. 30cm tall. May-August.

Trees

Conifers

Scots pine

Short, blue-green, needles in pairs, and small pointed buds. The bark is red at the top of the tree, and grey and furrowed below. The young tree has a pointed shape, becoming flat-topped with age.

Small bud
Short needles in pairs 5-7cm
Green, pointed cone turns brown in second year.
The bark flakes off in "plates".

Long bare trunk is red near top of tree.
35m

Maritime pine

Long, stout, grey-green needles in pairs; long spindle-shaped buds; and long, shiny brown cones grouped in clusters. Rugged bark on a long, bare trunk.

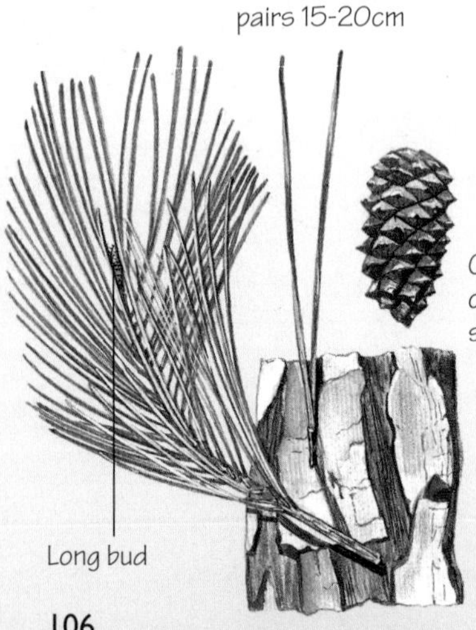
Long needles in pairs 15-20cm
Cones stay on tree for several years
Long bud

22m

⬆ Stone pine

Umbrella-shaped tree with a flat top, found on the Mediterranean coast. Long dark-green, paired needles, small buds, and broad cones with edible seeds.

⬆ Shore pine

Tall, narrow, fast-growing, with small cones in clusters. Yellow-green needles in pairs on twisted shoots, scaly bark, and sticky, bullet-shaped buds.

Conifers

Branches grow at regular intervals.
36m
Paired needles 12-18cm
Cones take two years to ripen.
Young shoot
Paired needles
Rare in Britain.
10m
Shiny, reddish cones stay on tree for many years.

↑ Corsican pine

Tall, fast-growing Mediterranean tree, found on rocky hillsides. Long, dark-green, paired needles; onion-shaped buds; and large lop-sided brown cones. Blackish bark.

↑ Aleppo pine

Small, round-topped Mediterranean tree, with bright-green, paired needles and small round buds. Its cones usually come in groups of two or three.

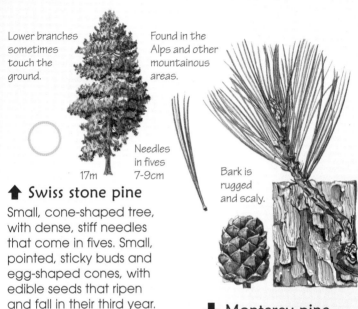

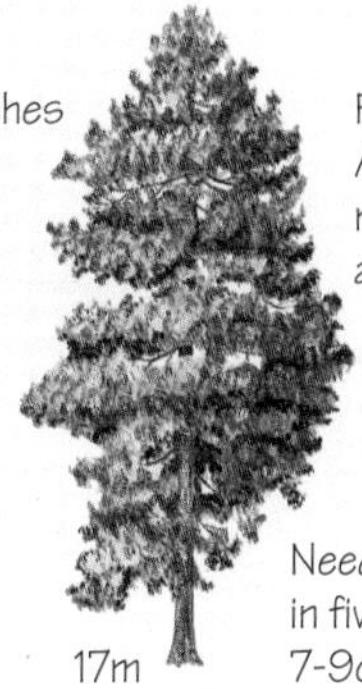

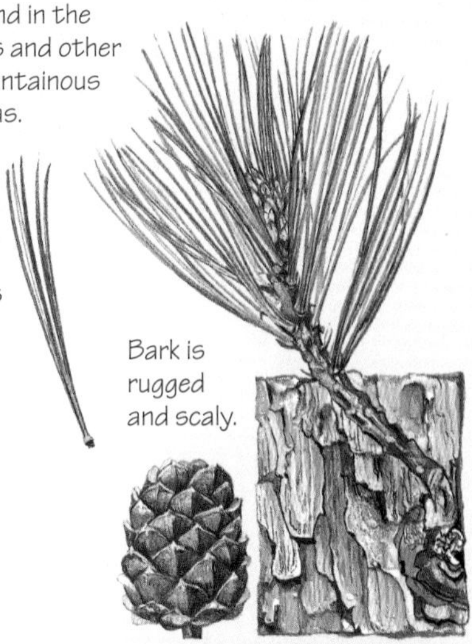

Lower branches sometimes touch the ground.
17m
Needles in fives 7-9cm

Found in the Alps and other mountainous areas.
Bark is rugged and scaly.

⬆ Swiss stone pine

Small, cone-shaped tree, with dense, stiff needles that come in fives. Small, pointed, sticky buds and egg-shaped cones, with edible seeds that ripen and fall in their third year.

Needles in threes – about 10cm
Large, pointed sticky buds

Cones uneven at base.

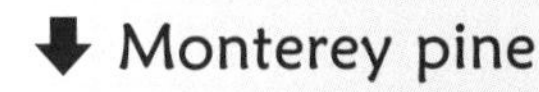

⬇ Monterey pine

Slender, grass-green needles in threes. Large, pointed, sticky buds and squat cones growing flat against the branches, staying on the tree for many years.

30m

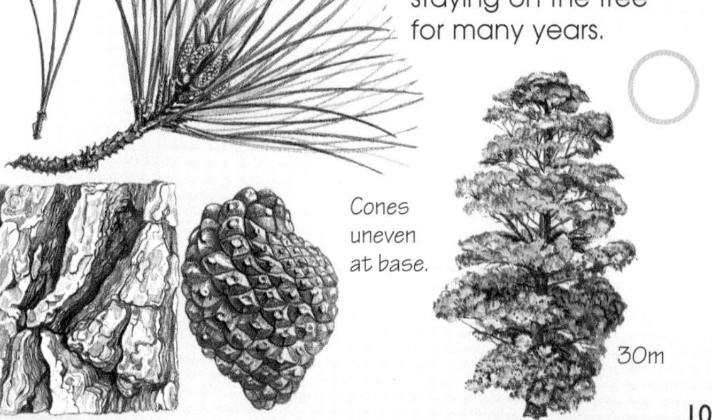

Conifers

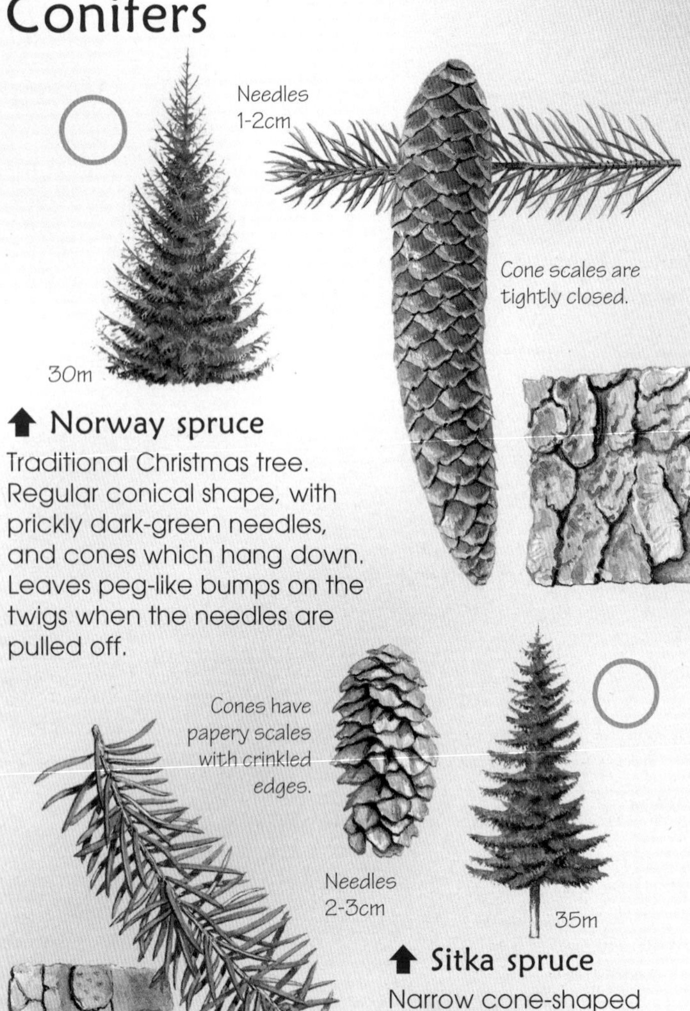
Needles
1-2cm
Cone scales are
tightly closed.
30m
Cones have
papery scales
with crinkled
edges.
Needles
2-3cm
35m

⬆ Norway spruce

Traditional Christmas tree. Regular conical shape, with prickly dark-green needles, and cones which hang down. Leaves peg-like bumps on the twigs when the needles are pulled off.

⬆ Sitka spruce

Narrow cone-shaped tree, with prickly blue-green needles and fat yellow buds. Small knobs left on yellow twigs when needles are pulled off.

Grey, scaly bark flakes off in "plates".

⬆ European larch

Bunches of soft, light-green needles, which turn yellow and fall in winter, leaving small barrel-like knobs on twigs. Small, egg-shaped cones and reddish female flowers.

⬇ Japanese larch

Bunches of blue-green needles, which fall in winter, leaving orange twigs. Pinkish-green female flowers and small, flower-like cones.

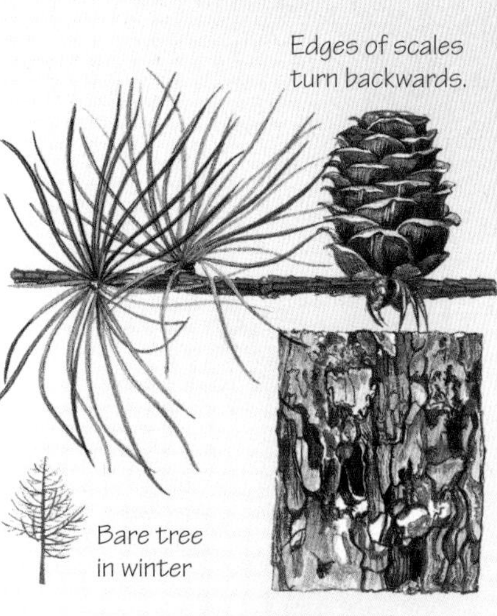

Conifers

Young cones are green, turning plum-coloured with age.

Cone

⬆ Nootka cypress

Fern-like sprays of dull green, scale-like leaves grow on either side of the twigs. Plum-coloured cones have prickles on their scales. Cone-shaped crown.

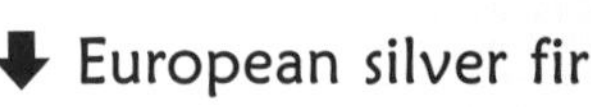

⬇ European silver fir

Flat single needles, green above and silvery below. Flat, round scars left on twigs when needles drop. Cones shed their scales when ripe, leaving a brown spike.

Large, upright cones

Bracts showing

The twigs are smooth and the needles have notched tips.

Rare in Britain, but common in central Europe.

Very tall, narrow tree

40m

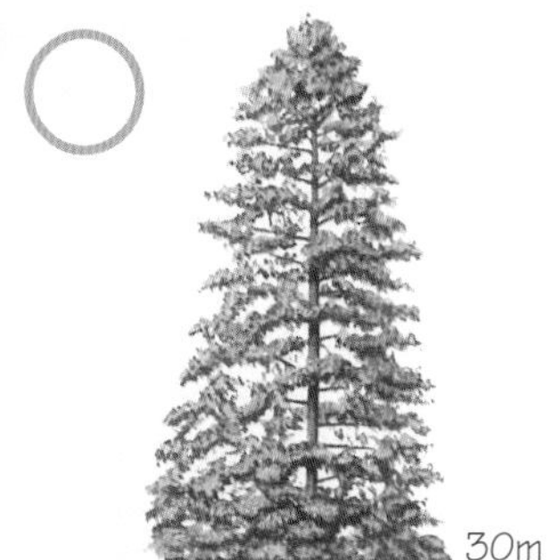
30m

The needles have pointed tips.
Bark flakes off in "plates".

⬆ Greek fir

Shiny green, spiny-tipped needles all around twig. Tall, narrow cones shed scales to leave bare spikes on tree. Found only in parks in Britain.

⬇ Spanish fir

Short, blunt, blue-grey needles all around twig. Cylindrical, upright cones, which shed scales when ripe, like the European silver fir.

The needles have blunt tips.
The tree has a conical shape.
28m

Conifers

The needles are shorter at the top of the twig.
40m
Bracts do not show.

⬆ Grand fir

Tall tree, with dark, shiny green needles, arranged like the teeth of a comb, fragrant when crushed. Whitish buds and small, upright cones.

⬇ Noble fir

Level branches and dense silver-blue needles, curving up. Enormous shaggy cones with down-turned bracts. Scales fall off, leaving tall spikes.

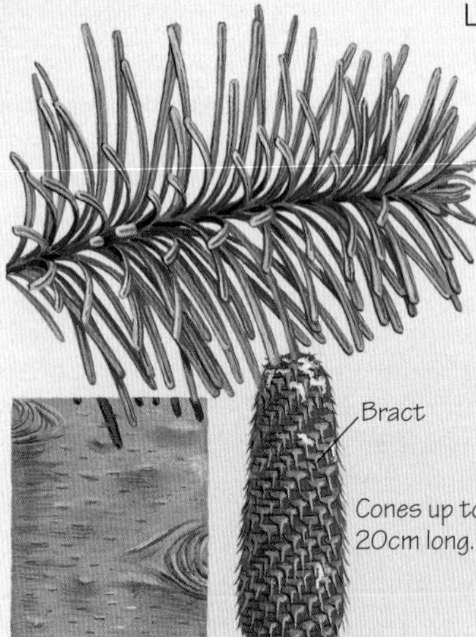
Bract
Cones up to 20cm long.

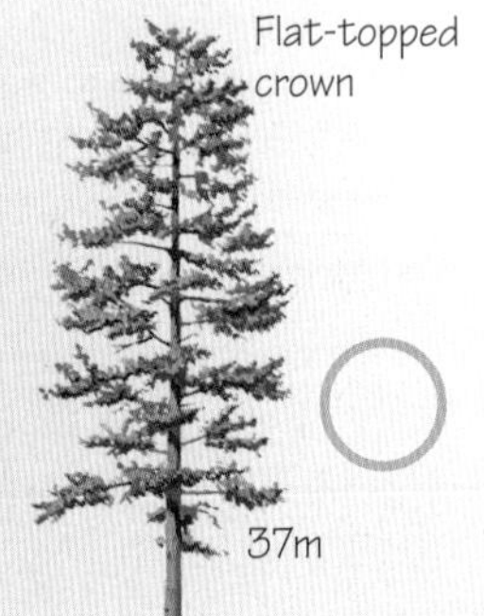
Flat-topped crown
37m

40m

Bract

⬆ Douglas fir

Soft, scented needles, copper-brown buds with long points, and light-brown hanging cones with three-pointed bracts. Its bark is thick and grooved when old.

⬇ Western hemlock

Smooth, brown scaly bark, drooping branch tips and top shoots with small cones. Needles of various lengths, green above and silver below.

Tips of branches droop.
Older cones are brown.
Flattened needles
Young cones are green.
35m

Conifers

⬇ Western red cedar

Small, flower-shaped cones and smooth, finely furrowed bark. The twigs are covered with flattened sprays of scented, scale-like leaves.

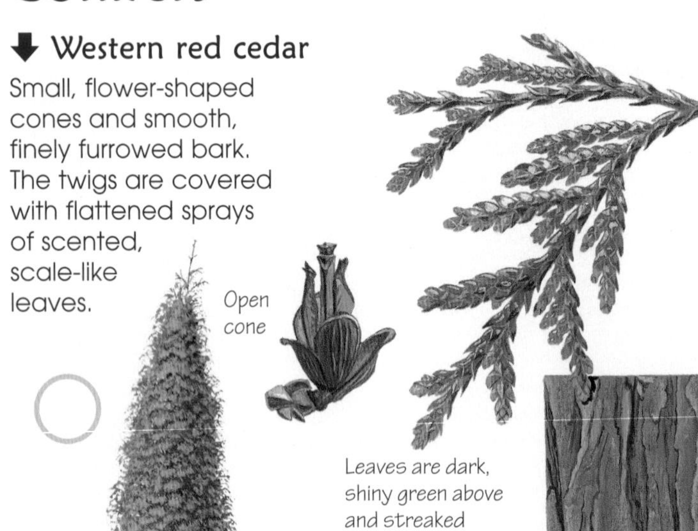

⬇ Lawson cypress

Sprays of fine, scale-like leaves, green and other colours. Small, round cones and smooth, reddish bark. The leader shoot (at tree top) often droops.

⬇ Italian cypress

An upright, narrow crowned, mainly ornamental tree. Small, dark, dull-green, scale-like leaves, closely pressed to stem. Large, rounded cones.

Cones are shiny pale-green at first, dull grey when older.

Leaves are smaller than Monterey cypress (below).

15m

⬇ Monterey cypress

Dense sprays of small, scale-like leaves and large, purplish-brown, rounded cones with knobs on scales. Column-shaped, becoming flat-topped when old, and the bark is often peeling.

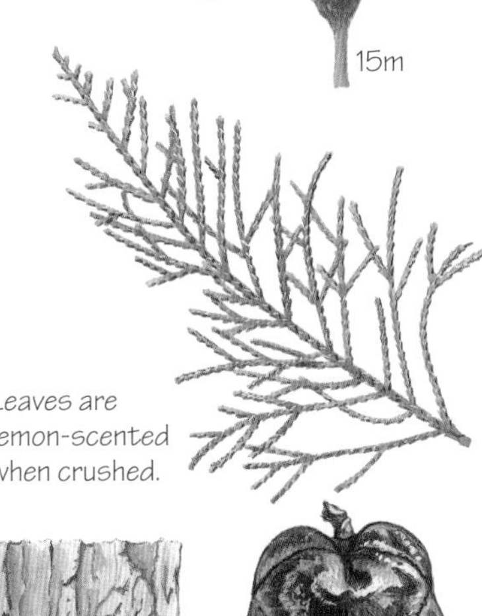
Leaves are lemon-scented when crushed.

25m

Peeling bark

Knob

Conifers

↑ Swamp cypress

Soft, feathery, light-green needles that appear late and drop in winter, leaving orange twigs. Reddish-brown spiralled bark, often peeling. Round, purplish-brown cones.

↓ Leyland cypress

Sprays of dense, bright-green, scale-like leaves. Rare, round grey-brown cones. Thick, column shape, often seen as a hedge.

↑ Japanese red cedar

Long, bright-green, spiky needles, which curve away from the twig. Round, spiky, green cones, ripening to brown. Red-brown peeling bark.

↓ Juniper

Often found as a shrub. Sharp blue-green needles in threes around shoot, with a white band on the upper surface. Berry-like fruit, turning purplish-black in second year.

Conifers

Wide, spreading branches

15m

Leaves and berries are poisonous.

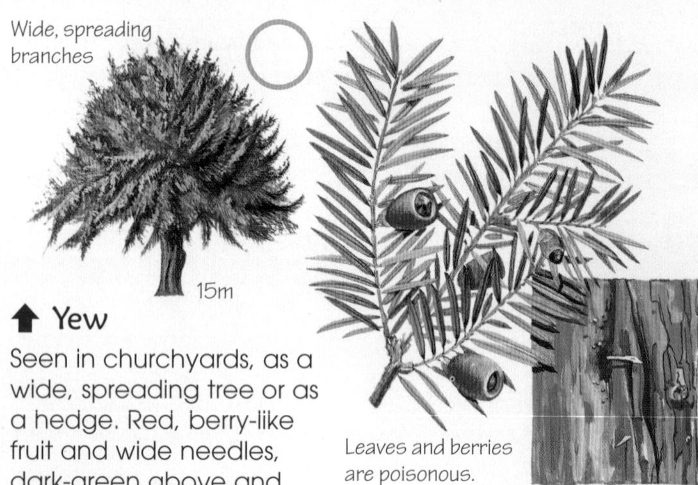

⬆ Yew

Seen in churchyards, as a wide, spreading tree or as a hedge. Red, berry-like fruit and wide needles, dark-green above and yellowish below. Orange-brown flaking bark.

⬇ Dawn redwood

Soft, light-green needles, similar to the swamp cypress (see page 104), but larger, turning reddish in autumn. Bark is orange in young trees, flaking and furrowed in older ones.

The cones are on long stalks, but rare.

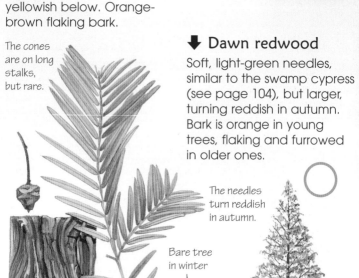

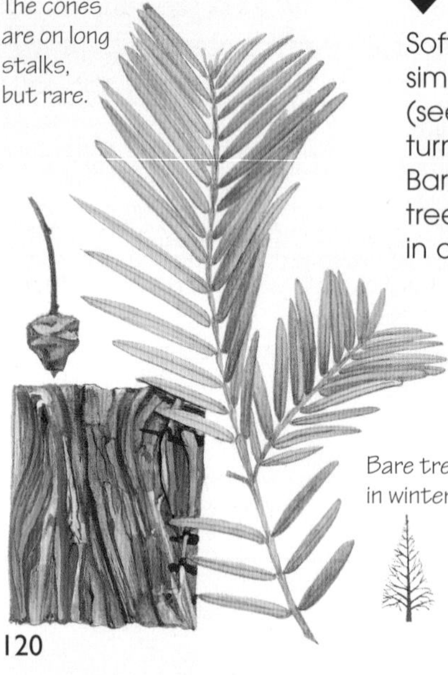

The needles turn reddish in autumn.

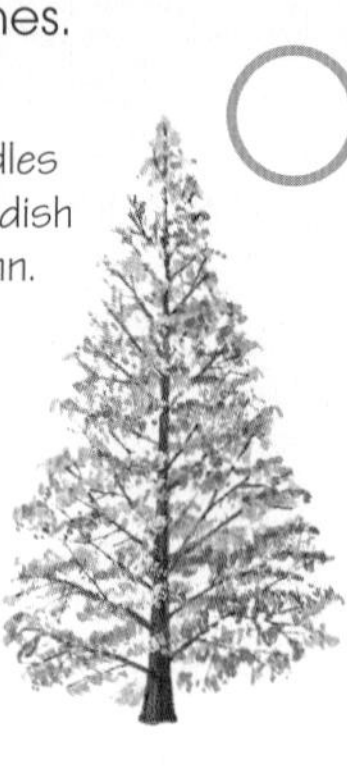

Bare tree in winter

20m

Coast redwood

Tall tree, with thick, reddish, spongy bark. Hard, sharp-pointed, single needles, dark-green above and white-banded below. Small, round cones.

Wellingtonia

Tall, with soft, thick, deeply furrowed bark. Deep-green, scale-like, pointed leaves, hanging from upswept branches. Long-stalked, round, corky cones. Also called giant sequoia.

Conifers

⬇ Atlas cedar

Large, spreading tree with dark-green needles, in bunches on the older shoots. Large, barrel-shaped, upright cones with sunken tops.

Leaves are blue-green in the common garden variety, dark green in the wild.

Sunken top

Top not sunken

Cones are covered with sticky resin.

30m

⬆ Cedar of Lebanon

Similar to Atlas cedar, but without sunken tops on cones. Branches spread out into level, leafy platforms.

Leaves overlap each other.

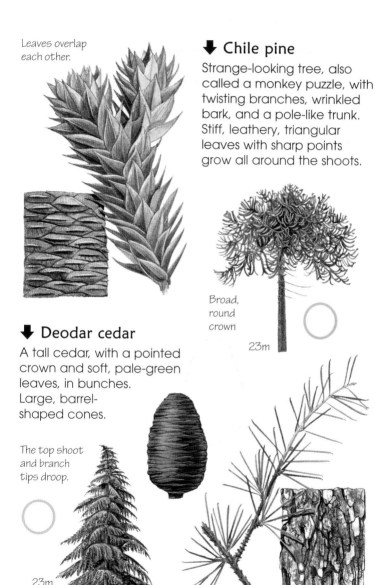

⬇ Chile pine

Strange-looking tree, also called a monkey puzzle, with twisting branches, wrinkled bark, and a pole-like trunk. Stiff, leathery, triangular leaves with sharp points grow all around the shoots.

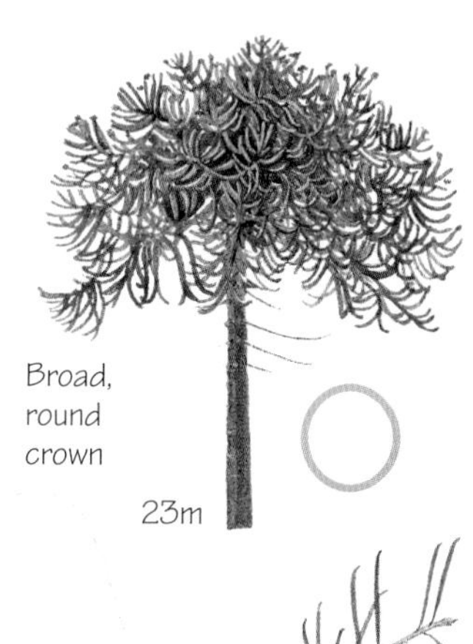

⬇ Deodar cedar

A tall cedar, with a pointed crown and soft, pale-green leaves, in bunches. Large, barrel-shaped cones.

The top shoot and branch tips droop.

23m

Broadleaved trees

Tall acorns on long stalks
23m
Acorn cup
Stalk

Lobe

⬆ English oak

Broad-crowned tree with many large branches growing upwards from the same point. Leaves are short-stalked with ear-like lobes at the base.

All veins go to tips of lobes.

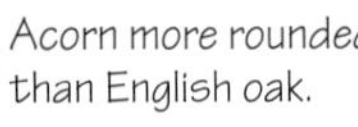
Acorn more rounded
than English oak.

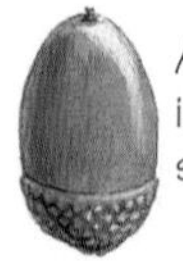
Acorn is often stalkless.

⬇ Sessile oak

Thick, dark, long-stalked leaves tapering to the base. Branches grow from stem at different levels and point up in a narrow crown.

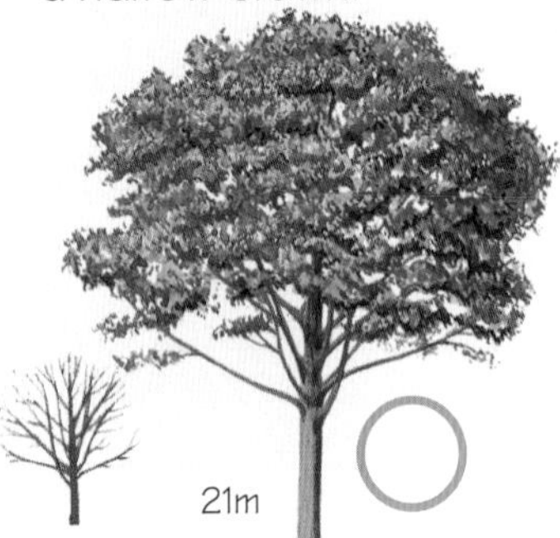
21m

Holm oak

Ornamental tree with a broad dense crown. Shiny, evergreen leaves, greyish-green beneath, sometimes with shallow teeth like holly.

Teeth

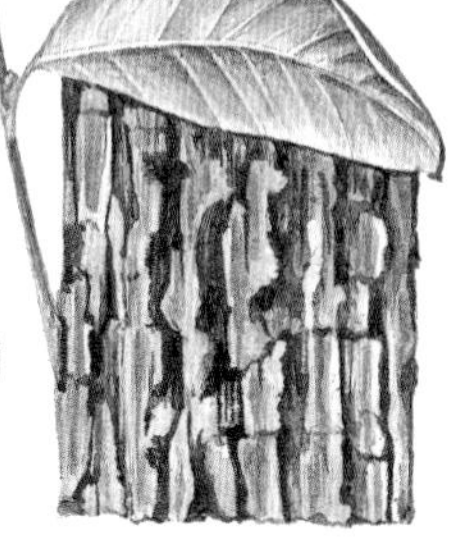

Turkey oak

Leaves unevenly lobed. Whiskers on buds and at base of leaves. Acorns ripen in second autumn. Acorn cups mossy and stalkless.

Broadleaved trees

Twisted trunk
and branches
16m

Cork is obtained
from the bark.
Acorn

⬆ Cork oak

Common in southern Europe, but extremely rare in Britain. Smaller than other oaks, it has thick, corky, whitish bark and shiny, evergreen leaves with wavy edges.

⬇ Red oak

Smooth, silvery bark, and squat acorns in shallow cups that ripen in second year. Large leaves, with bristly-tipped lobes, turn reddish brown in autumn.

The leaves turn
reddish in
autumn.
Acorn

20m

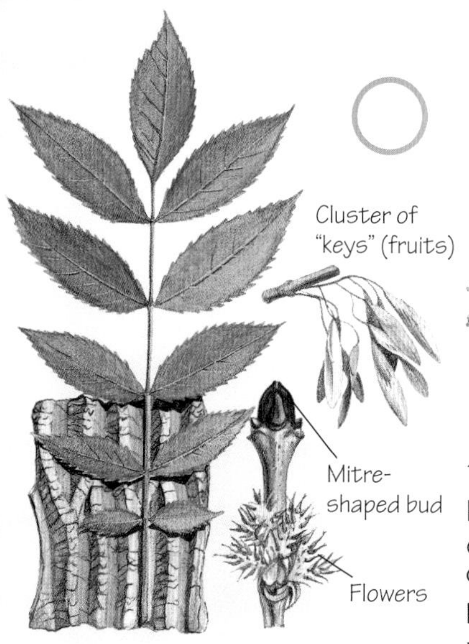

⬆ Common ash

Pale-grey bark and compound leaves of 9-13 leaflets, appearing late, after bunches of purplish flowers. Clusters of seeds stay on the tree into winter.

⬇ Manna ash

Smooth grey bark oozing a sugary liquid called manna. Leaves of 5-9 stalked leaflets appear with clusters of white flowers in May.

Broadleaved trees

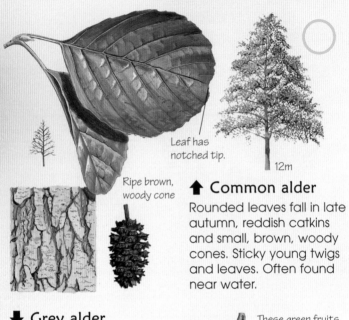

Leaf has notched tip.

12m

Ripe brown, woody cone

⬆ Common alder

Rounded leaves fall in late autumn, reddish catkins and small, brown, woody cones. Sticky young twigs and leaves. Often found near water.

⬇ Grey alder

Fast-growing, with catkins and fruit like the common alder. Pointed oval leaves, with sharply-toothed, edges, soft and grey beneath.

These green fruits ripen into brown, woody "cones".

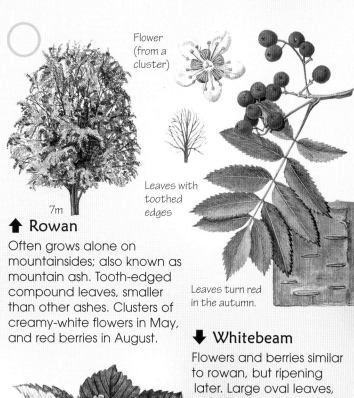

Flower (from a cluster)

Leaves with toothed edges

7m

Leaves turn red in the autumn.

⬆ Rowan

Often grows alone on mountainsides; also known as mountain ash. Tooth-edged compound leaves, smaller than other ashes. Clusters of creamy-white flowers in May, and red berries in August.

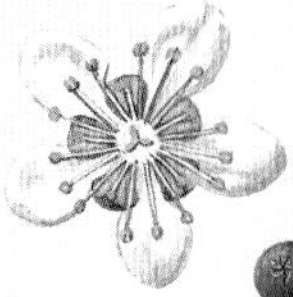

⬇ Whitebeam

Flowers and berries similar to rowan, but ripening later. Large oval leaves, with toothed edges, dark-green above, white and furry underneath.

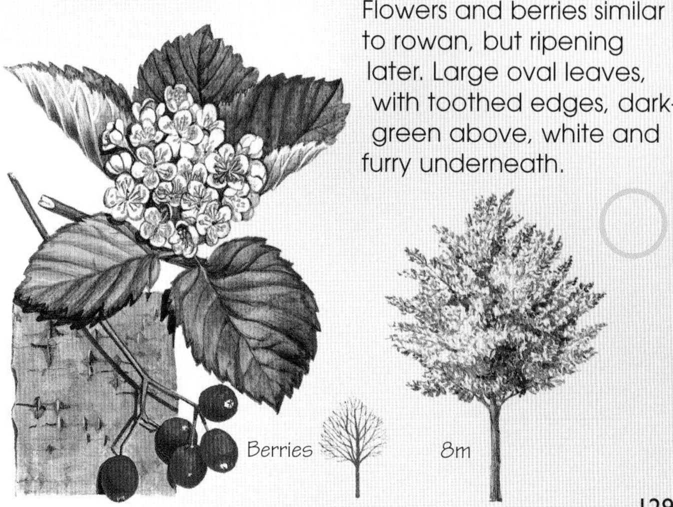

Broadleaved trees

Leaf stalks are long and flattened.

⬆ Aspen

Rounded leaves with wavy edges, deep-green on top, paler beneath. White downy catkins. Grey bark with large irregular markings. Often found growing in thickets.

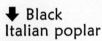

⬇ Black Italian poplar

Dark-green, triangular, pointed leaves appearing late. Red catkins and deeply furrowed bark. Trunk and crown often lean away from the wind.

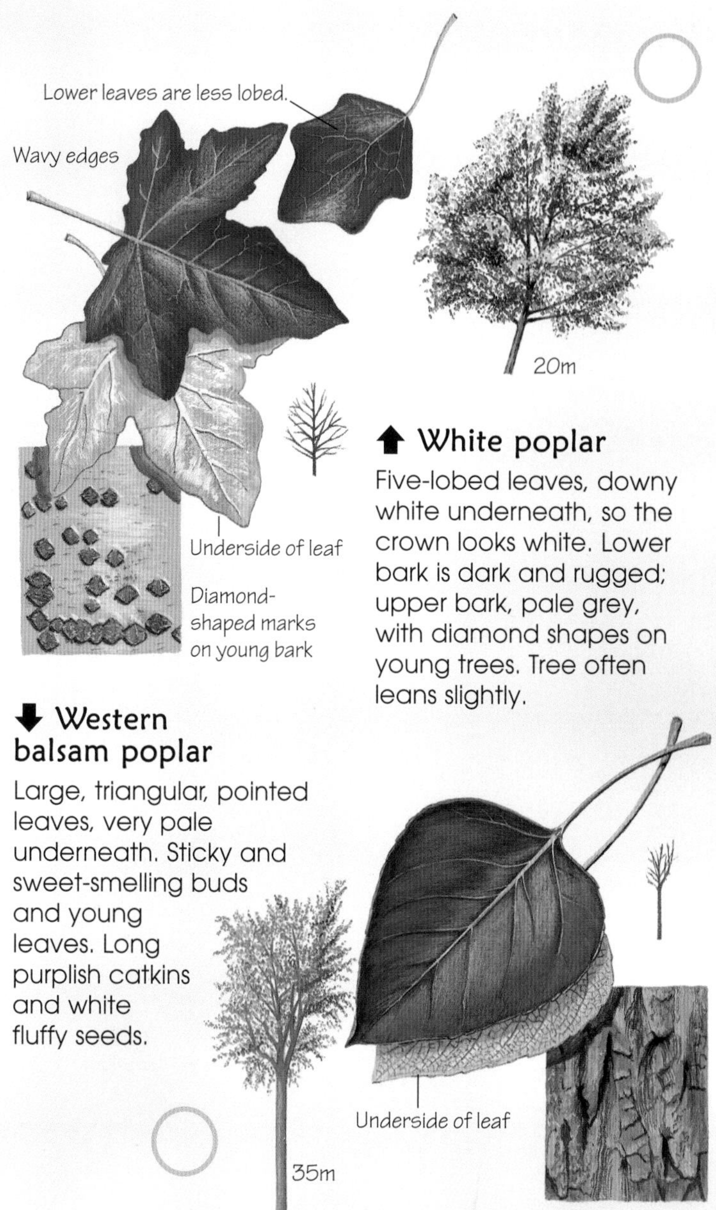

⬆ White poplar

Five-lobed leaves, downy white underneath, so the crown looks white. Lower bark is dark and rugged; upper bark, pale grey, with diamond shapes on young trees. Tree often leans slightly.

⬇ Western balsam poplar

Large, triangular, pointed leaves, very pale underneath. Sticky and sweet-smelling buds and young leaves. Long purplish catkins and white fluffy seeds.

Broadleaved trees

Leaf shape varies slightly.
28m
15m
Catkin
Silvery bark peels off in ribbons.

Lombardy poplar

Tall, narrow tree, often found along roadsides on the European continent. Pointed, triangular leaves, furrowed bark, and branches that grow upwards from the ground.

Silver birch

Slender tree with silvery bark and drooping branches. Small, diamond-shaped leaves, with toothed edges, and long "lamb's tail" catkins in April.

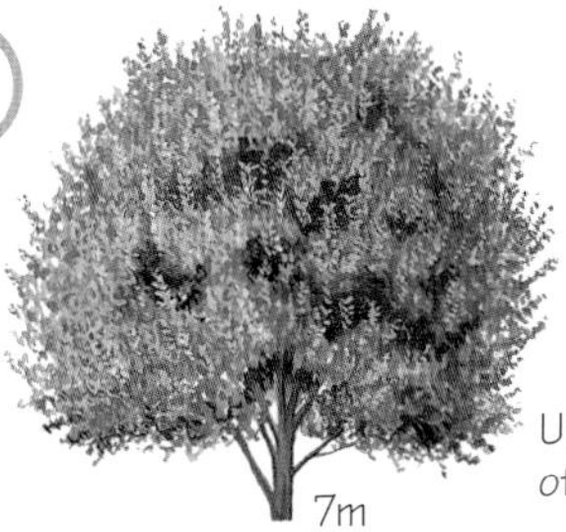

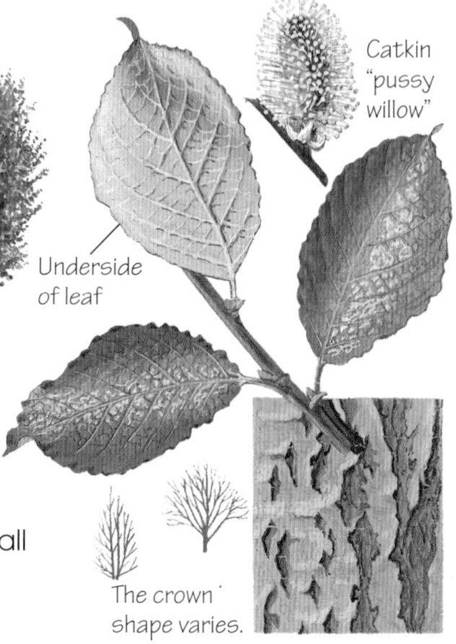

Catkin "pussy willow"

Underside of leaf

7m

Goat willow

Broad, rounded, rough, grey-green leaves. Silvery-grey upright catkins, known as "pussy willow", in late winter. Small bushy tree. Common on damp waste ground.

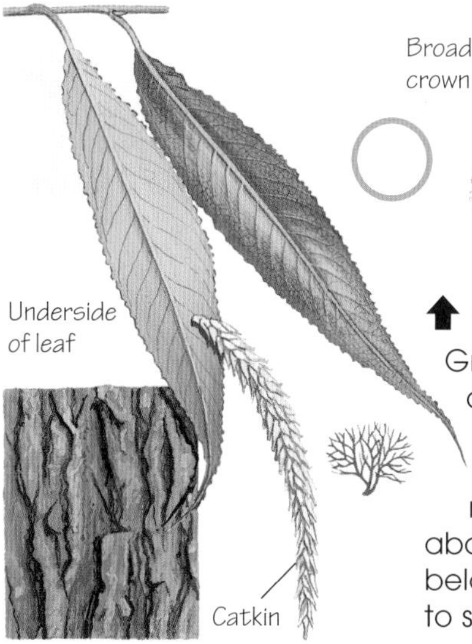

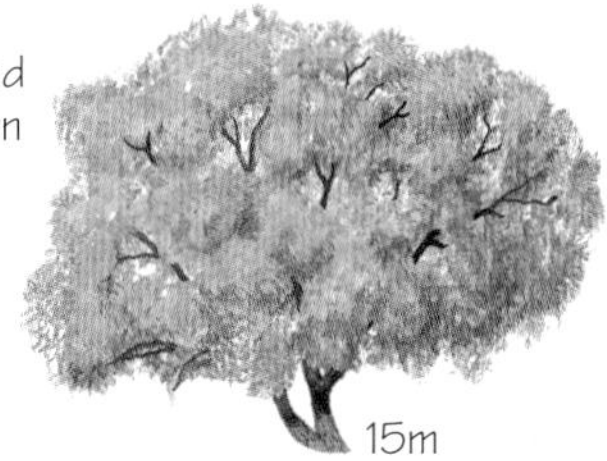

The crown shape varies.

Broad crown

15m

Crack willow

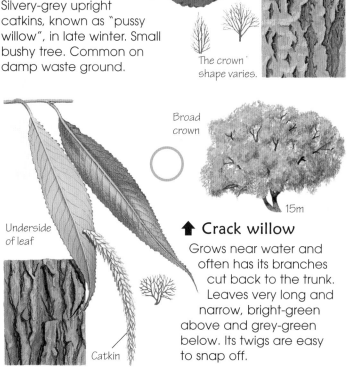

Grows near water and often has its branches cut back to the trunk. Leaves very long and narrow, bright-green above and grey-green below. Its twigs are easy to snap off.

Underside of leaf

Catkin

Broadleaved trees

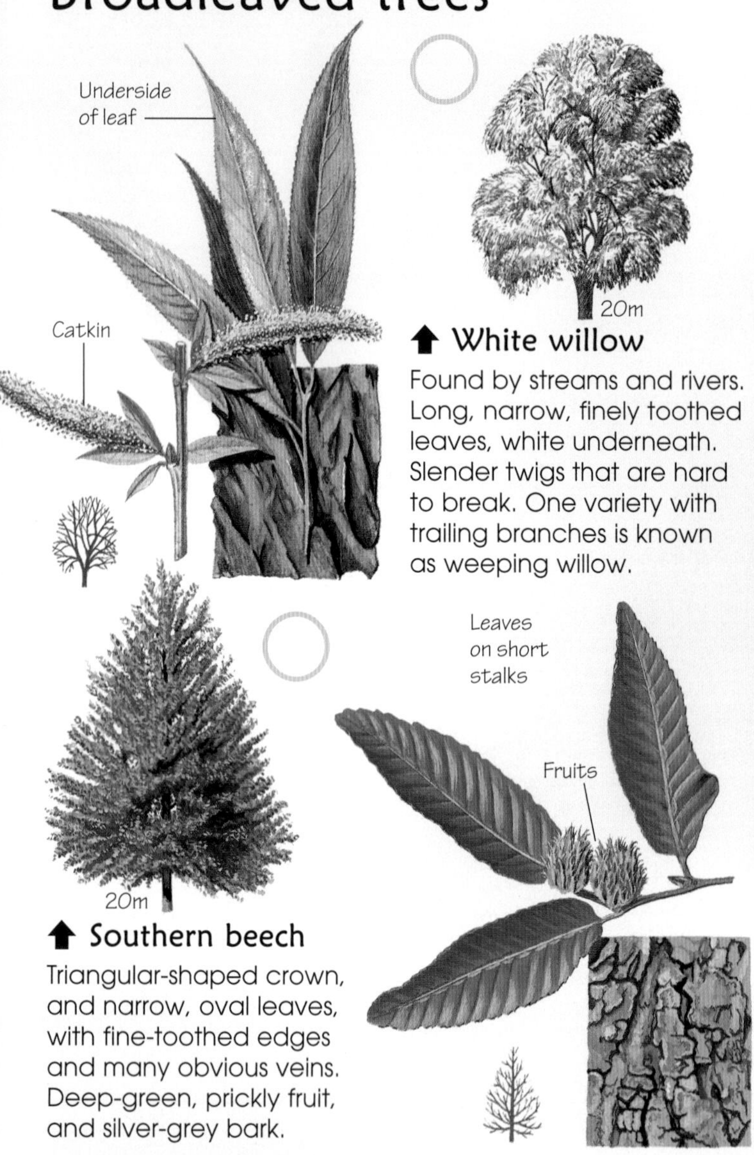

⬆ White willow

Found by streams and rivers. Long, narrow, finely toothed leaves, white underneath. Slender twigs that are hard to break. One variety with trailing branches is known as weeping willow.

⬆ Southern beech

Triangular-shaped crown, and narrow, oval leaves, with fine-toothed edges and many obvious veins. Deep-green, prickly fruit, and silver-grey bark.

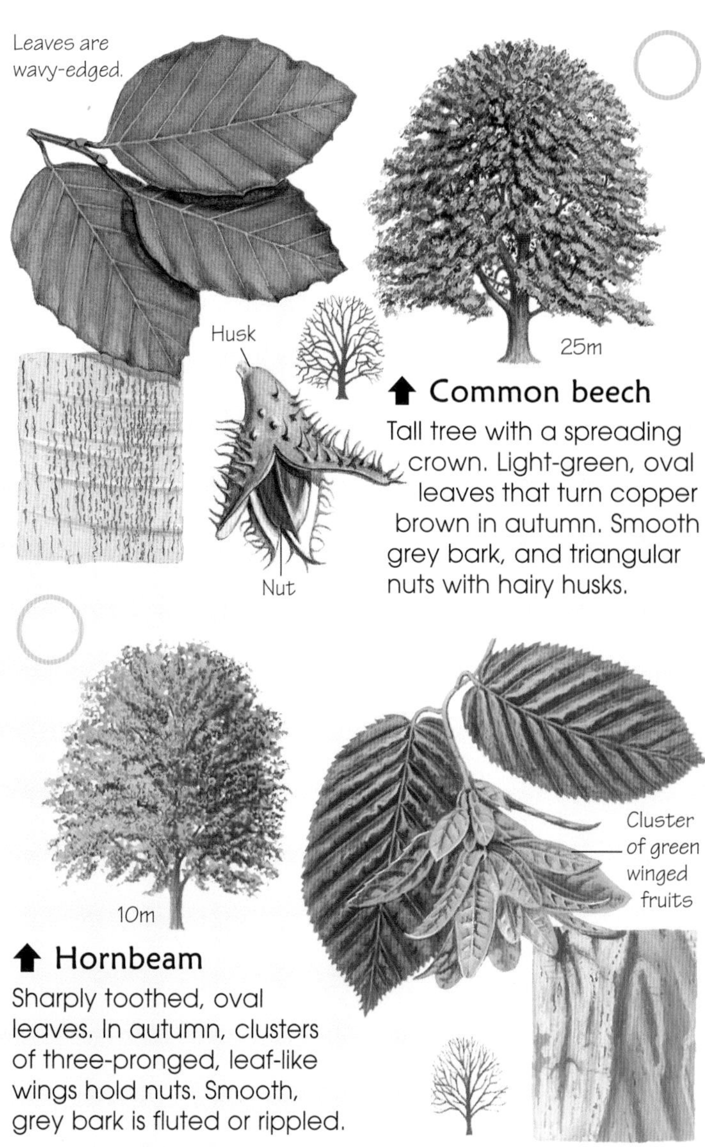

Common beech

Tall tree with a spreading crown. Light-green, oval leaves that turn copper brown in autumn. Smooth grey bark, and triangular nuts with hairy husks.

Hornbeam

Sharply toothed, oval leaves. In autumn, clusters of three-pronged, leaf-like wings hold nuts. Smooth, grey bark is fluted or rippled.

Broadleaved trees

Crab apple

Small, bushy tree, found in hedges. Small, rounded leaves with toothed edges. Pinkish-white flowers in May. Small, sour, speckled reddish-green apples that can be used in cooking.

Apple tastes sour even when ripe.

10m

Common pear

Found in woods and hedgerows. Large, white flowers in April. Small pears that are gritty to eat. Small, dark-green leaves, with finely toothed edges and long stalks.

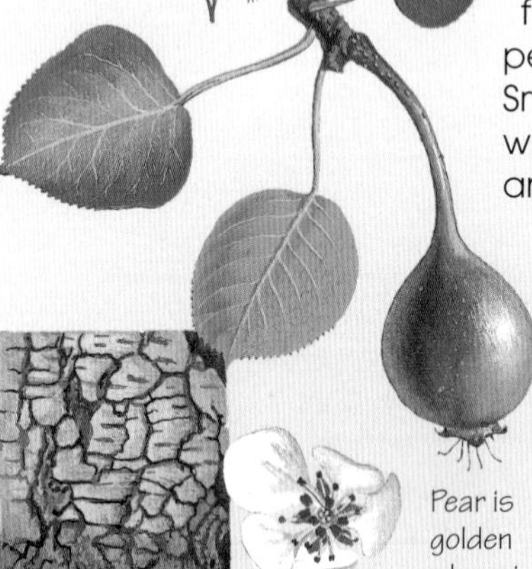

Pear is golden when ripe.

15m

Blackthorn

Small tree, with oval leaves. Foamy, white flowers on bare twigs in March. Small, blue-black fruit, called sloes, in September.

Berries called haws.

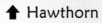

Hawthorn

Shiny, deeply lobed, dark-green leaves and thorny twigs. Clusters of small, white flowers in May, and dark-red berries. Rounded crown.

Broadleaved trees

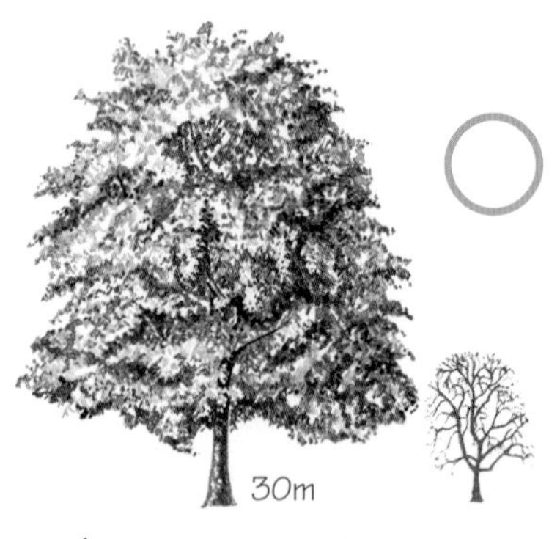
30m

Fruit

↑ London plane

Large, broad leaves in pairs, with pointed lobes. Spiny "bobble" fruits hang all winter. Flaking bark, leaving yellowish patches. Often found in towns.

Leaves have toothed edges.
Fruits twist as they fall.

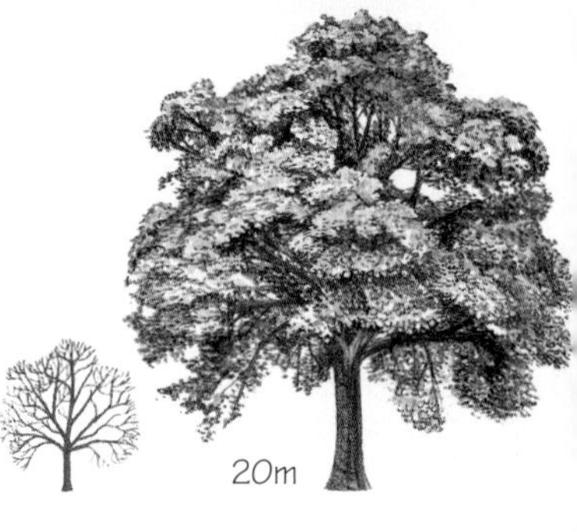
20m

↑ Sycamore

Large spreading tree, with dark-green leathery leaves with toothed edges and five lobes. Paired, right-angled, winged fruits. Smooth brown bark, becoming scaly.

⬆ Norway maple

Light-green, thin leaves, with bristle-tipped lobes and teeth. Wide-angled, paired fruits and finely furrowed, grey bark.

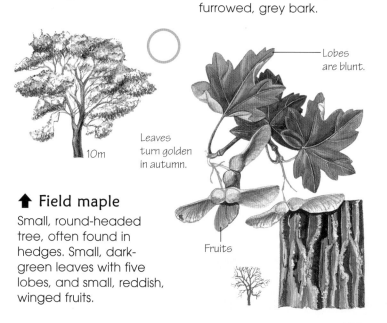

Lobes are blunt.

10m

Leaves turn golden in autumn.

⬆ Field maple

Small, round-headed tree, often found in hedges. Small, dark-green leaves with five lobes, and small, reddish, winged fruits.

Fruits

Broadleaved trees

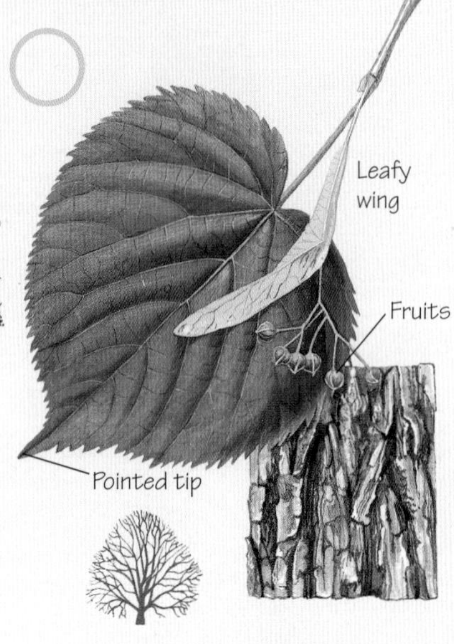

⬆ Common lime

Heart-shaped leaves with toothed edges. Yellowish-green, scented flowers in July. Small, round, hard, grey-green fruits hang from a leafy wing.

⬇ Silver lime

Like the common lime, but with a more rounded crown. Dark-green leaves, silvery-grey below. Fruits hang from a leafy wing.

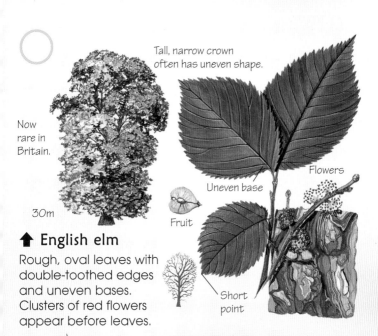

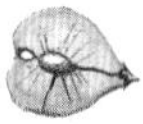

Tall, narrow crown often has uneven shape.

Now rare in Britain.

Flowers

Uneven base

Fruit

30m

Short point

⬆ English elm

Rough, oval leaves with double-toothed edges and uneven bases. Clusters of red flowers appear before leaves.

⬇ Wych elm

Like the English elm, but with a round, even crown; larger, rougher, stalkless leaves; and larger seeds. Now very rare in Britain.

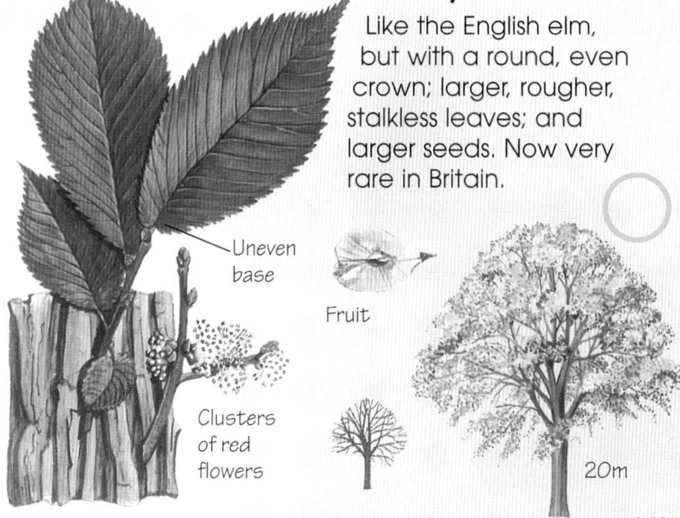

Broadleaved trees

⬇ Horse chestnut

Brown, inedible "conkers" in green, spiny cases. Compound leaves of 5-7 large leaflets. "Candles" of white or pink flowers in May.

⬇ Sweet chestnut

Clusters of edible brown chestnuts in prickly cases. Long, narrow leaves with saw-toothed edges. Bark sometimes spiral-furrowed.

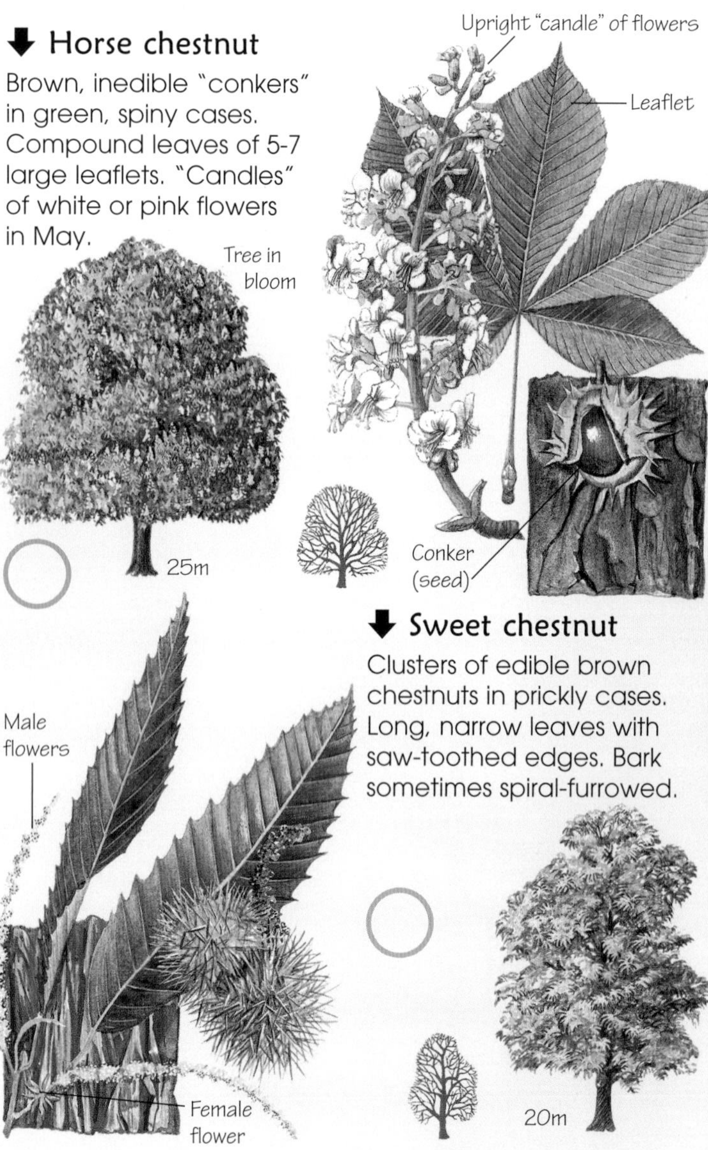

Wild cherry

White blossom in April and red, edible (though sour) cherries. Large, pointed, oval leaves with toothed edges. Reddish-brown bark peels in ribbons.

Bird cherry

Leathery, finely toothed, oval leaves, followed by drooping spikes of small white flowers. Small black cherries attract birds.

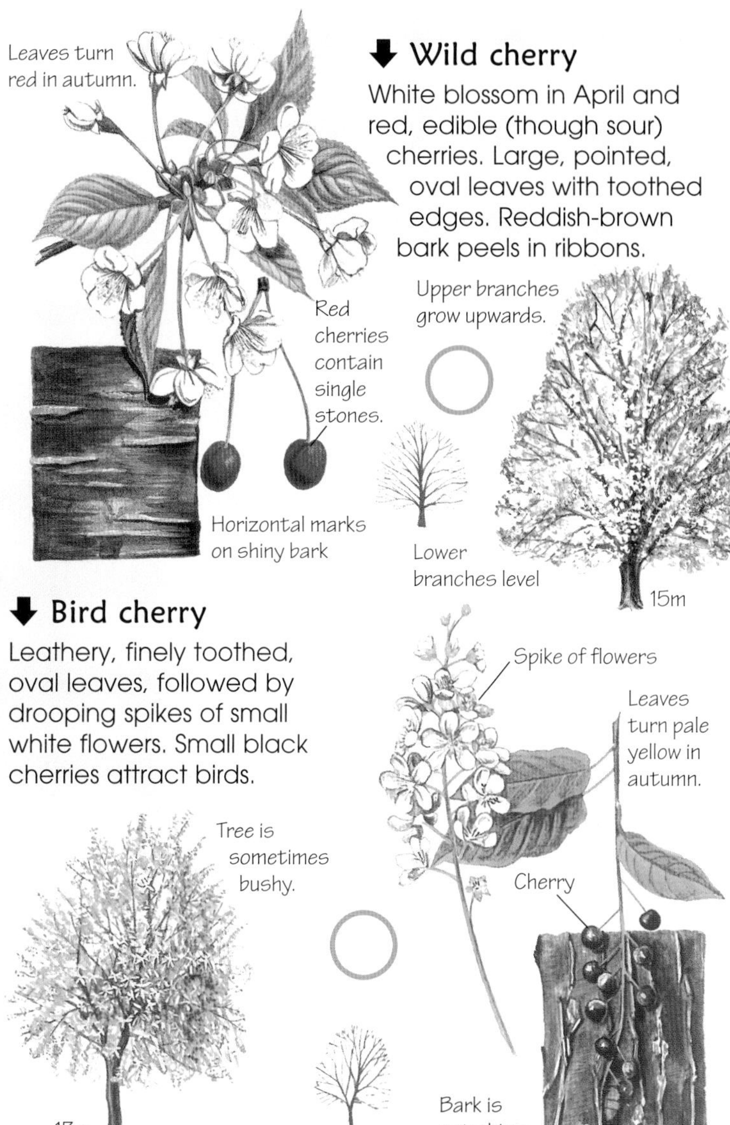
Leaves turn red in autumn.
Red cherries contain single stones.
Horizontal marks on shiny bark
Upper branches grow upwards.
Lower branches level
15m
Spike of flowers
Leaves turn pale yellow in autumn.
Tree is sometimes bushy.
Cherry
Bark is not shiny.
13m

Broadleaved trees

⬆ Black mulberry

Rough, heart-shaped leaves with toothed edges. Blackish-red berries. Short trunk, twisted branches. Flowers in short spikes.

⬇ Common walnut

Broad crown. Smooth, grey bark, with some cracks. Compound leaves of seven to nine leaflets, and hollow twigs.

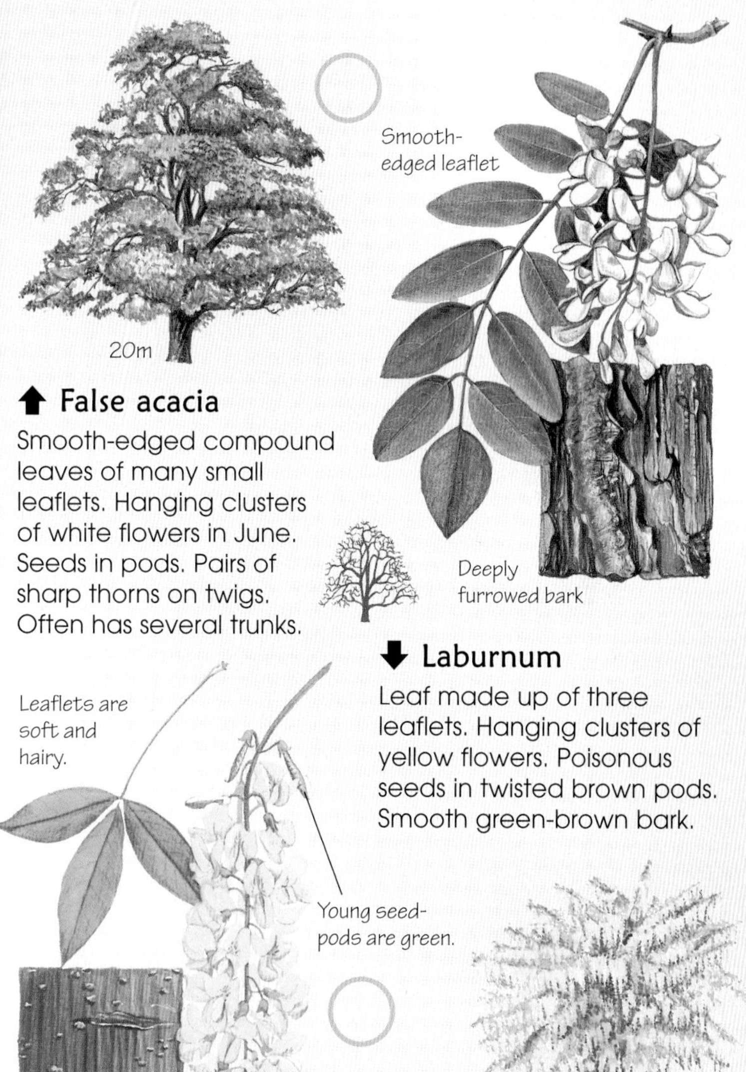

⬆ False acacia

Smooth-edged compound leaves of many small leaflets. Hanging clusters of white flowers in June. Seeds in pods. Pairs of sharp thorns on twigs. Often has several trunks.

⬇ Laburnum

Leaf made up of three leaflets. Hanging clusters of yellow flowers. Poisonous seeds in twisted brown pods. Smooth green-brown bark.

Broadleaved trees

⬇ Holly

Small tree with shiny, dark, evergreen leaves with thorny prickles. Small, white flowers. Round red berries. Smooth grey-green bark.

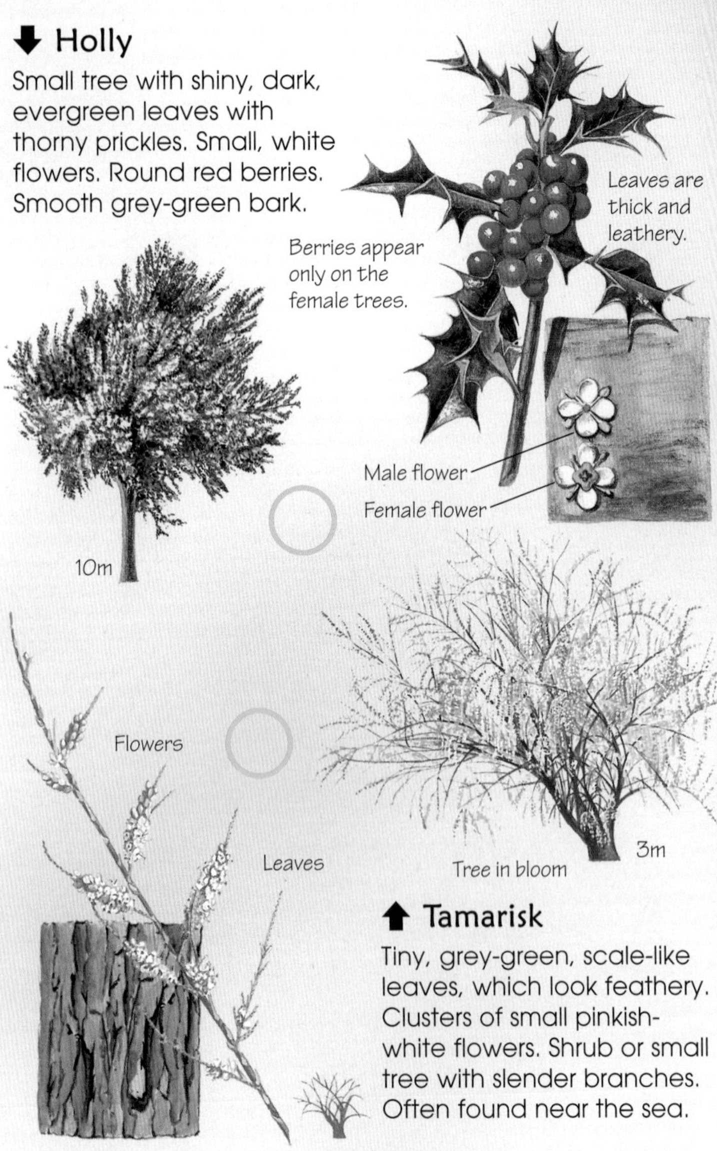

⬆ Tamarisk

Tiny, grey-green, scale-like leaves, which look feathery. Clusters of small pinkish-white flowers. Shrub or small tree with slender branches. Often found near the sea.

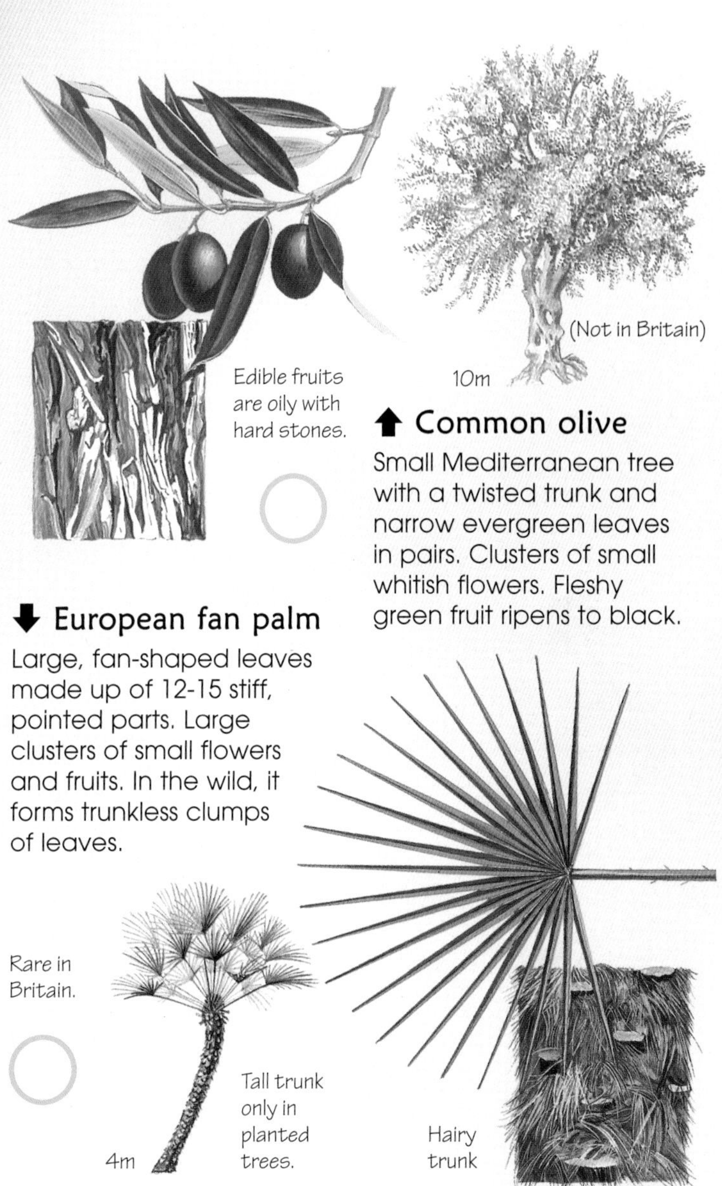

⬆ Common olive

Small Mediterranean tree with a twisted trunk and narrow evergreen leaves in pairs. Clusters of small whitish flowers. Fleshy green fruit ripens to black.

⬇ European fan palm

Large, fan-shaped leaves made up of 12-15 stiff, pointed parts. Large clusters of small flowers and fruits. In the wild, it forms trunkless clumps of leaves.

Broadleaved trees

Tulip tree

Smooth, four-lobed leaves, golden in autumn. Large tulip-like flowers in June. Upright, brown, cone-like fruits.

Maidenhair tree

Tall, slender tree. Double-lobed, fan-shaped leaves with deep cleft, bright yellow in autumn. Female trees have hanging fruit, but male trees are more common.

Maidenhair tree is neither a conifer nor a broadleaved tree. It is in a group on its own.

Fruit looks like a small plum.

23m

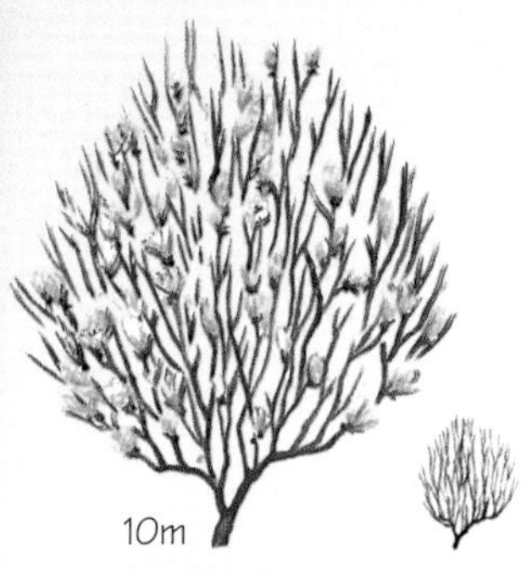

🡅 Magnolia

Wide, spreading tree. Large white flowers on naked twigs in March, before large, smooth, dark-green, oval leaves.

🡅 Tree of Heaven

Large compound leaves made up of 5-20 pairs of stalked leaflets. Large clusters of greenish flowers in July, followed by clusters of winged fruits.

Birds

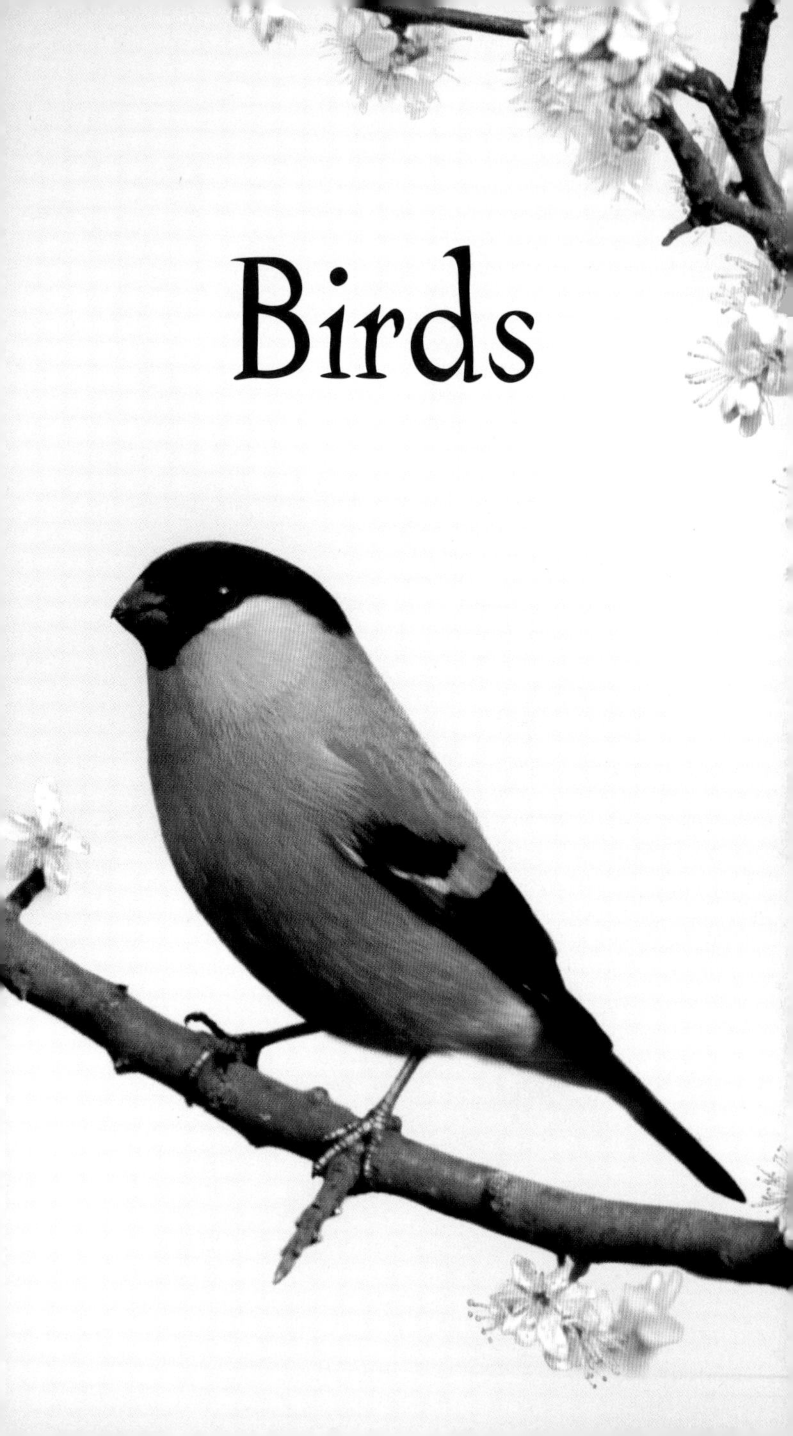

Geese

➡ Brent goose

Look for this small, dark goose on estuaries in winter. 58cm.

Brent goose

Canada geese were brought here from North America.

⬅ Canada goose

A large, noisy goose. Look in parks. Nests wild in Britain. 95cm.

➡ Greylag goose

Nests wild in Scotland and others have been released further south. Wild birds from Iceland visit Scotland in winter. 82cm.

⬅ Barnacle goose

Look for barnacle geese on the west coasts of Britain and Ireland in winter. Feeds in flocks on farmland. 63cm.

Barnacle goose has more white on head than Canada goose.

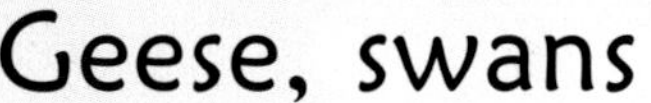

Geese, swans

➡ Pink-footed goose

A winter visitor. Seen in large numbers on fields in Scotland and near coasts in England. 68cm.

⬅ Bean goose

A rare winter visitor from northern Europe. Grazes on farmland away from the coast. 80cm.

➡ White-fronted goose

A winter visitor to estuaries, marshes and farmland. Look for white at base of bill. 72cm.

⬅ Swans

Mute swans are often seen in parks or on rivers. The others come to Britain in winter and can be seen on lakes or flooded fields.

Ducks

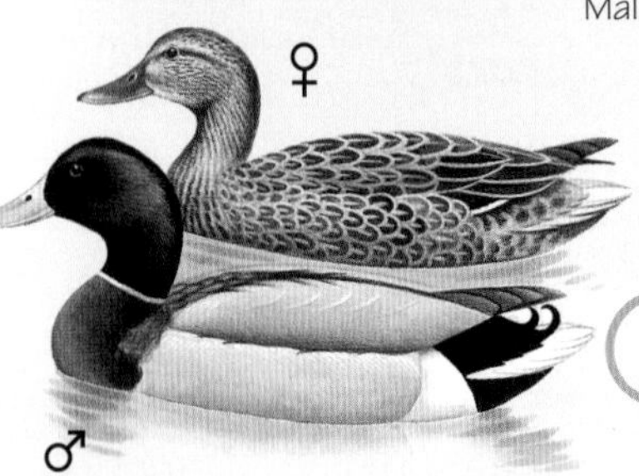

⬅ Mallard

Found near most inland waters. Only the female gives the familiar "quack". 58cm.

➡ Teal

Smallest European duck. A very shy bird. It prefers the shallow edges of lakes. Flies with fast wing-beats. 35cm.

⬅ Wigeon

Sometimes seen grazing on fields near water. Forms flocks in winter especially near the sea. Male's call is a loud "wheeo". 46cm.

➡ Pintail

Uses its long neck to feed on plants under the water. Look for these birds in winter, often near sea. 66cm.

➡ Shoveler

Likes quiet lakes and shallow water. Uses its long, flat bill to filter food from the surface of the water. Call is low "quack". 51cm.

⬅ Pochard

Spends much of its time resting on open water and diving for food. More likely to be seen in winter. 46cm.

➡ Tufted duck

Another diving duck which is more common in winter. Can sometimes be seen on park lakes. 43cm.

⬅ Eider

Breeds around rocky northern coasts. Forms large flocks on the sea in winter. 58cm.

Ducks

➡ Goldeneye

A few nest in Scotland, but mainly a winter visitor from northern Europe. Seen on the sea and inland lakes, often in small flocks. Dives frequently. 46cm.

⬅ Red-breasted merganser

Breeds by lakes and rivers. Seldom seen inland in winter, but visits many coastal areas and open sea. Dives for fish. 58cm.

➡ Goosander

Most British goosanders nest in the north and west. Likes large lakes in winter. Dives for fish. Look for shaggy crest on female. 66cm.

Female has no lump on bill.

⬅ Shelduck

Common around most sandy coasts, especially estuaries. Often in flocks. Groups of young join together in late summer. Looks slow and heavy in flight. 61cm.

Grebes, heron, stork

➡ Great crested grebe

Found on inland waters. Dives for fish. Beautiful courtship displays in spring. May be seen on sea in winter. 48cm.

⬅ Little grebe or dabchick

Common on inland waters, but secretive and hard to spot. Call is a shrill trill. 27cm.

➡ Grey heron

Usually seen near water. Nests in colonies in trees. Stands motionless for long periods. 92cm.

Head drawn back and legs stick out when flying.

⬅ White stork

Very rare in Britain. Likes wet areas. Will nest on buildings and pylons in Europe. 102cm.

Rails, crake

➡ Moorhen

A water bird that lives near ponds, lakes or streams. Notice red bill and white tail. Young are brown. 33cm.

⬅ Coot

Dives a lot. Prefers large lakes. Look for white bill and forehead. Young are grey with pale throats and breasts. Flocks in winter. 38cm.

➡ Corncrake

Difficult to see as it lives in long grass. Repeats "crex-crex" cry monotonously, especially after dark. Rare in Britain. 27cm.

⬅ Water rail

Secretive bird that lives in reed beds. Listen for its piglet-like squeal. Legs trail in flight. Swims for short distances. 28cm.

Cormorant, gannet, shag, chough

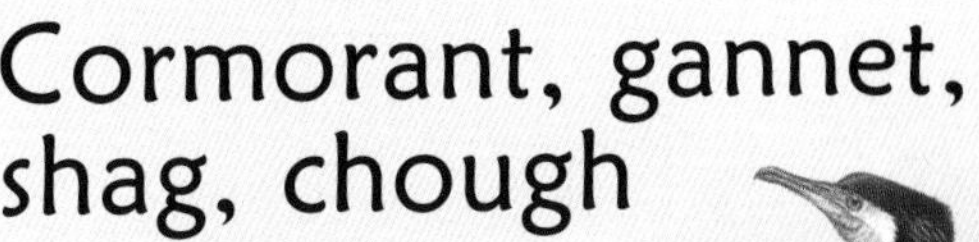

➡ Cormorant

Perches upright, often with its wings spread out to dry. Some have grey head and neck in breeding season. 92cm.

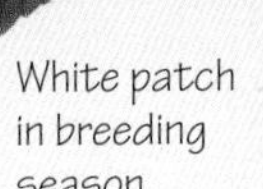

White patch in breeding season.

⬅ Gannet

Look for gannets out to sea, close to waves. Plunges head-first into water to catch fish. 92cm.

Crest only in nesting season.

⬋ Shag

Lives near the sea. Nests in colonies on rocky coasts. Dives for fish. Young are brown. 78cm.

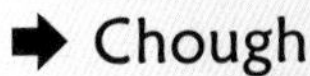

➡ Chough

A crow which lives on high, rocky sea cliffs and in mountains. Like a jackdaw, but has red feet and red beak. 38cm.

Waders

← Oystercatcher

Usually seen near the sea, especially in winter. Nests inland in Scotland and parts of England. Feeds on shellfish. 43cm.

→ Lapwing

A farmland bird which flocks in winter. Looks black and white from a distance. Displays in the air in breeding season. Calls "pee-wit". 30cm.

← Turnstone

Likes shingle or rocky shores. Turns stones over to find food. Does not nest in Britain, but can be seen most months. 23cm.

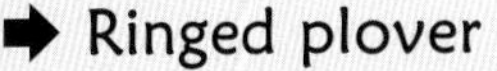

➡ Ringed plover

Usually found near the sea, but sometimes by inland lakes. Likes sandy or shingle shores. Seen all the year round. 19cm.

Notice yellow eye-ring.

⬅ Little ringed plover

Summer visitor. Most common in southeast England. Likes gravel pits and shingle banks inland. Legs are yellowish. 15cm.

➡ Golden plover

Breeds on upland moors, but found in flocks on coastal marshes or lowland farms in winter. 28cm.

Waders

➡ Redshank

Breeds on seashores and wet meadows. Look for white on rump and back edges of wings in flight. 28cm.

⬅ Greenshank

Rarer and slightly bigger than redshank. Seen in spring and autumn on coasts or inland. Some nest in northern Scotland. 30cm.

➡ Common sandpiper

Summer visitor to upland streams and lakes. Visits wet areas in lowland Britain in spring and autumn. Wags tail and bobs. 20cm.

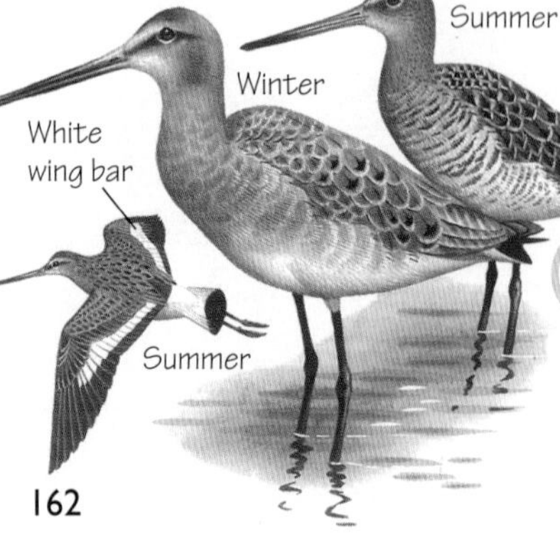

⬅ Black-tailed godwit

A few nest in wet meadows in Britain, but more seen on coasts during autumn and winter. 41cm.

➡ Bar-tailed godwit

Smaller than black-tailed godwit. Most are seen in spring and autumn, but some winter on east coast mud flats or estuaries. 37cm.

⬅ Curlew

Britain's largest wader. Nests on moors and upland farmland. Seen on coasts at other times of year. Song is "courli". 48-64cm.

➡ Whimbrel

Like a small curlew. A few nest in heather in northern Scotland. Many more visit Britain's coasts in spring and autumn. 40cm.

Waders

← Dunlin

A common visitor to seashores, but nests on moorland in the north. Often seen in flocks. Beak straight or down-curved. 19cm.

Winter

→ Knot

Seen in huge flocks in winter. Likes sand or mud flats in estuaries. Rare inland. Mainly a winter visitor. Breeds in the Arctic. 25cm.

← Sanderling

Seen on coasts in winter. Runs along water's edge on sandy beaches where it catches small animals washed up by waves. 20cm.

Winter

→ Ruff

Seen in autumn and spring, but also winter in wet places and a few stay to nest. Male 29cm. Female 23cm.

➡ Woodcock

Secretive bird of damp woods. Watch out for its bat-like display flight over woods at dusk in early summer. 34cm.

⬅ Snipe

Lives in wet fields, marshes or lake edges. Hard to see on the ground, but rises up with a zig-zag flight when disturbed. 27cm.

➡ Avocet

Nests on coastal marshes in eastern England. Flocks winter on southern estuaries. Rare inland. 43cm.

Gulls

➡ Black-headed gull

Common near the sea and inland. Nests in colonies. Look for white front edge of long wings. 37cm.

⬅ Lesser black-backed gull

Mainly summer visitor to coasts or inland. Some winter in Britain. Head streaked with grey in winter. 53cm.

➡ Great black-backed gull

Britain's largest gull. Not very common inland. Nests on rocky coasts. Often solitary. Legs pinkish. 66cm.

⬅ Common gull

Some nest in Scotland and Ireland. Seen further south and often inland in winter. 41cm.

Gull, terns

⬅ Herring gull

Nests in large colonies, often on the ground, sometimes on buildings and rocky cliffs. Young's plumage is mottled brown for first three years. 56cm.

Arctic tern in summer

➡ Arctic tern
➡ Common tern

Both species most likely to be seen near the sea, but common tern also nests inland. Both dive into water to catch fish. 34cm.

Common tern's bill has black tip.

Summer

⬅ Black tern

A spring and autumn visitor. Can be seen flying low over lakes, dipping down to pick food from surface. 24cm.

Summer

Autumn

➡ Little tern

Summer visitor. Nests in small groups on shingle beaches. Dives for fish. 24cm.

Summer

Yellow bill with black tip

Auks, fulmar

Neck and throat are white in winter.
Summer

← Razorbill

Look for its flat-sided bill. Nests on cliffs and rocky shores in colonies. Winters at sea. Dives for fish. Often with guillemots. 41cm.

→ Guillemot

Nests on cliffs in large groups. Slimmer than razorbill. Northern birds have white eye-ring and line on heads. 42cm.

Neck and throat are white in winter.
Summer

← Fulmar

Nests in colonies on ledges on sea cliffs. Often glides close to the waves on stiff wings. Can be seen near cliffs all round our coasts. 47cm.

→ Puffin

Rocky islands and sea cliffs in the north and west. Nests between rocks or in burrows in the ground. 30cm.

Colourful beak and reddish feet in summer.

Birds of prey

➡ Hobby

Catches large insects and birds in the air. Summer visitor to southern England. Look on heaths and near water. 33cm.

Tail shorter and wings longer than kestrel.

⬅ Goshawk

Looks like a large sparrowhawk. Lives in woods. Rare in Britain. Male 48cm. Female 58cm.

➡ Peregrine

Sea cliffs or inland crags. Hunts over estuaries and marshes in winter. Dives on flying birds at great speed. 38-48cm.

⬅ Honey buzzard

Summer visitor to British woodlands. Eats mainly grubs of wasps and bees. Rare. 51-59cm.

Birds of prey

➡ Osprey

Rare summer visitor to Britain. Some nest in Scotland but seen further south on its migration to Africa. Plunges into water to catch fish. 56cm.

⬅ Golden eagle

Lives in Scottish Highlands. Young birds have white on wings and tail. Glides for long distances. Bigger than buzzard. 83cm.

➡ Red kite

This rare bird nests in oak woods in Mid Wales. Recently released in Scotland and England and increasing in numbers. Soars for long periods. 62cm.

Long forked tail

Notice the pale wing patches.
Female is larger and browner than male.
♀
♂
Long, pointed wings and tail
♀
♂

⬅ Buzzard

Large bird of prey with broad wings. Often seen soaring over moors and farmland as it hunts. Rarer in southern and eastern England. 54cm.

➡ Sparrowhawk

Broad-winged hawk. Hunts small birds along hedges and woodland edges. Never hovers. Male 30cm. Female 38cm.

⬅ Kestrel

Well-known for the way it hovers when hunting, especially alongside motorways. Some nest in towns. Eats birds, insects and small mammals. 34cm.

Owls

➡ Barn owl

Its call is an eerie shriek. Often nests in old buildings or hollow trees. Hunts small mammals and roosting birds at night. 34cm.

Birds with dark faces and breasts are found in north and east Europe.

Bouncing flight

⬅ Little owl

Small, flat-headed owl. Flies low over farmland and hunts at dusk. Nests in tree-holes. Bobs up and down when curious. 22cm.

➡ Tawny owl

Calls with familiar "hoot". Hunts at night where there are woods or old trees. Eats small mammals or birds. 38cm.

⬅ Pygmy owl

The smallest European owl. Found in mountain forests, but not in Britain. Has a whistling "keeoo" call. Hunts small birds in flight. 16cm.

➡ Short-eared owl

Hunts small mammals in daylight and at dusk. Likes open country. Perches on the ground. Fierce-looking. 37cm.

⬅ Long-eared owl

A secretive night-hunting owl of thick pine woods. Roosts during the day. Long "ear" tufts cannot be seen in flight. 34cm.

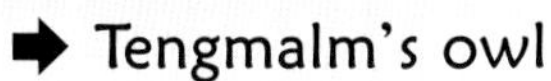

➡ Tengmalm's owl

Small owl that lives in northern and central European forests. Very rare visitor to Britain. Hunts at night. Nests in tree-holes. 25cm.

⬅ Scops owl

Very rare visitor from southern Europe. Gives monotonous "kiu" call from hidden perch. Hunts only at night. 19cm.

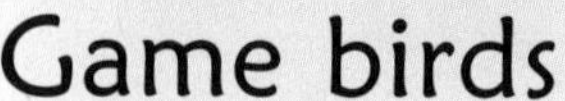

Game birds

➡ Red grouse
➡ Willow grouse

Red grouse lives on moors in Britain. Willow grouse lives in northern Europe. Willow grouse is white in winter. 36cm.

In summer, the male's plumage is browner and the female's yellower than in autumn.

Winter

Autumn

⬅ Ptarmigan

Lives on barren mountain tops in the north. Has three different plumages and is well camouflaged. Allows people to get close. 34cm.

➡ Black grouse

Found on edge of moorland, sometimes perched in trees. Groups of males display together at an area known as a "lek". Male 53cm. Female 41cm.

➡ Capercaillie

Lives in pine forests in parts of Scotland. Eats pine shoots at tips of branches. Male 86cm. Female 61cm.

⬅ Grey partridge

Often in small groups. Likes farmland with hedges. Its call is a grating "kirr-ic". Rare in Ireland. 30cm.

➡ Pheasant

Lives on farmland with hedges. Often reared as game. Roosts in trees. Male 87cm. Female 58cm.

Young birds are similar in appearance to the female.

Look for long tail.

⬅ Red-legged partridge

Common in southern and eastern Britain. Fields and open sandy areas. Often runs rather than flies. 34cm.

Hoopoe, nightjar, cuckoo, kingfisher

➡ Hoopoe

Rare visitor to Britain, seen mainly in spring. More common in southern Europe. Probes ground for insects with its long bill. 28cm.

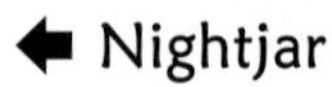

⬅ Nightjar

Rarely seen in daylight. Listen for churring call at night when it hunts insects. Summer migrant to heathland. 27cm.

Male has white spots on wings.

➡ Cuckoo

Male's song well known. Female has bubbling call. Found all over Britain in summer. Looks like a sparrowhawk in flight. 30cm.

Juvenile cuckoo

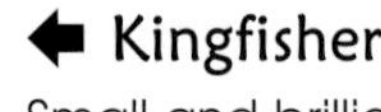

⬅ Kingfisher

Small and brilliantly coloured. Seen near lakes and rivers. Dives for fish. Listen for shrill whistle. 17cm.

Usually flies low and straight over water.

Woodpeckers

➡ Black woodpecker

Size of a rook. Found in forests in Europe, especially old pine woods, but not in Britain. Can be confused with crow in flight. 46cm.

Male (shown here) has red crown. Female has red patch on back of head.

Large white patches on wings

⬅ Great spotted woodpecker

Size of a blackbird. Found in woods all over Britain. Drums on trees in spring. 23cm.

➡ Lesser spotted woodpecker

Sparrow-sized. Lacks white wing patches of great spotted woodpecker. Male has red crown. Open woodland. Not in Scotland. 14cm.

Stripy back

Yellow-green rump

⬅ Green woodpecker

Pigeon-sized. Often feeds on ground. Open woods and parks. Quite common in England and Wales. Rare in Scotland. Has a laugh-like call. 32cm.

Woodpeckers do not live in Ireland. They all have bouncing flight.

Swift, swallow, martins

➡ Swift

A common migrant that visits Britain from May to August. Flies fast over towns and country, often in flocks. Listen for its screaming call. 17cm.

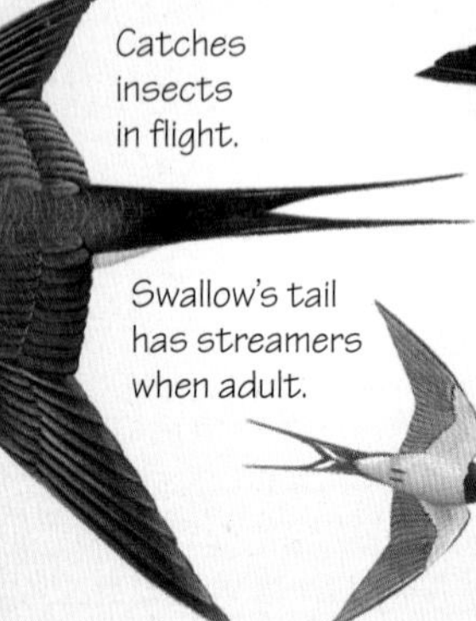

⬅ Swallow

Summer migrant, seen from April to October. Prefers country, often near water. Nests on rafters or ledges in buildings. 19cm.

➡ House martin

Summer migrant. Builds cup-shaped nest under eaves. Found in town and country. Catches insects in flight. 13cm.

⬅ Sand martin

Summer migrant. Groups nest in holes in sandy cliffs and other soft banks. Often seen in flocks, catching insects over water. 12cm.

Larks, pipits, dunnock

⬅ Skylark

Lives in open country, especially farmland. Rises to a great height, hovers, and sails down, singing. 18cm.

➡ Crested lark

Not often in Britain, but widespread in central and southern Europe. Open, often barren, areas. 17cm.

⬅ Meadow pipit

Most common on upland moors, but also in fields, marshes and other open areas, especially in winter. 14.5cm.

➡ Tree pipit

Summer migrant to heaths and places with scattered trees or bushes. Often perches on branches. 15cm.

⬅ Dunnock

Common, even in gardens. Feeds under bird tables. Mouse-like walk. Often flicks wings. 14.5cm.

Wagtails

➡ Pied wagtail
➡ White wagtail

The white wagtail is widespread in Europe, but only the pied wagtail is usually seen in Britain. Common, even in towns. 18cm.

⬅ Grey wagtail

Usually nests near fast-flowing water in hilly areas. Paler yellow in winter, when it visits lowland waters. 18cm.

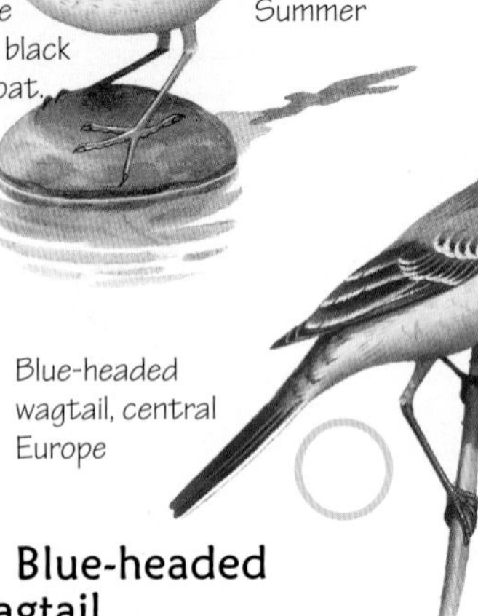

➡ Blue-headed wagtail
➡ Yellow wagtail

Two different forms of the same species. Summer visitor to grassy places near water. Yellow wagtail only seen in Britain. 17cm.

Spanish wagtail, Spain and Portugal

Ashy-headed wagtail, southern Europe

All the birds on this page wag their tails up and down.

Waxwing, dipper, wren, shrikes

⬅ Waxwing

Rare winter visitor from northern Europe. Feeds on berries. May be seen in towns. 17cm.

Resembles a starling in flight.

➡ Dipper

Fast-flowing rivers and streams in hilly areas. Bobs up and down on rocks in water. Walks underwater to find food. 18cm.

⬅ Wren

Very small. Found almost everywhere. Loud song finishes with a trill. Never still for long. 9.5cm.

Flies fast and straight on tiny, rounded wings.

➡ Red-backed shrike

Rare visitor to Britain. Catches and eats insects and small birds. 17cm.

Sticks food on thorns to store it.

⬅ Great grey shrike

Winter visitor to open country in Britain. Feeds on birds and mammals. Often hovers. 24cm.

Warblers

➡ Sedge warbler

Summer migrant. Nests in thick vegetation, usually near water, but also in drier areas. Sings from cover and is often difficult to see. 13cm.

White stripe over eye

Reddish-brown rump

⬅ Reed warbler

Summer visitor. Nests in reed beds or among waterside plants, mainly in the south of England. Hard to spot. Look for it flitting over reeds. 13cm.

➡ Garden warbler

Summer visitor. Sings from dense cover and is hard to see. Likes undergrowth or thick hedges. Song can be confused with blackcap's. 14cm.

Brown above, paler below

Female's cap is reddish-brown.

♂ ♀

⬅ Blackcap

Common summer visitor to woods or places with trees. Always moving from perch to perch as it sings. 14cm.

Male has grey head and white throat. Females and young have brown heads.

⬅ Whitethroat

A summer migrant, which hides itself in thick, low bushes. Sometimes sings its fast, scratchy song in flight. Flight is short and jerky. 14cm.

➡ Willow warbler

Summer migrant. Most common British warbler. Its song, which comes down the scale, is the best way of telling it from the chiffchaff. 11cm.

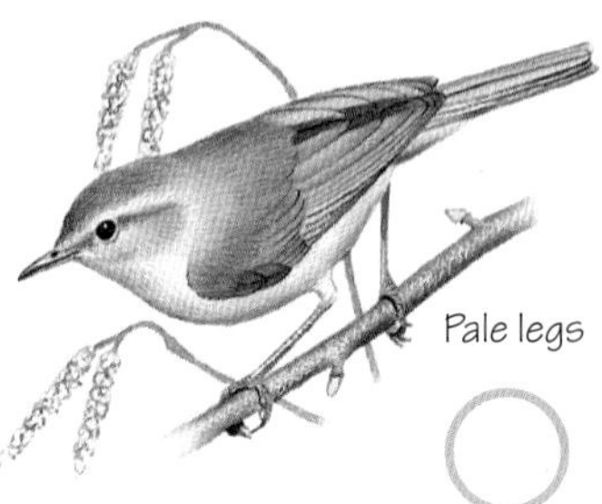

⬅ Chiffchaff

Summer migrant, often arriving in March. A few spend the winter in Britain. Its repetitive "chiff-chaff" song can be heard in woods and from bushes. 11cm.

➡ Wood warbler

Summer migrant to open woods. Sings from a branch, repeating a note faster and faster until it becomes a trill. 13cm.

Flycatchers, chats

⬅ Pied flycatcher

Catches insects in air. Also feeds on the ground. Summer migrant to old woodland. 13cm.

➡ Whinchat

Summer migrant, found in open country. "Tic-tic" call. Perches on tops of bushes and posts. 13cm.

Flicks wings and tail

⬅ Stonechat

"Tac-tac" call sounds like stones being knocked together. Found on heaths with gorse, especially near the sea. 13cm.

Colour is duller in winter.

➡ Wheatear

Summer migrant to moors and barren areas, but also seen elsewhere in the spring and autumn. 15cm.

White rump and black tail

➡ Spotted flycatcher

Summer migrant. Likes open woods, parks and country gardens. Catches insects in flight. 14cm.

Sits upright, often on a bare branch.

⬅ Redstart

A summer migrant to open woods, heaths and parks. Constantly flickers its tail. 14cm.

➡ Black redstart

A few nest on buildings or on cliffs in Britain. Some winter in south of England. Flickers its tail. 14cm.

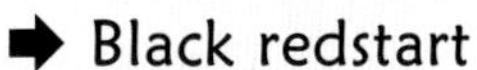

⬅ Robin

Woodland bird that is familiar in gardens. Sings in winter and spring. "Tic-tic" is its call of alarm. 14cm.

Male and female look alike.

➡ Nightingale

Secretive summer migrant. Best found by listening for its song in May and June. 17cm.

Reddish tail

Thrushes, oriole

➡ Fieldfare

Winter visitor, but a few nest in England and Scotland. Flocks can be seen in autumn, eating berries. 25.5cm.

⬅ Ring ouzel

Summer migrant to moors and mountains. Visits lower areas on migration. Shyer than blackbird. Loud piping call. 24cm.

Young are lighter and spottier than female.

➡ Blackbird

Lives where there are trees and bushes, often in parks and gardens. Loud musical song. Clucking alarm call. 25cm.

⬅ Golden oriole

Rare summer migrant most often seen in woods of eastern England. Hard to see as it spends a lot of time in tree-tops. 24cm.

Thrushes, starling

⬅ Redwing

Winter migrant, but a few nest in Scotland. Feeds on berries in hedges and hunts worms. 21cm.

➡ Song thrush

Found near or in trees or bushes. Well-known for the way it breaks open snail shells. Often in gardens. 23cm.

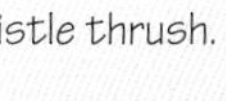

White under wing

White outer tail feathers

⬅ Mistle thrush

Large thrush found in most parts of Britain. Seen on the ground in fields and on moors. 27cm.

➡ Starling

A familiar garden bird. Often roosts in huge flocks. Mimics songs of other birds. 22cm.

Tits

➡ **Long-tailed tit**

Hedgerows and the edges of woods are good places to see groups of these tiny birds. 14cm.

⬅ **Crested tit**

Widespread in Europe but in Britain only found in a few Scottish pine woods, especially in the Spey Valley. 11cm.

➡ **Coal tit**

Likes conifer woods, but often seen in deciduous trees. Large white patch on back of head. 11cm.

⬅ **Blue tit**

Seen in woods and gardens. Often raises its blue cap to form a small crest. Young are less colourful. 11cm.

➡ **Marsh tit**

A bird of deciduous woods, like the willow tit (not illustrated). Rarely visits gardens. 11cm.

Tit, nuthatch, crests, treecreeper

➡ Great tit

Largest tit. Lives in woodlands and gardens. Nests in holes in trees or will use nestboxes. 14cm.

⬅ Nuthatch

Deciduous woods in England and Wales. Climbs up and down trees in a series of short hops. Very short tail. Nests in tree-holes. 14cm.

➡ Treecreeper

Usually seen in woods climbing up tree trunks and flying down again to search for food. Listen for high-pitched call. 13cm.

⬅ Firecrest

⬅ Goldcrest

Smallest European birds. Goldcrests are found in woods, especially of pine, all over Britain. Firecrests are much rarer. 9cm.

Finches

➡ Chaffinch

Found in gardens and wherever there are trees and bushes. Often seen in flocks on farmland in winter. 15cm.

♀

♂

♀

Male's head is brown in winter.

♂

⬅ Brambling

Winter migrant from northern Europe. Flocks feed on grain and seeds. Likes fruit from beech trees. 15cm.

♀

➡ Greenfinch

A frequent visitor to gardens, especially in winter. Likely to nest wherever there are trees and bushes. 15cm.

♂

♀

♂

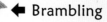

⬅ Siskin

A small finch which nests in conifers. It sometimes visits gardens in winter to feed on peanuts. 11cm.

Bullfinch

Secretive bird often found on edges of woods, and in hedges or gardens. Eats seeds and also buds from fruit trees. 15cm.

Linnet

Lives on heathland and farmland, but also found in towns, where it may visit gardens. Feeds on the seeds of weeds. Flocks in winter. 13cm.

Lesser redpoll
Common redpoll

The lesser redpoll is common in birch woods and forestry plantations in Britain. The common redpoll lives in northern Europe. 12cm.

Goldfinch

Feeds on thistle seeds and other weed seeds in open places. Nests in trees. 12cm.

Crossbill, crows

← Crossbill

Nests in pine woods. A slightly different species nests in Scotland. Eats pine cone seeds. 16cm.

Crossbills are sparrow-sized, with large heads and bills.

→ Jay

Secretive woodland bird. Will visit gardens. Listen for harsh screeching call. Look for white rump in flight. 32cm.

← Raven

This large crow lives in wild rocky areas or on rocky coasts. Look for its wedge-shaped tail and huge bill. Croaks. 64cm.

→ Jackdaw

Small member of the crow family. Found where there are old trees, old buildings, or cliffs. Nests in colonies. Often seen with rooks. 33cm.

⬅ Carrion crow
⬅ Hooded crow

Carrion crow is more often seen alone or in pairs. Hooded crows form flocks. Carrion is more widespread than hooded. 47cm.

➡ Rook

Nests in "rookeries" in tops of trees. Is usually seen in flocks on farmland. Young lack bare skin round beak. Call is harsh "kaw". 46cm.

⬅ Magpie

Seen in both town and country. Eats many eggs and young birds in spring. Long tail is very noticeable in flight. 46cm.

Pigeons, doves

➡ Woodpigeon

Largest of the pigeons. Common on farmland and in woods and towns. Forms large flocks. 41cm.

⬅ Stock dove

Nests in holes in trees or in rock faces. Feeds on the ground, often with woodpigeons. Sometimes seen in flocks. 33cm.

➡ Rock dove
➡ Town pigeon

Town pigeons are descended from rock doves which are usually found in small groups on sea cliffs. 33cm.

⬅ Collared dove

Found in parks, large gardens, or near farm buildings. Feeds mainly on grain. 30cm.

➡ Turtle dove

Summer visitor to England and Wales. Woods, parks and farmland. Listen for purring call. 28cm.

Sparrows, buntings

➡ House sparrow

Very familiar bird. Lives near houses and even in city centres. Builds domed nests. 15cm.

⬅ Tree sparrow

Usually nests in holes in trees or cliffs. Much less common than house sparrow. 14cm.

➡ Yellowhammer

Found in open country, especially farmland. Feeds on ground. Forms flocks in winter. Sings from the tops of bushes. 17cm.

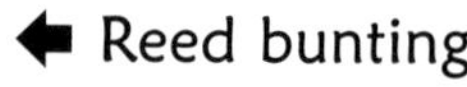

⬅ Reed bunting

Most common near water, but some nest in dry areas with long grass. May visit bird tables in winter. 15cm.

➡ Corn bunting

Nests in cornfields. Sings from posts, bushes or overhead wires. 18cm.

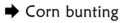

Bugs & Insects

Butterflies

➡ Meadow brown

Meadows and grassy places where it visits thistles, knapweed and bramble flowers. Active even on dull days. Caterpillar eats grasses. W.S. 50-55mm.

⬅ Ringlet

Keeps to damp, grassy places and sunny woodland paths. Visits thistles, knapweed and bramble flowers. W.S. 48-52mm.

⬋ Small heath

Not fussy about where it lives, and found in open woods, on marshes and on dry hillsides. Likes hawkweed. W.S. 33-35mm.

➡ Gatekeeper or hedge brown

Basks in sunshine on roadside hedges, especially on bramble. Most common in the south. W.S. 40-46mm.

Butterflies fly around during the day, unlike moths, which are active at night.

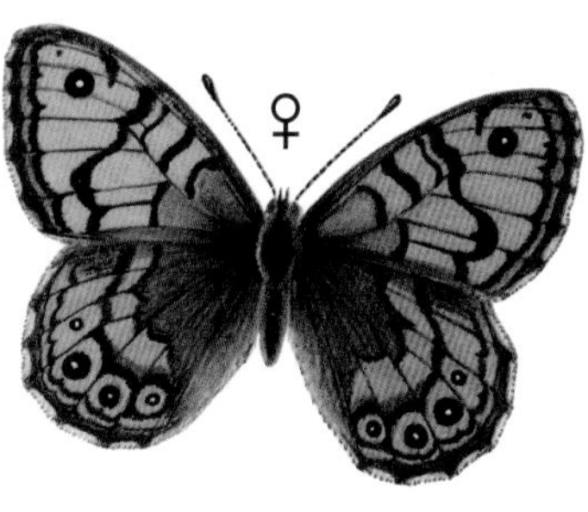

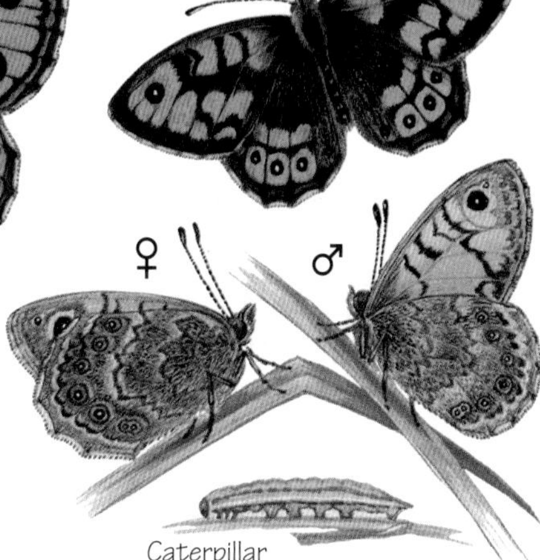

➡ Wall brown

Often rests on walls and paths. Likes rough, open ground and woodland glades. Flies slowly. Caterpillar eats grasses. W.S. 44-46mm.

Butterflies

← Dark green fritillary

Likes thistle and bramble flowers. Open grassland near woods, and high rough ground. Flies fast. W.S. 63-70mm.

→ Peacock

Common in gardens. One of five British species that hibernates in adult stage, in hollow trees, sheds, etc. Caterpillar eats nettles. W.S. 62-68mm.

The markings are like the "eyes" on a peacock's tail.

← Painted lady

Arrives in spring from North Africa. Lays eggs on thistles. Adult insects can be seen in autumn, but do not survive the winter. W.S. 62-65mm.

→ Red admiral

Common in gardens on buddleia and Michaelmas daisies. Migrates to Britain from the Mediterranean. Caterpillar feeds on nettles. W.S. 66-68mm.

← Small tortoiseshell

Name comes from pattern on wings. Visits many flowers and is common all over Britain. On the wing from April to November. W.S. 48-52mm.

Butterflies

➡ Small white

Appears in May and August. Lays single eggs on cabbages and nasturtiums. Common in gardens. W.S. 48-50mm.

⬅ Green-veined white

Pattern on underwing helps to protect the butterfly from enemies when it sits on grass. Caterpillar eats leaves and seed pods of Jack-by-the-hedge. W.S. 47-50mm.

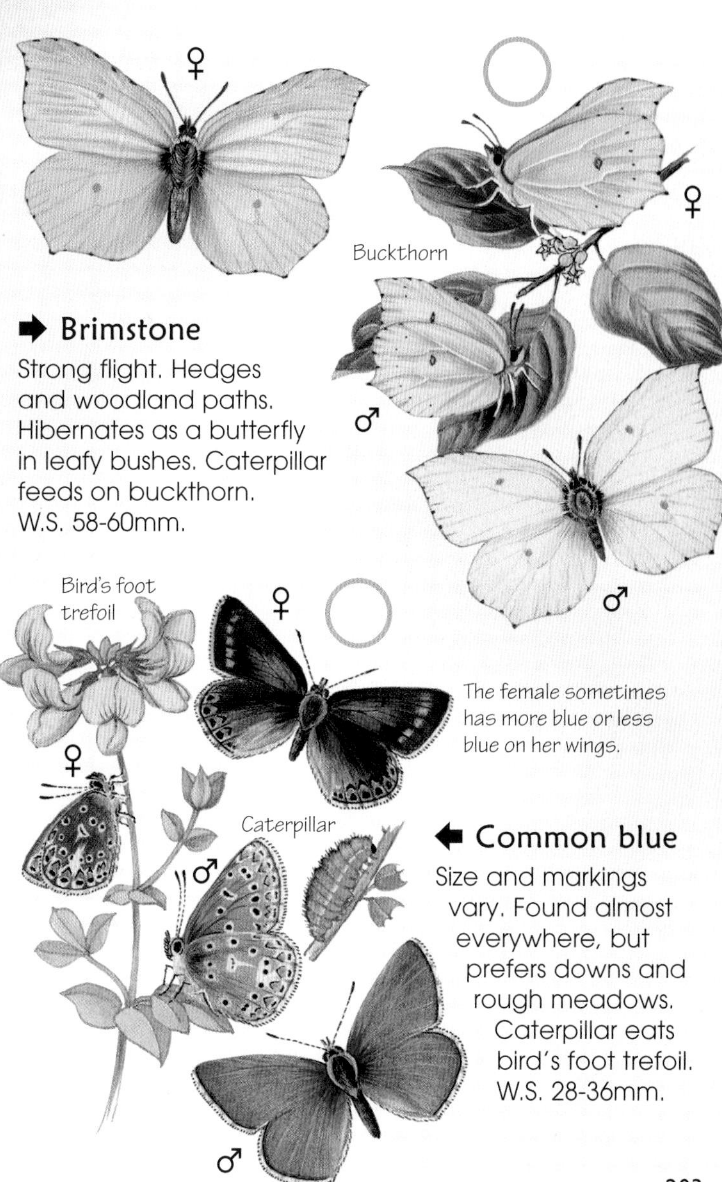

➡ Brimstone

Strong flight. Hedges and woodland paths. Hibernates as a butterfly in leafy bushes. Caterpillar feeds on buckthorn. W.S. 58-60mm.

⬅ Common blue

Size and markings vary. Found almost everywhere, but prefers downs and rough meadows. Caterpillar eats bird's foot trefoil. W.S. 28-36mm.

Moths

Most moths are nocturnal, which means they are active at night. Moths' antennae don't have swellings at the ends like those of butterflies.

➡ Death's-head hawk

Occasionally visits Britain from southern Europe and northern Africa. Lays eggs on potato leaves. Larva is seen in late summer and pupates underground. W.S. 100-125mm.

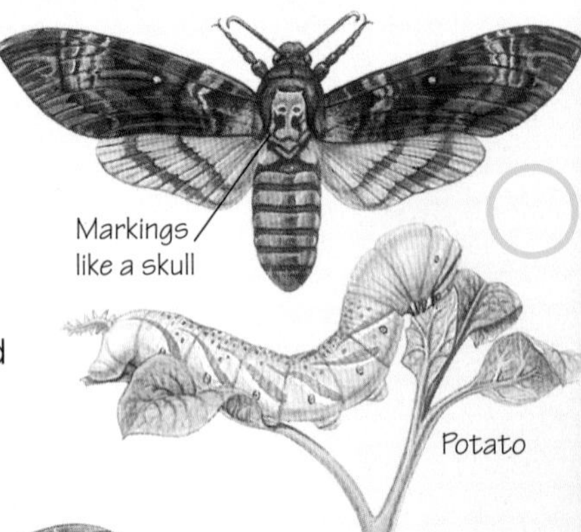

⬅ Privet hawk

Most common in southern England and the Midlands. Larva eats privet leaves in July and August. Moth emerges the following summer. W.S. 90-100mm.

Privet

➡ Lime hawk

One of Britain's most common hawk moths. Larva eats leaves of lime trees in late summer. W.S. 65-70mm.

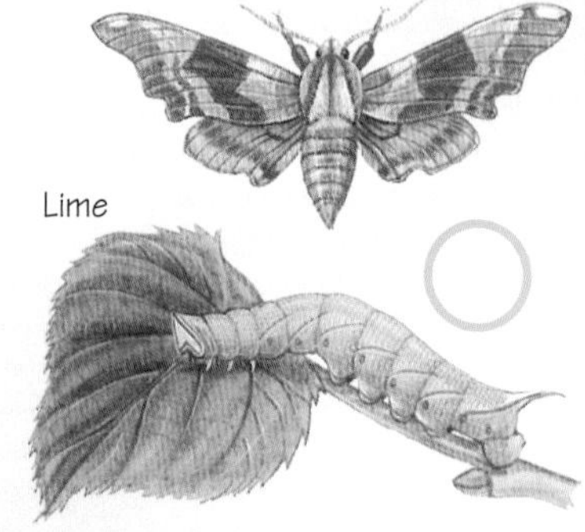

➡ Eyed hawk

Flashes markings on its underwings to frighten birds and other enemies. Larva feeds on sallow and leaves of plum and apple trees. W.S. 75-80mm.

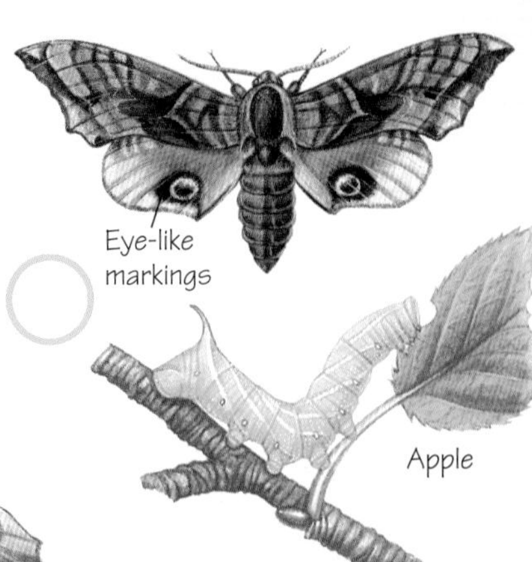

Yellow points

Poplar

⬅ Poplar hawk

Common all over Britain. Larva feeds on poplar or willow and, like eyed hawk, has rough skin surface. Notice yellow markings. W.S. 75-80mm.

➡ Hummingbird hawk

Visitor to Britain. Found in gardens during day. Hovers over flowers to feed, beating its wings like a hummingbird. Lays eggs on bedstraw plants. W.S. 45mm.

Moths

➡ Elephant hawk

Widespread, but scarce in Scotland. Larva is shaped like an elephant's trunk. It feeds on willowherb and bedstraw plants. W.S. 65mm.

⬅ Emperor

Found all over Britain. Male flies by day over moorland, looking for female which comes out at dusk. Lays eggs on heather and brambles. Appearance of larva changes each time its skin is shed. W.S. female 70mm. Male 55mm.

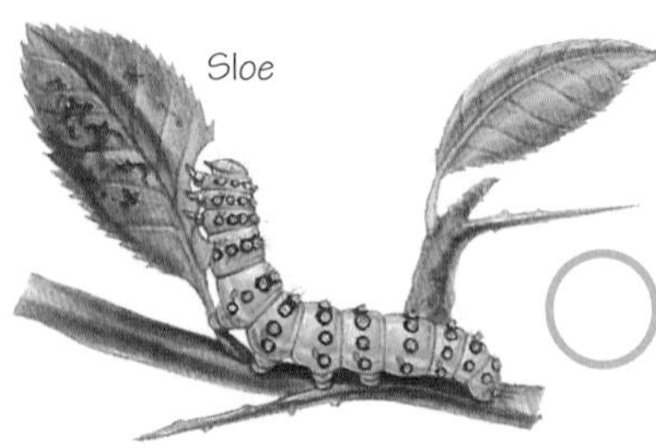

➡ Puss

Widespread in Britain. Lays eggs, usually singly, on willow in May-June. Thin red "whips" come out of larva's tails, perhaps to frighten birds. W.S. 65-80mm.

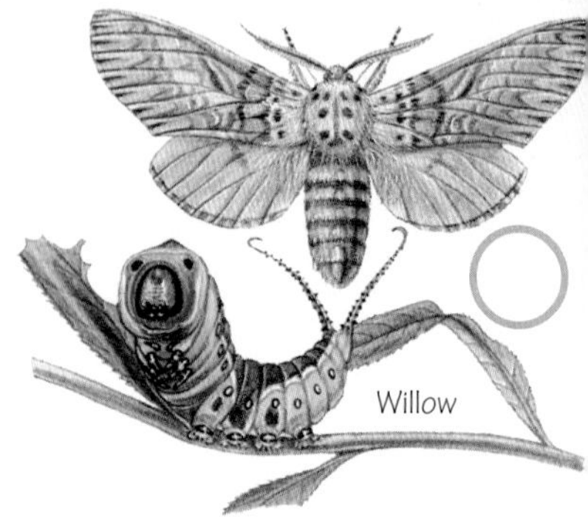

➡ Lobster

Can be seen in southern England, Wales and parts of southern Ireland. Name comes from the shape of the larva's tail end. Larva eats beech leaves. W.S. 65-70mm.

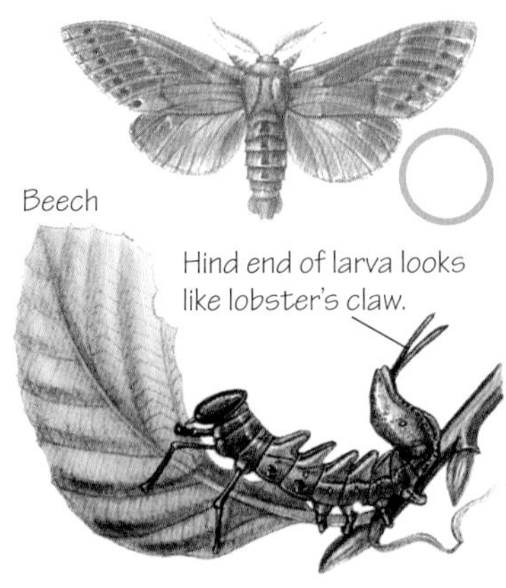

⬅ Vapourer

Common all over Britain, even in towns. Female has only wing stubs and can't fly. Larva feeds on a variety of trees. W.S. 35mm.

➡ Peach blossom

Found in woodland areas. Its name comes from the peach blossom pattern on its wings. Larva feeds on bramble. W.S. 35mm.

Moths

← Yellow-tail

Brightly coloured larvae are often found in hedgerows of hawthorn, sloe and bramble in May and June. W.S. 32-40mm.

→ Merveille-du-jour

Lives in oak woodlands. Forewings match oak tree bark, making moth difficult for enemies to see. Larva eats oak leaves. W.S. 45mm.

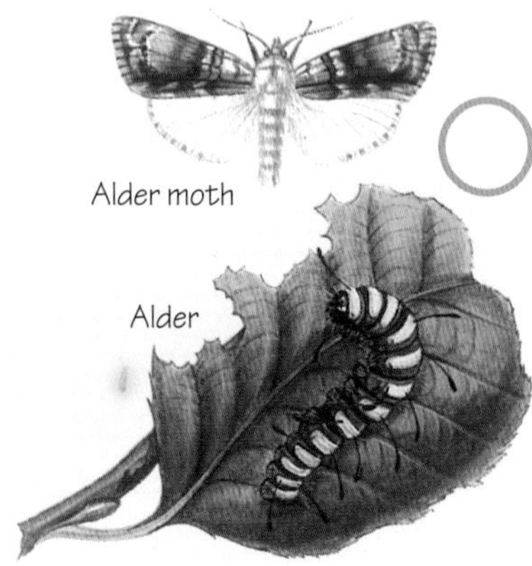

← Alder

Like many other species, the larva is more striking than the adult moth. It feeds on a variety of trees, including alder and oak. W.S. 37mm.

➡ Clifden nonpareil or blue underwing

Breeds in a few places in Kent, but sometimes visits other parts of Britain, usually in late summer. Stick-like larva feeds on black poplar and aspen.

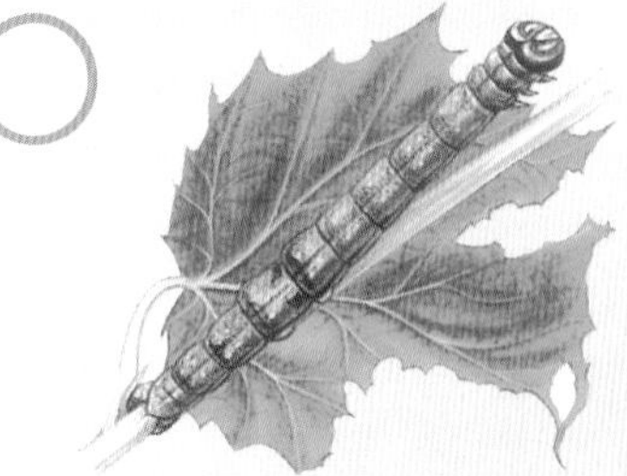

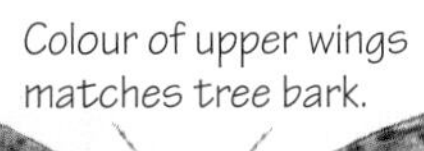

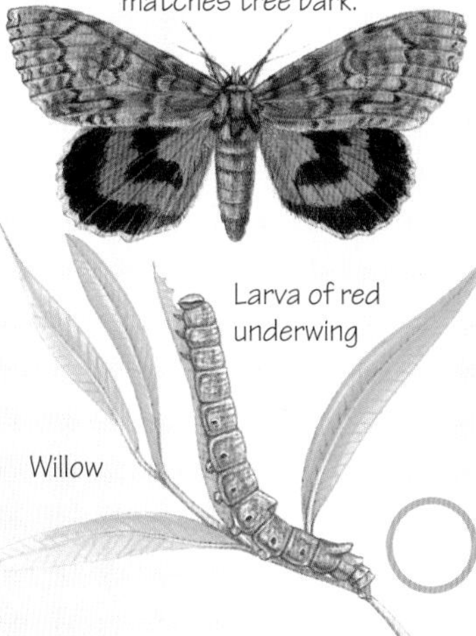

⬅ Red underwing

Quite common in southern England and the Midlands. Flashes underwings when threatened by birds. Rests in daytime on trees. Larva eats poplar and willow. W.S. 80mm.

➡ Mother Shipton

Flies on sunny days. Look on railway banks and in meadows May to June. Larva eats vetches and clover. Named after a woman who was believed to be able to see into the future. W.S. 35mm.

Moths

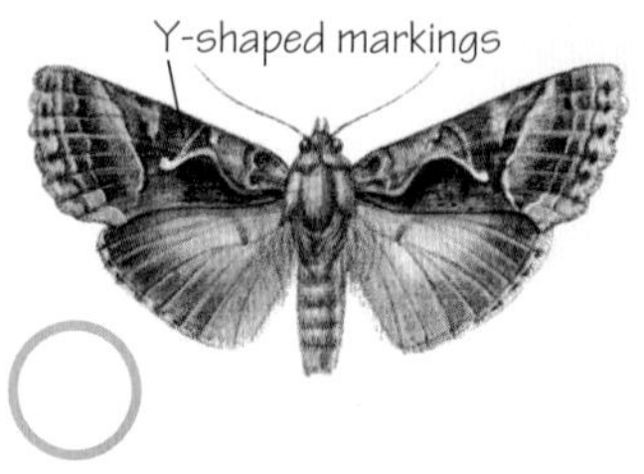

⬅ Silver Y

Visitor to Britain, some years in great numbers. Feeds on garden flowers with long proboscis. Flies fast. Larva eats nettle and thistle. W.S. 40mm.

➡ Herald

Widespread in Britain. Hibernates during the winter in barns, sometimes in small groups. Mates in spring and female lays eggs on various kinds of willow. W.S. 40mm.

Larva of herald

Willow

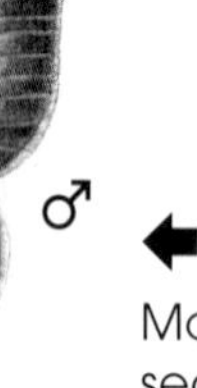

♂

⬅ Oak eggar

Male flies by day, searching for female who rests in heather on moorland. Larva eats heather, bramble and hawthorn. W.S. 50-65mm.

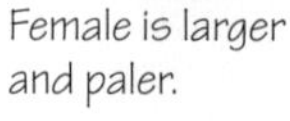

Female is larger and paler.

Hawthorn

➡ Lappet

Name comes from "lappets" on larva. Feeds on apple, willow and hawthorn. Adult's brown colour, ragged wing edges and veined wings make it look like a bunch of leaves. W.S. 60-70mm.

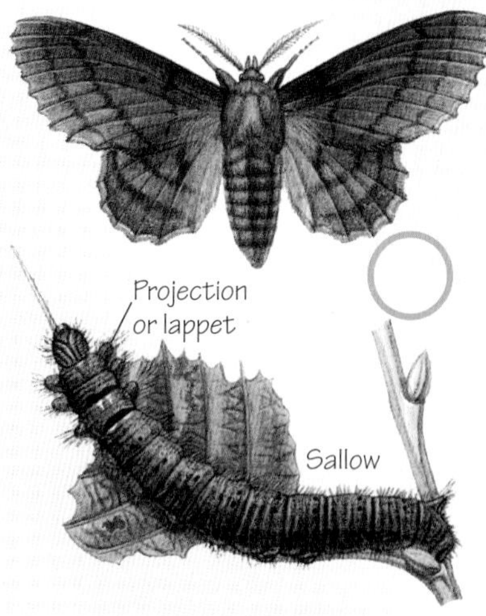

Wing pattern varies

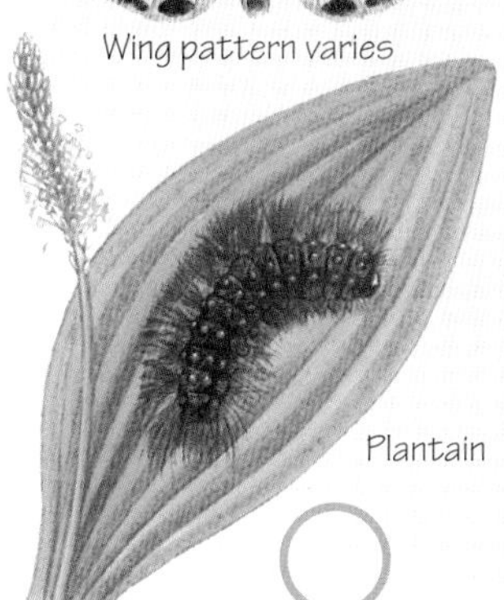

⬅ Wood tiger

Smaller and more local than garden tiger. Widespread on hillsides, heaths and open woodland. Larva eats violets and forget-me-nots, and hibernates. W.S. 35-40mm.

➡ Garden tiger

Common, but larva more often seen. Feeds on many low-growing plants and hibernates when young. Feeds again in spring and is fully grown by June. W.S. 60-70mm.

Larva is called a woolly bear.

Moths

➡ Cinnabar

Sometimes flies by day, but weakly. Striped larvae feed in groups on ragwort. Common on waste ground and railway banks. W.S. 40-45mm.

Ragwort

⬅ Goat

Widespread, but well camouflaged and rarely seen. Larva eats wood of ash and willow. Spends three or four years in a tree trunk and pupates a silk-bonded cocoon made of wood shavings. Larva smells like goats. W.S. 70-85mm.

Larva inside tree trunk

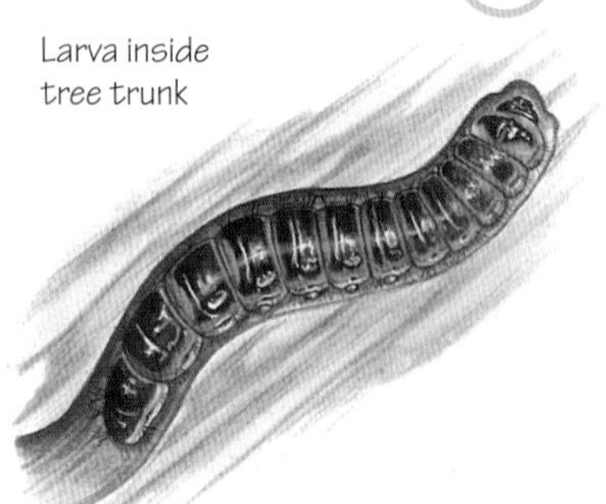

➡ Swallow-tailed

Looks like a butterfly. Weak, fluttering flight. Stick-like larva feeds on leaves of ivy, hawthorn and sloe. W.S. 56mm.

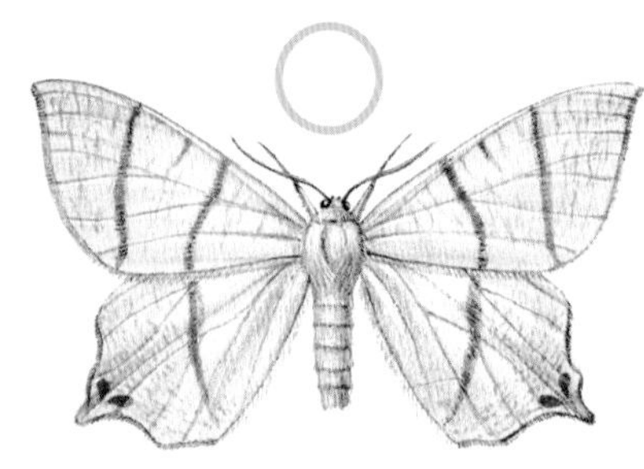

⬅ Six-spot burnet

The most common British burnet. Flies over grassy areas during the day. Larva eats trefoil, clover and vetch. Boat-shaped cocoons are found attached to plant stems. W.S. 35mm.

♀

➡ Ghost

Very common. Males often seen after dusk searching for larger females in dense grass. Female clings without moving to grass stem until male approaches. Larva eats plant roots. W.S. 50-60mm.

Female is better camouflaged than male.

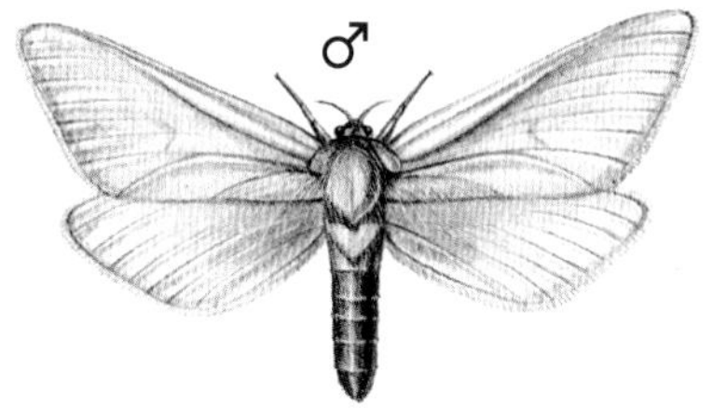

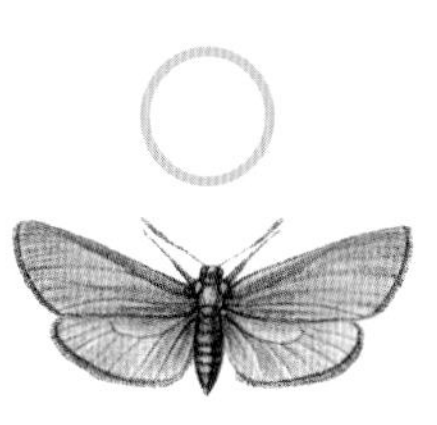

⬅ Forester

Widely distributed. Flies over lush meadows. Stubby larva feeds on sorrel. W.S. 25-27mm.

Beetles

➡ Green tiger beetle

Fierce, sharp-jawed predator. Open woodland and sandy areas in early summer. Larva catches ants when they approach its burrow. 12-15mm long.

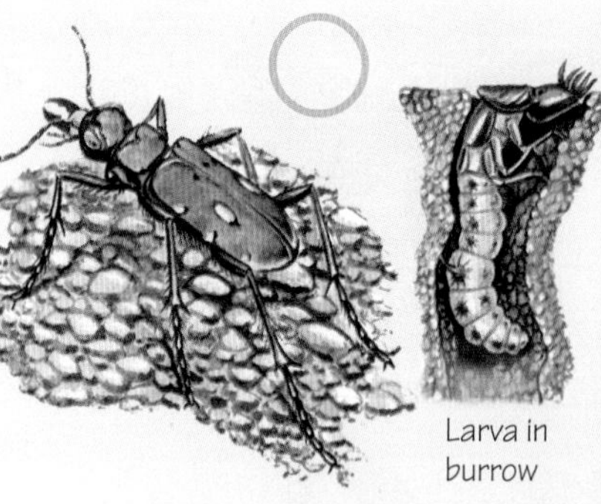

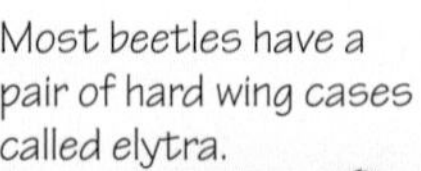
Most beetles have a pair of hard wing cases called elytra.

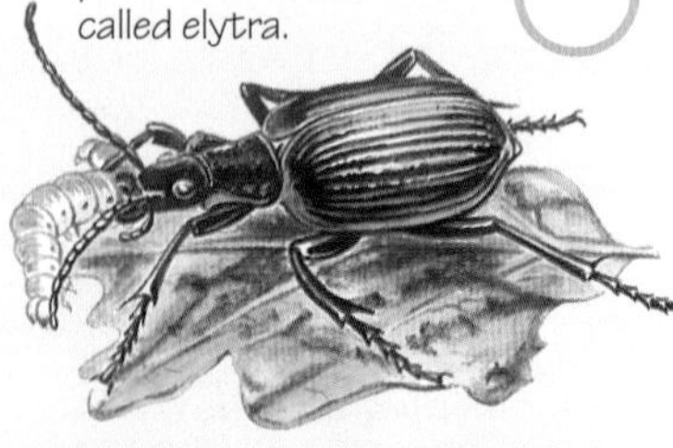

⬅ Large green ground beetle

Adults live in oak trees. Both adults and larvae feed on leaf-eating caterpillars and other larvae. 16-20mm long.

➡ Violet ground beetle

Found under large stones in gardens, and common in woods and under hedges. Adult and larva eat other insects and worms. Larva pupates in soil. 30-35mm long.

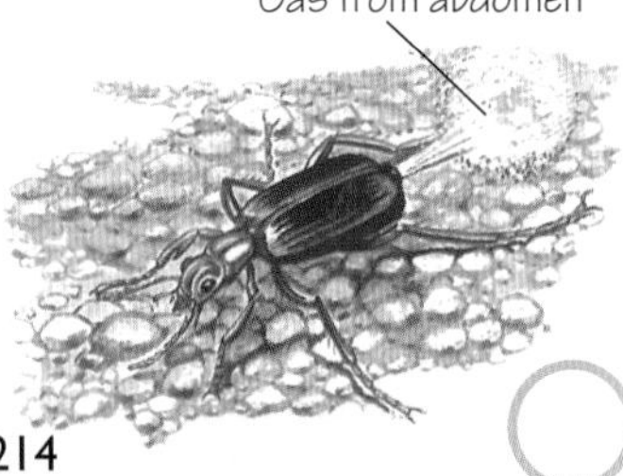

⬅ Bombardier beetle

Lives under stones in chalky areas in southern England. When threatened, it shoots irritating gas from end of its abdomen with a popping sound. 7-10mm long.

⬅ Devil's coach horse or cocktail beetle

Common in gardens. When challenged, raises tail and spreads jaws. Can ooze poisonous liquid from end of abdomen. 25-30mm long.

➡ Rove beetle

Feeds mainly on dead animals and birds. Most common in southern England. Related to Devil's coach horse. 20mm long.

⬅ Red and black burying beetle

Feeds on dead animals, kneading and biting the flesh and then burying the body. Female lays eggs in burrow beside the body. Larvae feed on it and pupate in a chamber in soil. 15-20mm long.

➡ Ant beetle

Small, fast-moving beetle found on elms and conifers. Larvae live under loose bark. Adults and larvae eat larvae of bark beetles. 7-10mm long.

Beetles

➡ Great diving beetle

Lives in lakes and large ponds. Eats tadpoles, small fish and other insects. Collects air from surface and stores it between wing covers and end of abdomen. 30-35mm long.

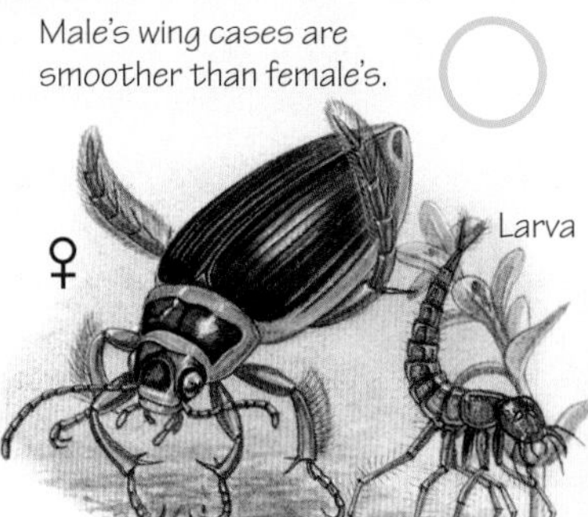

Carries bubble of air under body.

⬅ Great silver water beetle

Largest British water beetle. Eats mainly water plants, but larva is a predator and eats water snails. Can fly to other waters if its home dries up. 37-48mm long.

➡ Whirligig beetle

Seen in groups on surface of ponds, lakes and slow rivers in bright sunshine. Darts in all directions. Carnivorous, eating mosquito larvae. 6-8mm long.

⬅ Water beetle

Lives under water, among vegetation of lakes and rivers, where it lays its eggs. Colour may be darker, sometimes all black. Widespread. 7-8mm long.

➡ Glow-worm

Likes grassy banks, hillsides, open woods. Most common in southern England. Wingless female attracts male with her glowing tail. Male 15mm long. Female 20mm long.

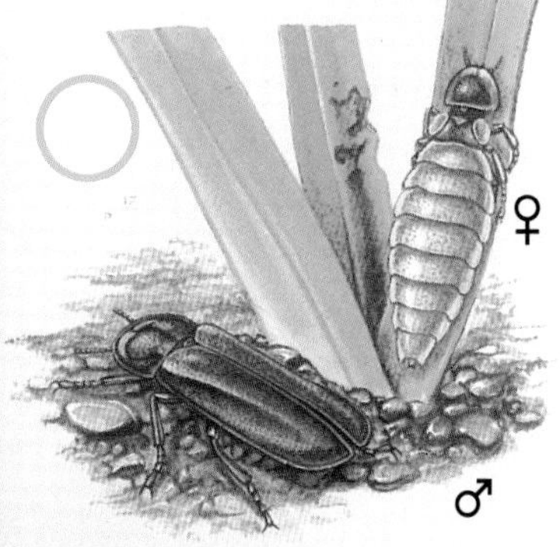

⬅ Lesser glow-worm

Seen near streams on damp grassy banks. Male and larva have small lights on tip of abdomen. Found in central and southern Europe, but not in Britain. 8-10mm long.

➡ Scarlet-tipped flower beetle

Most common in southern England. Look in buttercups and other flowerheads. Blows up scarlet bladders on its underside when handled. 7-10mm long.

Buttercup

⬅ Click beetle or skipjack

Found in dense vegetation or in flowers. Larvae live in soil, eating plant roots. Other species of click beetle do much damage to crops. 14-18mm long.

Beetles

➡ Two-spot ladybird

Very common. Colour pattern often varies and some individuals are shiny black with red spots. 4-5mm long.

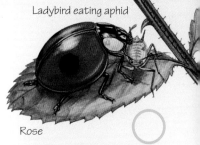

Ladybird eating aphid

Rose

⬅ Seven-spot ladybird

Very common. Hibernates in large numbers in sheds, houses or tree bark. Emerges on sunny spring days to find aphids and lay its eggs. 6-7mm long.

➡ Eyed ladybird

Largest ladybird in Britain. Found near or on fir trees. Both adults and larvae hunt for aphids. 8-9mm long.

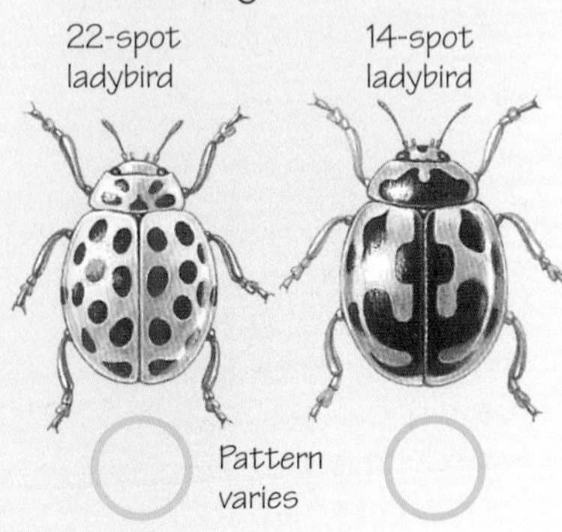

⬅ 22-spot ladybird
⬅ 14-spot ladybird

22-spot is found in many areas and habitats. 2-3mm long. 14-spot is rare in the north. Likes trees and bushes. 3-4mm long.

➡ Death watch beetle

Larva eats timber in buildings. The sound the adult makes when it taps its head against its tunnel walls was once believed to foretell a death. 7-10mm long.

⬅ Cardinal beetle

Found on flowers and under bark. Whitish larvae feed on bark and wood. 15-17mm long.

➡ Oil beetle

This beetle cannot fly. The larva waits in a flower for a special kind of solitary bee to carry it to its nest where the larva feeds and grows. 15-30mm long.

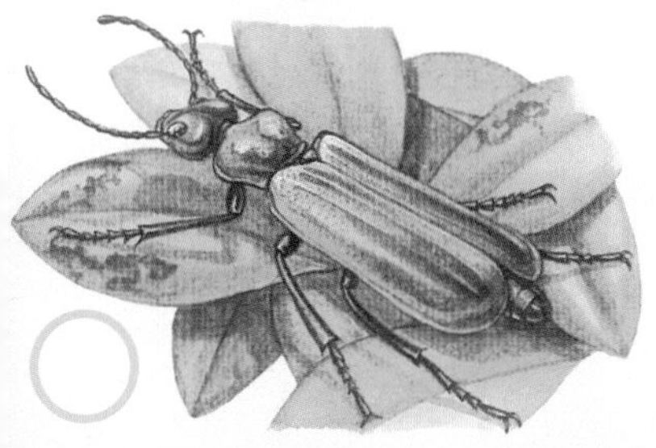

⬅ Blister beetle

Rare. Name comes from a fluid in the insect's blood which causes blisters on human skin. Larvae live as parasites in the nests of some types of bee. 12-20mm long.

Beetles

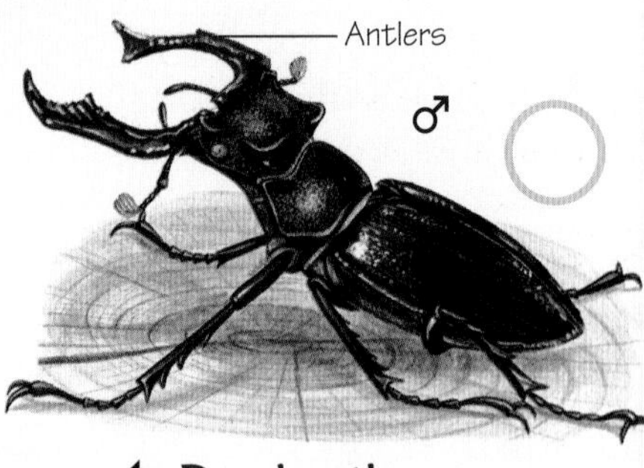

➡ Stag beetle

Largest British beetle. Only male has antlers. Larvae feed on tree stumps for three years or more. Most common in southern England. 25-27mm long.

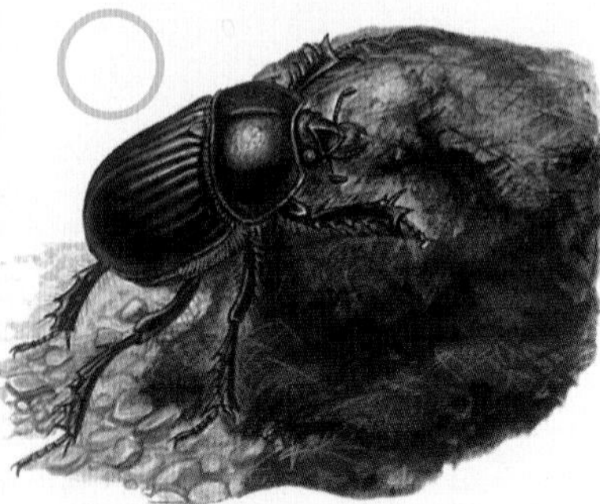

⬅ Dor beetle

Common. Seen flying at night to dung heaps where it lays its eggs. Makes a loud droning sound when it flies. 16-24mm long.

➡ Horned dung beetle or Minotaur beetle

Found in sandy places where rabbits live. Eats their dung and fills tunnels with it for larvae to eat. 12-18mm long.

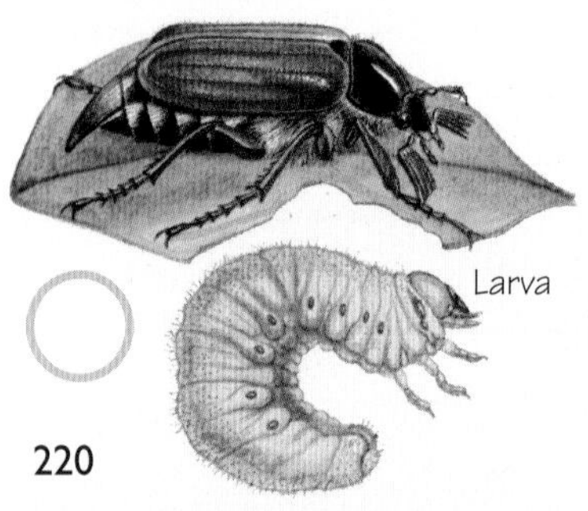

⬅ Cockchafer or May bug

Common. Flies round tree tops in early summer and sometimes down chimneys and at lighted windows. Larvae may be dug up in gardens. 25-30mm long.

➡ Rose chafer

Sometimes found in roses and other flowers. Larvae feed on old timber and roots. Found all over Britain. 14-20mm long.

⬅ Bee beetle

Found mainly in Scotland and Wales. Found in flowers. Mimics colouring of bees (see page 39). Larvae eat rotting wood. 10-13mm long.

➡ Musk beetle

Longhorn beetles have long antennae, perhaps so they can recognize each other when they emerge from their pupae in wood tunnels. 20-32mm long.

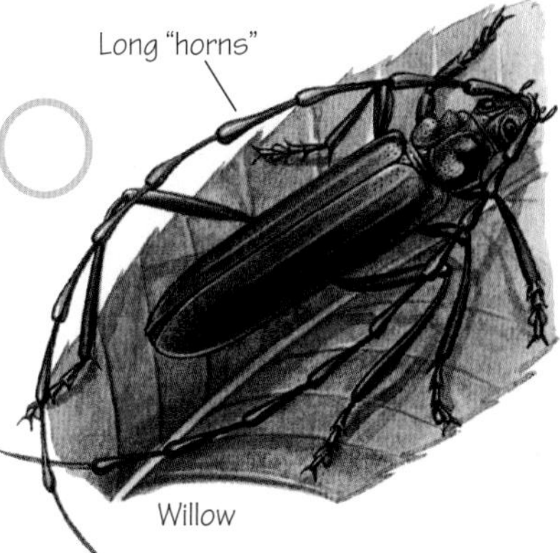

⬅ Wasp beetle

Harmless, but looks and behaves like a wasp. Flies in bright sunshine visiting flowers. Common all over Britain. 15mm long.

Beetles

➡ Colorado beetle

Damages potato crops. Introduced by accident from America. Some still appear in Europe. You should tell the police if you spot one. 10-12mm long.

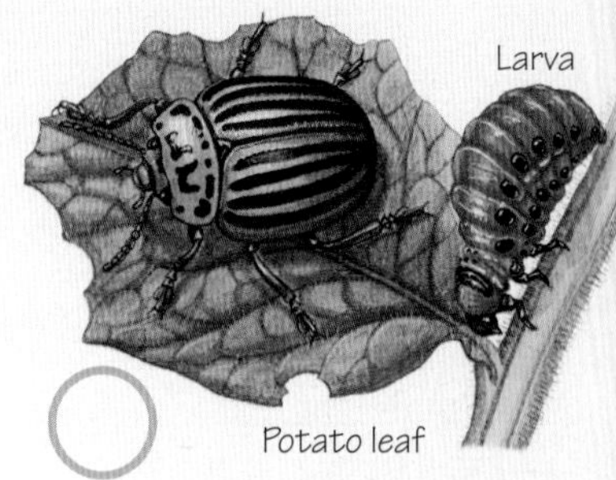

⬅ Bloody-nosed beetle

Like oil beetle and blister beetle, it reacts when threatened, spurting bright red fluid from its mouth. This is called "reflex-bleeding". Found in low, dense foliage. 10-20mm long.

➡ Green tortoise beetle

Legs and antennae often hidden so it looks like a tortoise. Well camouflaged on thistles where it feeds, and where larvae pupate. 6-8mm long.

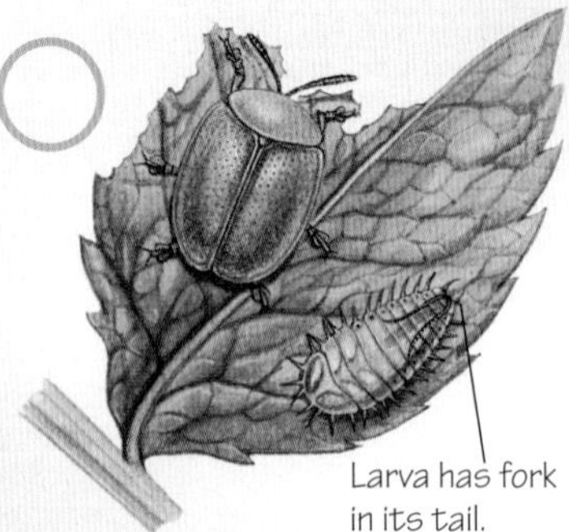

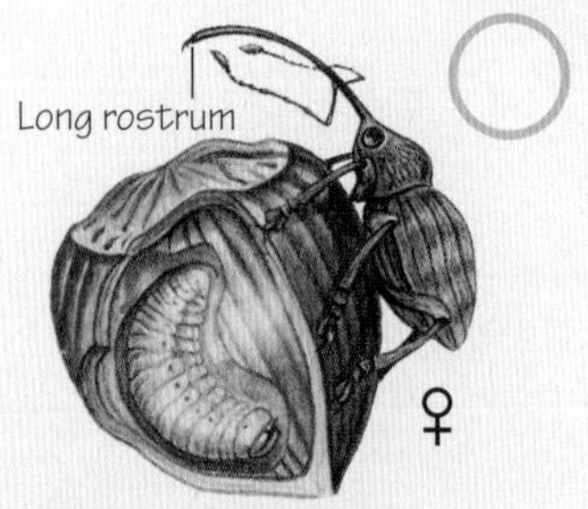

⬅ Nut weevil

Found in parks and gardens with oak and hazel trees. Female has longer rostrum than male. Black, diamond shaped body with brown, hair-like scales. 10mm long.

Bugs

➡ Green shieldbug

Lives on trees such as hazel and birch. Lays eggs in batches. Nymphs mature in late summer after several moults. 12-14mm long.

Birch

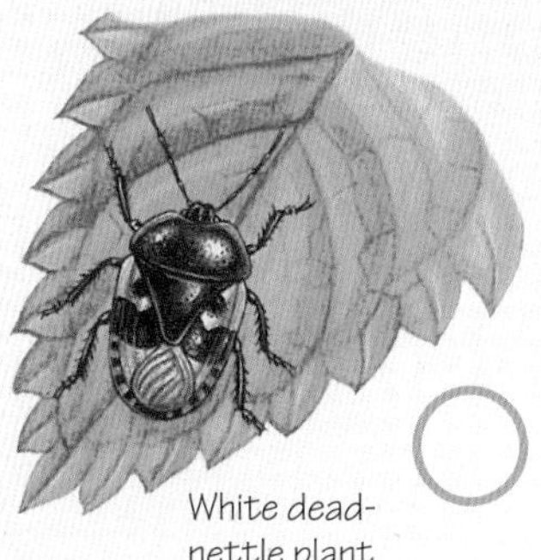

White dead-nettle plant

⬅ Pied shieldbug

Lays eggs in soil and female looks after them. When they hatch out, she leads the nymphs to their food plant. Rare in the north. 6-8mm long.

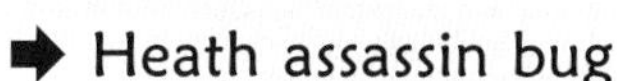

➡ Heath assassin bug

Common on open heath and sand dunes. Adults and nymphs suck body fluids out of prey. Most adults are wingless. 9-12mm long.

Oak

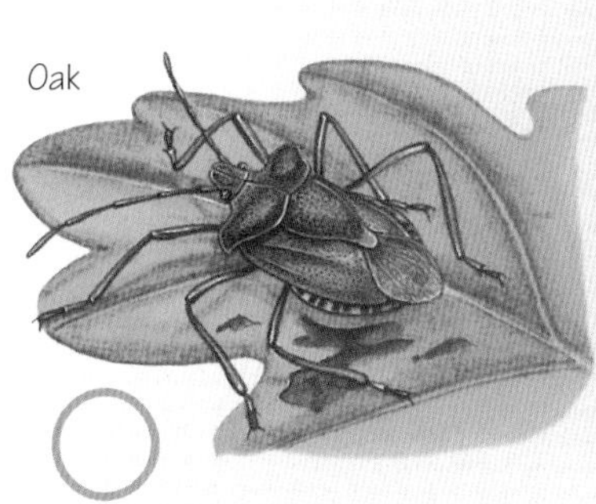

⬅ Forest bug

Common on oak or orchard trees. Feeds on leaves, fruits and caterpillars. Female lays batches of eggs on leaves. 11-14mm long.

Bugs

➡ Water cricket

Common on still and slow-moving water. Runs on water surface, eating insects and spiders. Lays eggs out of water on moss. 6-7mm long.

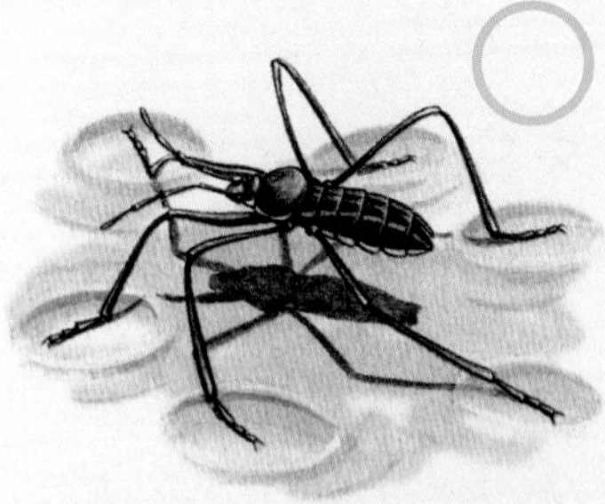

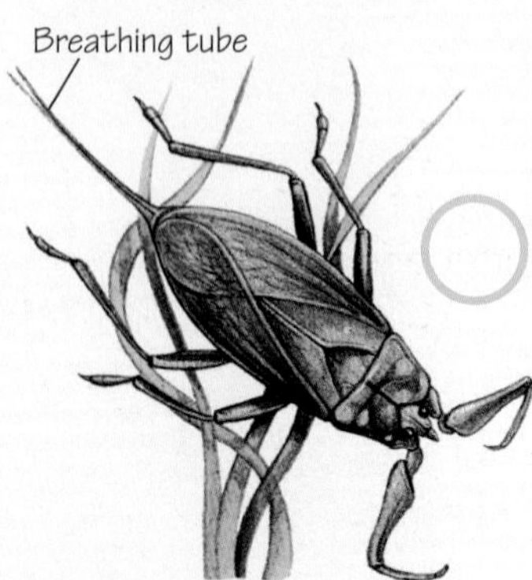

⬅ Water scorpion

Found in ponds and shallow lakes. Seizes small fish, tadpoles and insect larvae with its forelegs. Lays eggs in algae or on water plants. 18-22mm long.

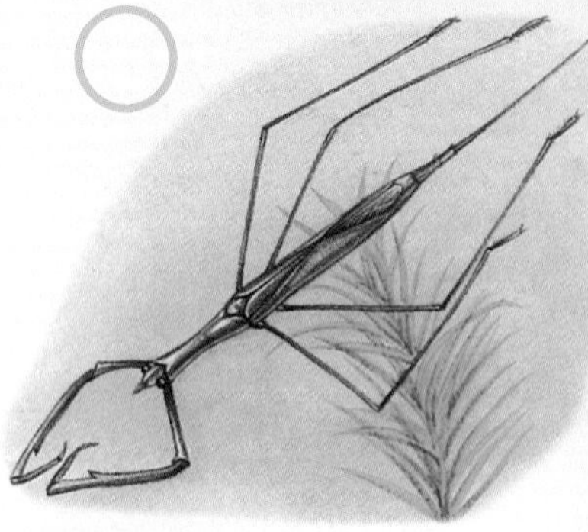

➡ Water stick insect

Not related to true stick insects, but like them it is hard to see among plants. Most common in southern Wales and southern England. 30-35mm long.

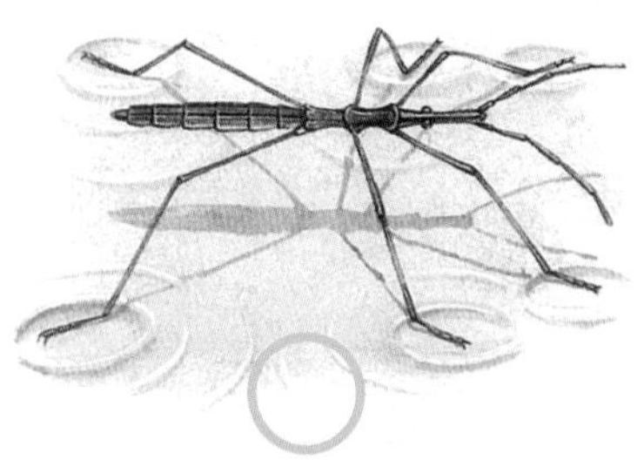

⬅ Water measurer

Found at edges of ponds and slow rivers and streams. Stabs at mosquito larvae and water fleas with its rostrum. Also eats dead insects. 9-12mm long.

➡ Water boatman or backswimmer

Lives in pools, canals, ditches and water tanks. Jerks along with its hind legs, usually on its back. Eats tadpoles and small fish. Can fly away if its home dries up. 15mm long.

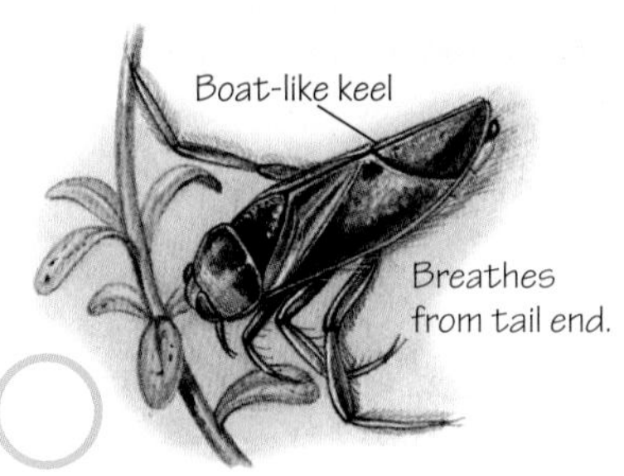

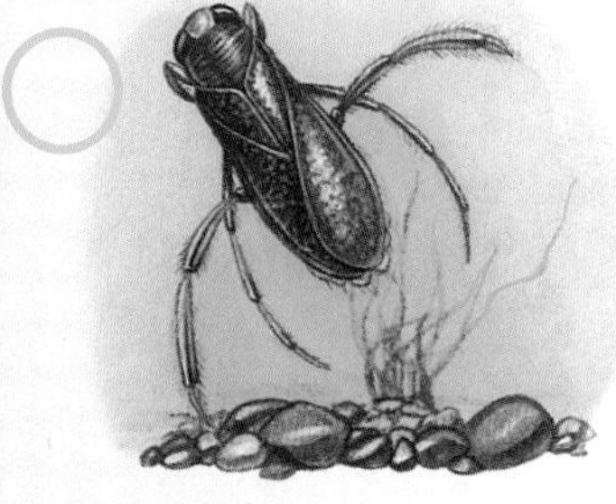

⬅ Lesser water boatman

Flatter and rounder than water boatman, with shorter legs. It uses its front legs to swim. Sucks up bits of animal and plant material at bottom of ponds. Common. 12-14mm long.

➡ Pond skater

Front legs adapted to catch dead or dying insects that fall on water's surface. Some can fly; others have no wings. Common in ponds. 8-10mm long.

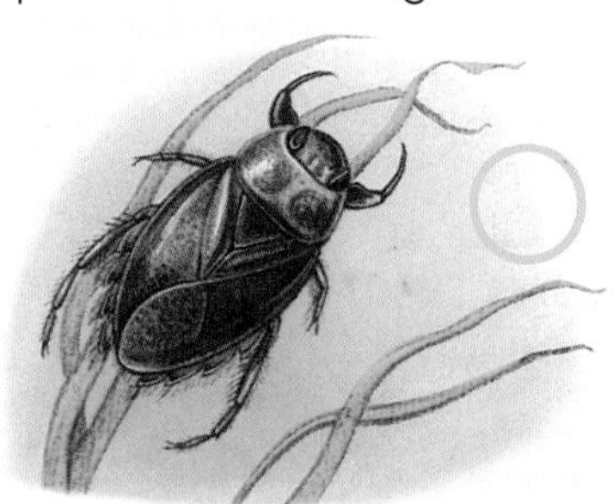

⬅ Saucer bug

Lives in vegetation at bottom of muddy pools and canals. Like the water boatman, it can stab with its rostrum. Hibernates in winter, as do most water bugs. 12-16mm long.

Bugs

➡ New Forest cicada

Male makes high-pitched buzzing sound that is very difficult to hear. Nymphs live underground for several years eating plant roots. The only British cicada. 25mm long.

Adult sucking sap from tree

Birch

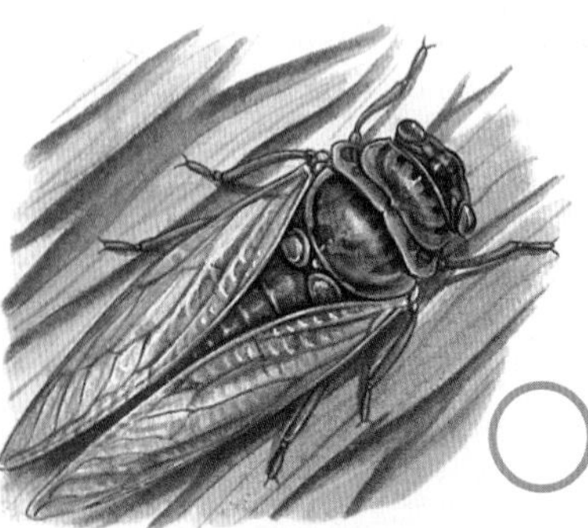

⬅ Southern cicada

Larger and noisier than British cicada. Common in southern Europe. Adult eats the sap of ash, pine and olive trees. 50mm long.

➡ Horned treehopper

Found on tree branches and low vegetation, such as bracken, in woods. Adult and larva feed on oak leaves and other plants. 9-10mm long.

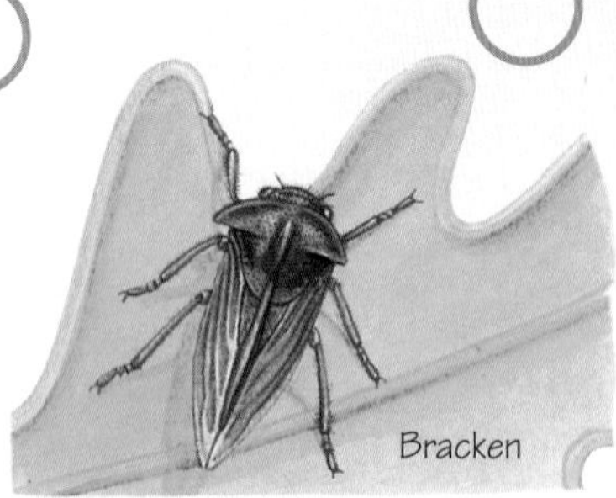

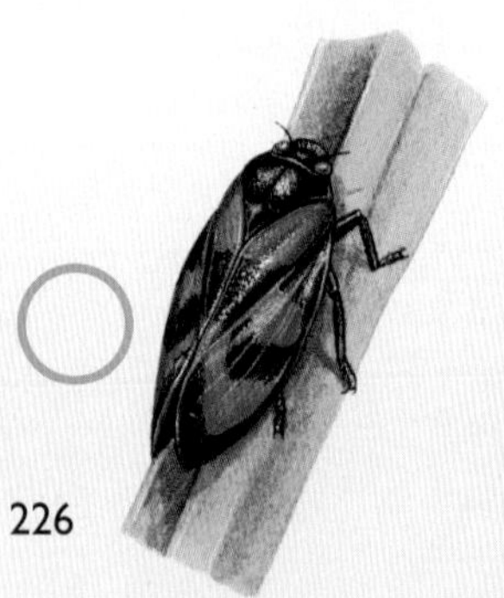

⬅ Black and red froghopper

Common in dense grass and on trees. Jumps if disturbed. Larvae secrete froth which covers them when they feed underground. 9-10mm long.

➡ Eared leafhopper

Seen on lichen-covered oak or other trees where it is well hidden. Adults appear about June. Moves slowly. Local in southern England. 13-17mm long.

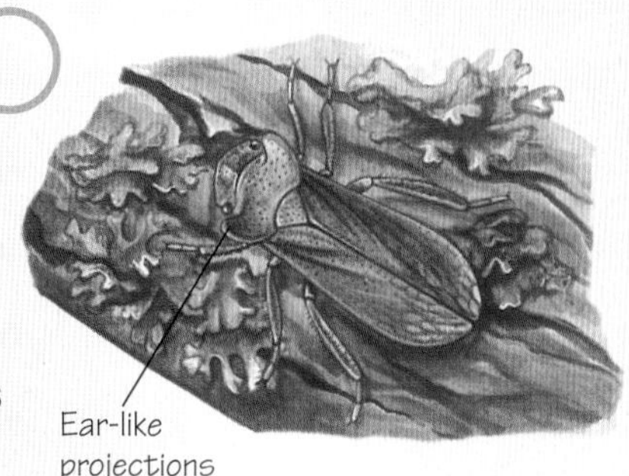

⬅ Green leafhopper

Common throughout Britain. Feeds on grasses and rushes in damp meadows and marshy places. 6-9mm long.

➡ Rose aphid or greenfly

Green or pinkish. Feeds on roses in spring, then moves to other plants. Excretes honeydew which ants feed on. Pest on roses. 2-3mm long.

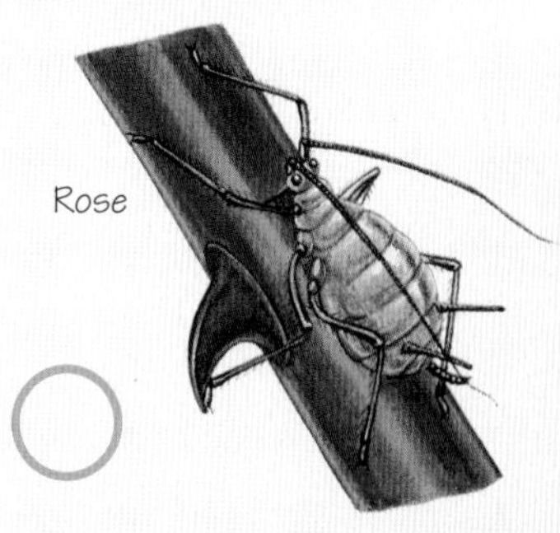

⬅ Bean aphid or blackfly

Common on broad bean, but also on thistle and other plants. Lays eggs on spindle trees. Adults produce fully formed young which eat beans. 2-3mm long.

Dragonflies and damselflies

➡ Downy emerald

This dragonfly flies fast and hovers over ponds, lakes and slow-moving streams and rivers in summer. Quite common in southern England. W.S. 68mm.

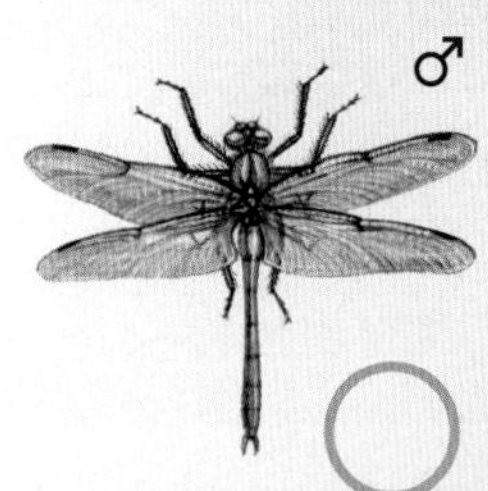

♂

Female is longer than male.

⬅ Golden-ringed dragonfly

Lives near streams and rivers, but like many dragonflies, it is sometimes seen far from water. Female lays eggs in mud. W.S. 100mm.

➡ Broad-bodied chaser

Seen over ponds and lakes with plenty of plants. Flies in short bursts. Most common in southern England. W.S. 75mm.

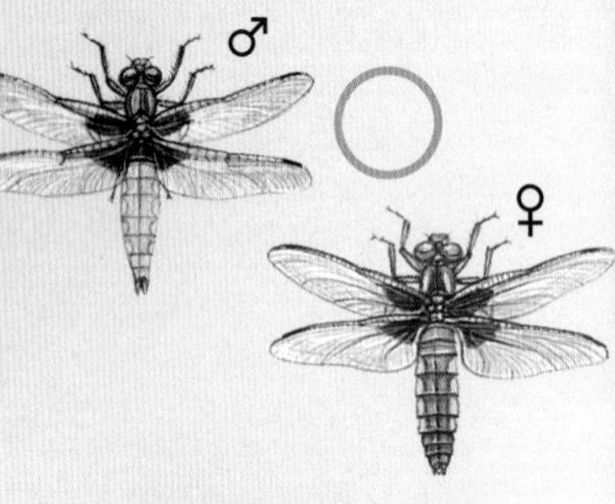

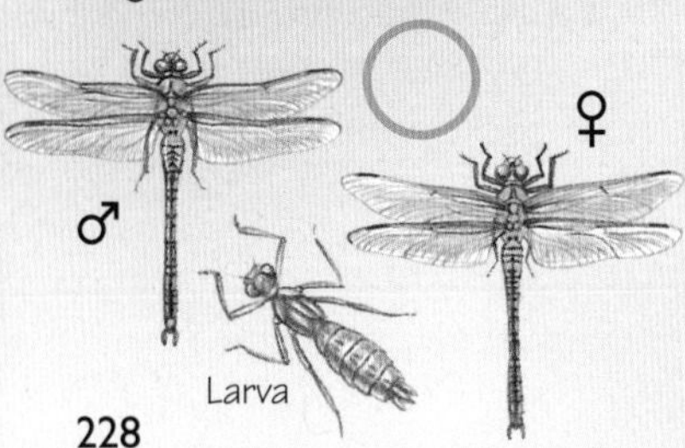

⬅ Emperor dragonfly

Seen over large ponds, lakes and canals in the summer. Adult catches flies in flight. W.S. 105mm.

➡ Ruddy darter

Found near weedy ponds or ditches in marshy areas. Nymphs mature more quickly than the larger dragonflies, which may take 2-3 years. W.S. 55mm.

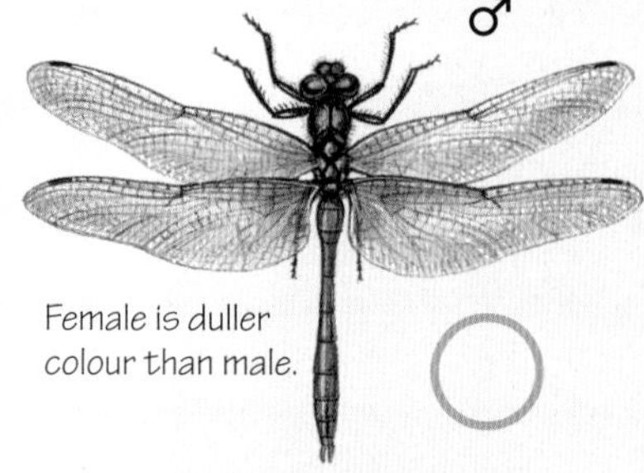

Female is duller colour than male.

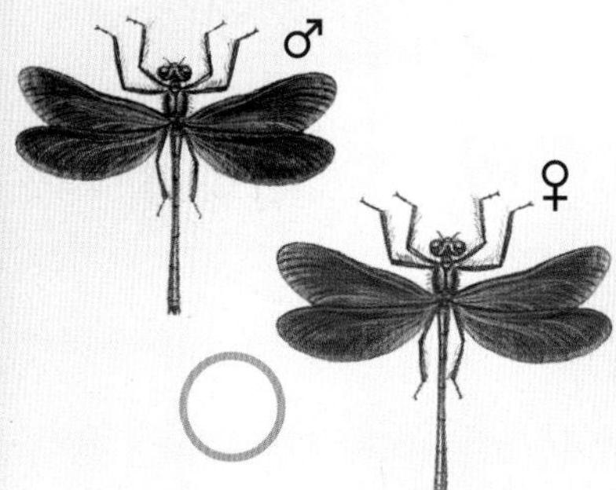

⬅ Beautiful demoiselle

Found near fast-flowing streams with sandy or stony bottoms. Damselflies usually rest with wings together, not spread out like dragonflies. W.S. 58-63mm.

➡ Banded demoiselle

More common than the beautiful demoiselle, but rare in northern England and not recorded in Scotland. Usually seen by streams and rivers with muddy bottoms. W.S. 60-65mm.

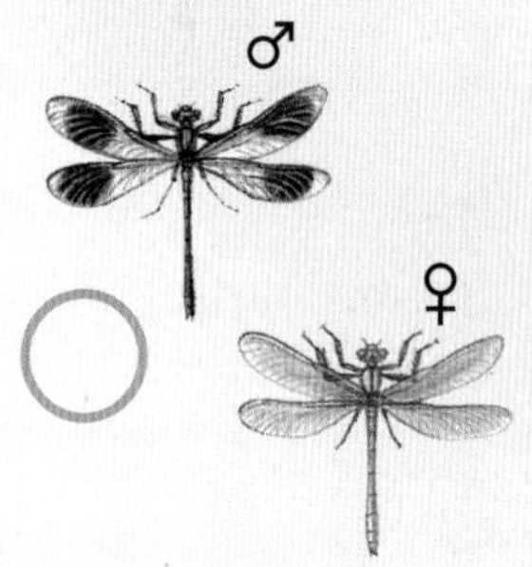

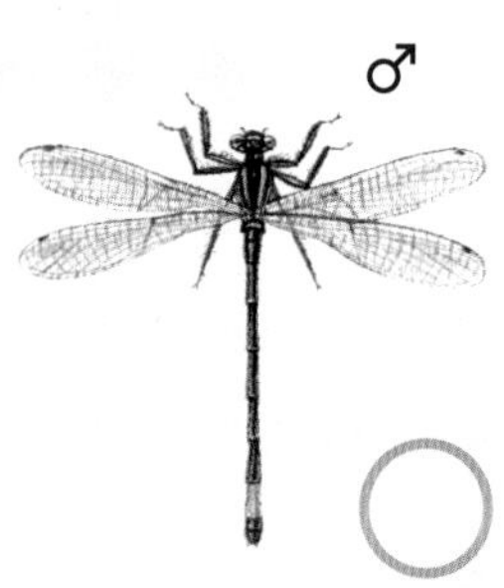

⬅ Blue-tailed damselfly

Found on plants by ditches, canals, lakes, ponds and slow-moving rivers and streams. Common in most of Britain. W.S. 35mm.

Bees, wasps, ants

Some bees, wasps and ants are solitary creatures. Others are "social insects", living in colonies. These colonies include queens, drones and workers.

➡ Red-tailed bumblebee

Common in gardens. The queen makes a nest in a hole in the ground. Eggs develop into colonies of queens, workers and drones. Queen 22mm long.

⬅ Leaf-cutter bee

Cuts pieces from rose leaves to make cylinders where female lays an egg. Solitary species. Male 10mm long. Female 11mm.

➡ Potter wasp

Makes clay pots for its larvae. Each one has a separate pot, stocked with smaller caterpillars (paralysed with a sting) for food. Sandy heaths. Male 12mm long. Female 14mm.

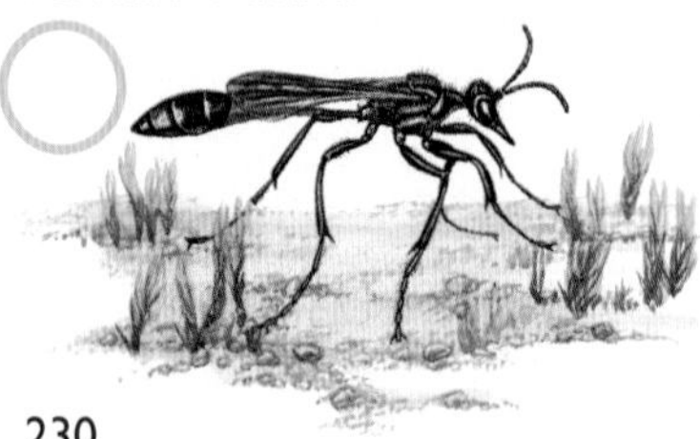

⬅ Sand wasp

Makes a nest burrow in sand where it lays a single egg on top of a paralysed caterpillar. Larva eats the caterpillar. 28-30mm long.

➡ Ruby-tailed wasp

Also called a cuckoo-wasp because female lays egg in nest of a solitary bee or wasp. When larva hatches it eats its host's food and its egg or larva. 12mm long.

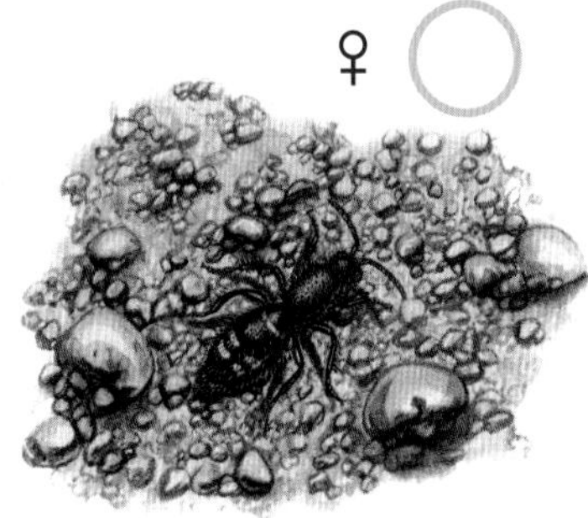
♀

⬅ Velvet ant

Actually a wasp, but female is wingless. She lays her egg in a bee larva which is eaten by her own larva when it hatches. Can sting painfully. 15mm long.

➡ Ichneumon wasp

Female pierces pine trees with her ovipositor (egg layer) and lays an egg on a horntail larva or in its burrow inside the tree. 22-30mm long.

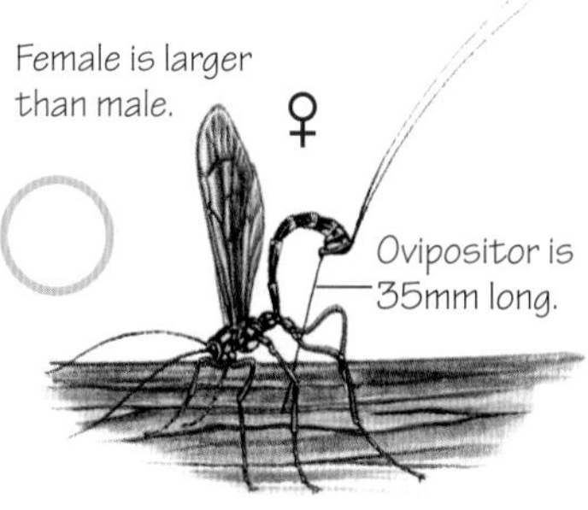
Female is larger than male.
♀
Ovipositor is 35mm long.

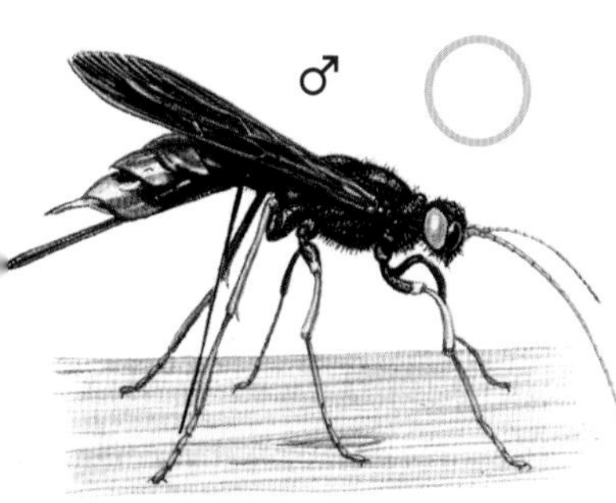
♂

⬅ Giant wood wasp or horntail

Female lays eggs in sickly or felled conifers. Larvae feed on wood for up to three years. 25-32mm long.

Wasps

➡ Blue horntail

Male is like male horntail except his head, thorax and the first two segments of his abdomen are deep metallic blue. Female is all blue and has only a short ovipositor. 20-25mm long.

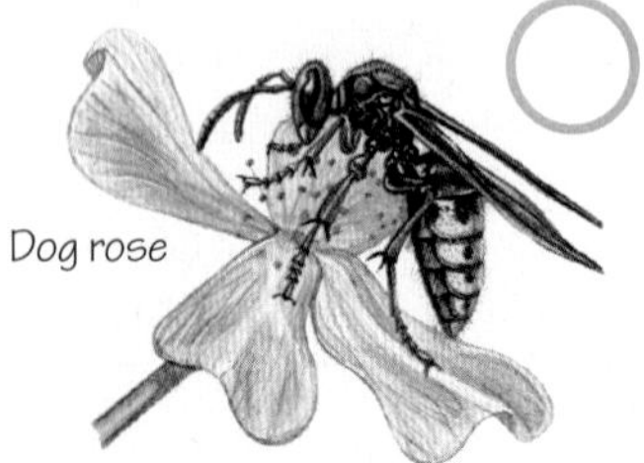

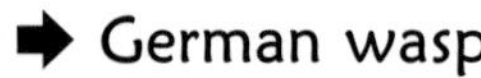

➡ German wasp

One of the most common British species. Most likely to sting in late summer when larvae are mature. 15-20mm long.

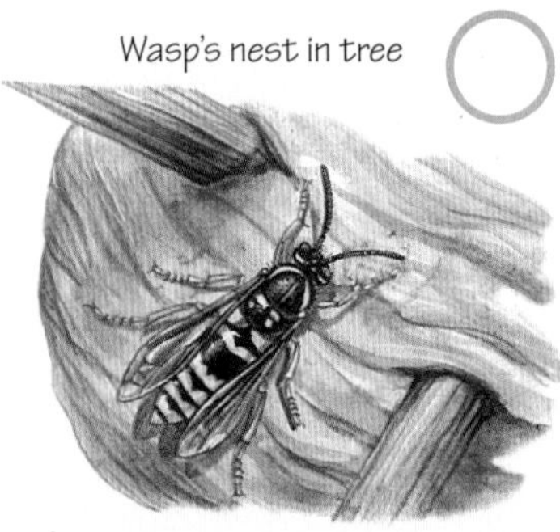

Ovipositor

⬅ Hornet

Not as likely to sting as the German wasp. Nests in hollow trees, banks or roofs. Preys on soft-bodied insects which it feeds to its larvae. Also feeds from flowers in woods. 22-30mm long.

Marmalade

⬅ Tree wasp

Likes to nest in woods, often hanging its oval nest from a tree branch. More locally distributed than German wasps. 15-20mm long.

Ants

➡ Carpenter ant

Hollows out pine tree trunks where it nests, often making the tree fall down. Not in Britain. 8-18mm long.

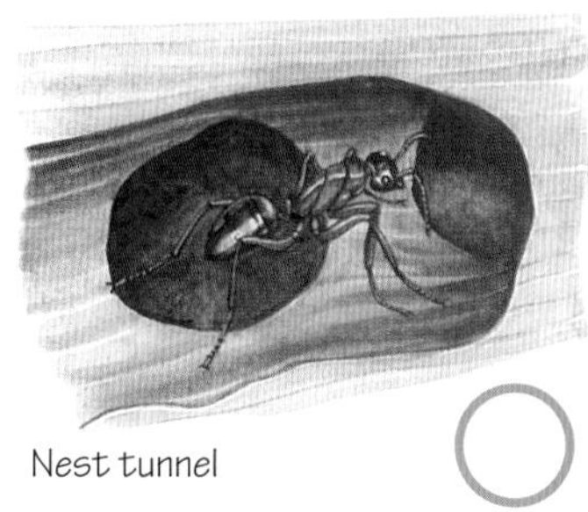
Nest tunnel

⬅ Wood ant

Makes large conical nest from twigs and leaves in pine woods. Useful to foresters as it eats leaf-eating larvae. Cannot sting, but sprays formic acid at intruders. 5-11mm long.

➡ Red ant

Nests under stones or in rotting wood. Rears aphids in its nest and feeds on the sugary liquid they produce. 3-6mm long.

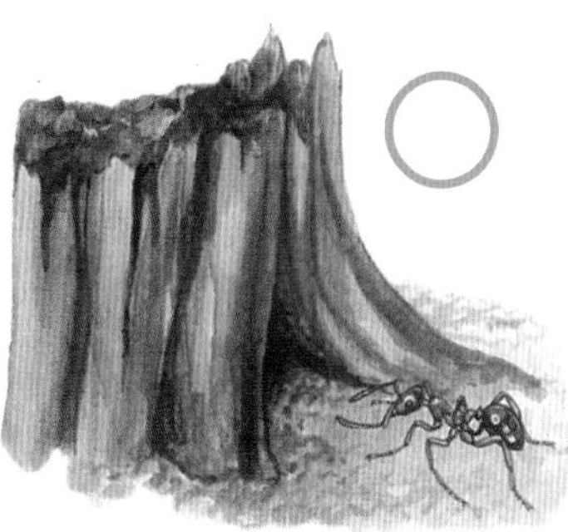
Nest in tree stump

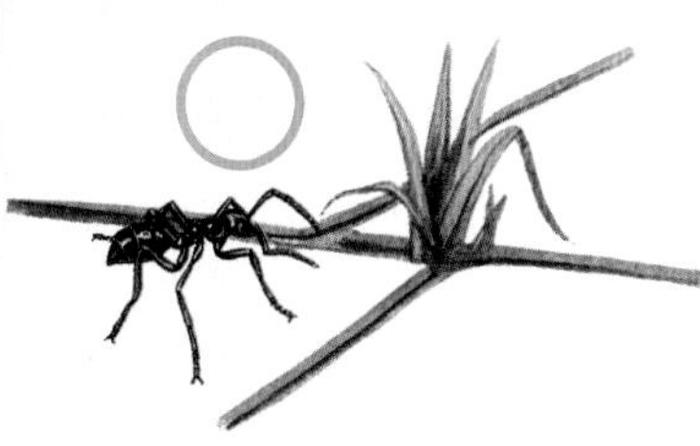

⬅ Black ant

Common in gardens. Like all ants, only queens and males have wings. Males die after mating and queens start a new colony. 3-9mm long.

Ant, sawfly, gall-wasps

➡ Yellow meadow ant

Makes small mounds in meadows. Sometimes "farms" other small insects, such as aphids, for a sugary liquid that they produce. 2-9mm long.

⬅ Birch sawfly

Name "sawfly" comes from female's saw-like ovipositor. Larva feeds on birch leaves in late summer. It makes a large oval cocoon and the adult emerges the next spring. 20-23mm long.

Sawfly larva has nine pairs of legs.

➡ Oak marble gall-wasp

Female lays egg in a leaf bud. Larva's feeding causes the tree to "blister" around it. Only one larva lives in each "marble". 4mm long.

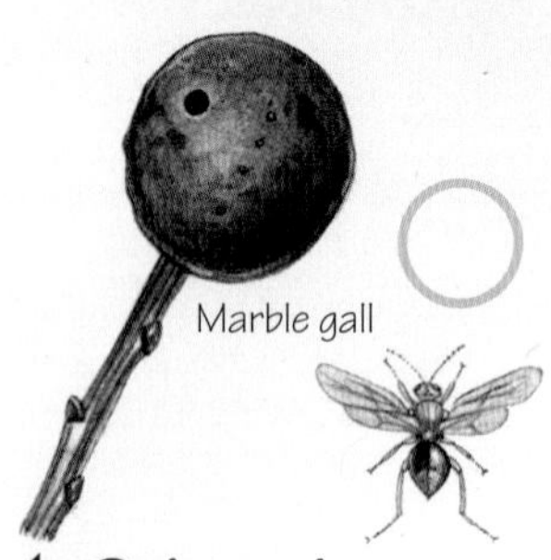

Marble gall

⬅ Oak apple gall-wasp

These galls can be 40mm across and are at first red and green and then later darken. Each gall contains many larvae. Insect is 3mm long.

Oak apple gall

True flies

True flies have only one pair of wings. The second pair are replaced by two "halteres", which are like tiny drumsticks. Flies probably use them for balance. The insects that appear on pages 238-240 are not true flies.

➡ Grey flesh fly

Common. Lays eggs in carrion. White, legless larvae (known as maggots) feed on flesh before turning into oval brown pupae. 6-17mm.

⬅ Greenbottle fly

Most species lay eggs in carrion. Adults seen on flowers. One species lays eggs in skin or fleece of sheep. Its larvae eat the sheep's flesh. 7-11mm long.

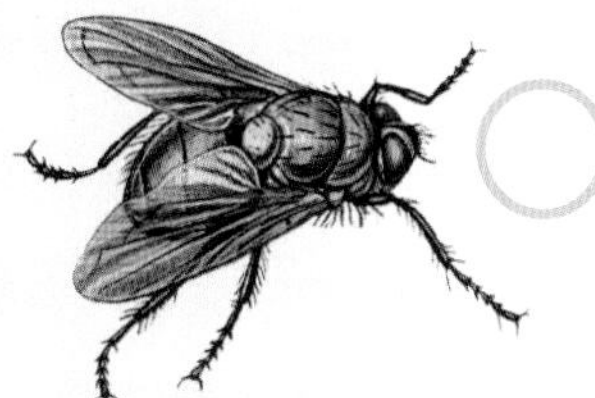

➡ Drone fly

Makes a loud, bee-like droning in flight. Visits flowers for nectar and pollen. Larva rests on pond bottom and breathes through a long tube. 15mm long.

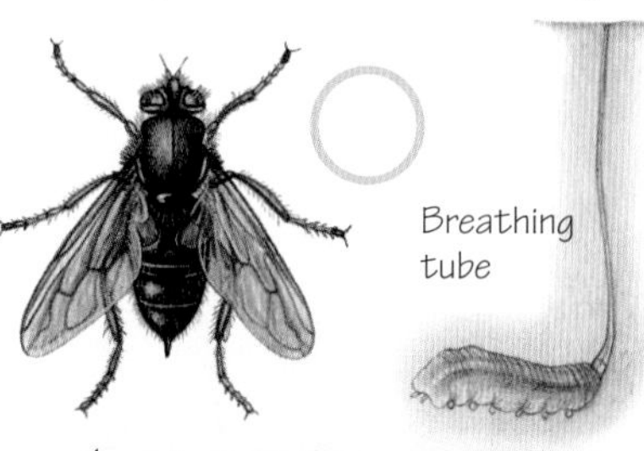

⬅ Hover fly

Hovers as though motionless. Common in summer. Female lays eggs among aphids and the legless larvae eat them. 10-14mm long.

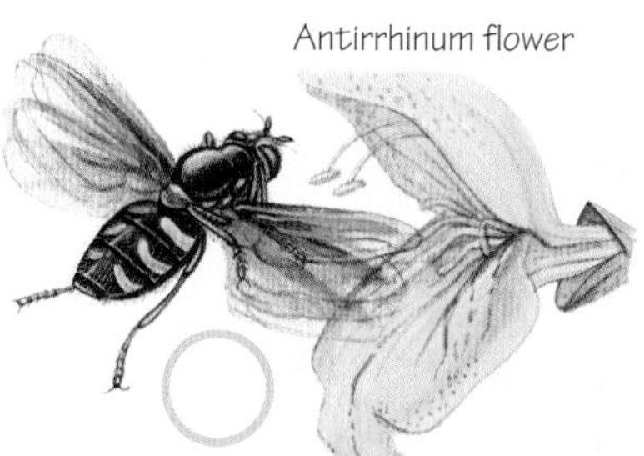

True flies

➡ Dung fly

Visits fresh cowpats where female lays eggs. Many rise in a buzzing mass if disturbed, but soon settle again. Larvae eat dung but adults are predators on other flies. 10-12mm long.

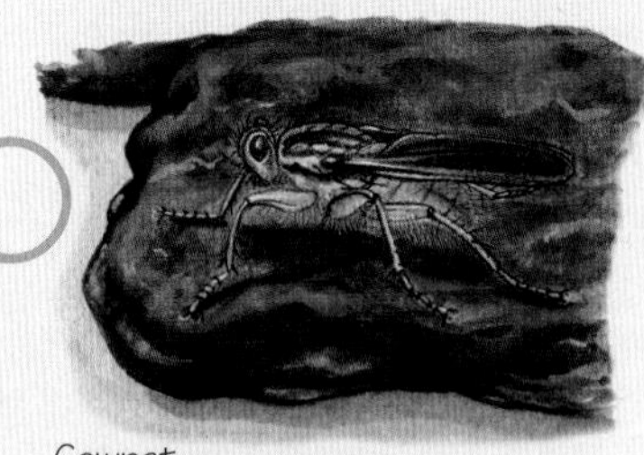

Cowpat

Robber fly killing damsel fly

⬅ Robber fly

Preys on other insects by capturing them and sucking out their body fluids. Larvae feed on animal dung as well as vegetable matter. 18-26mm long.

➡ Bee fly

Probes flowers in gardens for nectar in spring. Lays eggs near bees' nests and its larvae eat the bees' larvae. Most common in southern England. 10-11mm long.

Sweet woodruff

A horse fly piercing someone's arm

⬅ Horse fly

Female sucks blood, but her loud hum warns you before you get bitten. Smaller species are more silent and stab before being noticed. Found in old forests in southern England. 20-25mm long.

➡ Fever fly

Does not bite or cause fever. Most noticeable in spring and summer. Males perform courtship dance in the air above females. 8mm long.

Water violet

⬅ Giant cranefly or daddy-long-legs

Often found near water. Other species found in gardens where larvae (called leatherjackets) eat root crops and grass roots. 30-40mm long.

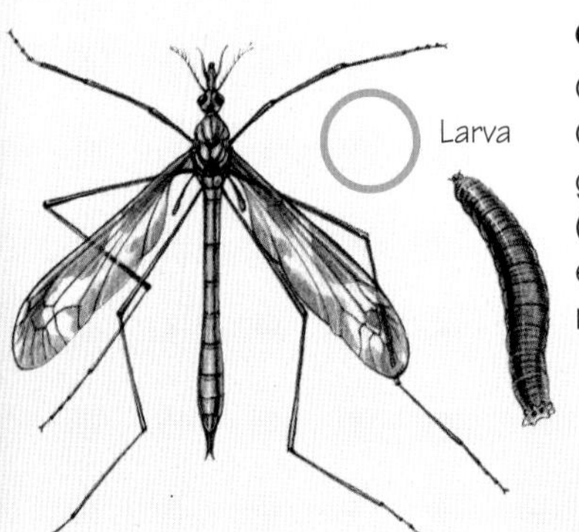

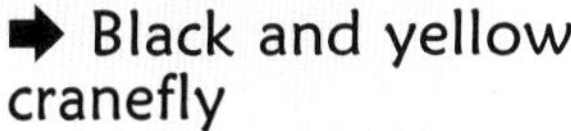

➡ Black and yellow cranefly

Found in low vegetation. Craneflies mate end to end and can be seen joined like this in summer. Female lays eggs in soil with her pointed ovipositor. 18-20mm long.

⬅ Common gnat or mosquito

Female sucks people's blood. Lays eggs in clusters which float on water. Larvae hang down below surface. 6-7mm long.

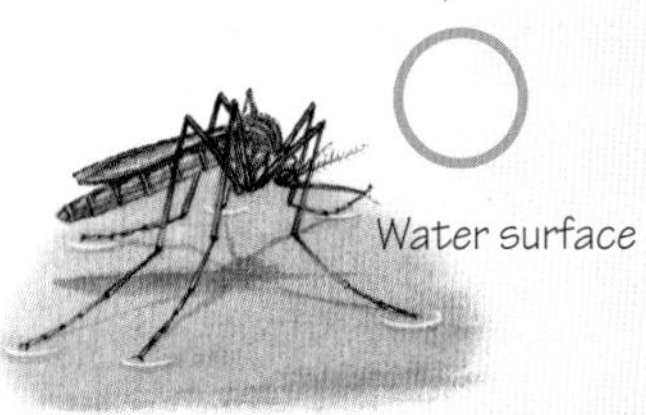

Ant-lion, lacewings

➡ Ant-lion

Name refers to larva which traps ants and other insects in a sandy hollow. Grabs them in its sickle-like jaws and sucks them dry. Not in Britain. Adult 35mm long.

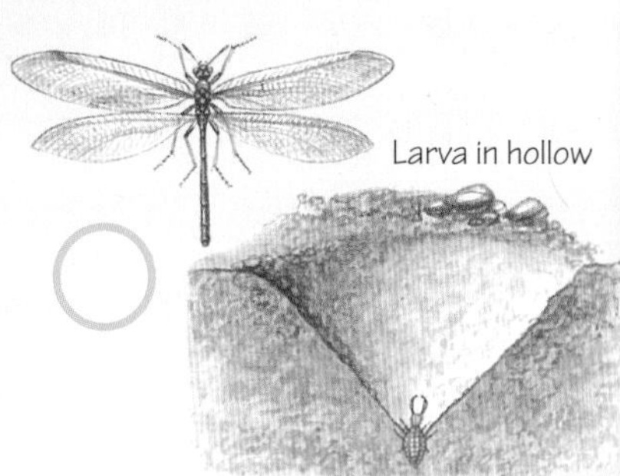

⬅ Giant lacewing

Mainly nocturnal. Larvae eat small midge larvae they find in wet moss at the water's edge. Pupates in yellowish, silken cocoons. 15mm long.

➡ Green lacewing

Found in gardens and hedges and sometimes attracted to house lights. Weak fluttering flight. Larvae feed on aphids. 15mm long.

Larva catching an aphid

⬅ Brown lacewing

Smaller than green lacewing, with dark brownish transparent wings. Look near water in lush vegetation and on trees. Throughout Britain. 10mm long.

Scorpion fly, alder fly, snake fly

➡ Scorpion fly

Name comes from the scorpion-like shape of male's tail. Both adults and larvae eat dead insects and waste matter. 18-22mm long.

♂

♀

Notice shape of tail.

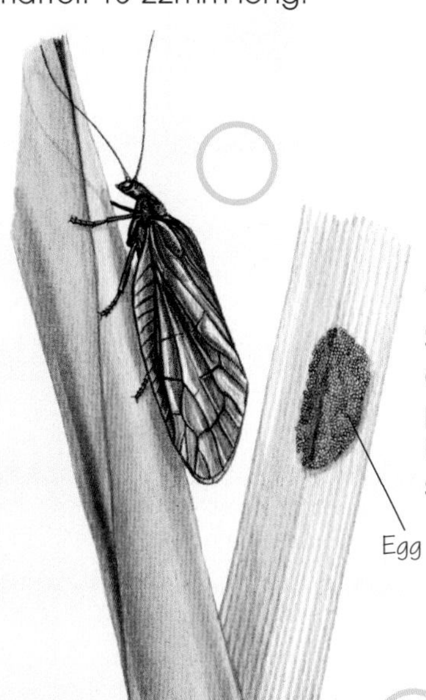

⬅ Alder fly

Slow, heavy flier. Lays eggs on stems of water plants. Larvae live on water bottom where they eat small animals. 20mm long.

➡ Snake fly

Name comes from long head and thorax, which can bend, making the insect look like a cobra snake. 15-20mm long.

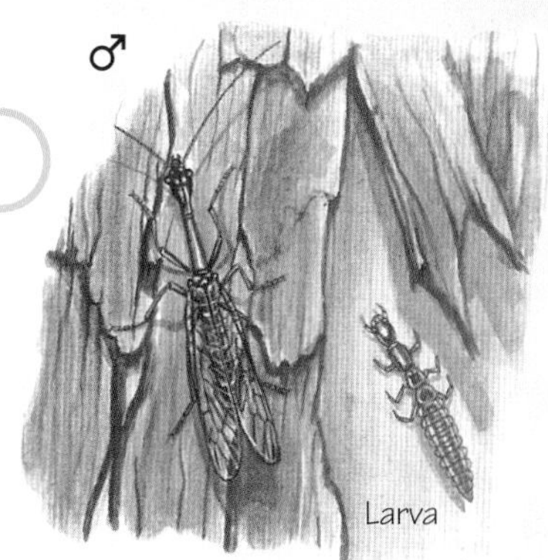

Caddis fly, stonefly, Mayfly

➡ Caddis fly

Found near lakes and slow rivers. Many caddis larvae make a protective case from bits of twigs and tiny shells. 15-20mm long.

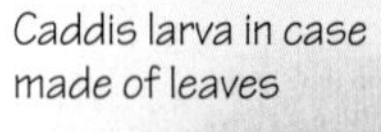

Wings overlap

⬅ Stonefly

Found mainly in fast-flowing rivers. Larvae live at river bottom feeding on other small animals. 22mm long.

Larva on river bottom

Long tails

➡ Mayfly

Adults live for a short time, perhaps only a few hours. In this time they mate and female lays her eggs in river water. 40mm long.

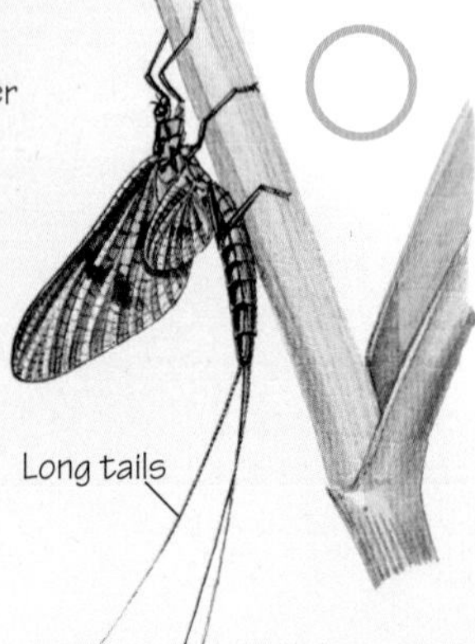

Crickets

Crickets and bush crickets have very long antennae, while grasshoppers' are short. The third pair of legs on these insects is adapted for leaping. Males "sing" to attract females by rubbing their wing-cases together.

➡ Field cricket

Very rare. Lives in grassy banks and meadows in sandy or chalky areas. Male sings to attract female. 20mm long.

⬅ House cricket

Found in heated buildings and greenhouses, garden rubbish heaps and bigger tips. Rarely flies. Shrill song. 16mm long.

➡ Mole cricket

Burrows like a mole with its large spade-like forefeet. Lives in damp meadows. Male has a whirring call. Rare. 38-42mm long.

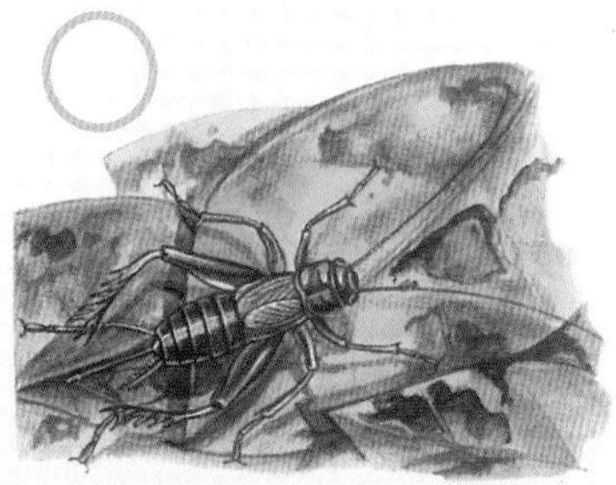

⬅ Wood cricket

Found in dead leaves in ditches and banks in southern England. Male has quiet, churring song. Flightless. 8-9mm long.

Grasshopper, bush crickets

Wings look silvery in flight.

⬅ Large marsh grasshopper

Found in bog and fenland in southern England, Norfolk Broads and Ireland. Flies a long way when disturbed. Male makes slow ticking sound. 27-32mm long.

➡ Great green bush cricket

Harsh, shrill, penetrating song. Moves slowly and never flies far. Eats small insects found in dense vegetation. 45-47mm long.

⬅ Speckled bush cricket

Flightless adults seen in late summer or early autumn. Found in old gardens where shrubs grow. Male's song is hard to hear. 11-13mm long.

➡ Wart-biter

May bite when handled. Some people used to use it to bite their warts off. Seen in coarse grassland on downs. Preys on small insects. 34-35mm long.

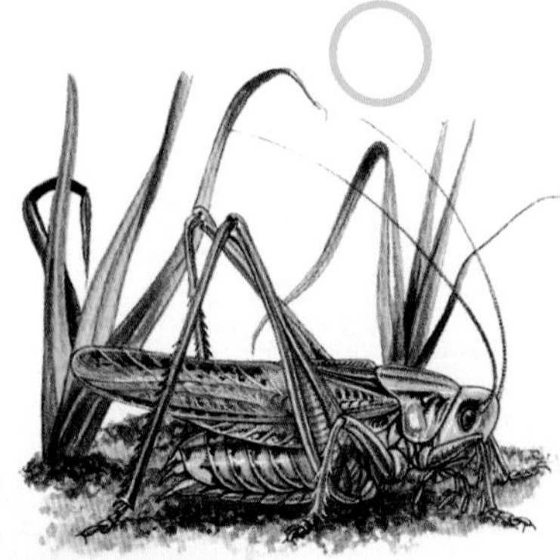

Cockroaches, mantis

➡ Common cockroach

Found in houses and other warm buildings, where it eats waste. Female lays eggs in purse-like containers. Does not fly. 25mm long.

Old bread

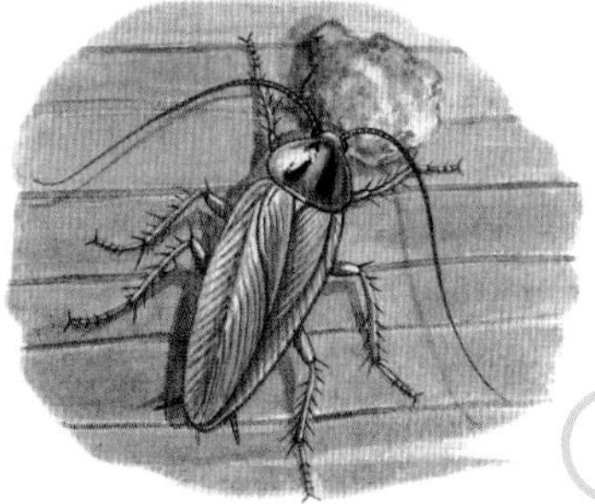

⬅ German cockroach

Not from Germany – it probably originated in northern Africa or the Middle East. Lives in heated buildings. 13mm long.

➡ Dusky cockroach

Lives out-of-doors, unlike its larger relatives. Found mainly in woodlands on leaves of trees. 7-10mm long.

⬅ Praying mantis

Holds its forelegs together, as if praying, while waiting for its insect prey to come close. Found in scrub and tall grass in southern Europe. Not in Britain. 60-80mm long

Stick insect, earwigs

➡ Stick insect

Lives in bushes in southern Europe. Eats vegetation. Another species is commonly kept as a pet. Not found in Britain. Up to 90mm long.

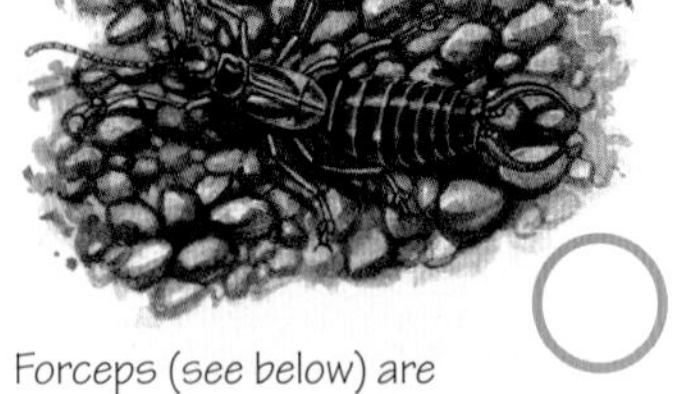

⬅ Common earwig

Eats small insects (usually dead), as well as leaves and fruits. Female guards nymphs until they can look after themselves. 15mm long.

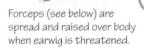

Forceps (see below) are spread and raised over body when earwig is threatened.

➡ Lesser earwig

Flies during the day, but is rarely noticed because it is small. Not rare, but less common than common earwig. 10mm long.

Some other small insects

The insects on these pages are mostly very small and the pictures are greatly enlarged. The sizes given are very approximate.

Water springtail

Lives on the surface of ponds and lakes. Can make spectacular jumps by flicking its tail (usually folded beneath its body). About 2mm long.

Fleas

Many different species. Wingless, but can jump powerfully. Feed on blood of many mammals and birds. Closely related to flies. Average length is 2mm.

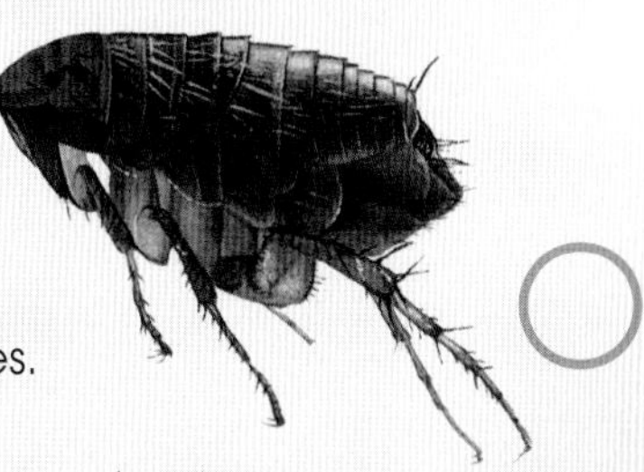

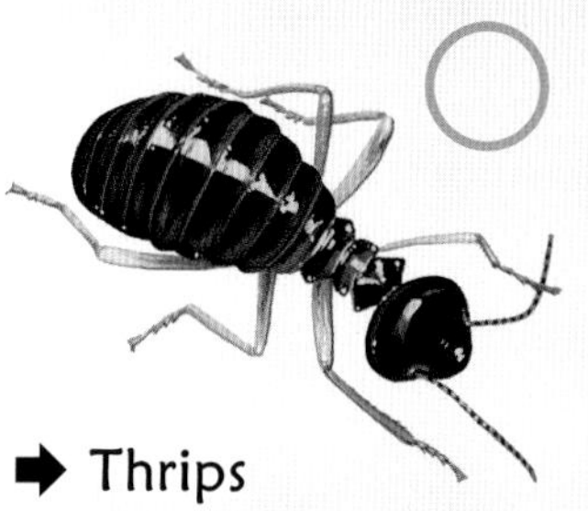

Termites

Like ants, termites are social insects with queens, soldiers and workers. Live in colonies in rotting wood. Not found in Britain. Average length is 10-15mm.

Thrips

Tiny insects. Often settle on arms in hot summers and tickle. They are known as "thunder flies" because they are associated with thundery weather. About 1-2mm long.

Mushrooms & Fungi

Cap fungi with pores

White flesh does not change colour when cut.
Pores come away easily from cap.

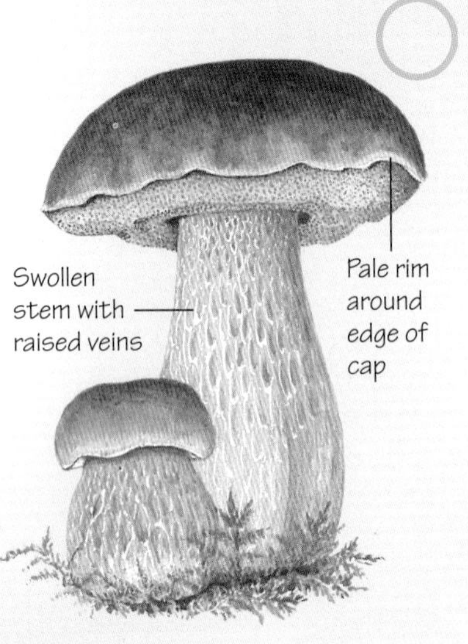
Swollen stem with raised veins
Pale rim around edge of cap

➡ Penny bun, cep or porcini

Boletus edulis

Light to dark brown cap feels greasy when wet. Pores white at first, then pale yellow when mature. Grows in broadleaved woods. Cap 5-18cm. Sept-Nov.

Cap often flat when mature.
Yellow pores turn blue when bruised.
Flesh turns blue when cut.

⬅ Bay bolete

Boletus badius

Dark brown cap feels velvety when dry, sticky when wet. White pores when young. Usually under conifers. Cap 5-12cm. Aug-Nov.

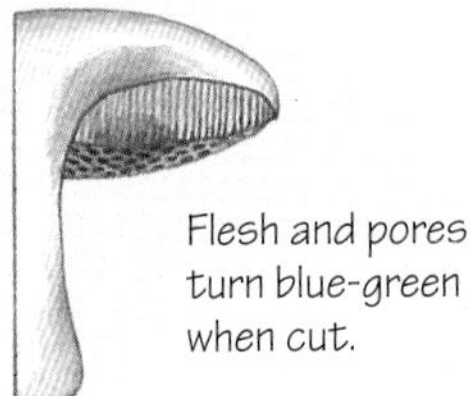

➡ Red-cracked bolete

Boletus chrysenteron
When mature, red-brown cap flattens and cracks to show red flesh. Grows in broadleaved woods. Cap 4-12cm. Aug-Nov.

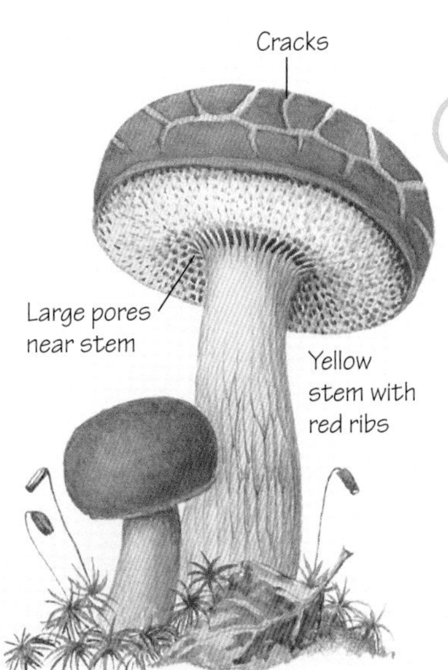

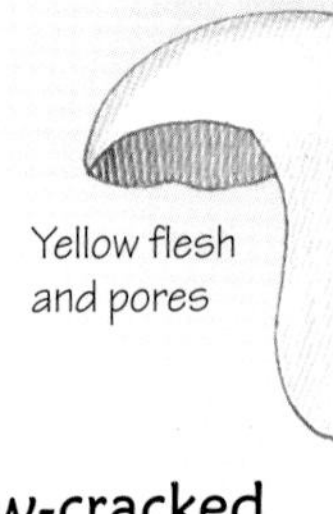

⬅ Yellow-cracked or suede bolete

Boletus subtomentosus
Light to olive brown cap feels velvety and when mature, often cracks to show yellow flesh. Broadleaved woods. Cap 4-12cm. Aug-Nov.

Cap fungi with pores

Dry velvety cap

Pale pink flesh when mature.

Pink pores turn brown when bruised.

⬅ Tylopilus felleus

Cap feels velvety. Pores white at first, turning pink when mature. Honeycomb patterns on stem. In mixed woods. Cap 5-15cm. Aug-Nov.

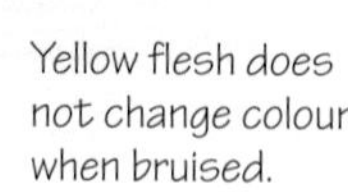

➡ Suillus granulatus

Tiny granules on stem near cap. Yellow pores ooze milky drops. Grows under pine trees. Cap 5-15cm. Aug-Nov.

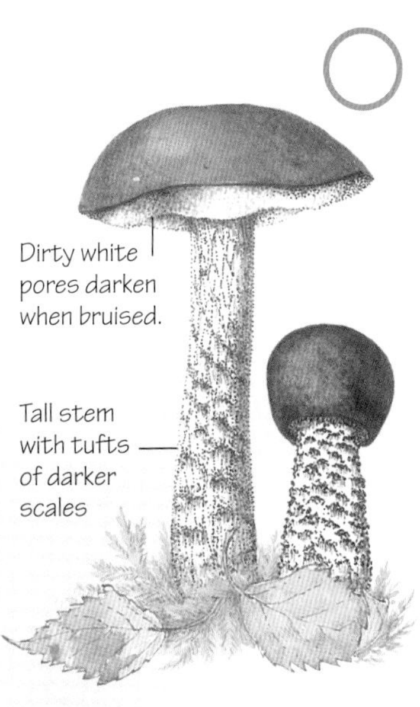
Dirty white
pores darken
when bruised.
Tall stem
with tufts
of darker
scales

White flesh turns
pink when cut.

⬅ Brown birch bolete

Leccinum scabrum
Stem covered with tufts of scales. Pores off-white. Under birch trees. Cap 6-20cm. Aug-Nov.

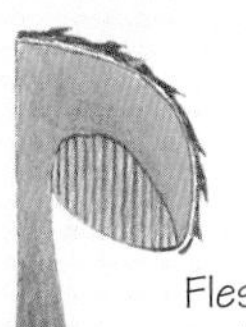
Flesh turns
red then black
when bruised.

➡ Old man of the woods

Strobilomyces strobilaceus
Cap covered with scales, which are black at first, then brown-black when mature. Dries out without rotting. Broadleaved woods. Cap 8-15cm. Sept-Nov.

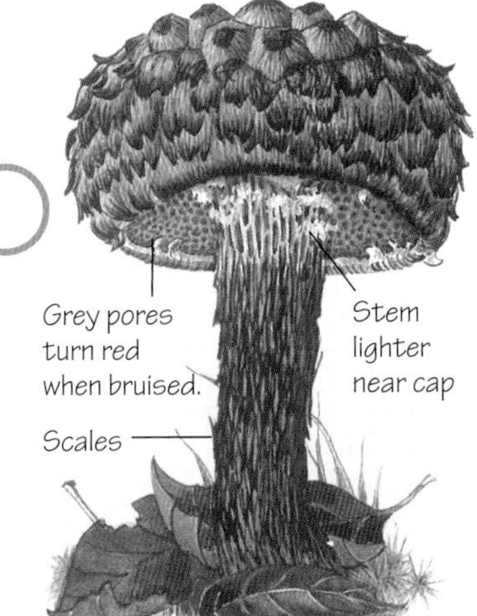
Dark woolly scales on cap
Grey pores
turn red
when bruised.
Stem
lighter
near cap
Scales

Cap fungi with gills

Amanitas, pages 252-254, grow from an "egg" enclosed in a white veil that splits, as the stem grows, to form a volva. Another veil splits from the gills to form a ring. Amanitas have white, free gills and white spores. Some are poisonous.

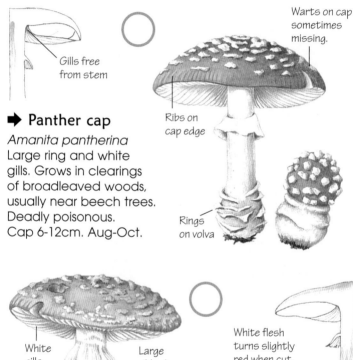

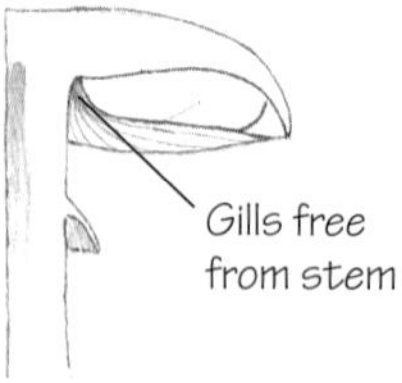

Gills free
from stem

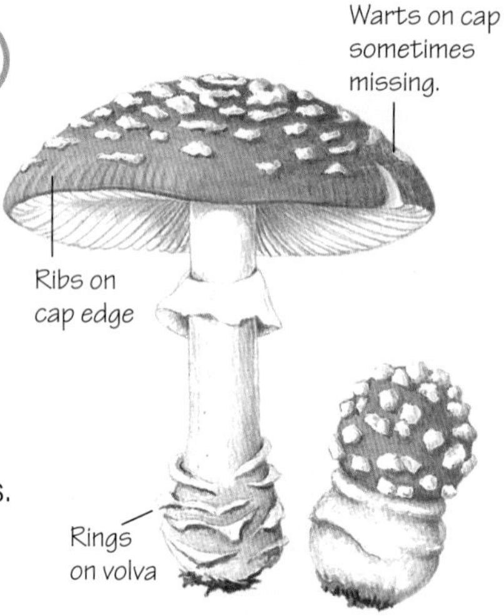

Warts on cap
sometimes
missing.
Ribs on
cap edge
Rings
on volva

➡ Panther cap

Amanita pantherina
Large ring and white gills. Grows in clearings of broadleaved woods, usually near beech trees. Deadly poisonous.
Cap 6-12cm. Aug-Oct.

White
gills
Large
ribbed
ring
Warty
scales
on volva

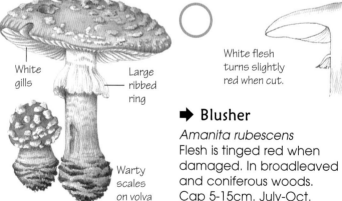

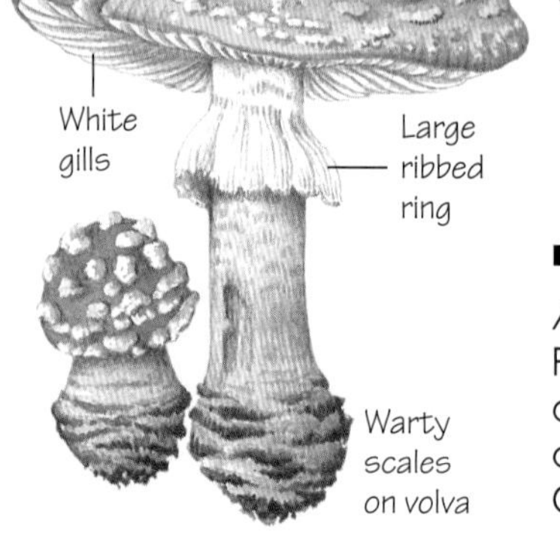

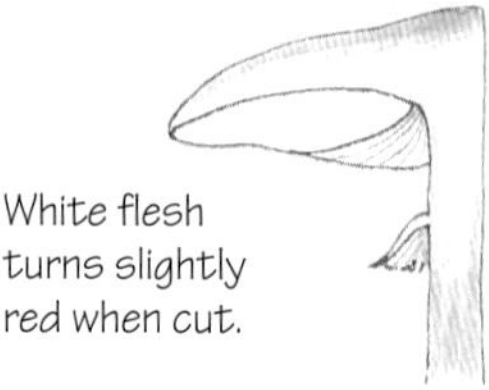

White flesh
turns slightly
red when cut.

➡ Blusher

Amanita rubescens
Flesh is tinged red when damaged. In broadleaved and coniferous woods.
Cap 5-15cm. July-Oct.

Paler orange-red, and fewer warts when mature.

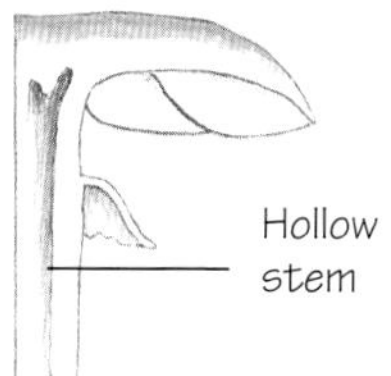
Hollow stem

➡ Fly agaric

Amanita muscaria
Grows under birch and pine trees, often on sandy soil. Poisonous. Cap 6-12cm. Aug-Nov.

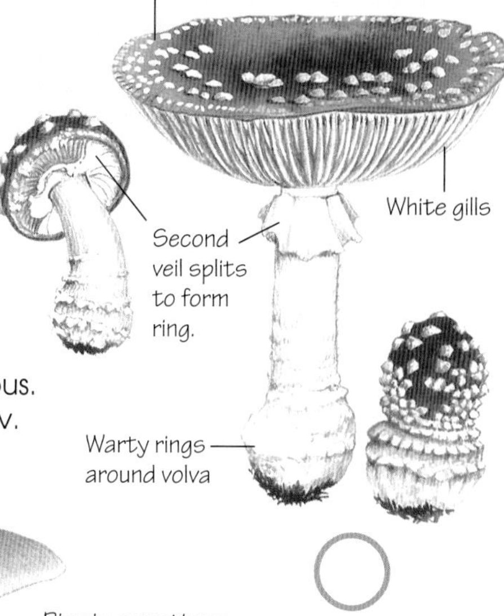
Second veil splits to form ring.
White gills
Warty rings around volva

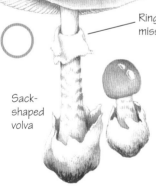

Ring is sometimes missing.

Sack-shaped volva

⬅ Death cap

Amanita phalloides
Cap is white to olive green. Broadleaved woods. Deadly poisonous. Cap 4-16cm. June-Oct.

➡ False death cap

Amanita citrina
Smells of potatoes. Broadleaved and conifer woods. Cap 6-12cm. July-Nov.

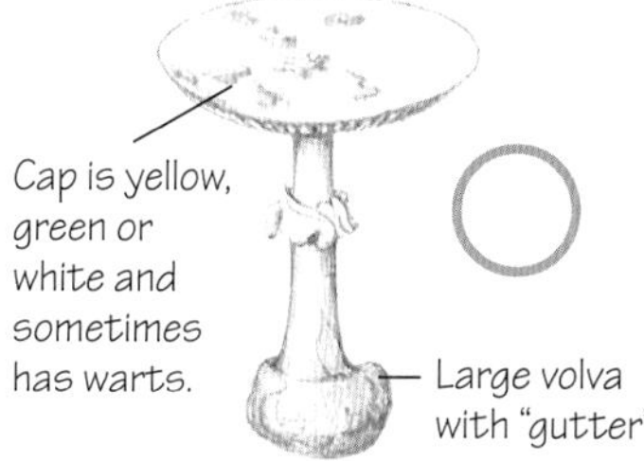
Cap is yellow, green or white and sometimes has warts.
Large volva with "gutter"

Cap fungi with gills

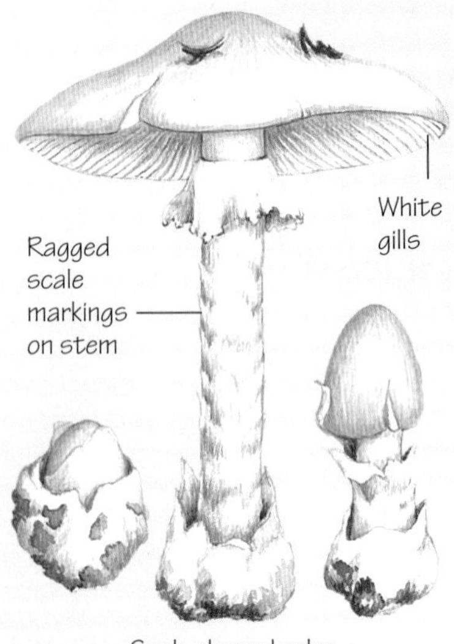

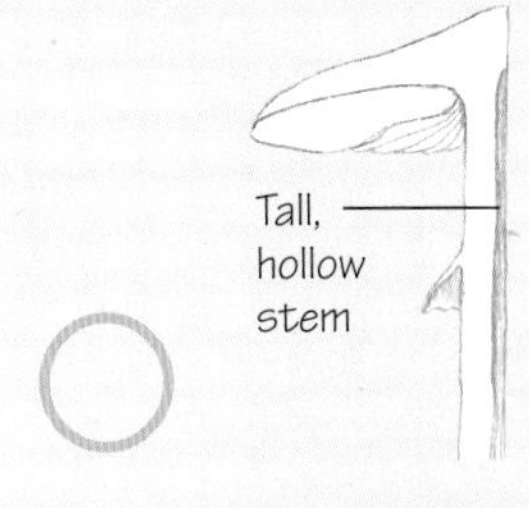

⬅ Destroying angel

Amanita virosa
Cap is conical at first, and expands with age. In conifer and broadleaved woods. Rare. Deadly poisonous. Cap 6-12cm. July-Oct.

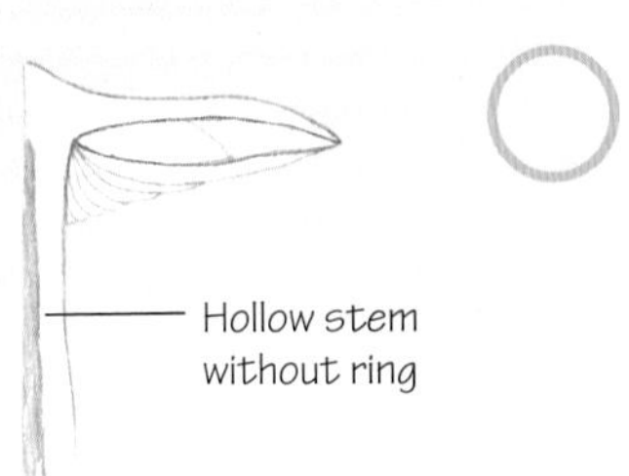

➡ Tawny grisette

Amanita fulva
Grows in broadleaved woods, especially under birch, on poor soil. Cap 3-10cm. May-Nov.

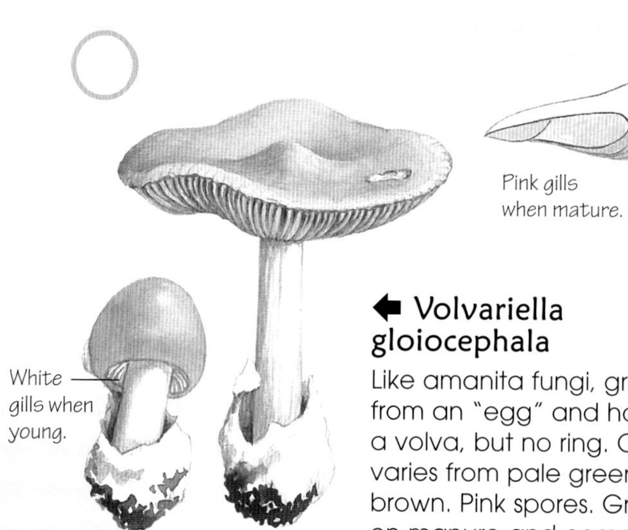
Pink gills
when mature.
White
gills when
young.
Large sack-shaped
volva may be left
behind when picked.

⬅ Volvariella gloiocephala

Like amanita fungi, grows from an "egg" and has a volva, but no ring. Cap varies from pale green to brown. Pink spores. Grows on manure and compost heaps. Caps 5-10cm. July-Oct.

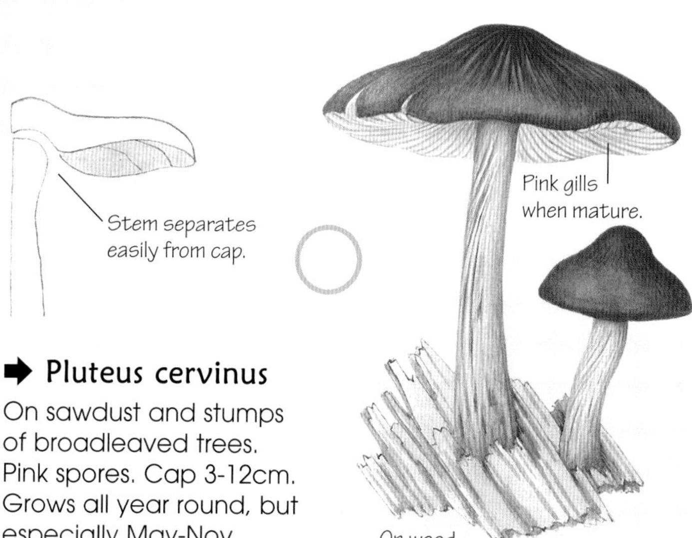
Stem separates
easily from cap.
Pink gills
when mature.
On wood

➡ Pluteus cervinus

On sawdust and stumps of broadleaved trees. Pink spores. Cap 3-12cm. Grows all year round, but especially May-Nov.

Cap fungi with gills

Mushrooms (*Agaricus* group), pages 256-257, grow from a "button" and have a ring around the stem. The gills are free from the stem, and pink or grey at first; dark brown when mature. They have brown spores. Not all are edible.

➡ Field mushroom

Agaricus campestris
Ring on stem often falls off. In grass fields and on roadside verges.
Cap 5-15cm. Aug-Nov.

⬅ Horse mushroom

Agaricus arvensis
Cap at first white, turning yellow with age and when bruised. Smells of aniseed. In grass fields.
Cap 6-18cm. Aug-Nov.

Flesh turns slightly red when cut.
Scales on cap
Hollow stem
Gills at first pink then dark brown.
Cap turns yellow when bruised.
Base of stem turns yellow when it's cut.
Pink gills when young.

➡ Scaly wood mushroom

Agaricus silvaticus
Cap is covered with small fibrous scales. Base of stem slightly swollen. In mixed woods, often in beds of pine needles.
Cap 6-16cm.
Sept-Nov.

⬅ Yellow stainer

Agaricus xanthodermus
Turns yellow when bruised or cut. Unpleasant smell. In fields and hedges. Poisonous. Cap 5-12cm. Aug-Nov.

Cap fungi with gills

Parasols have whitish gills that are free from the stem, and white spores. They have a ring, but no volva. The stem and cap separate easily.

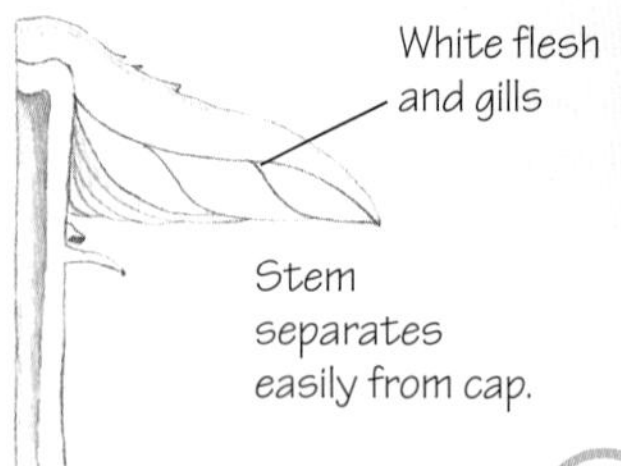
White flesh and gills
Stem separates easily from cap.

➡ Parasol

Macrolepiota procera
Stem has snake-like patterns and is swollen at the base. In woods and grassy places.
Cap 5-15cm. July-Nov.

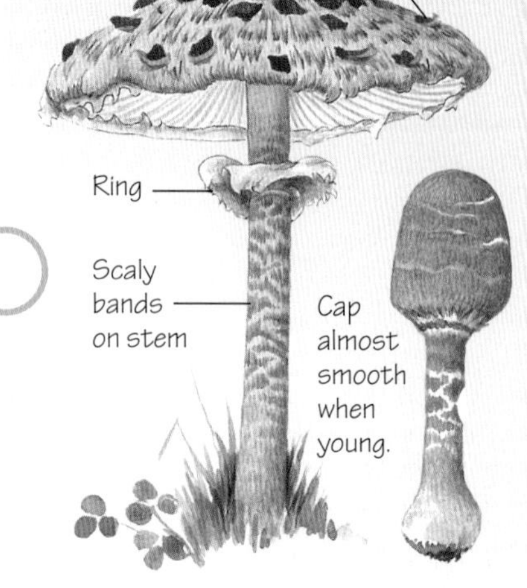
Scales
Ring
Scaly bands on stem
Cap almost smooth when young.

Scales
Ring
Smooth stem turns red when bruised.

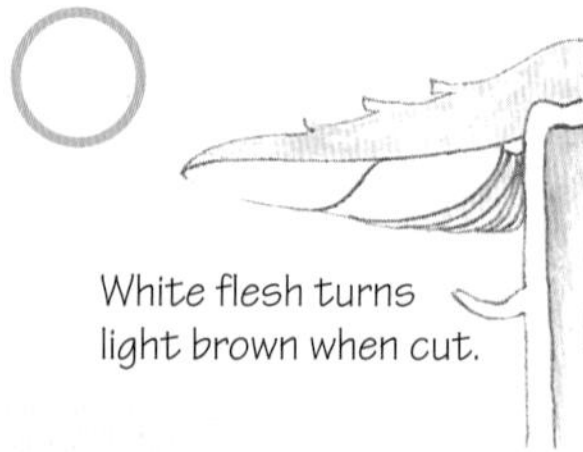
White flesh turns light brown when cut.

➡ Shaggy parasol

Macrolepiota rhacodes
Smooth stem, swollen at base. In clearings, in woods and grassy places.
Cap 5-15cm. July-Nov.

Ink caps, pages 259-260, have thin, crowded gills that often dissolve into a black, inky liquid with age. The spores are black.

Gills white at first, then pink, and finally black.
Cap dissolves with age.
White scales

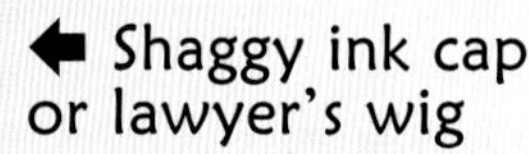

⬅ Shaggy ink cap or lawyer's wig

Coprinus comatus
Slender, hollow stem separates easily from the cap. Often in groups in fields and on roadside verges. Cap 5-10cm high. May-Nov.

White veil covers cap when young.

➡ Magpie ink cap

Coprinus picaceus
Brown-black cap with white patches. Gills at first white, then pale brown, and finally black. Broadleaved woods. Cap 5-10cm high. Sept-Nov.

Cap dissolves with age.

Cap fungi with gills

➡ Common ink cap

Coprinus atramentarius
Gills at first dirty white, turning brown then black. Cap dissolves with age. Usually grows in groups at the base of trees, in fields, or in woods. Cap 3-7cm. May-Dec.

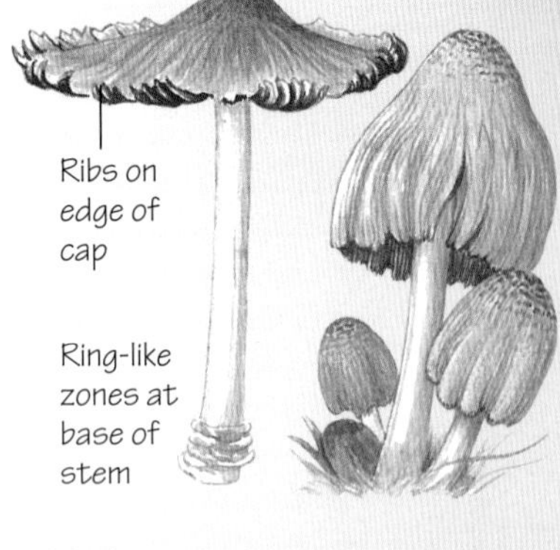

⬅ Glistening ink cap

Coprinus micaceus
Tiny granules on cap when young. Gills at first white then black, only dissolving slightly. Grows in groups on tree stumps. Cap 2-5cm high. May-Dec.

➡ Snowy ink cap

Coprinus niveus
Gills at first grey, then black. Cap curls and dissolves with age. On cow or horse dung. Cap 1-3cm. May-Nov.

⬅ Psathyrella multipedata

Grows in groups of ten or more from a common "root". Chocolate-brown spores. By paths in woods. Cap 2-3cm. July-Oct.

Bright yellow cap with ribbed edge

➡ Bolbitius vitellinus

Cinnamon-coloured spores. On grass and straw. Cap 2-5cm. July-Oct.

Rust-brown gills

Small ring is sometimes torn or missing.

⬅ Dung roundhead

Paneolus semiovatus
Bell-shaped cap feels sticky when wet. Black spores. On dung. Cap 2-5cm. July-Nov.

Cap fungi with gills

Yellow flesh

Dark brown gills when old.

⬅ Sulphur tuft

Hypholoma fasciculare
Faint ring on stem. Yellow flesh. Grows in clusters on broadleaved tree stumps, often in large numbers. Purple-brown spores. Cap 4-10cm. Aug-Nov.

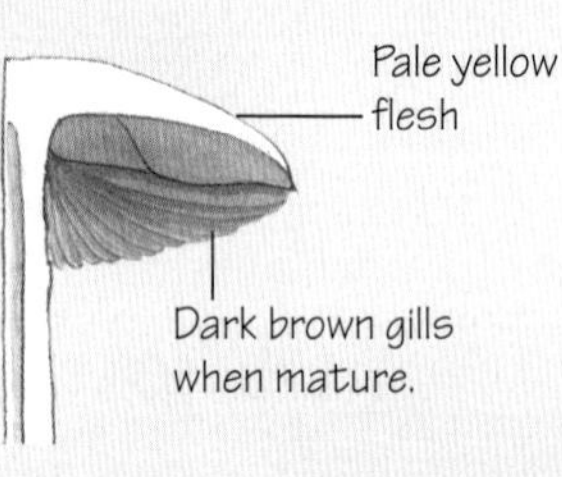

➡ Brick-red cap

Hypholoma lateritium
Gills at first yellow, then lilac-grey, finally dark brown. Purple-brown spores. Grows in clusters on tree stumps.
Cap 3-8cm. Sept-Dec.

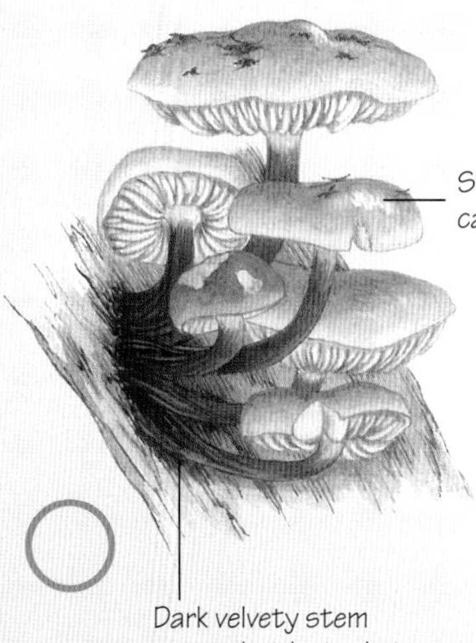

⬅ Velvet shank

Flammulina velutipes
Stem ends in a root-like thread. Gills turn brown with age. On trunks, stumps and branches of broadleaved trees.
Cap 3-8cm. Sept-March.

➡ Cluster fungus

Kuehneromyces mutabilis
Cap is dark brown when wet, has dark and light orange-brown zones when dry. Thin white gills turn pale brown with age. Grows in clusters on tree stumps. Cap 4-10cm.
All year round.

Cap fungi with gills

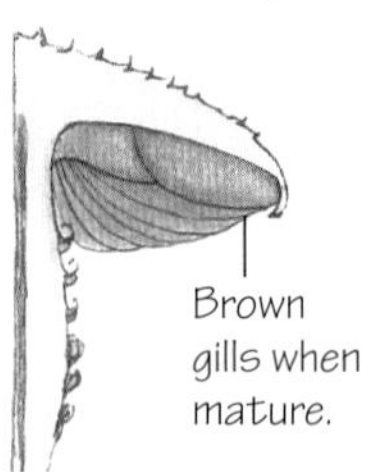

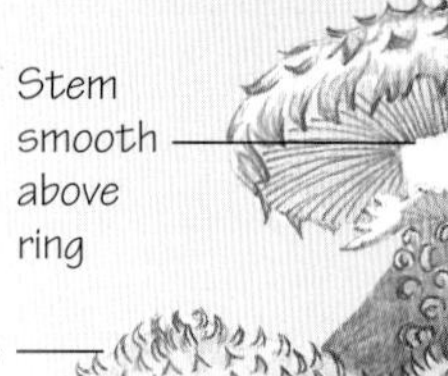

➡ Shaggy pholiota

Pholiota squarrosa
Yellow gills turn brown with age. Grows in groups at the base of broadleaved trees. Cap 3-8cm. Sept-Nov.

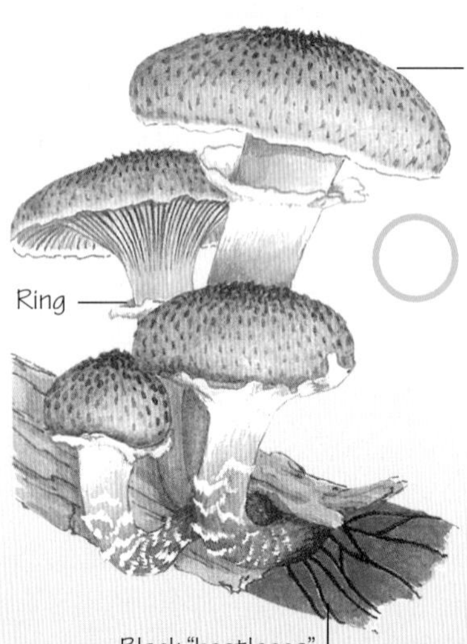

⬅ Honey fungus

Armillaria mellea
Cream-coloured gills turn brown with age. Grows at the base of broadleaved or conifer trees, which it eventually kills.
Cap 3-10cm. July-Dec.

Both the fungi on this page are **wax caps**. These are mainly white or brightly coloured fungi that look waxy, and have well-spaced gills and white spores.

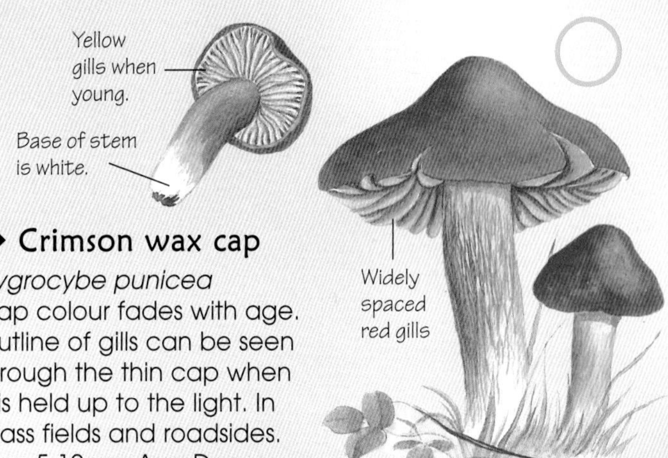
Yellow gills when young.
Base of stem is white.
Widely spaced red gills

➡ Crimson wax cap

Hygrocybe punicea
Cap colour fades with age. Outline of gills can be seen through the thin cap when it is held up to the light. In grass fields and roadsides. Cap 5-12cm. Aug-Dec.

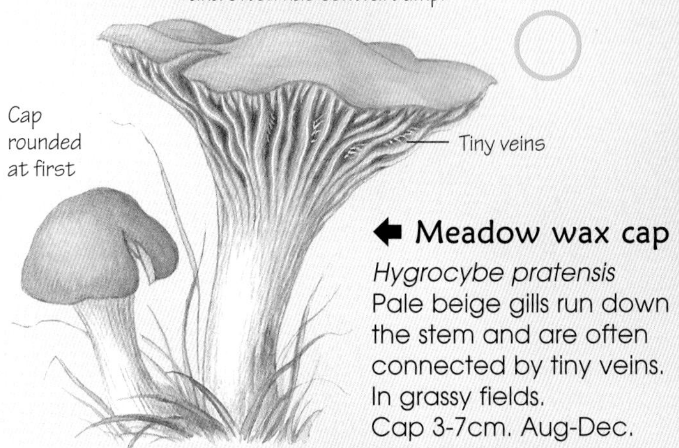
Cap flattens when mature and often has central bump.
Cap rounded at first
Tiny veins

⬅ Meadow wax cap

Hygrocybe pratensis
Pale beige gills run down the stem and are often connected by tiny veins. In grassy fields. Cap 3-7cm. Aug-Dec.

Cap fungi with gills

Clitocybes, pages 266-267, have whitish or pale gills that run down the stem, and the cap is often funnel-shaped. They have white spores.

Gills run down stem.

Base of stem is swollen and woolly.

⬅ Aniseed toadstool

Clitocybe odora
Blue-green cap with central bump. Amongst dead leaves in broadleaved woods. Smells of aniseed. Cap 3-7cm. Aug-Nov.

Cap darker grey at centre.

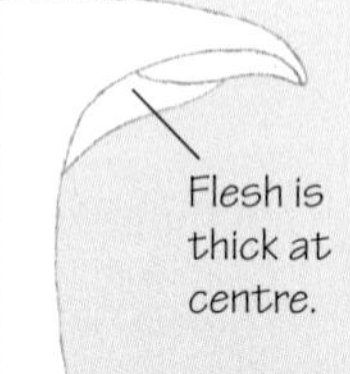
Flesh is thick at centre.

Edge of cap curves under.

➡ Cloudy funnel cap

Clitocybe nebularis
Grey to grey-brown cap. Grows in woods, especially under pine. Putrid smell. Cap 6-25cm. Aug-Nov.

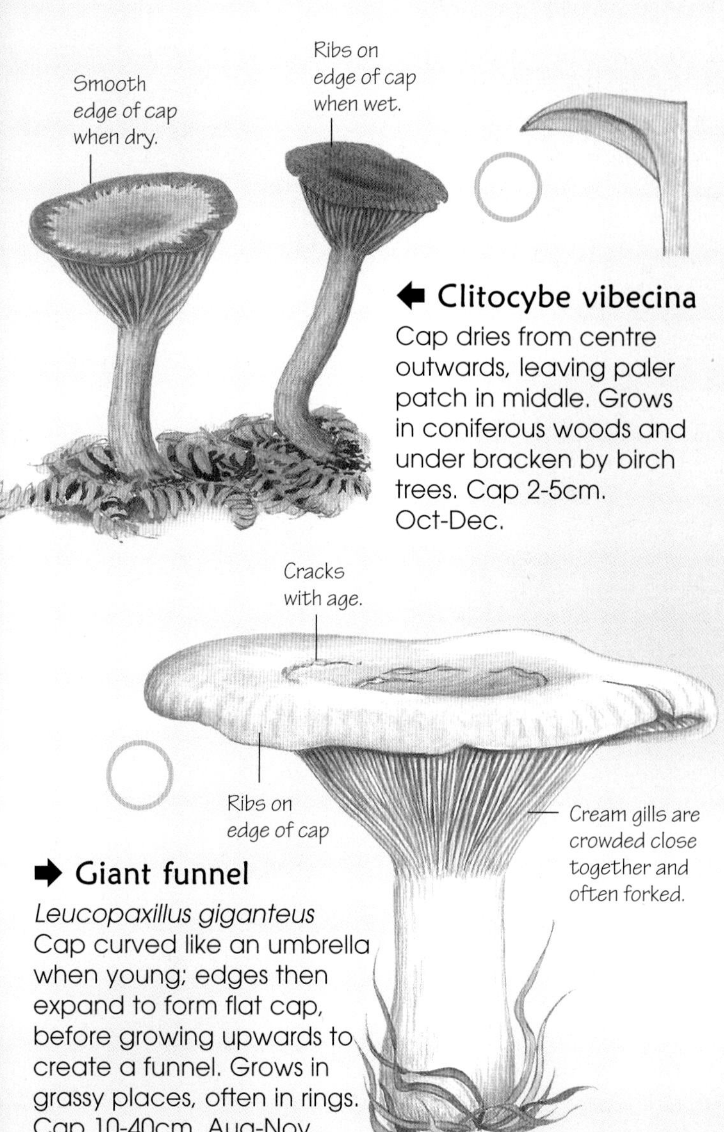
Smooth edge of cap when dry.
Ribs on edge of cap when wet.
Cracks with age.
Ribs on edge of cap
Cream gills are crowded close together and often forked.

← Clitocybe vibecina

Cap dries from centre outwards, leaving paler patch in middle. Grows in coniferous woods and under bracken by birch trees. Cap 2-5cm. Oct-Dec.

→ Giant funnel

Leucopaxillus giganteus
Cap curved like an umbrella when young; edges then expand to form flat cap, before growing upwards to create a funnel. Grows in grassy places, often in rings. Cap 10-40cm. Aug-Nov.

Cap fungi with gills

➡ False champignon or fool's funnel

Clitocybe rivulosa
Gills run down the stem and are crowded together. In grass fields and lawns, often with fairy ring champignon. Poisonous. Cap 2-6cm. Aug-Nov.

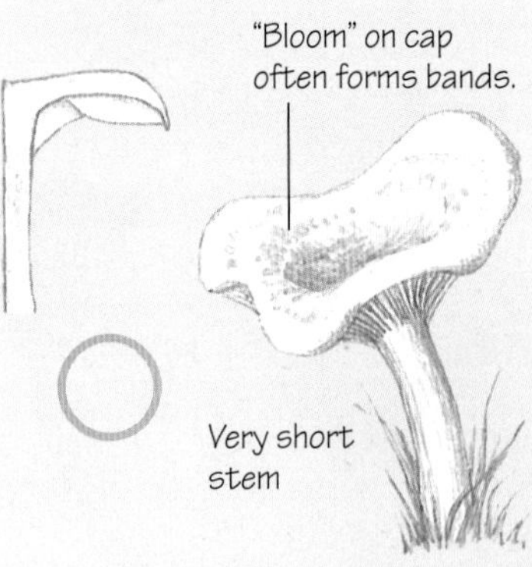
"Bloom" on cap often forms bands.
Very short stem

Cap darker at centre.
Gills do not run down stem.

⬅ Fairy ring champignon

Marasmius oreades
Well-spaced gills with many intermediates. In grass, often in rings. Cap 3-6cm. June-Nov.

➡ Inocybe erubescens

Gills white at first, then yellow-brown. Flesh turns deep pink when cut. Brown spores. Broadleaved woods, especially under beech. Deadly poisonous. Cap 3-8cm. June-Nov.

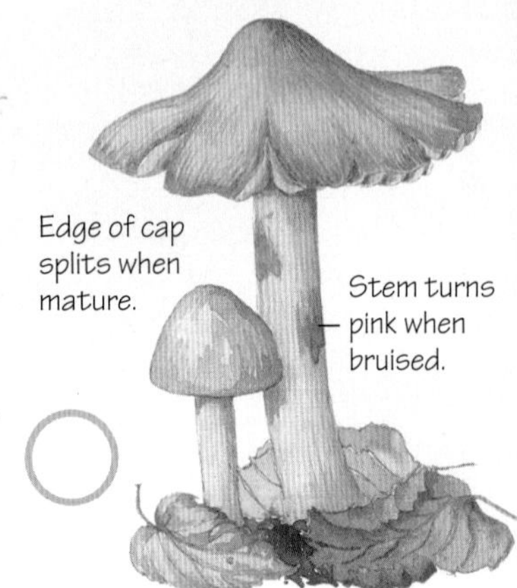
Edge of cap splits when mature.
Stem turns pink when bruised.

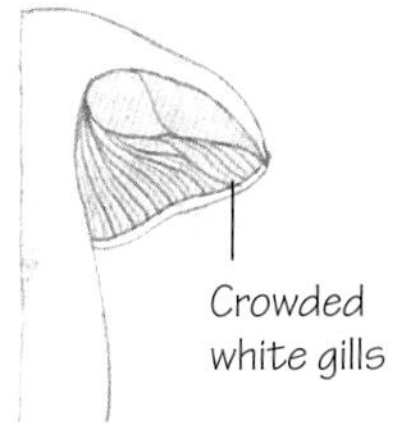

➡ Saint George's mushroom

Calocybe gambosa
Cream cap sometimes tinged with red spots. White spores. In grassy places, especially on chalk soil. Cap 5-16cm. April-June.

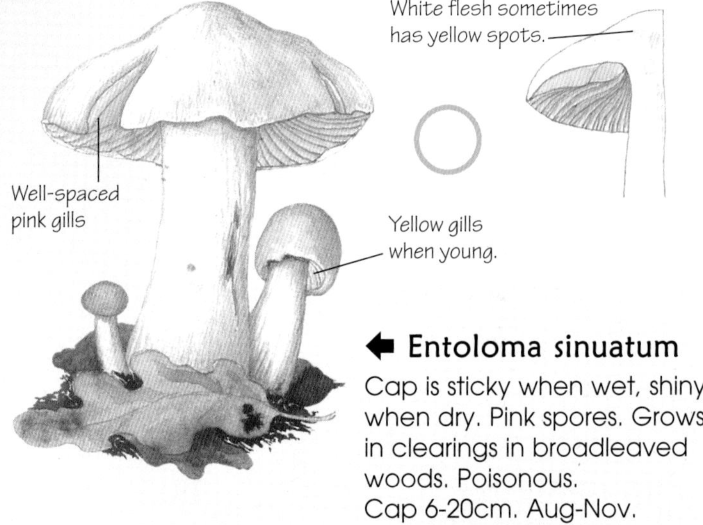

⬅ Entoloma sinuatum

Cap is sticky when wet, shiny when dry. Pink spores. Grows in clearings in broadleaved woods. Poisonous.
Cap 6-20cm. Aug-Nov.

Cap fungi with gills

⬅ Wood blewit

Lepista nuda
Tinged lilac all over. Cap colour fades with age. Gills crowded close together. Pale pink spores. Grows in broadleaved and coniferous woods. Cap 6-15cm. Sept-Feb.

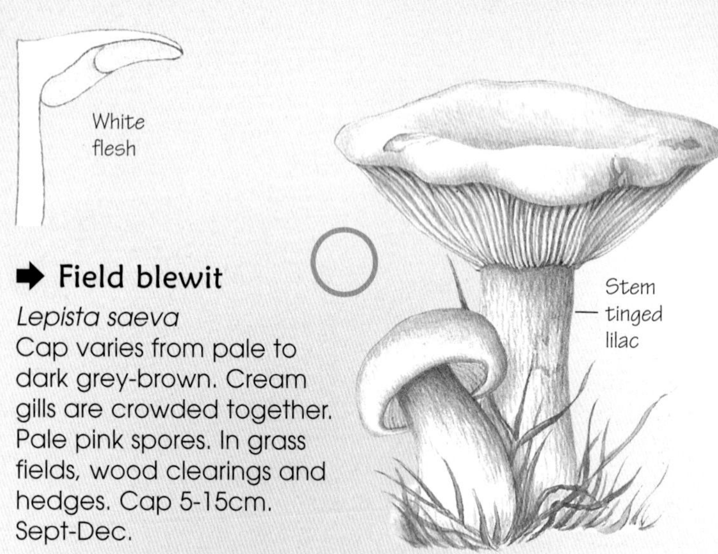

➡ Field blewit

Lepista saeva
Cap varies from pale to dark grey-brown. Cream gills are crowded together. Pale pink spores. In grass fields, wood clearings and hedges. Cap 5-15cm. Sept-Dec.

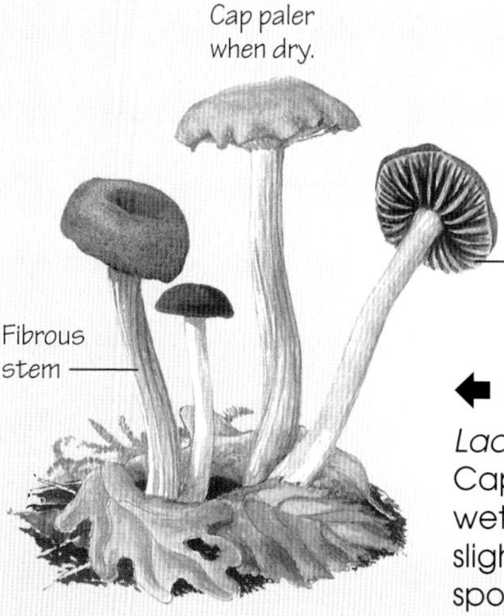

Cap paler when dry.

Thick widely spaced gills

Fibrous stem

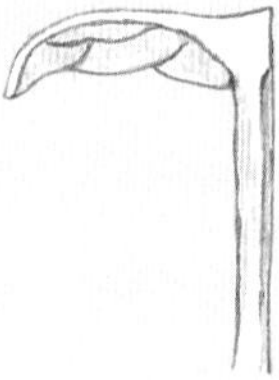

⬅ Amethyst deceiver

Laccaria amethystea
Cap deep violet when wet, paler when dry. Smells slightly of garlic. White spores. In broadleaved woods. Cap 2-4cm. Aug-Dec.

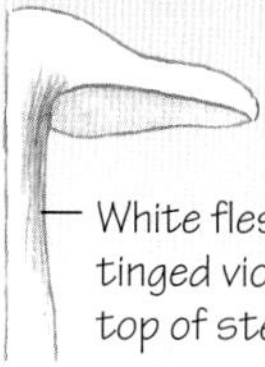

White flesh tinged violet at top of stem

Sometimes has fibres on edge of cap.

➡ Lilac thickfoot or pearly webcap

Cortinarius alboviolaceus
Well-spaced gills are violet at first, turning brown when mature. Rust-brown spores. Broadleaved woods, especially beech and oak. Cap 3-8cm. Aug-Dec.

Cap fungi with gills

Russulas, pages 272-273, have crumbly flesh. The spores and gills are white or cream, and gills run from the cap edge to the stem. Many gills are brightly coloured. There are about 100 species in Britain.

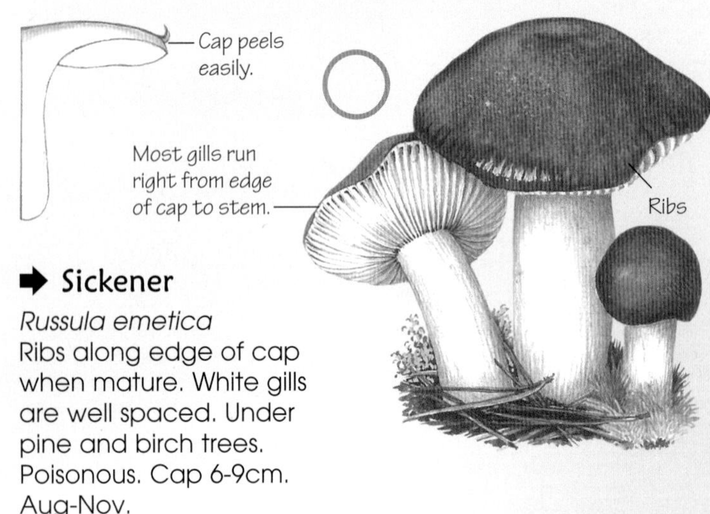
Cap peels easily.
Most gills run right from edge of cap to stem.
Ribs

➡ Sickener

Russula emetica
Ribs along edge of cap when mature. White gills are well spaced. Under pine and birch trees. Poisonous. Cap 6-9cm. Aug-Nov.

Gills sometimes have fine rust-coloured spots on edges.

Well-spaced cream gills
Thick stem

⬅ Purple brittlegill

Russula atropurpurea
Centre of cap is darker in colour and often depressed. Broadleaved woods. Cap 5-15cm. July-Nov.

➡ Ochre brittlegill

Russula ochroleuca
White to pale cream gills break easily. White flesh turns light grey with age. All types of wood, but especially under pine. Cap 4-10cm. Aug-Nov.

Ribs on edge of cap
White stem with faint veins

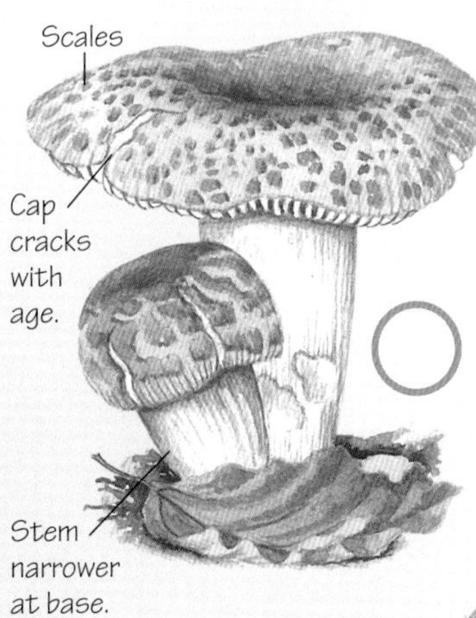
Scales
Cap cracks with age.
Stem narrower at base.

⬅ Green-cracked brittlegill

Russula virescens
Green cap with darker scales. White gills break easily and are crowded. Broadleaved woods, especially beech. Cap 5-12cm. July-Oct.

Cream gills feel greasy and are elastic.

➡ Variable brittlegill or charcoal burner

Russula cyanoxantha
Cap varies from mottled green to violet or grey. Flesh is brown when cut. Broadleaved woods, especially beech. Cap 5-15cm. Aug-Nov.

Cap fungi with gills

Milk caps, pages 274-275, have crumbly flesh and white or pale yellow gills and spores. They ooze milky drops when broken.

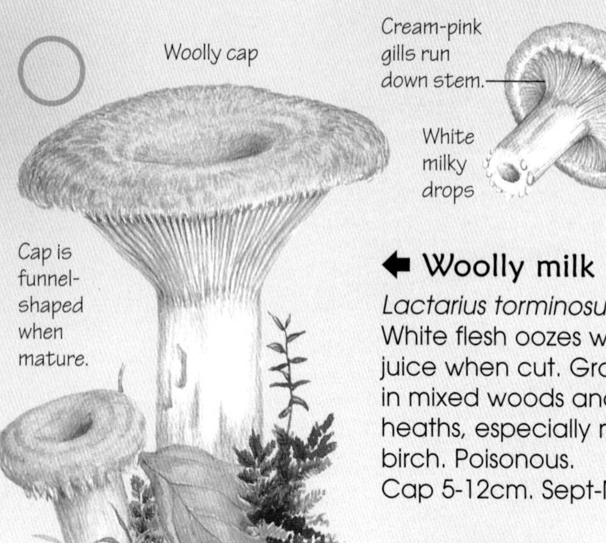

⬅ Woolly milk cap

Lactarius torminosus
White flesh oozes white juice when cut. Grows in mixed woods and on heaths, especially near birch. Poisonous.
Cap 5-12cm. Sept-Nov.

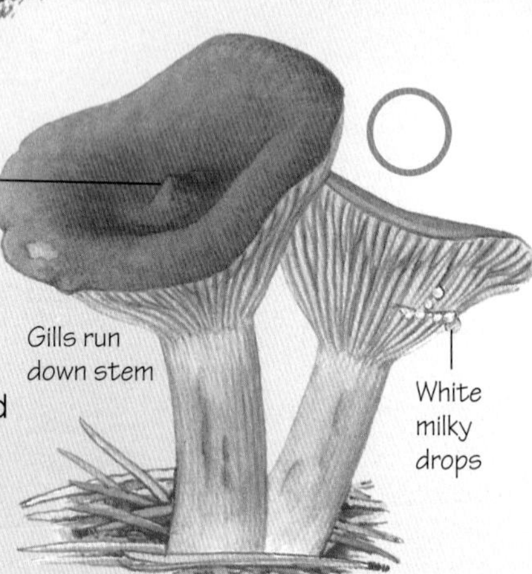

➡ Red milk cap

Lactarius rufus
Cap at first covered with downy hairs, later smooth. Cream coloured gills when young, turning pale and red-brown with age. Under pine.
Cap 3-10cm. Aug-Nov.

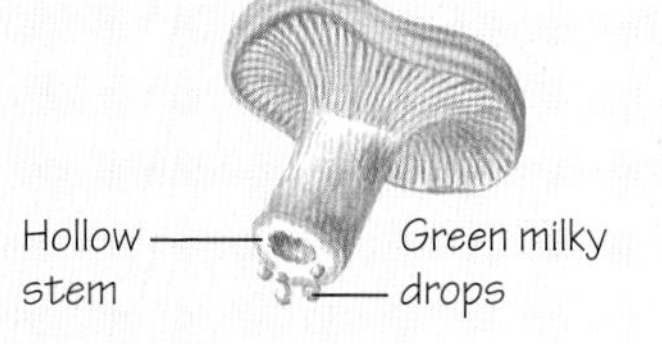

➡ Saffron milk cap

Lactarius deliciosus
Orange to fawn, funnel-shaped cap with light and darker rings. Oozes green "milk" when cut. Grows in coniferous woods. Cap 4-10cm. Aug-Nov.

White "milk"

Edge of cap turns under

Short thick stem

⬅ Fleecy milk cap

Lactarius vellereus
Cap depressed at centre and feels velvety. Yellowy-white gills run down stem and may be tinged brown. Often in groups in broadleaved woods. Cap 8-20cm. Sept-Nov.

➡ Ugly milk cap

Lactarius turpis
Cap covered with thick yellow down when young. White flesh turns violet-grey when cut. Cream gills have brown edges. Under conifers and birch. Cap 8-24cm. Aug-Nov.

Cap fungi with gills

Yellow flesh

Funnel-shaped cap when mature.

Edge of cap curves under, especially when young.

Gills and stem dark brown when bruised.

⬅ Brown roll-rim

Paxillus involutus
Gills are close together; at first beige, then brown. Brown spores. Broadleaved woods, especially birch. Poisonous. Cap 6-12cm. Aug-Nov.

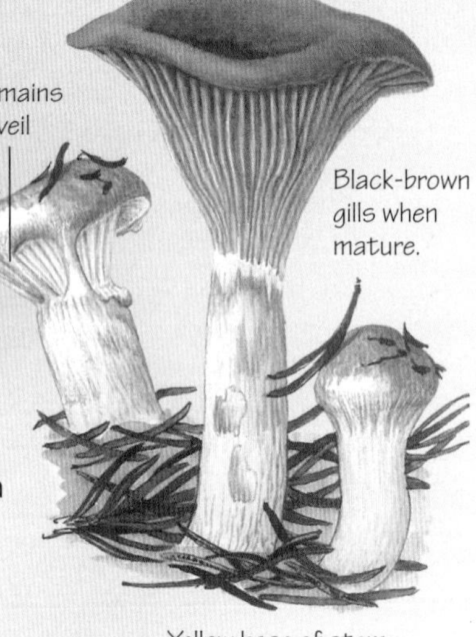

➡ Slimy spike cap

Gomphidius glutinosus
Cap at first conical, then depressed at centre when mature. Gills run down stem. Brown-black spores. Coniferous woods. Cap 5-12cm. July-Nov.

Cap fungi with spines

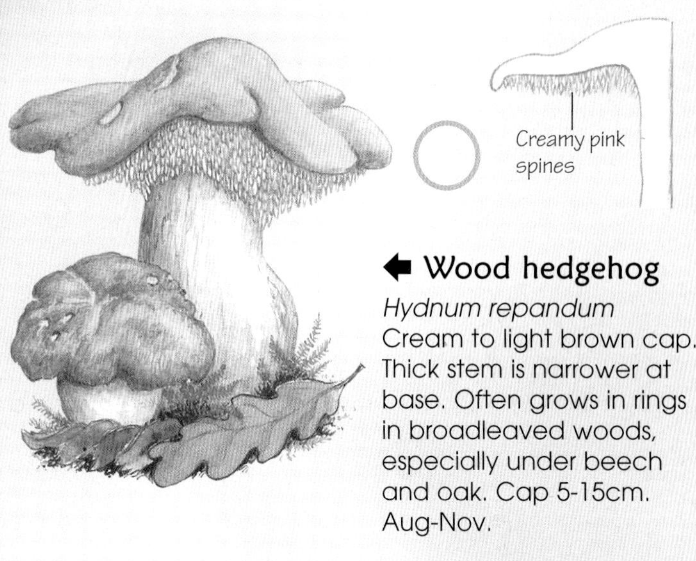

⬅ Wood hedgehog

Hydnum repandum
Cream to light brown cap. Thick stem is narrower at base. Often grows in rings in broadleaved woods, especially under beech and oak. Cap 5-15cm. Aug-Nov.

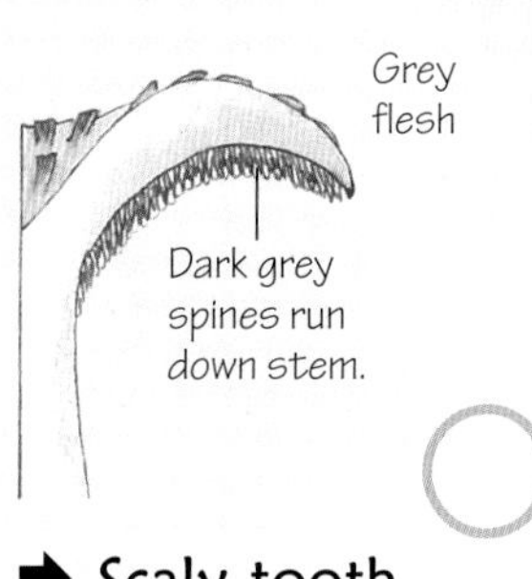

➡ Scaly tooth

Sarcodon imbricatum
Grey-brown cap with darker overlapping scales. Coniferous woods, usually on poor sandy soil. Cap 5-20cm. Sept-Nov.

Funnel-shaped fungi

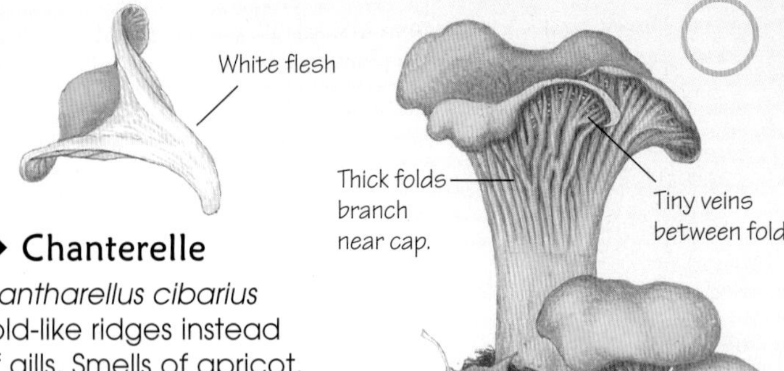
White flesh
Thick folds branch near cap.
Tiny veins between folds

➡ Chanterelle

Cantharellus cibarius
Fold-like ridges instead of gills. Smells of apricot. Broadleaved woods, especially beech and oak. Cap 3-10cm. May-Dec.

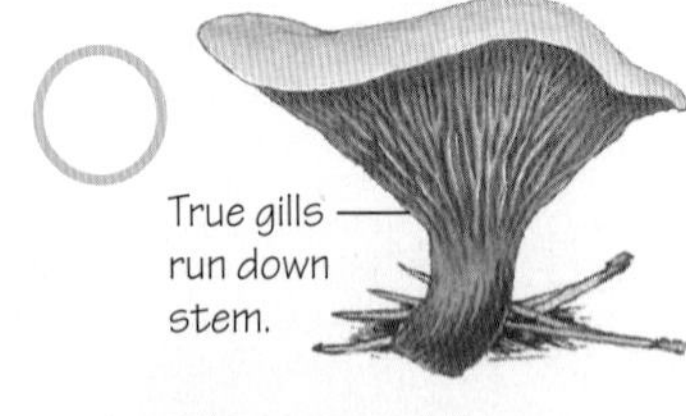
False chanterelle is deeper orange than chanterelle.
True gills run down stem.

⬅ False chanterelle

Hygrophoropsis aurantiaca
Forked, orange gills. Conifer woods and heaths. Poisonous. Cap 4-8cm. Aug-Nov.

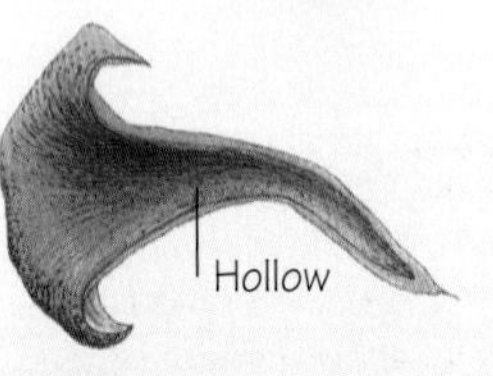
Hollow

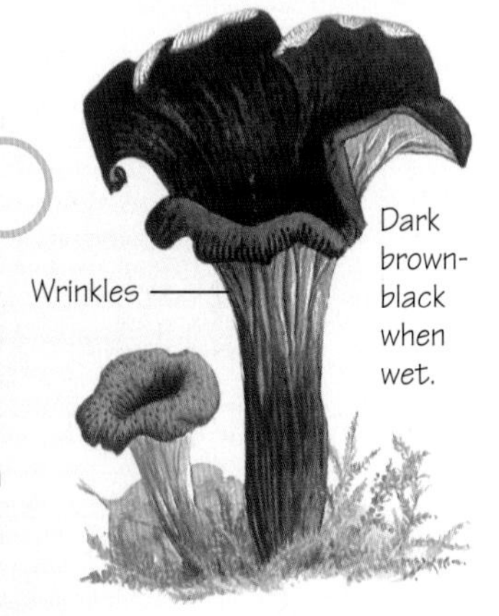
Wrinkles
Dark brown-black when wet.

➡ Horn of plenty

Craterellus cornucopioides
Funnel-shaped, with wrinkles on outer surface. Paler when dry. Broadleaved woods. 5-12cm high. Aug-Nov.

Bracket fungi with gills

Bracket fungi with gills grow on trees (living wood) or stumps (dead wood). The gills run down a short stem that is usually to one side of the cap.

⬅ Little fan or splitgill

Schizophyllum commune
Grey, fan-shaped cap. Tough flesh. Mainly in southeast England. On dead branches and cut timber. Cap up to 3cm. All year round.

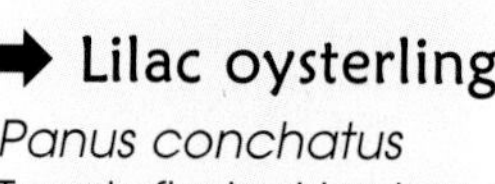

➡ Lilac oysterling

Panus conchatus
Tough flesh dries hard. Flesh-coloured gills run down stem. Grows on cut stumps of broadleaved trees. Cap 1-14cm. May-Oct.

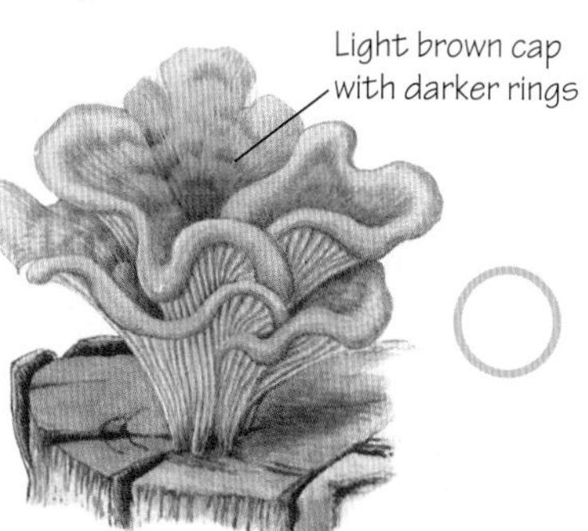

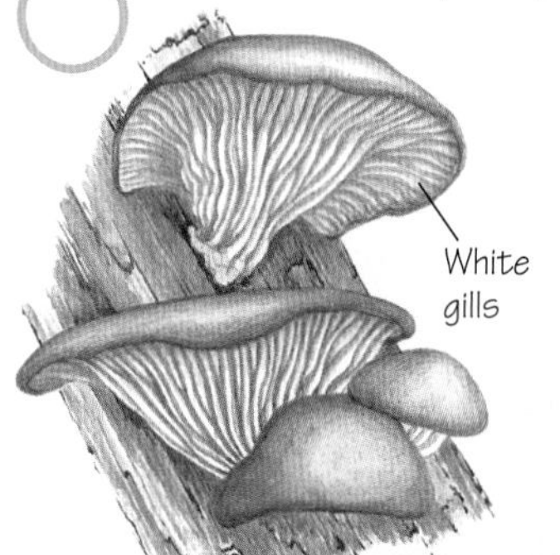

⬅ Oyster mushroom

Pleurotus ostreatus
Cap colour very variable, may be cream, pale brown, pale blue, chocolate or blue-black. White gills. Lilac spores. In groups on broadleaved, and sometimes coniferous, trees. Cap 5-25cm. All year round.

Bracket fungi with pores

These fungi all grow on trees or stumps, and have masses of fine tubes, opening as small pores on the undersurface of the cap. The spores are produced in these tubes.

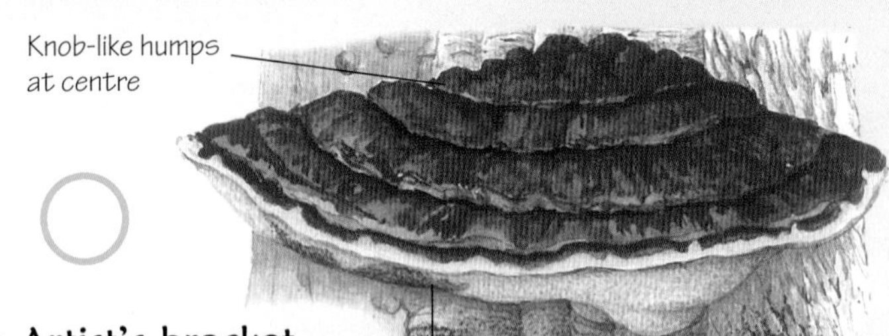

Knob-like humps at centre
Rust-coloured spores fall from pores.

➡ Artist's bracket

Ganoderma applanatum
Dark brown cap with paler margin. Once used as tinder for lighting fires. On trunks of broadleaved trees, especially beech. Kills the tree. Cap 5-60cm. All year round.

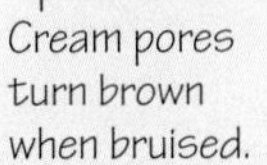

Cream pores turn brown when bruised.

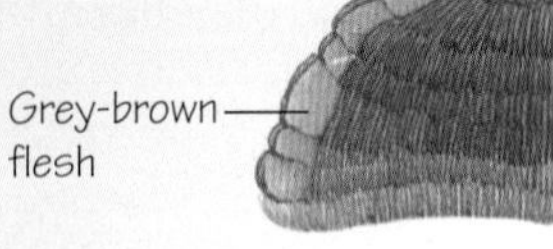

Grey-brown flesh

Surface is cracked like charcoal.
Pale margin

⬅ Tinder fungus

Phellinus ignarius
Very hard, grey to black-brown, cracked cap. Tiny pale grey pores turn light brown with age. On broadleaved trees, especially willow and poplar. Cap 10-30cm. All year round.

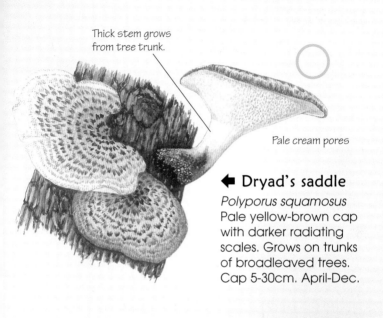

Thick stem grows from tree trunk.

Pale cream pores

⬅ Dryad's saddle

Polyporus squamosus
Pale yellow-brown cap with darker radiating scales. Grows on trunks of broadleaved trees. Cap 5-30cm. April-Dec.

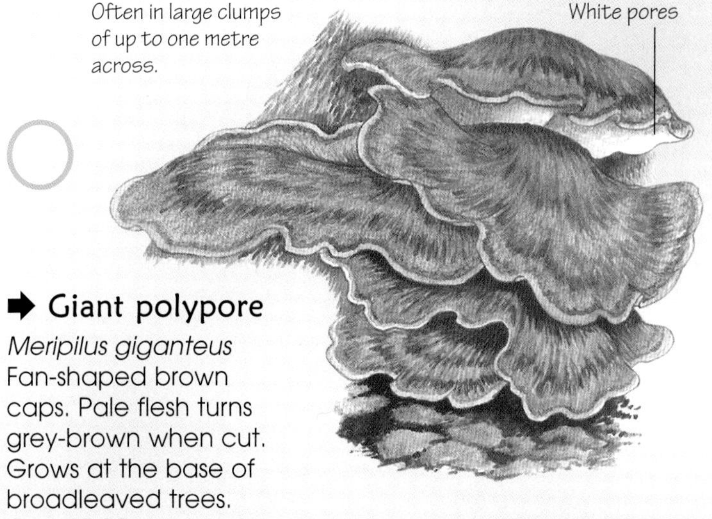

➡ Giant polypore

Meripilus giganteus
Fan-shaped brown caps. Pale flesh turns grey-brown when cut. Grows at the base of broadleaved trees. Cap 10-50cm. July-Jan.

Bracket fungi with pores

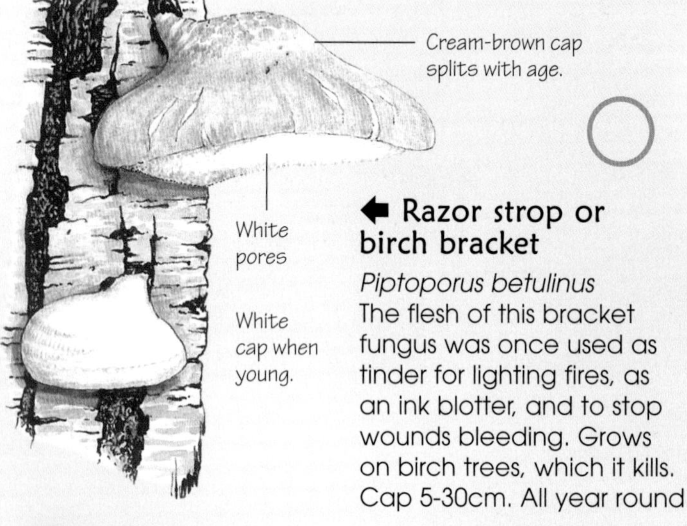

Cream-brown cap splits with age.
White pores
White cap when young.

⬅ Razor strop or birch bracket

Piptoporus betulinus
The flesh of this bracket fungus was once used as tinder for lighting fires, as an ink blotter, and to stop wounds bleeding. Grows on birch trees, which it kills. Cap 5-30cm. All year round.

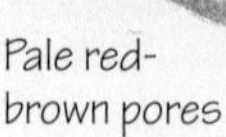

Pale red-brown pores

Flesh looks like raw meat.

➡ Beef steak fungus

Fistulina hepatica
Soft, fleshy fungus that oozes red drops when squeezed. Pores yellow at first, then turn a pale red-brown with age. At the base of broadleaved trees, especially oak and chestnut. Cap 5-30cm. Aug-Nov.

Small brackets, crust fungi

Many fungi form crusty layers on bark or on the ground. Some, such as *Antrodia serialis*, have pores. Others, such as *Stereum hirsutum*, produce spores on their undersurface.

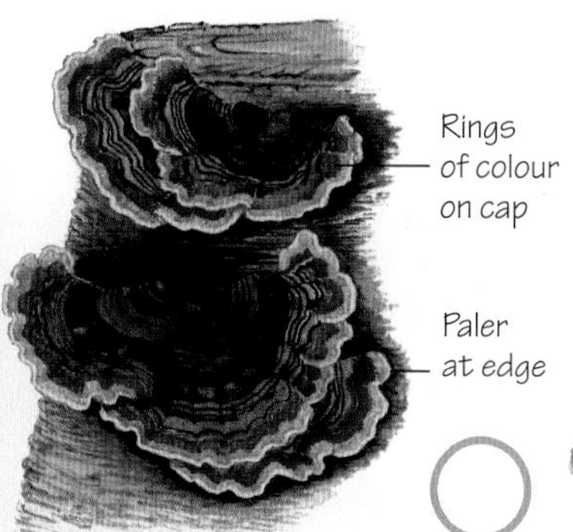

← Turkey tail

Trametes versicolor
Brightly coloured bracket with velvet-like cap. Grows in layers on cut stumps and branches of broadleaved trees. Cap 2-5cm wide. All year round.

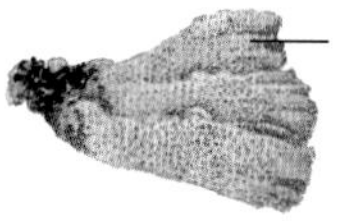

→ Antrodia serialis

Cream-coloured with small pores all over its surface. Forms a crust on conifer tree trunks and stumps. All year round.

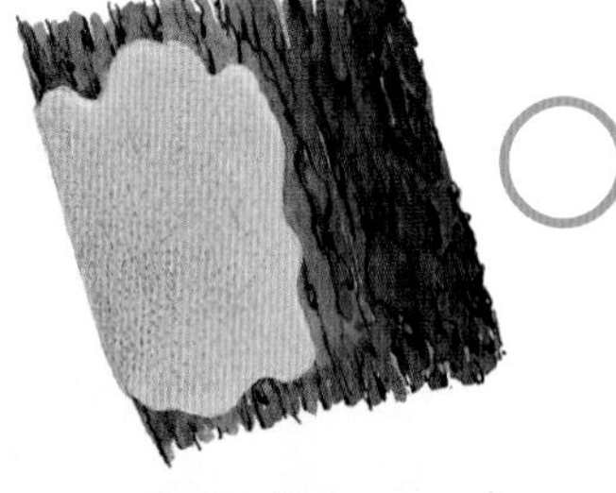

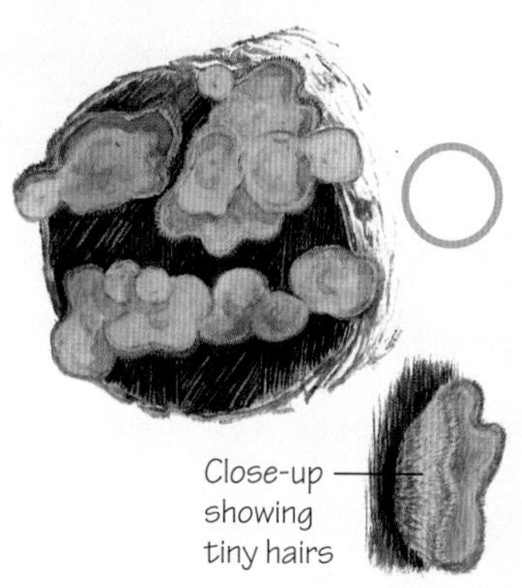

← Stereum hirsutum

Smooth yellowish upper surface, covered with tiny hairs. Very common on stumps, branches and cut wood. Causes white rot on stored timber. 1-4cm across. All year round.

Cup fungi

➡ Scarlet elf cup

Sarcoscypha coccinea
Smooth, scarlet surface inside cup; downy, cream or orange outer surface. On rotting branches of broadleaved trees. Cup 2-5cm wide. Dec-March.

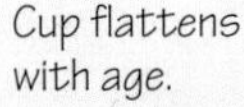
Cup flattens
with age.

⬅ Peziza badia

Outside surface of cup is paler brown than inside. On the ground, in broadleaved woods. Poisonous. Cup 3-7cm wide. Aug-Oct.

➡ Orange peel fungus

Aleuria aurantia
Smooth, orange surface inside cup; downy, paler orange outer surface. On gravel, lawns and on bare soil in woods. Cup 1-12cm wide. Aug-Dec.

Edge of cup often splits with age.

Cup fungi, truffle

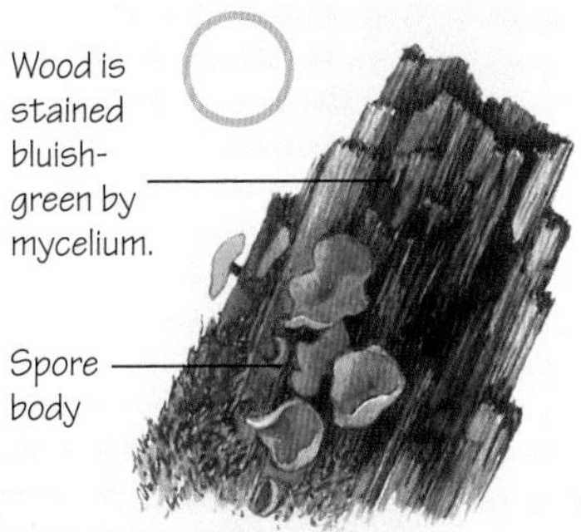

← Blue stain or green elf cup

Chlorosplenium aeruginascens
Tiny, bluish-green cup-shaped spore bodies. The wood on which it grows is permanently stained bluish-green. Grows on rotting wood, especially oak. Cup 0.5cm wide. May-Nov.

→ Common bird's nest

Crucibulum laeve
Small cup-shaped fungus, filled with several egg-shaped bodies that contain spores. Rain splashes the "eggs" out of the cup, dispersing the spores. On twigs. Cup 0.5-1cm high. Sept-Feb.

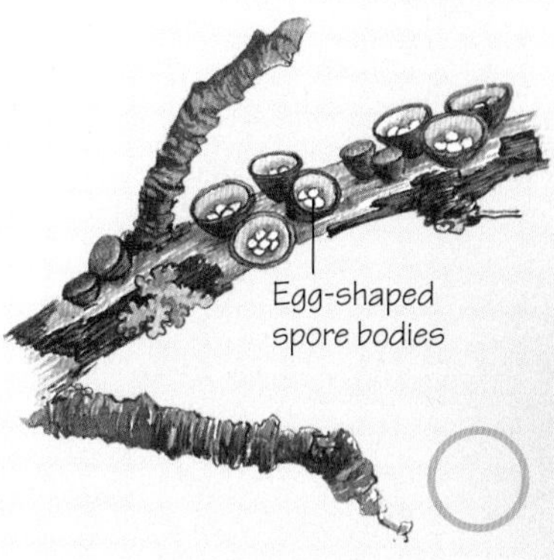

← Summer truffle

Tuber aestivum
This is one of several kinds of truffle. Grey flesh, sometimes tinged lilac, streaked with paler veins. Grows in soil (especially chalk soil), just below ground level, in beech woods. 3-8cm across. Aug-Oct.

Puffballs

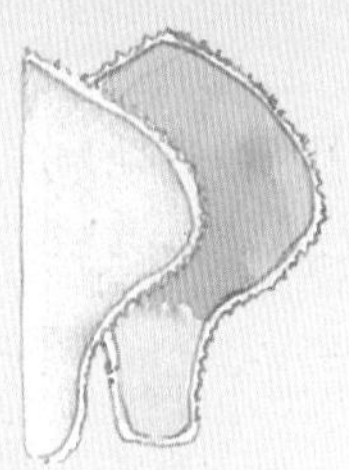

Flesh at first white, then yellow.

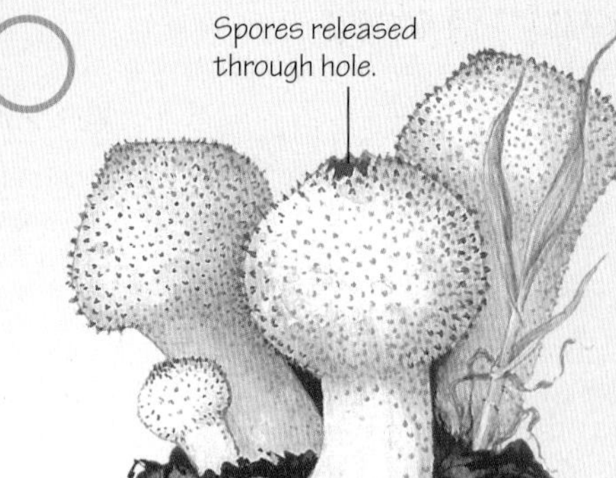
Spores released through hole.

⬆ Common puffball

Lycoperdon perlatum
Covered with small warts. White flesh turns yellow-green as spores ripen. When mature, small hole forms at top. In woods. 4-7cm high. July-Nov.

➡ Giant puffball

Calvatia gigantea
One of the world's largest fungi. Flesh at first white, then yellow. Splits when mature. In fields, woods and hedgerows. 15-100cm. across. Aug-Nov.

Puffball, earthball, earthstar

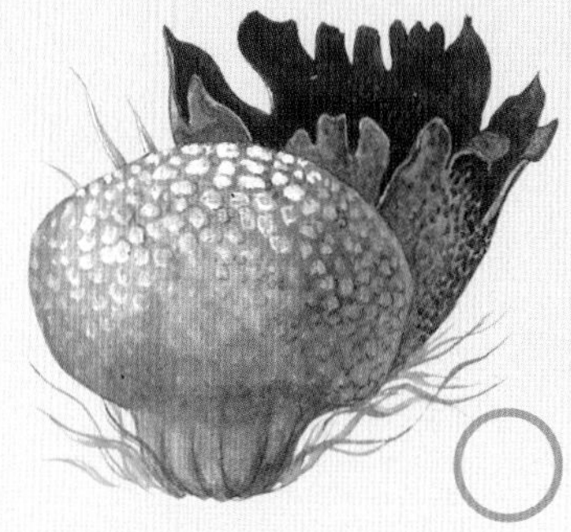

⬅ Mosaic puffball

Handkea utriformis
Grey-brown at first, turning dark brown with age. Top opens out to release dark brown spores. In fields and woods on sandy soil. 6-10cm across. July-Nov.

➡ Common earthball

Scleroderma citrinum
Looks like a young puffball, but is much harder, and forms no hole. Centre is at first cream, then yellow, and finally black. In woods, especially under birch. 4-8cm across. July-Dec.

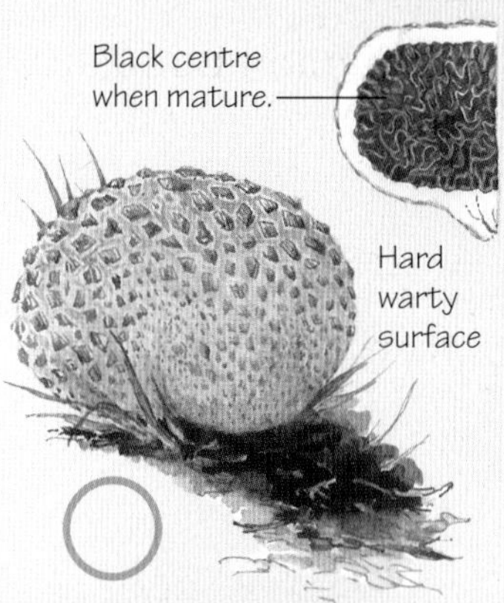

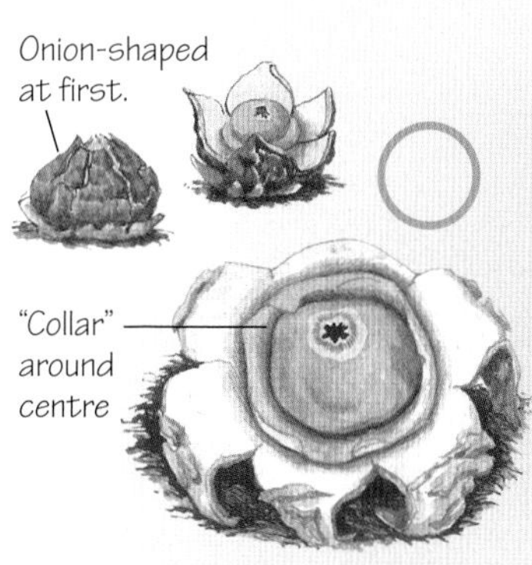

⬅ Collared earthstar

Geastrum triplex
Onion-shaped at first, then outer layer peels back forming 5-7 pointed fringe. Broadleaved woods, especially beech. 6-8cm across. Aug-Nov.

Note: There are other kinds of earthballs and earthstars.

Soot fungi

➡ King Alfred's cakes

Daldinia concentrica
Hard, brown or black ball-shaped fungus with a shiny surface. Has dark and pale circular zones inside. Grows on dead trees, especially ash. 2-8cm across. All year round.

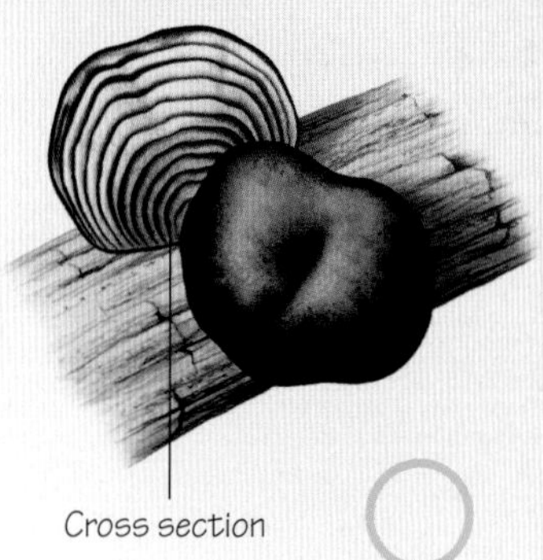

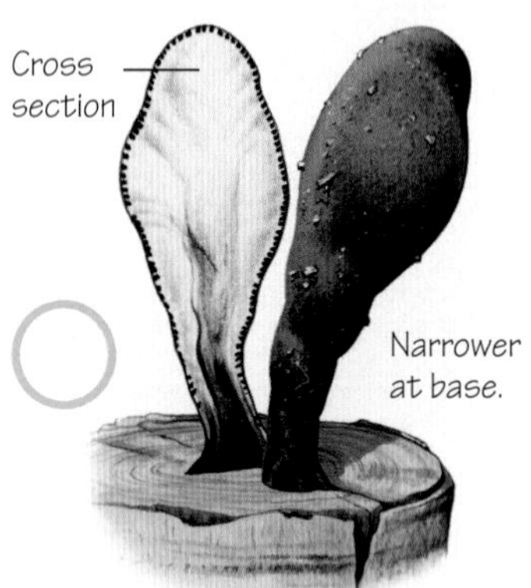

⬅ Dead man's finger

Xylaria polymorpha
Hard, black, finger-shaped fungus with white flesh inside. Usually grows in groups from the stumps of broadleaved trees. 3-8cm high. All year round.

➡ Candle snuff

Xylaria hypoxylon
Black stem with white tip that turns black with age. On dead wood and tree stumps. 2-6cm high. All year round.

Jelly fungi

➡ Witch's butter

Exidia glandulosa
Deep olive to black coloured jelly. Grows in a mass of varying size on rotting stumps of broadleaved trees. All year round, but mainly Oct-Dec.

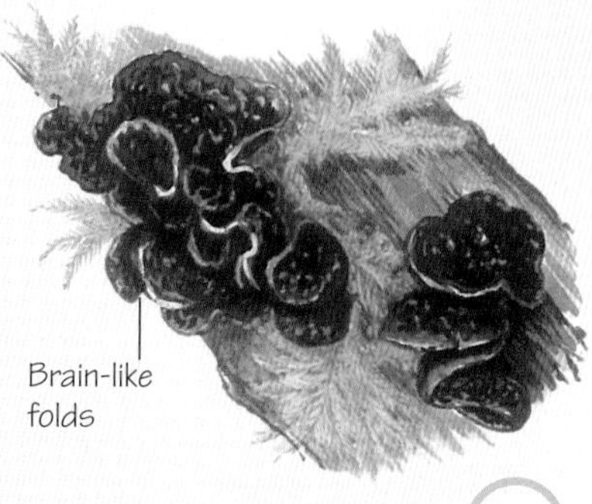

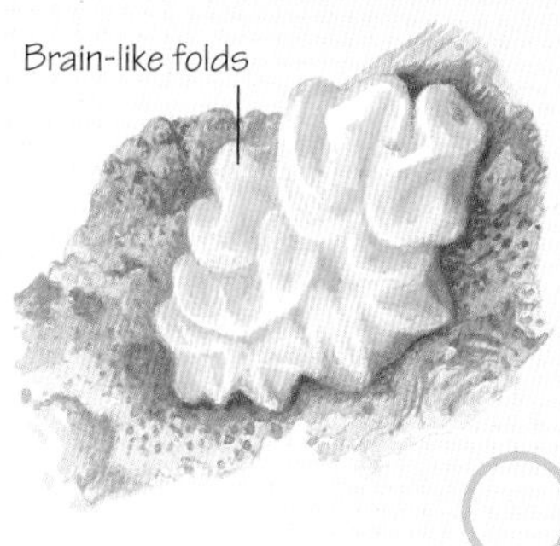

⬅ Yellowbrain

Tremella mesenterica
Slimy when wet, drying to a hard, orange crust. Grows in a mass of varying size on dead branches and tree stumps. All year round, but mainly Sept-Dec.

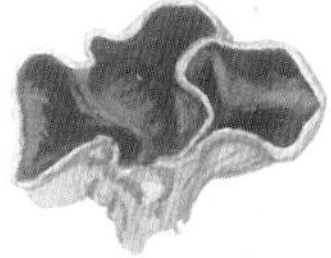

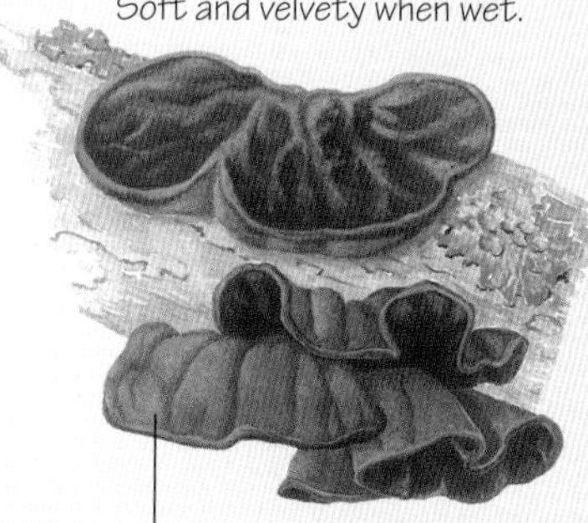

➡ Jelly ear

Auricularia auricula
Mainly on branches of elder trees. Each "ear" 3-10cm across. All year round.

Morel, turban fungus

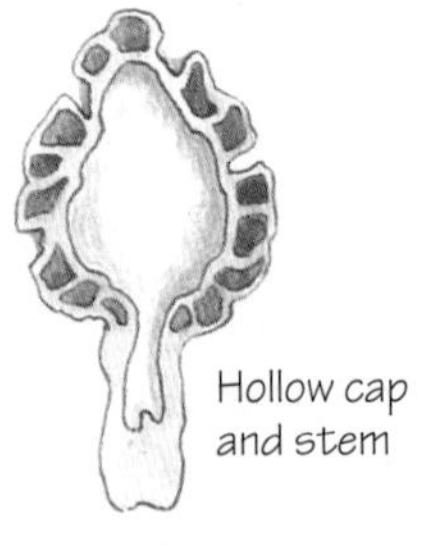

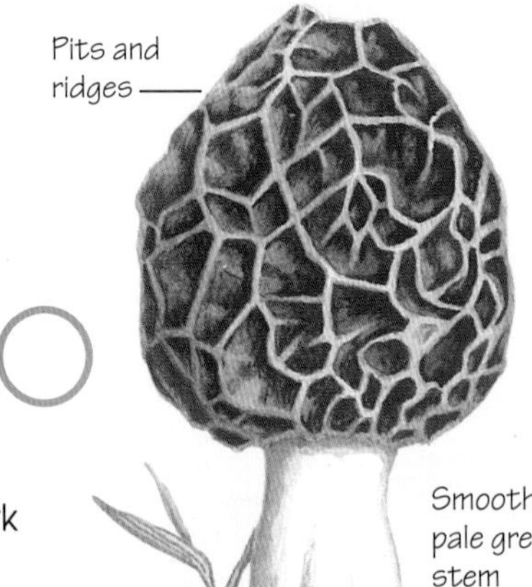

 Morel

Morchella esculenta
Stem is capped by a dark brown mass of ridges and pits, which are shiny when wet. In broadleaved woods and grassy places. 12-24cm high. May-July.

Brain-like folds

Cream or pink stem with ridges

⬅ False morel or turban fungus

Gyromitra esculenta
Mass of cream-brown, brain-like folds on a hollow stem. Grows on sandy soil in coniferous woods. Very poisonous. 5-15cm high. March-May.

Stinkhorn, saddle cap

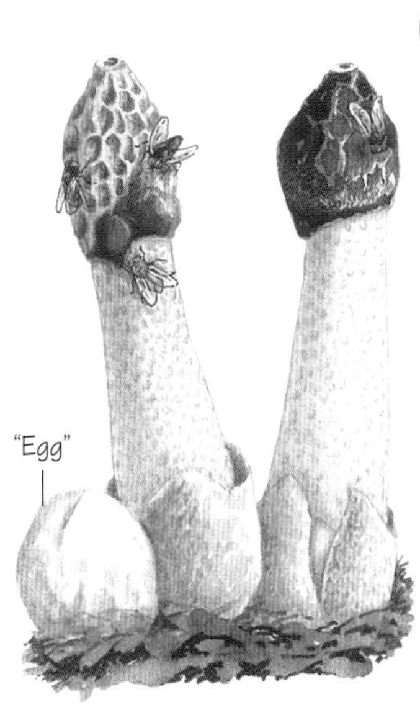

⬅ Stinkhorn

Phallus impudicus
Develops from a white "egg", buried in leaves or moss. Dark slime on head of stem contains spores, and is soon eaten by flies. Very strong, unpleasant smell. Grows in woods and hedgerows. 6-12cm high. July-Oct.

➡ White saddle cap

Helvella crispa
Hollow stem is capped by folds that are off-white on the upper side and pale fawn underneath. Beside paths in broadleaved woods. 5-10cm high. March, April and Aug-Oct.

How cap fungi grow

Both the mycelium buried in the soil and the spore body above ground are made of tiny tubes called hyphae. These hyphae develop from spores dropped from fungus caps. In a mycelium they are arranged loosely, while in a spore body they are tightly packed. The picture below shows the cycle from spore to spore body.

1. Thousands of spores ripen and fall from the fungus cap and are carried away by the wind. The parent spore body then quickly decays.

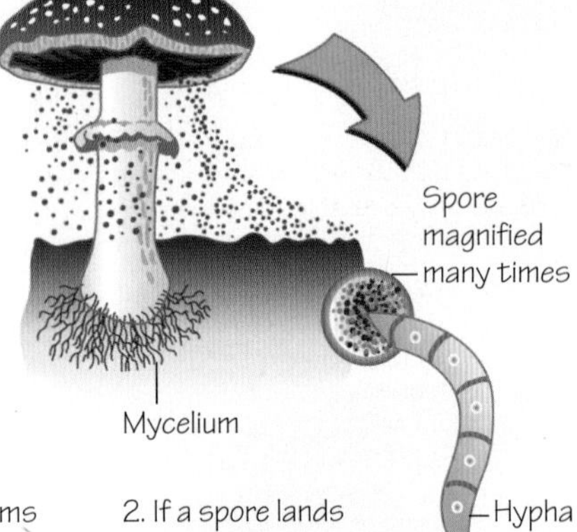

5. Eventually, the mycelium forms a "button", which pushes up out of the soil. From this, a new spore body quickly develops.

2. If a spore lands on a suitable surface, it starts to produce a hypha.

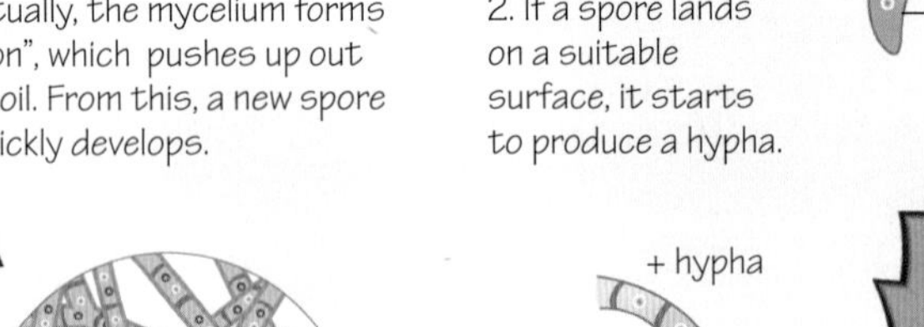

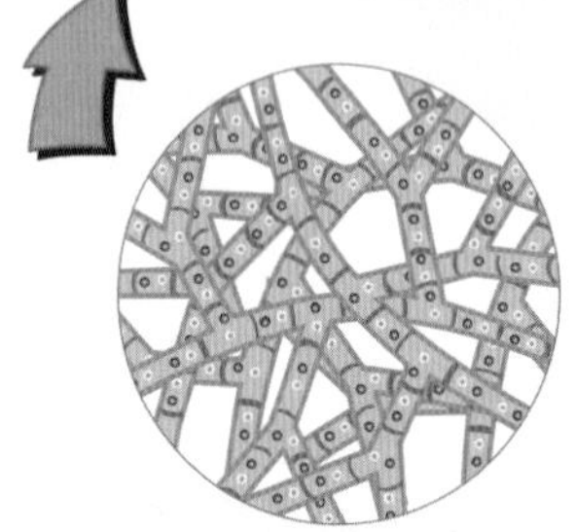

4. If there is enough food and moisture this new, combined hypha grows and forms a mycelium.

3. There are two types of hypha, positive (+) and negative (-). A fungus forms when a + and - hypha join together.

Fairy rings

A fairy ring is a circle of toadstools that sometimes forms when a fungus uses up all the nutrients in its area and spreads out to find more.

1. The mycelium spreads outwards in a circle underground, as it searches for food in the soil. It lives on decaying leaves and other dead plants and animals.

2. It breaks the food down to absorb its nutrients, and forms a ring of toadstools. Fed by the same nutrients, the grass around the toadstools grows thick and lush.

3. When the fungus uses up all the nutrients in its area, the mycelium spreads out farther still, and often leaves behind a circle of withered, exhausted grass.

4. Eventually, lush grass may grow in the centre, where the ring began, because the old mycelium has died and the nutrients it had absorbed have been released back into the soil.

Fairy ring
Earlier fairy ring grew here.

Fairy rings can be hundreds of years old. You can get an idea of their age from their size: they grow by about 10-20cm a year. In English folklore, the rings were formed by fairies dancing in a circle by the light of the moon.

How fungi live

Most plants contain chlorophyll, a green chemical that enables them to make their own food. Fungi are not plants, and they have to "feed" on plant or animal matter to get the energy they need to grow and reproduce. Some fungi feed only on dead matter, while others get their food from living plants or animals.

Symbiotic fungi grow on living plants, but don't damage them. The fungus and the plant help each other to live and grow.

Parasites feed on living things. Parasitic fungi harm, and some even kill, the plant or animal on which they live.

Saprophytes are very useful because they decompose the dead plants and animals they feed off.

Turkey tail is a saprophytic fungus that grows on dead trees.

Birch tree
Birch polypore is a parasitic fungus that kills birch trees.
The tree provides fly agaric with sugars, and the fungus provides the tree with nutrients.

Useful fungi

Without some fungi, life could not exist, because they break down dead matter and return its nutrients to the soil. Fungi also have uses in medicine and food production.

Penicillium is a saprophytic mould that's used to make the medicine penicillin. Another type of penicillium mould forms the tangy veins in blue cheese.

Yeast is a saprophytic fungus that lives on sugars. It makes dough rise by breaking down its sugars to release gas. The alcohol in wine and beer is also produced when yeast breaks down the sugar in fruit juices or grain.

Truffles are symbiotic fungi that grow under the ground. They have been a rare and expensive food delicacy for thousands of years, but there are many poisonous "false" truffles, so never eat anything you have found without expert advice.

Summer truffle

Harmful fungi

Parasitic fungi can destroy crops, and kill animals and plants.

Cordyceps fungi live inside an insect, digesting it, until the spore body emerges. Before killing an ant by erupting through its head, *Cordyceps unilateralis* makes its host climb up to a high place, so its spores will be spread over the largest possible area.

Fungus feeding on a beetle

Rose mildew is a parasitic fungi that grows inside rose bush leaves. Blotches appear on the leaves and the plant turns sickly.

Athlete's foot is caused by a fungus that lives on the skin of the soles of people's feet. The skin turns dry and hard.

Animals, Tracks & Signs

Deer

➡ Red deer

Lives in herds in open country and woods. In winter, the males and females separate into two herds. Young have spotted coats. Eats grass, fruit, heather and tree bark. May raid crops. 1.5m.

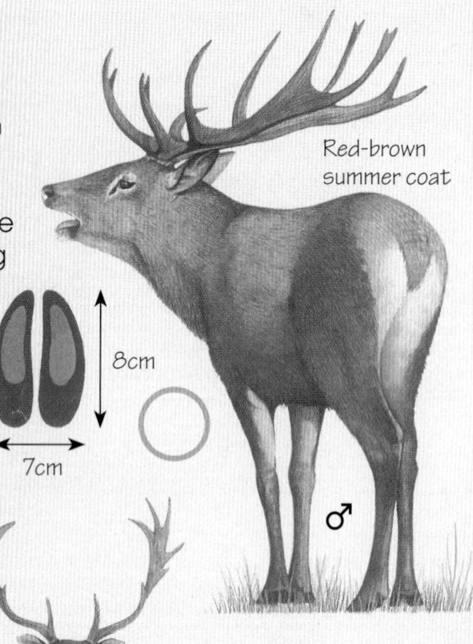

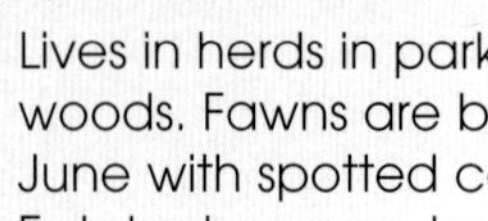

⬅ Fallow deer

Lives in herds in parks and woods. Fawns are born in June with spotted coats. Eats herbs, grass, berries, acorns and leaves. 1m.

➡ Muntjac

Lives on its own or in pairs, in thick undergrowth in woods. Quiet, but barks if frightened. Eats mainly bramble and wild herbs. 50cm.

➡ Roe deer

Red-brown in summer, grey-brown in winter. Lives on its own or in small family groups in woods. Eats leaves, herbs and berries. 70cm.

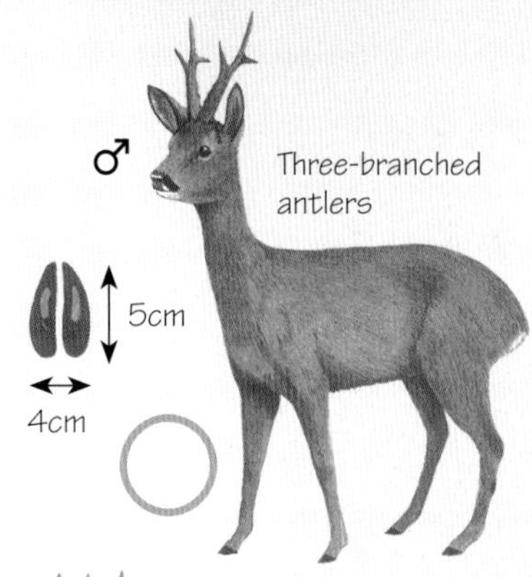

16cm

12cm

Flattened, palm-shaped antlers

Beard

⬅ Elk / moose

Largest European deer. Found in woods or marshes in northern and eastern Europe. Not found in Britain. Lives on its own in summer, and in herds in winter. Swims well. Eats water plants, grass and moss. 1.8m.

➡ Sika deer

Originally from Asia. Females live in small groups. Males are solitary. Eats heather and grass. May raid crops. 80cm.

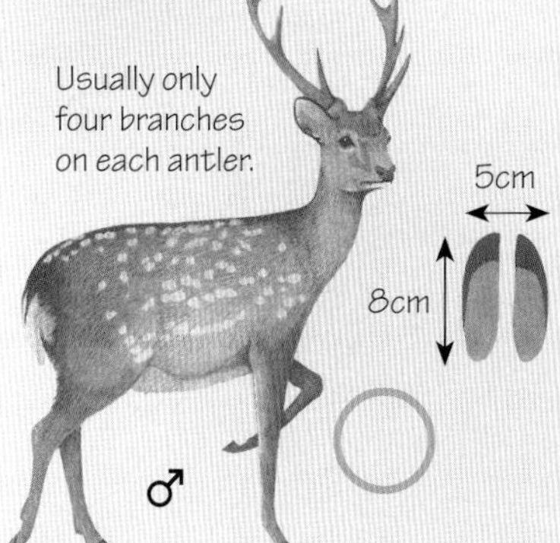

Deer and sheep

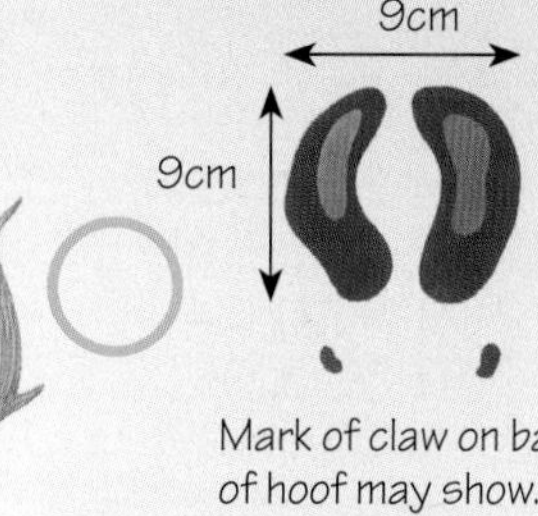

➡ Reindeer

Both sexes have antlers. Coat colour varies. Lives in herds in mountains and tundra of northern Scandinavia. A herd has been introduced to Scotland. Eats grass, heather and lichen. 1.1m.

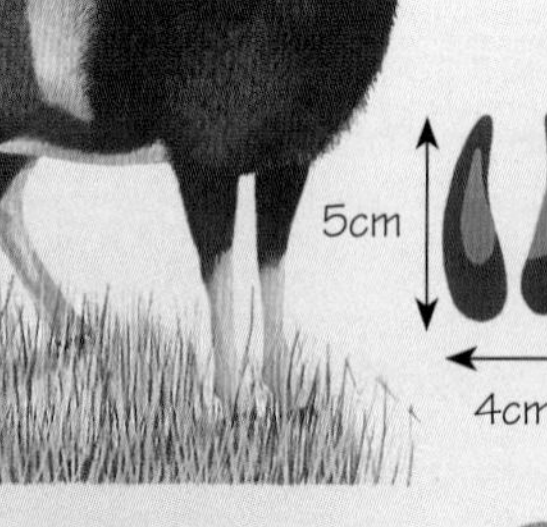

⬅ Mouflon / wild sheep

Ancestor of domestic sheep. Mainly nocturnal. Lives in small flocks in open mountain woods. Not found in Britain. Eats grass, moss, buds and berries. 70cm.

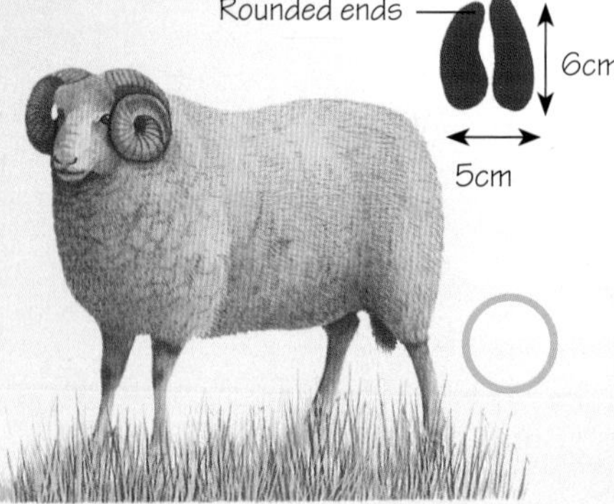

➡ Domestic sheep

Many different breeds. Kept in fields, open pastures, or mountains. Lives in flocks with an old female as leader. Eats mainly grass. Size varies with breed.

Goats and chamois

➡ Domestic goat

Many different breeds. Most are domesticated on farms, but some roam wild on mountains. Male usually has a beard. Size varies with breed.

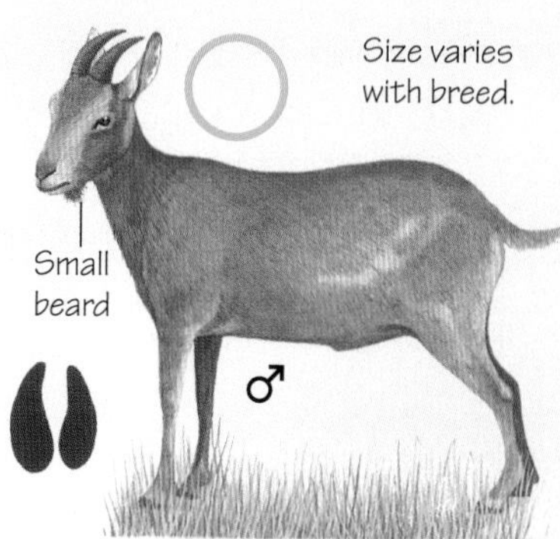

Similar to sheep tracks.

9cm

5cm

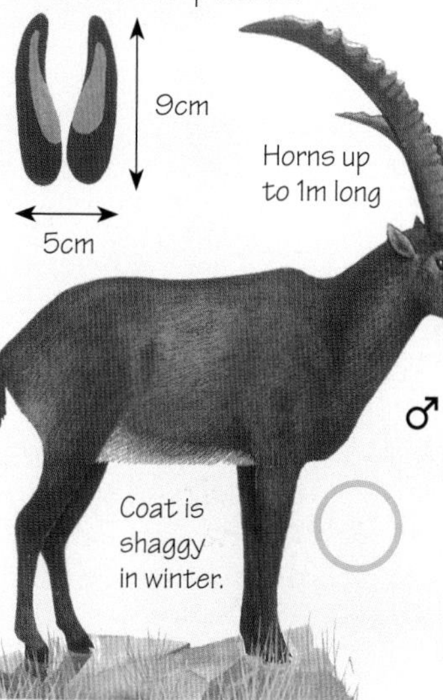

⬅ Ibex / wild goat

Lives in flocks on high mountains in Europe. Not found in Britain. Male has a beard. Very agile. Eats grass, lichen, moss and leaves. 75cm.

3.5cm

6cm

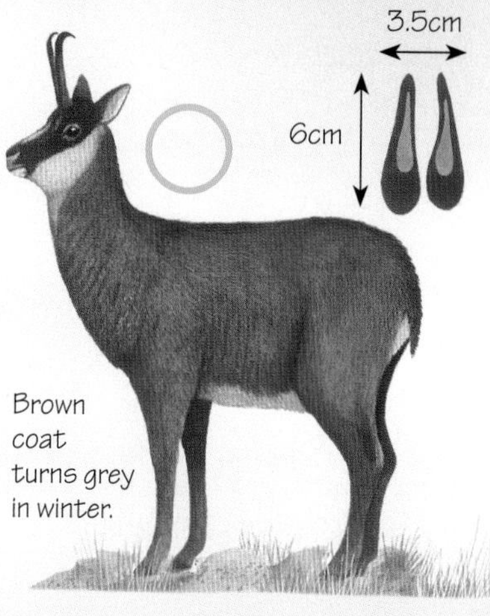

➡ Chamois

Both sexes have horns. Lives in flocks on wooded mountains. Not found in Britain. Males live on their own. Very agile. Eats grass, berries and buds. 75cm.

Cows, pigs and ponies

➡ Domestic cow

Colour and size vary with breed. Some have horns. Cows bred for beef can be seen roaming on moors and mountains.

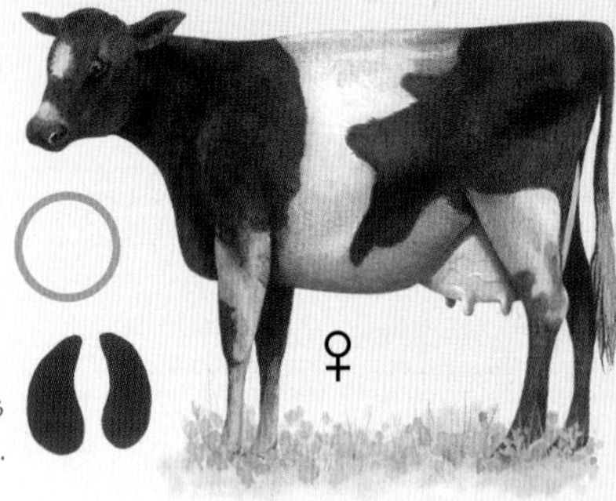

Size varies with breed.

7cm

Claw

Stiff, bristly fur

⬅ Wild boar

Ancestor of domestic pig. Lives in woods and marshes of Europe. Very rare in Britain. Males are solitary, females live in small groups. Eats roots, bark, and fallen fruit such as acorns. 90cm.

➡ Domestic pig

Size and colour vary with breed. Kept mainly on farms, but can be kept as pets. Omnivorous.

Size varies with breed.

⬅ Exmoor pony

Lives semi-wild in herds on Exmoor. There are no other semi-wild ponies in Britain. Eats grass, leaves and low-growing plants. 1.3m.

Track is made by one toe.

Wolves, dogs and bears

➡ Wolf

Usually lives on its own in remote forests in Spain, Scandinavia, Italy and Eastern Europe. In winter, lives in packs. Hunts silently for deer. 1.2m.

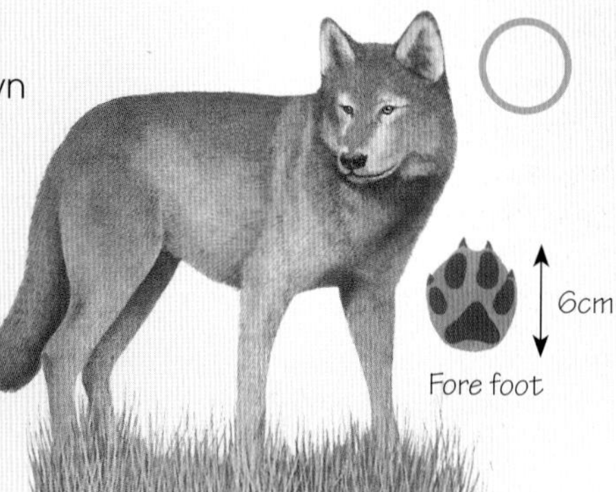

Size varies with breed.

Fore foot

⬅ Domestic dog

Size and colour vary with breed. Alsatians and huskies look similar to wolves. Eats mainly meat.

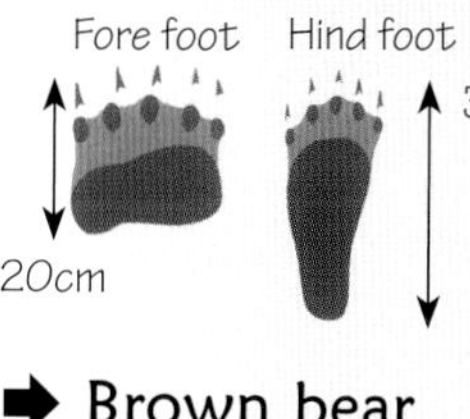

➡ Brown bear

Usually lives on its own in remote areas of Europe. Not found in Britain. Nocturnal. Hibernates in caves in winter. Omnivorous. 2m.

Foxes and badgers

➡ Red fox

Common on farmland and in woods, but also found on mountains and in towns. Usually nocturnal. Hunts and scavenges mammals, birds and insects. 65cm.

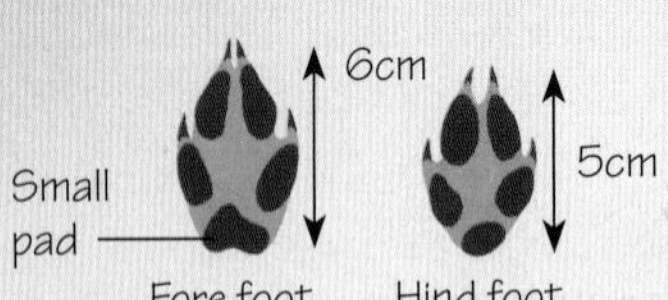

⬅ Arctic fox

Lives on tundra and mountains in northern Scandinavia. Not found in Britain. Coat is dull brown in summer; usually all white in winter, occasionally grey. Lives in small groups. Active by day and night. 60cm.

Tracks are 4.5cm, and similar to those of the red fox.

➡ Badger

Found mainly in woods, but also on mountains. Nocturnal. Lives in a large group, in networks of tunnels called setts. Eats mainly worms; also small mammals, insect larvae, wasp nests, cereals and roots. 80cm.

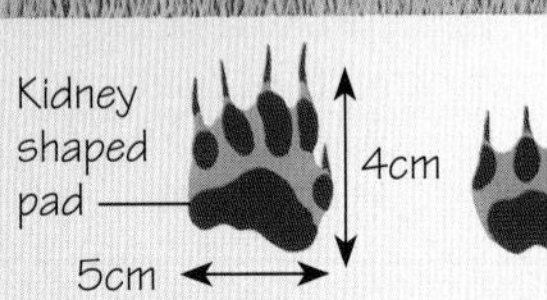

Stoats, weasels, mink and polecats

➡ Stoat

Found in woods, farmland and on mountains. Northern stoats, called ermines, are white in winter. Tip of tail is always black. Eats rabbits, small rodents, birds and eggs. 28cm.

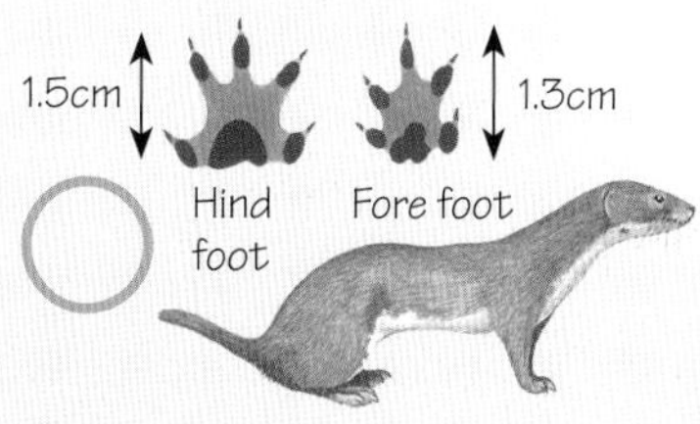

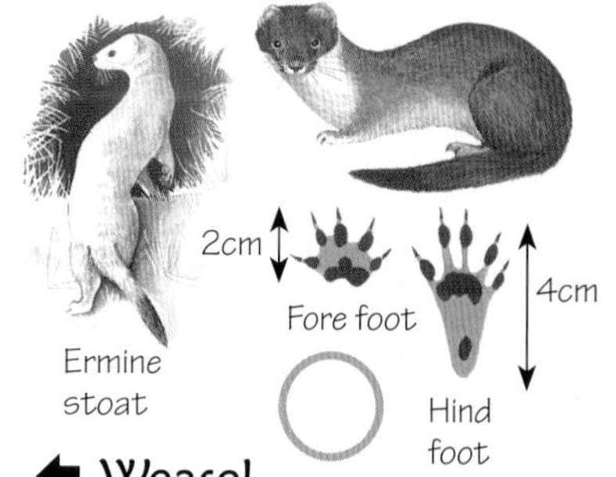

⬅ Weasel

Lives in similar areas to stoats; prefers dry places. Not found in Ireland. Nocturnal. Runs with an arched back. Eats small mammals and birds. 20cm.

➡ European mink

Native to France and Eastern Europe. American mink have escaped from fur farms in Britain and Europe. Lives near water and swims well. Stores food in its den. Eats fish, frogs, rabbits and birds. 38cm.

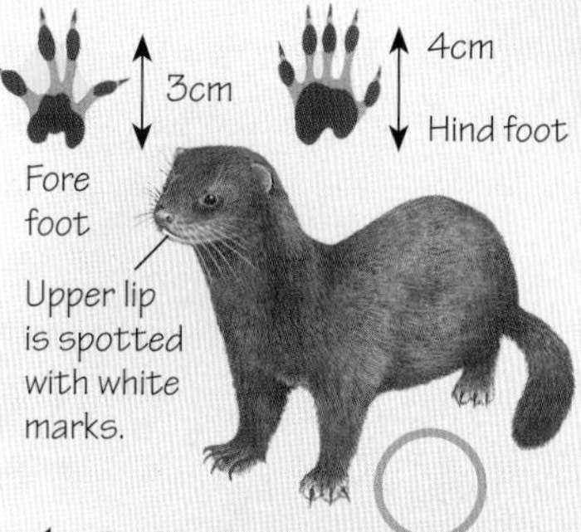

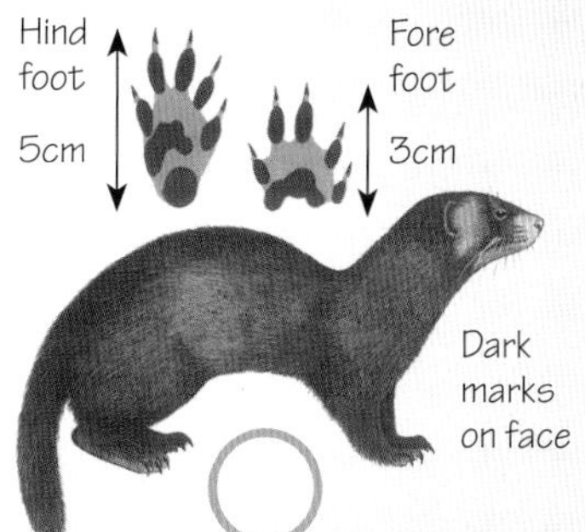

⬅ Polecat

Nocturnal. Found in wooded country, often near houses. Tame polecats are called ferrets. Eats rabbits, frogs, birds and rodents. 40cm.

Otters and martens

➡ Otter

Found along marshes, rivers, lakes, and coastal areas, and on offshore islands. Lives on its own. Nocturnal. Expert swimmer. Eats fish, crabs, eels, frogs, waterfowl and rabbits. 70cm.

⬅ Pine marten

Shy and nocturnal. Lives in mountain woods, usually amongst conifer trees. Good climber. Eats insects, berries, small mammals and birds. 50cm.

➡ Beech marten

Lives in woods and on farmland, often close to houses. Not found in Britain. Climbs well. Eats small mammals, birds and sometimes fruit. 45cm.

Cats

➡ Domestic cat

Many different breeds. Fed by people, but often hunts small mammals and birds. Active by day and night. Size varies with breed.

No claw marks

Fore foot   Hind foot

⬅ Wild cat

Found in remote, woody areas, or among rocks in Scotland and Europe. Nocturnal and shy. Eats mountain animals, such as hares, small deer, small rodents and grouse. 65cm.

Hind foot   6cm

Fore foot

➡ Lynx

Lives in remote mountain woods in Scandinavia and Eastern Europe. Nocturnal and solitary. Eats deer, hares, and game birds. 1.1m.

Hind foot

Fore foot

8cm

7cm

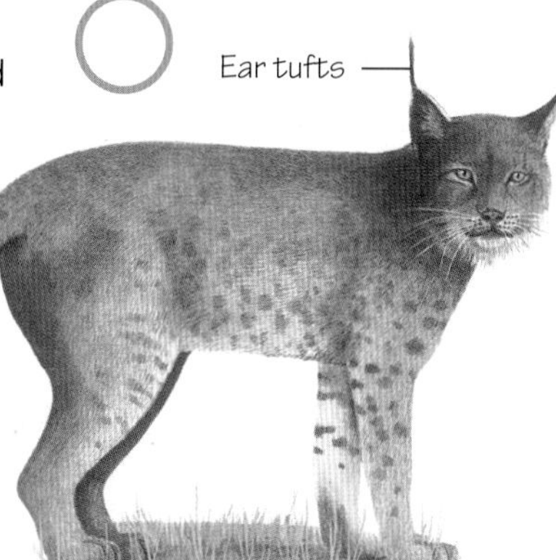

Beavers, coypu and muskrats

➡ Beaver

Small colonies can be seen in Europe. Builds a dam in a river or lake. Families live in a lodge, a large conical pile of branches. Eats water plants, bark and roots of aspen, willow and poplar trees. 85cm.

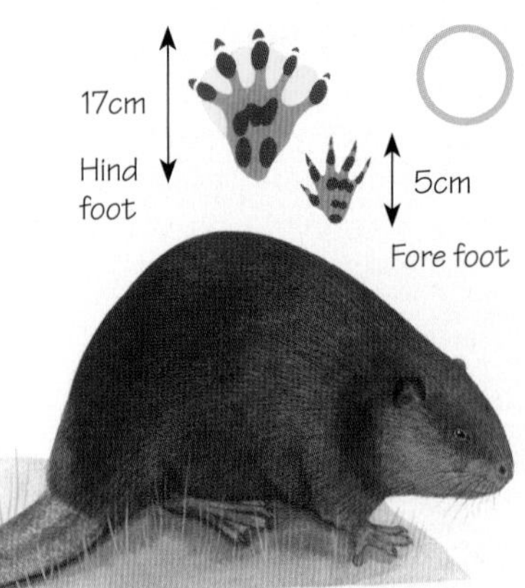

Webbed feet

⬅ Coypu

Originally from South America. Has escaped from fur farms in Europe. Not found in Britain. Lives beside water, burrowing into the banks. Eats waterside plants and root crops. 59cm.

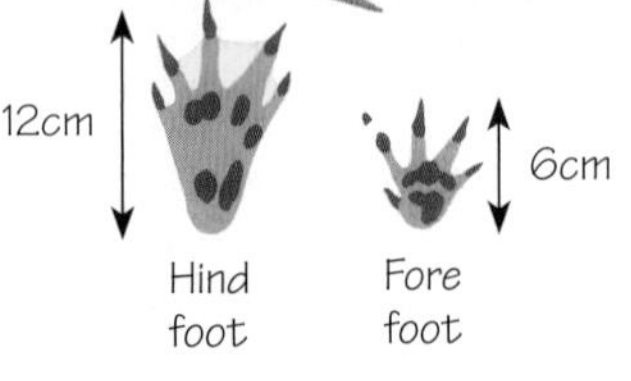

The sides of the tail are flattened.

➡ Muskrat

Lives beside fresh water. Has escaped from fur farms in Europe. Not found in Britain. Eats waterside plants. 33cm.

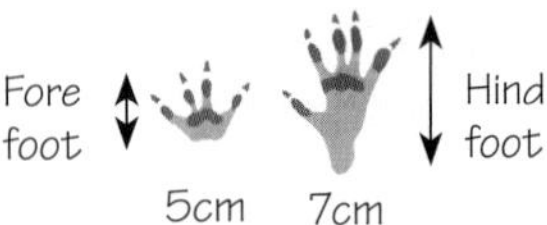

Squirrels and dormice

➡ Red squirrel

Lives mostly in conifer woods. Active by day, but shy. Eats seeds of cones, berries, buds, birds' eggs, nuts and fungi. 23cm.

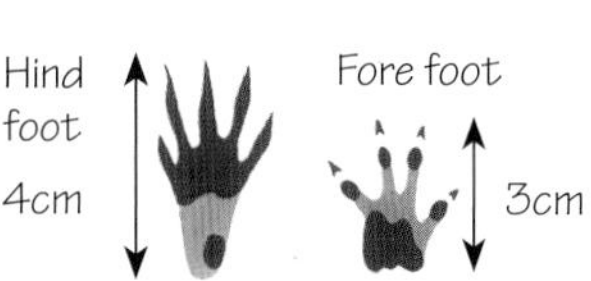

⬅ Grey squirrel

Similar habits to red squirrel, but is more common and less shy. Found in parks, gardens and woods. Eats seeds, acorns and nuts. 27cm.

➡ Edible dormouse

Native to Europe and Asia. Not found in Scotland. Found in deciduous woods, parks, and orchards. May live near houses. Nocturnal. Hibernates in winter. Eats nuts, fruit, insects, flowers, pollen and bark. 12cm.

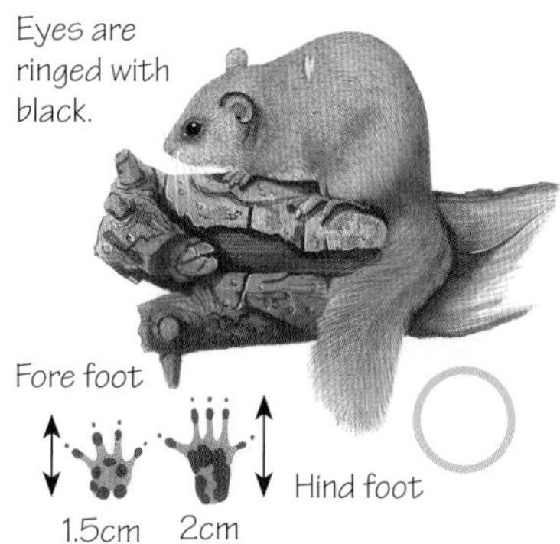

Dormice and hamsters

➡ Common dormouse

Lives in woods and hedges. Uses honeysuckle bark to build its hibernation and breeding nests. Nocturnal and solitary. Climbs well. Eats insects, berries, seeds, hazelnuts and chestnuts. 8cm.

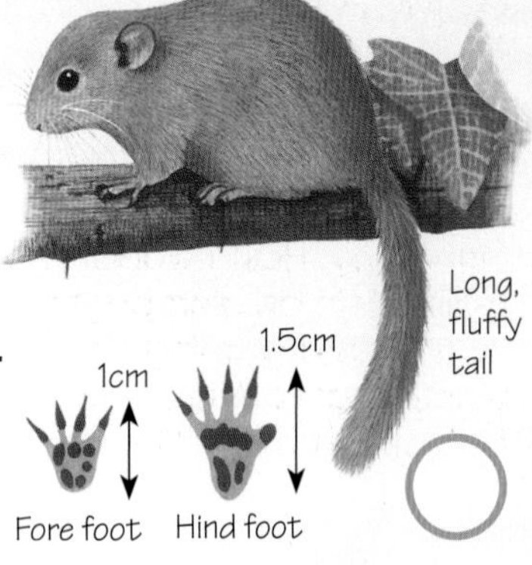

Black marks around eyes

Fore foot 1cm

Hind foot 1.5cm

⬅ Garden dormouse

Eats the same food and has the same habits as the common dormouse, but is larger, with a more pointed face. May enter buildings. Not found in Britain or Scandinavia. 13cm.

➡ European hamster

Lives on open grassland in Central Europe. Not found in Britain. Nocturnal. Lives on its own in a system of burrows. Hibernates. Stores food in its cheek pouches. 27cm.

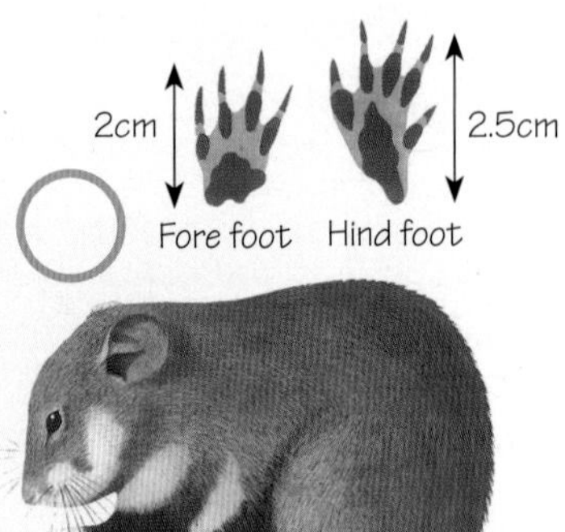

White cheeks and paws

Marmots and rats

➡ Alpine marmot

Families live in colonies in networks of long tunnels on the mountains of Europe. Not found in Britain. Active in the day. Has a waddling walk. Sits in an alert position and gives a warning whistle. Eats berries, seeds, nuts and insects. 55cm.

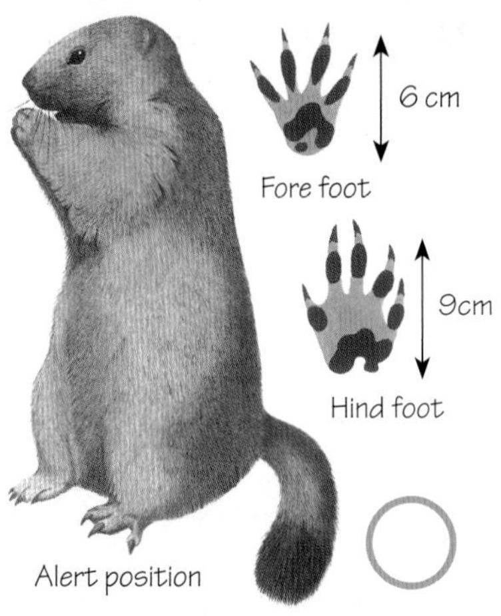

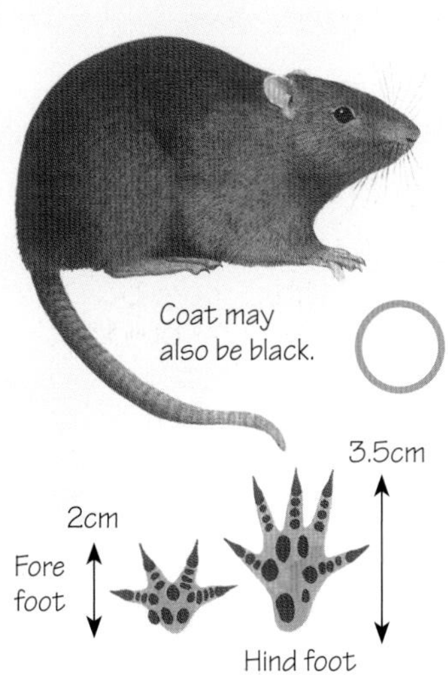

⬅ Common rat

Found worldwide. Lives in a colony, usually near houses. Makes a system of tunnels. Bold. Eats anything. 26cm.

Coat may also be shades of grey.

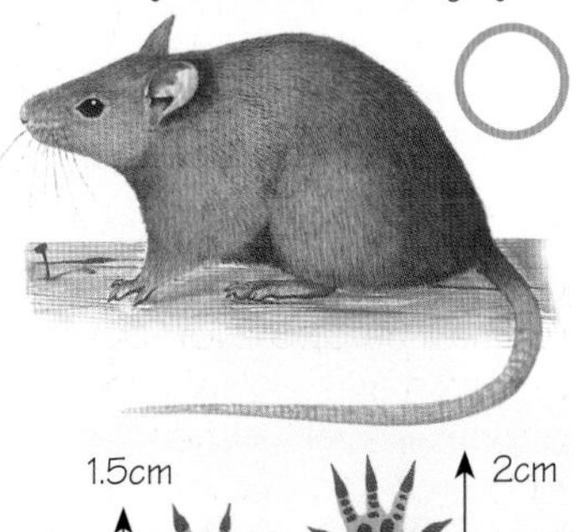

➡ Black rat / ship rat

Common near water, especially in ports and waterside buildings. Can climb well. Nocturnal and shyer than the common rat. Eats anything. 20cm.

Voles and lemmings

➡ Water vole

Found near water all over Western Europe, except Ireland. Active by day. Swims well and digs burrows in the banks of ponds, canals, streams and marshes. Eats waterside plants and snails. 19cm.

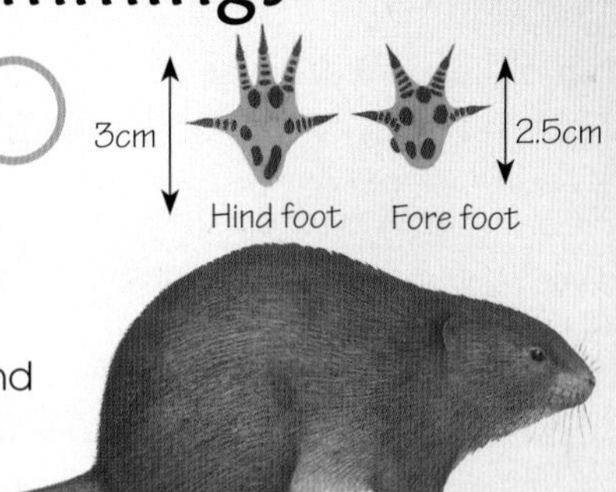

Coat may also be black.

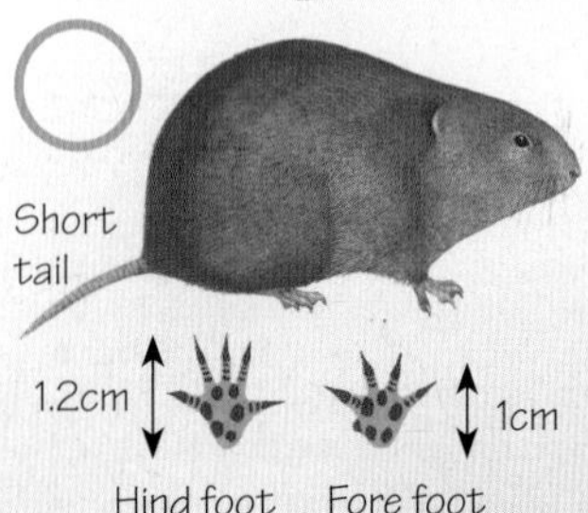

⬅ Short-tailed vole / field vole

Active by day. Makes tunnels below open ground. Not found in Ireland. Eats grass, leaves and moss. 11cm.

➡ Bank vole

Widespread in deciduous woods and hedgerows. Active by day. Climbs well and makes its burrows in banks. Eats leaves, buds, berries and insects. 10cm.

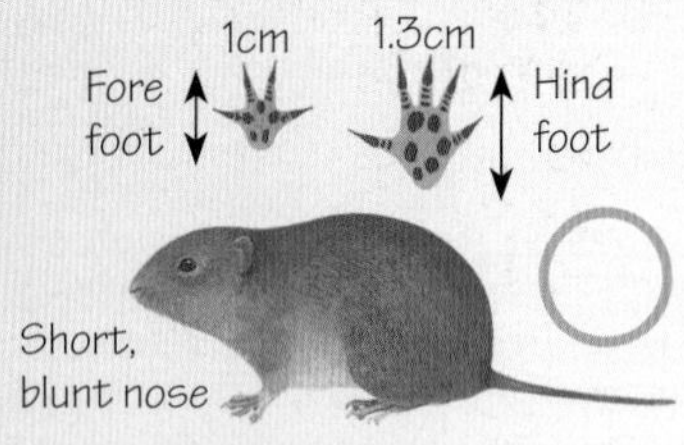

⬅ Norway lemming

Lives in colonies, usually on mountains. Not found in Britain. Migrates in large groups every two or three years. Eats berries, grass and bark. 14cm.

Mice

➡ House mouse

Found on farms and in buildings worldwide. Mostly nocturnal. Has a high squeak. Eats cereals, seeds, vegetables, fruit and stored fruit. 9cm.

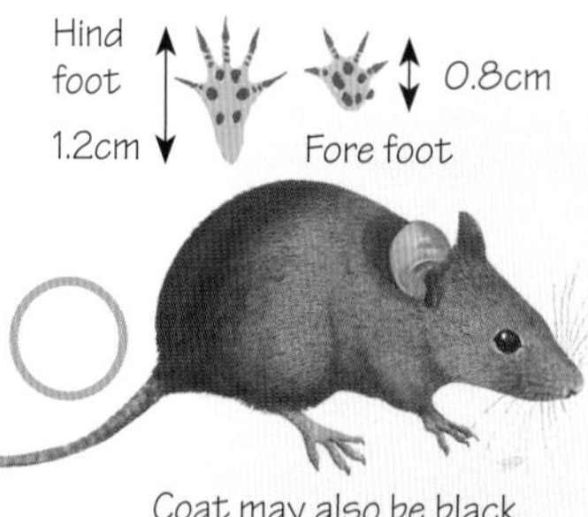

Coat may also be black.

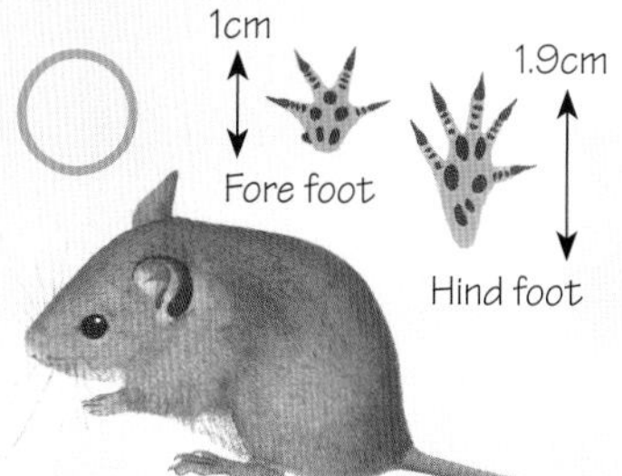

⬅ Wood mouse

Can be seen in gardens, hedgerows and woods. Digs burrows. Climbs and moves fast, making long leaps. Eats berries, buds, nuts, seeds and insects. 9cm.

➡ Yellow-necked field mouse

Similar habits to the wood mouse, but not usually found in the same areas. Lives in woodlands and may enter buildings. 10cm.

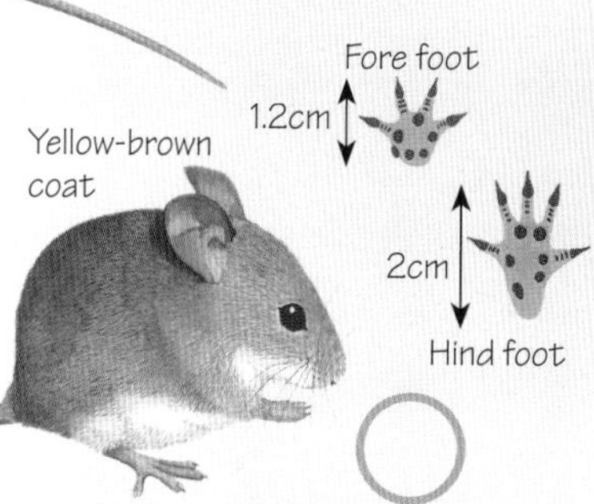

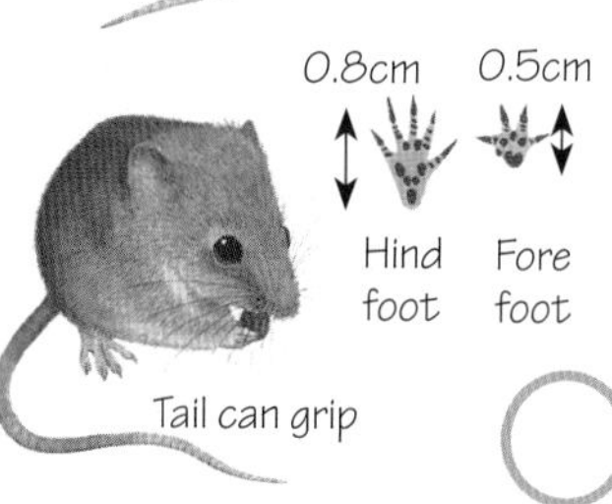

⬅ Harvest mouse

Active by day. Good climber. Builds its breeding nests around corn and grass stalks. Eats soft leaves, insects and seeds. 6cm.

Rabbits and hares

➡ Rabbit

Found on farmland, woodland, sand dunes, and hillsides. Lives in colonies in burrow systems. Active at dusk and dawn. Thumps the ground with its hind feet when alarmed. Eats grasses and plants. 40cm.

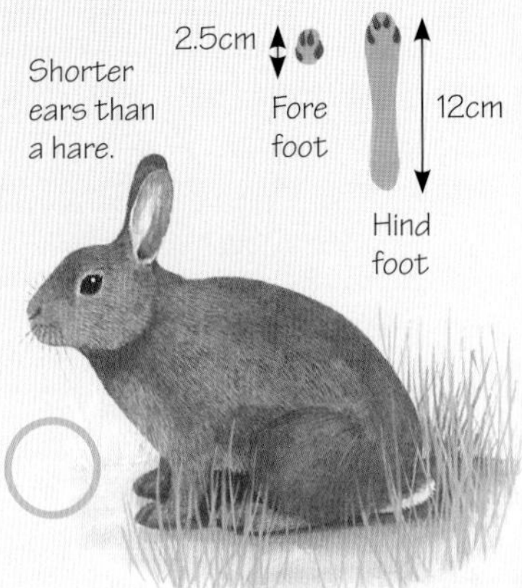

⬅ Blue hare

Active by day and night. Rests above ground. Lives on its own. Found on heather moorland in Britain, Scandinavia and the Alps. Eats heather and grasses. 50cm.

➡ Brown hare

Usually solitary and silent. Rests above ground, in a hollow called a form. Lives in open farmland and woodland. Not found in Norway, Sweden, or most of Ireland. 58cm.

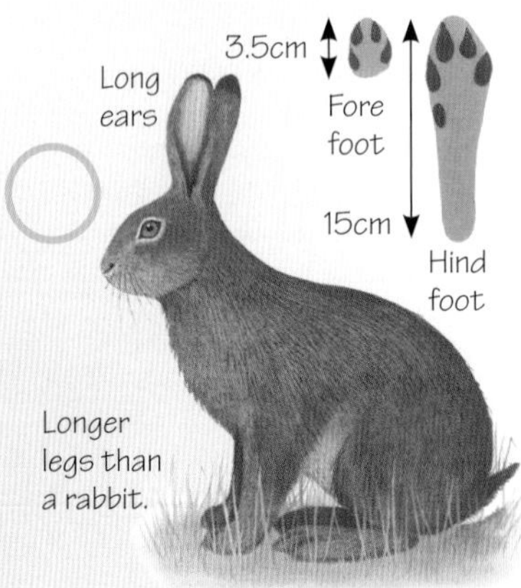

Seals

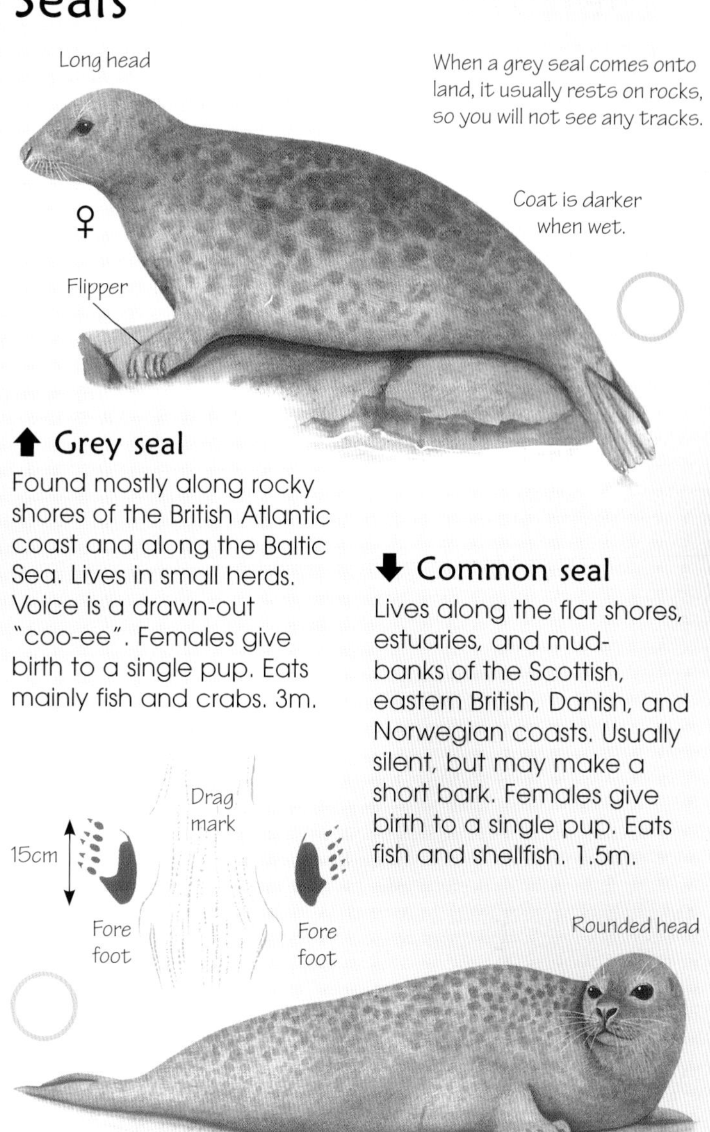
Long head
When a grey seal comes onto land, it usually rests on rocks, so you will not see any tracks.
♀
Coat is darker when wet.
Flipper
Drag mark
15cm
Fore foot
Fore foot
Rounded head

⬆ Grey seal

Found mostly along rocky shores of the British Atlantic coast and along the Baltic Sea. Lives in small herds. Voice is a drawn-out "coo-ee". Females give birth to a single pup. Eats mainly fish and crabs. 3m.

⬇ Common seal

Lives along the flat shores, estuaries, and mud-banks of the Scottish, eastern British, Danish, and Norwegian coasts. Usually silent, but may make a short bark. Females give birth to a single pup. Eats fish and shellfish. 1.5m.

Moles, hedgehogs and shrews

➡ Mole

Lives underground on farms and in woods. Not found in Ireland. Occasionally comes to the surface. Molehills are piles of waste earth from its tunnels. Sensitive to vibrations. Eats grubs, worms and insects. 13cm.

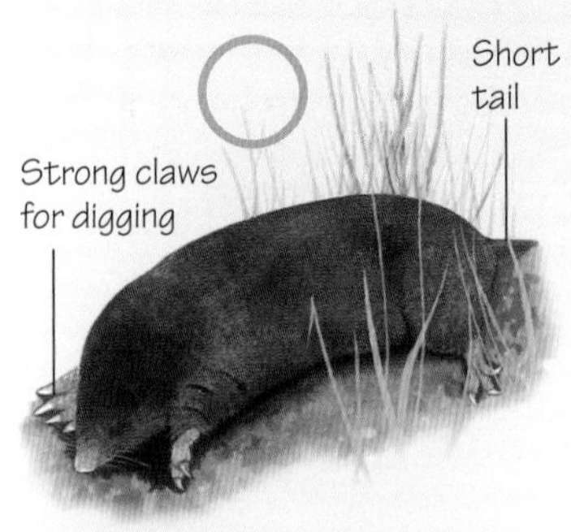

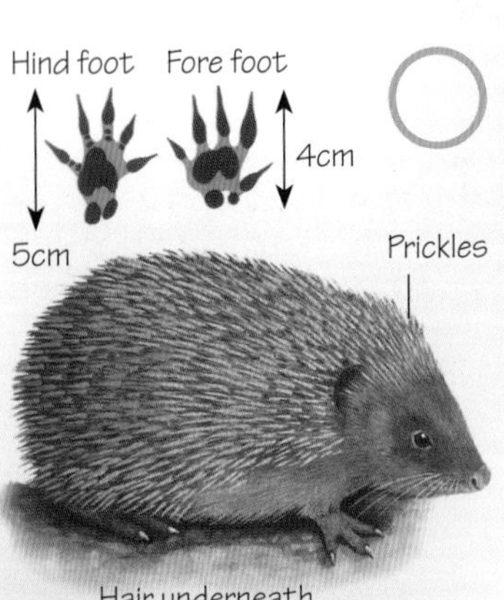

⬅ Hedgehog

Solitary and mainly nocturnal. Lives in ditches, hedgerows, parks and gardens. Spends winter hibernating. Makes snuffling, squealing, and snoring sounds. Rolls into a ball when alarmed. Eats worms and slugs. 25cm.

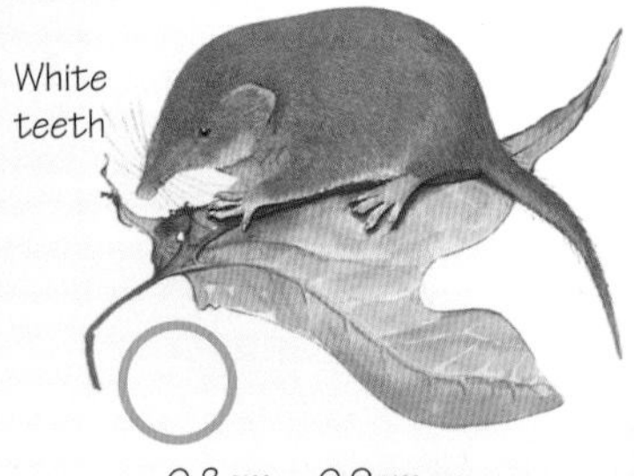

➡ Millet's shrew

Found on the Channel Islands, and the Isles of Scilly. Lives in hedges, gardens, and the edges of woods. Very active and mainly nocturnal. Eats earthworms, insects and spiders. 8cm.

0.8cm 0.9cm

Fore foot Hind foot

➡ Common shrew

Has a high, shrill squeak. Can be aggressive. Climbs and swims. Lives in rough pasture, woods, hedgerows. dunes, and marshes. Not found in Ireland. Eats insects and worms. 7cm.

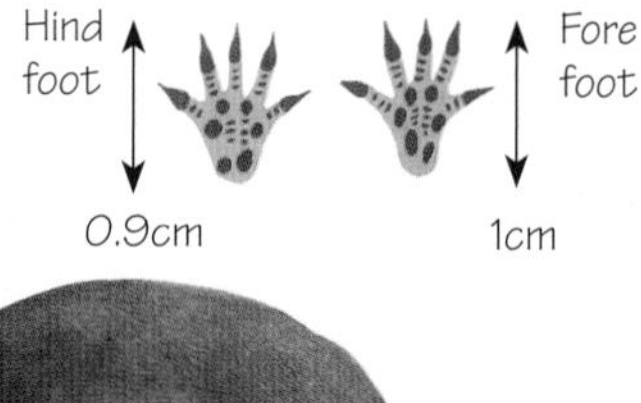

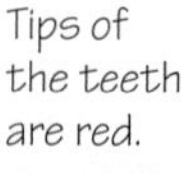

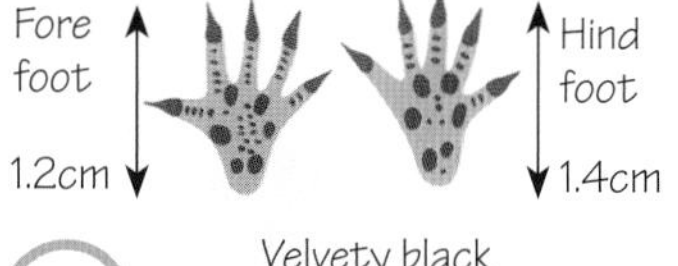

Velvety black fur on top

⬅ Water shrew

Lives close to water; makes tunnels in banks. A good swimmer. Active by day and night. Not found in Ireland. Eats small fish, worms and water insects. 8cm.

➡ Pygmy shrew

Habits and diet are similar to those of the common shrew. Found in woods and on grassland and moorland. 5cm.

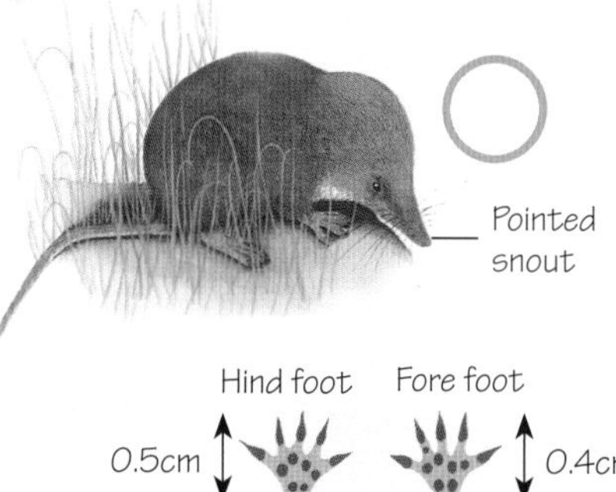

Bats

➡ Pipistrelle bat

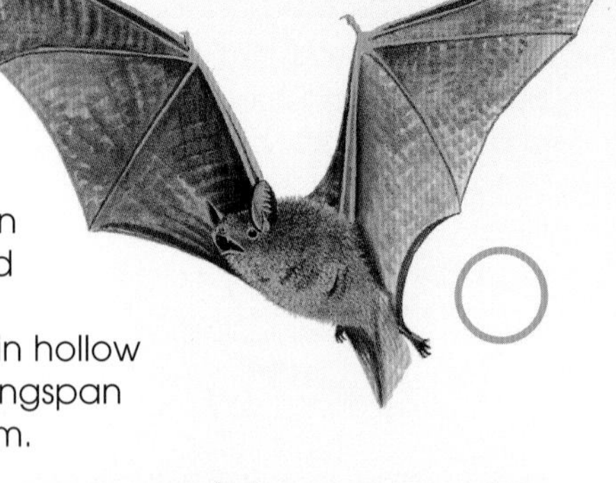

Rapid flight with jerky movements. Rusty to dark brown back, yellow-brown belly. Common in open woods, town parks and squares, and villages. Hibernates in a group in hollow trees and buildings. Wingspan 20cm; body length 5cm.

⬅ Long-eared bat

Yellow-brown back, paler belly. Not very common. Found in woodlands and orchards, and often near buildings. Flies in the late evening. Hibernates in cellars, caves and mine shafts. Ears fold up when at rest. Wingspan 25cm; body length 5cm.

➡ Daubenton's bat / water bat

May fly by day. Reddish-brown back, dirty white belly. Common in some places, usually near water. Large furry feet help to grab prey from the surface of water. Hibernates among rocks, cellars and roof-tops. Wingspan 24cm; body length 4cm.

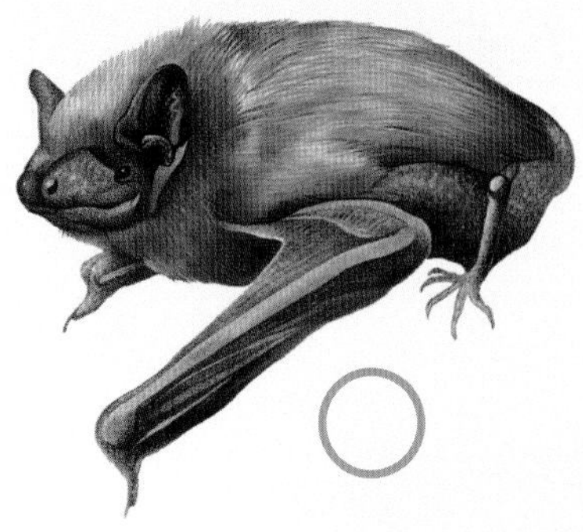

➡ Noctule bat

Seen in parks, woods and gardens. Reddish-brown back, paler belly. Narrow wings and widely spaced ears. Hibernates in trees and buildings. Wingspan 38cm; body length 7cm.

⬅ Whiskered bat

Dark grey-brown back, greyish belly. Long body hair. Often seen flying low near water. Has a fluttering flight. Hibernates in trees, caves and cellars. Males usually solitary. Wingspan 23cm; body length 5cm.

➡ Greater horseshoe bat

Common in mountainous areas. Flies fairly low and may glide. Grey-brown back, pale grey belly. Male is a reddish colour. Broad wings, horseshoe-shaped nose. Hibernates in rocks, caves, quarries and mine shafts. Wingspan 35cm; body length 6cm.

Grebes, cormorants and herons

➡ Great crested grebe

Usually seen on lakes and reservoirs. Sits low on the water and often dives. Builds a floating nest. Eats fish and water insects. 48cm.

Crest expands during courtship display.

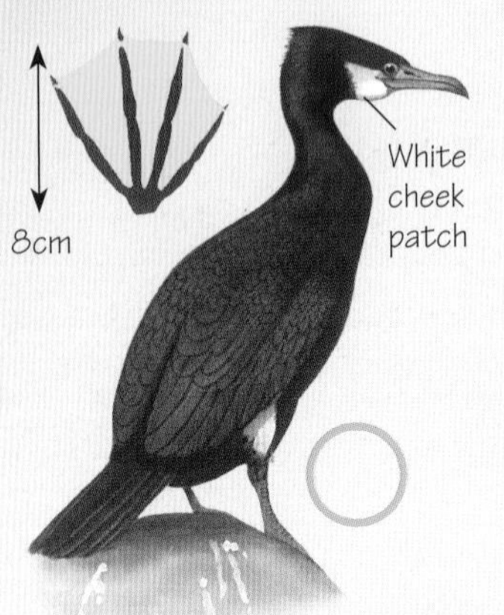

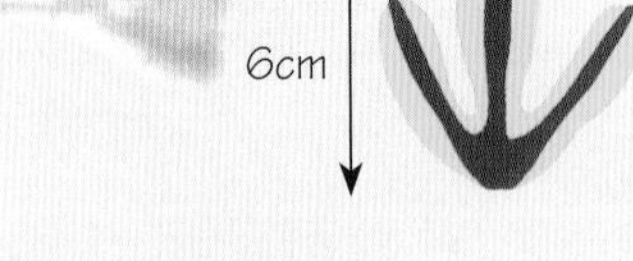

⬅ Cormorant

Found along coasts, usually on cliffs, sometimes on lake islands and rivers. May fly in flocks. Nests in colonies. Eats fish. 92cm.

➡ Grey heron

Found near water, by rivers, marshes, lakes and estuaries. Eats fish, frogs, voles, beetles and moles. Usually feeds by the bank, but may wade out into shallow water. 92cm.

Geese, ducks and pheasant

➡ Greylag goose

European birds may be seen near the coast. Lives in flocks which fly in a V formation. Nests on the ground. Eats grass and sometimes water plants. 82cm.

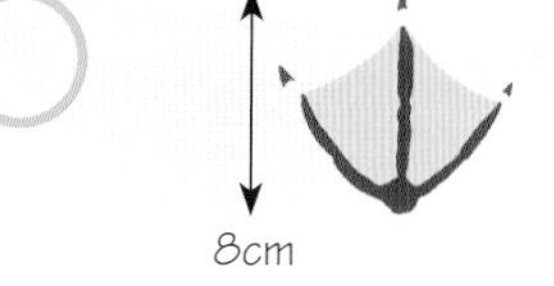

⬅ Mallard

Common on water. Female is mottled brown with a purple wing patch and greenish beak. Eats small water plants and sometimes water insects, snails and worms. 58cm.

➡ Pheasant

Spends most of the time on the ground. Roosts in trees to avoid foxes. Nests on the ground. Female is brown. Eats grain, berries, insects and worms. Male 87cm; female 58cm.

Males can vary in colour and often have a white neck ring.

Moorhens, coots and curlews

➡ Moorhen

Seen swimming with a jerky movement on ponds, marshes and streams. Nests among reeds. Eats water plants, fruit, seeds, insects, worms and slugs. 33cm.

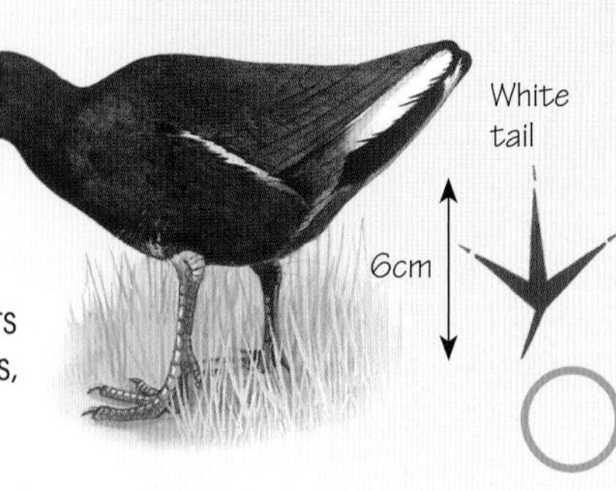

⬅ Coot

Usually found in groups on open water. Bobs its head when swimming. Nests among reeds or water plants. Eats water plants and some insects. 38cm.

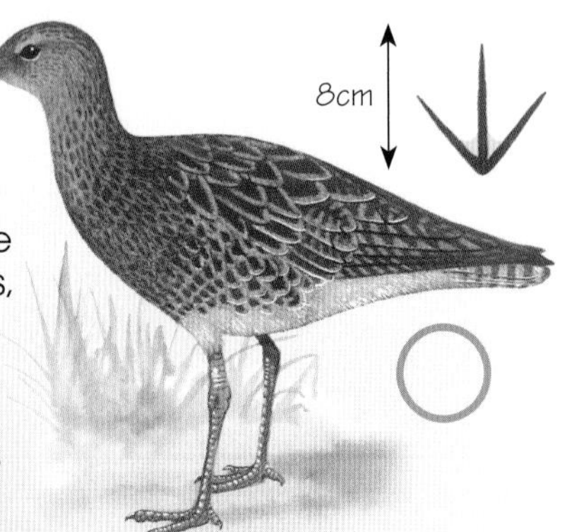

➡ Curlew

Flies fast and high in large flocks. Found on mudflats, estuaries, and coasts. Seen inland in summer. Eats insects, worms, berries, sea worms, crabs and small fish. 55cm.

Gulls, sparrows and rooks

➡ Herring gull

Comfortable living and nesting in areas of human activity. Most common gull on sea coasts; seen in ports and seaside towns. Feeds on shellfish, eggs, chicks, fish and food scraps scrounged from people. 56cm.

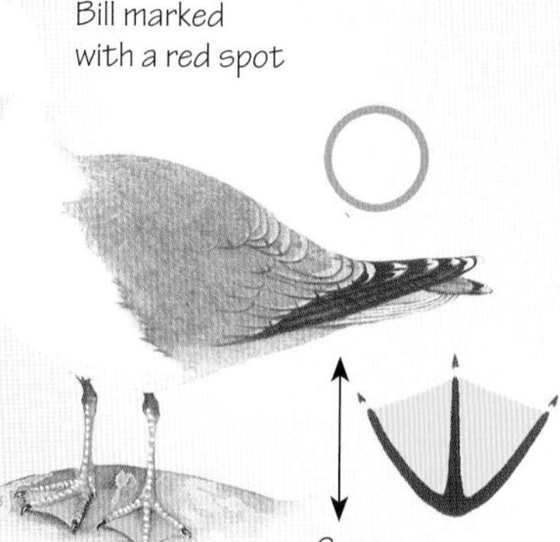

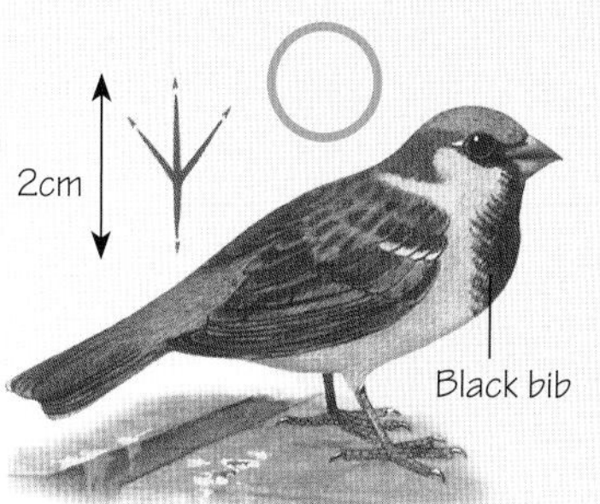

⬅ House sparrow

Lives on farmland, where it eats seeds, and in towns, where it feeds on scraps. May nest in buildings. Hops on the ground. Roosts in flocks. 15cm.

➡ Rook

Often builds nests with twigs stolen from other birds. Stores food for young in a stretchy pouch under bill. Feeds on fields and ploughed ground. Eats insects, grubs and grain. 46cm.

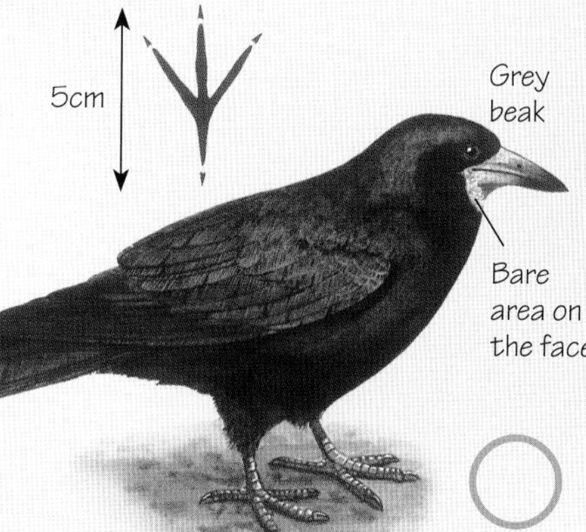

Insects

➡ Bark beetle

Bores into bark and makes a tunnel called a gallery, into which it lays eggs. On hatching, larvae bore side galleries of their own.

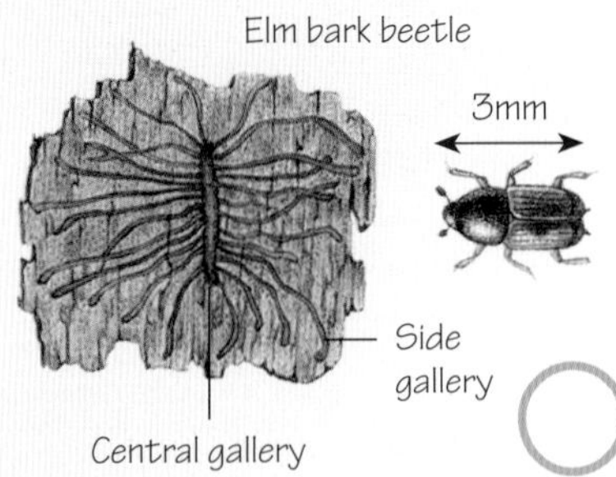

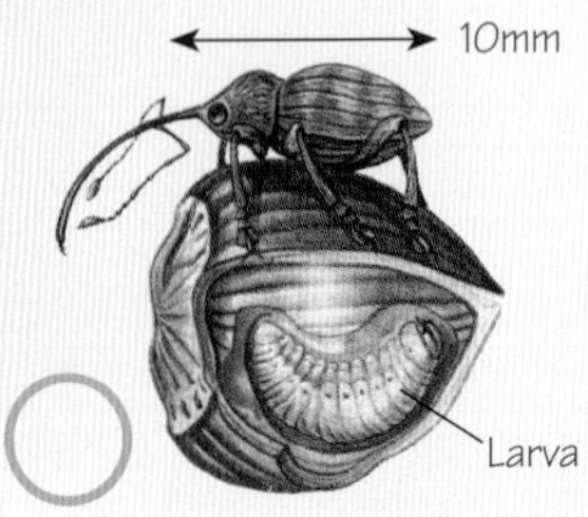

⬅ Nut weevil

Uses its long snout to drill into a hazelnut, then lays an egg inside. After larva hatches, it feeds on its hazelnut until autumn, when the nut falls to the ground. Larva then gnaws its way out.

⬇ Wood ant

Builds massive, cone-shaped nests from twigs and pine needles. Makes entrance holes in the roof, which it can close in cold weather.

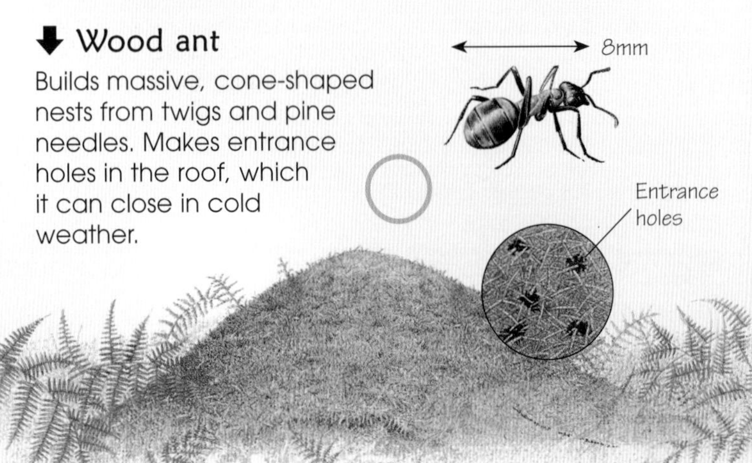

Galls

Galls are little growths produced by a tree in reaction to an irritation caused by a feeding larva. The gall grows around the larva, providing it with protection as it grows into an adult. Some galls house just one larva; others contain several, with each one inside its own chamber.

➡ Oak apple gall wasp

Females lay eggs on oak leaf buds. Red and green galls grow around larvae. Gall grows up to 4cm across and darkens as it ripens. Up to 30 larvae live inside a gall.

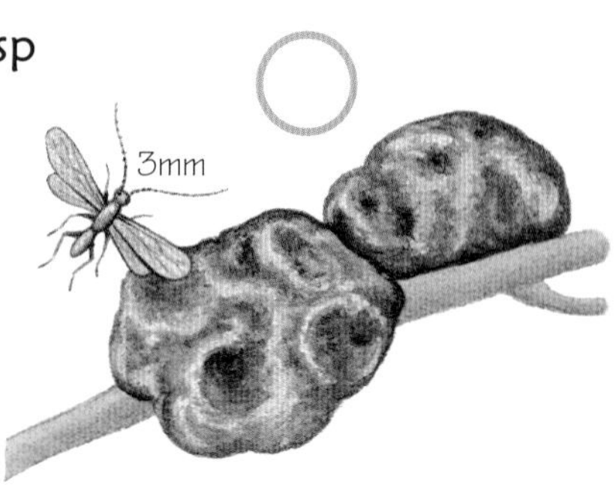

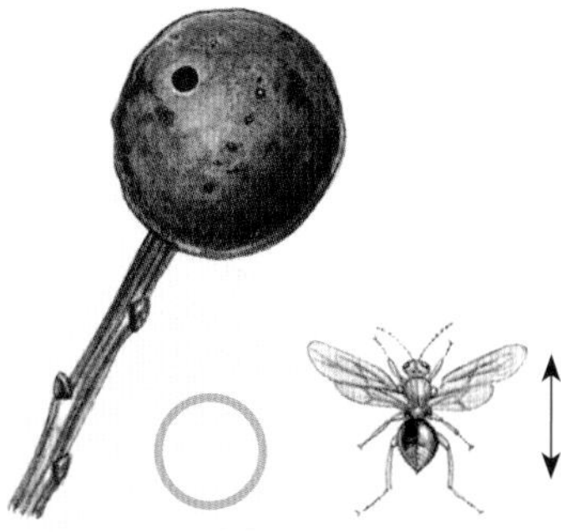

⬅ Oak marble gall-wasp

Larva grows inside a gall on an oak leaf or twig. Galls are green in summer; later ripen to brown, and stay on the branches throughout winter.

➡ Aphid

Cause pineapple-shaped galls to grow on spruce trees. In August, the galls break open, dry up and turn brown.

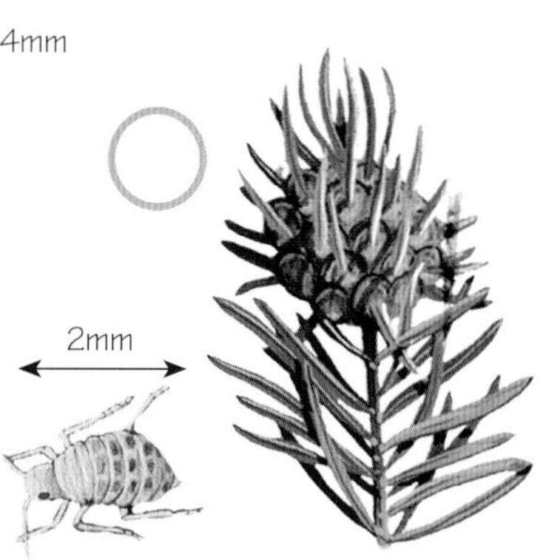

Mammal skulls

As you look for tracks and signs, you could find the bones of a dead animal. You might be able to identify what type of animal it is by looking closely at its skull.

➡ Mole

Insect-eater. Notice the long muzzle and the sharp teeth used for chewing hard insect bodies. The skull may be inside owl pellets.

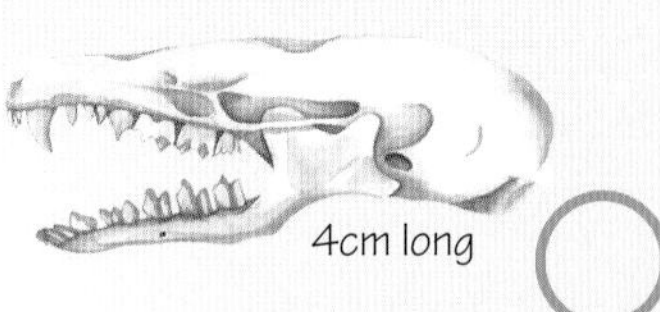

Moles usually have 36 teeth.

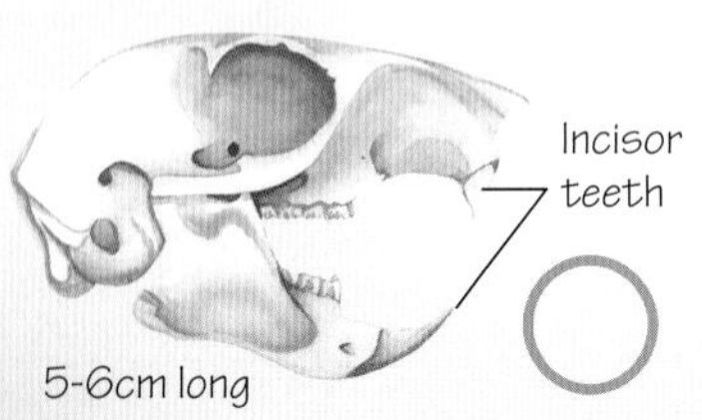

⬅ Grey squirrel

Plant-eater. Has strong front incisor teeth used for gnawing and biting hard plant material.

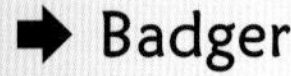

➡ Badger

Meat-eater. Notice the long canine teeth and sharp chewing teeth for tearing and chewing meat. Strong jaw muscles are attached to the ridge on top of the skull.

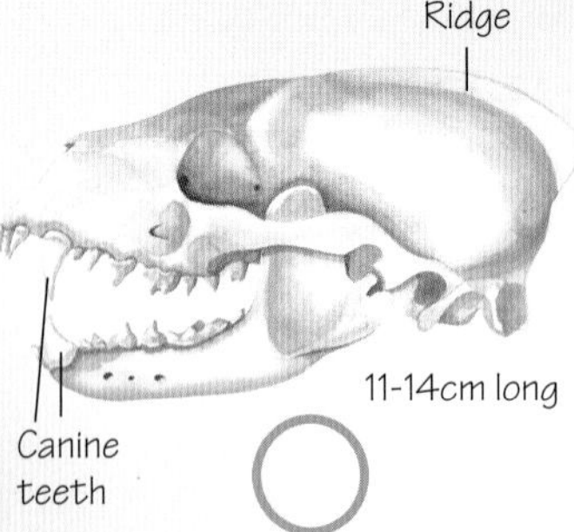

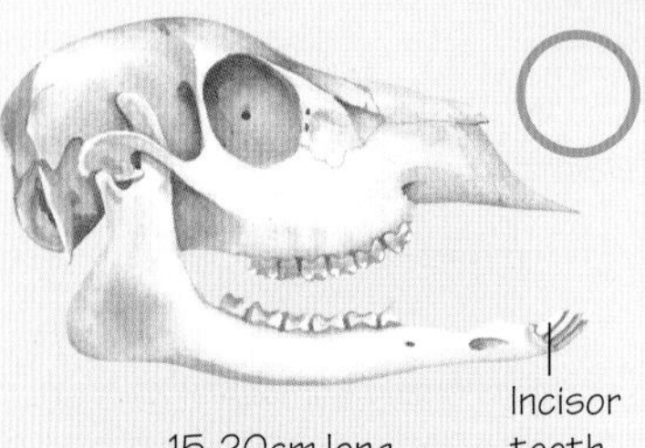

⬅ Roe deer

Plant-eater. Has long incisor teeth on lower jaw used for biting off bits of plants, and flat molar teeth for chewing them.

Bird beaks

If you find a bird skull, the shape of the beak will give you clues to what sort of food the bird ate.

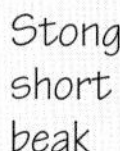

⬆ Hawfinch

Seed-eater. Finches have strong, stubby beaks used for cracking open seeds and nuts.

⬆ Oystercatcher

Feeds on animals that live in mud. Has a long, powerful beak that can probe for and prise open shells.

⬆ Mallard

Tiny plants and animals are caught in grooves on the beak as water is passed through its bill.

⬆ Tawny owl

Meat-eater. All owls use their hooked beaks to tear meat.

⬆ Green woodpecker

Insect-eater. Has a long, sharp, strong beak to probe for and pick up insects, and to chip wood.

⬆ Reed warbler

Insect-eater. Uses its thin, pointed beak to catch flying insects.

Long, stabbing beak

⬆ Grey heron

Fish-eater. Has a long, sharp beak used for stabbing fish and water animals.

Fur and feathers

Fur and hairs

Bits of fur or hair can be found in places where an animal has had to squeeze through or under something, usually wood or barbed wire. Fur on the ground may be a sign of a fight or the remains of an animal's meal.

⬇ Sheep wool

Usually found on barbed wire. Often in matted lumps.

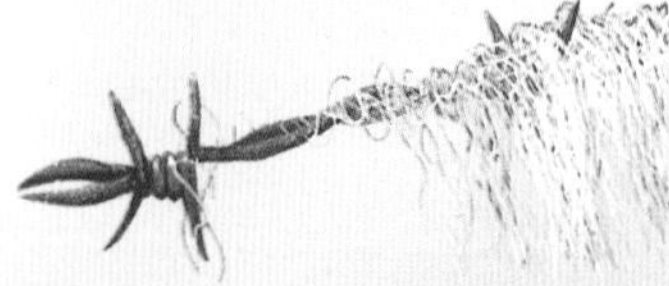

⬆ Badger hairs

Badgers tend to follow regular pathways. Where these pass under fences, look for hairs stuck to the wood.

Feathers

All birds shed old and worn out feathers, so feathers are usually easy to find, even in the busiest cities. Here are some of the types of feathers you might see.

Jay's wing feather

Pheasant's tail feather

Wood pigeon's wing feather

Mallard's wing feather

Pheasant's body feather

Meal remains of predators

Most animals eaten by predators are small, and so are gobbled down whole. If a predator is disturbed while it eats, it may leave remains of its meal. Some deliberately leave a part of their food if it is inedible, or they may store it for later.

↑ Stored food

Shrikes store food, such as insects, mice, lizards and small birds, by pinning it onto branches and barbed wire.

↑ Pierced eggs

Beech martens bite a hole in a bird's egg to reach the food inside.

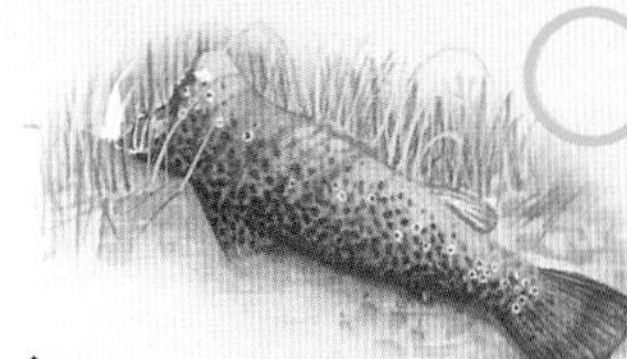

↑ Fish remains

Otters may leave remains of fish near water. They often eat the head first.

↑ Small birds

Many birds of prey eat smaller birds. They usually tear off the head, pluck out the feathers and peck at the flesh.

↑ Smashed snail shells

Song thrushes smash snail shells open on rocks, leaving bits of shell.

Meal remains of plant-eaters

Plant-eating animals, such as birds and rodents, leave signs of feeding in different parts of a plant. Look for marks in leaves, buds, fruit and even in bark.

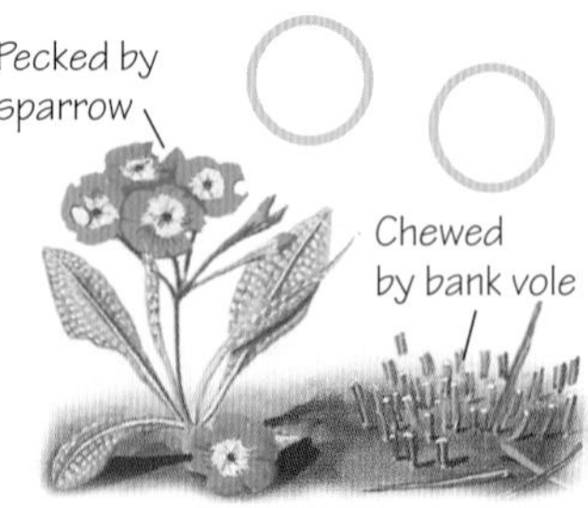

Young plants

Look for young plants in spring. Birds peck at leaves and flowers. Voles chew shoots, leaving tooth marks.

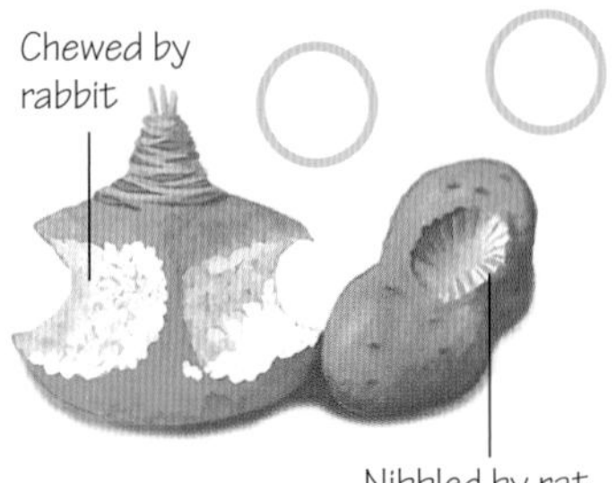

Root crops

Rats and voles gnaw at roots above and below ground. Hares, rabbits, and deer eat the parts above ground.

Bark

Deer, squirrels and voles tear strips of bark off tree trunks, leaving teeth marks. Deer leave the biggest marks.

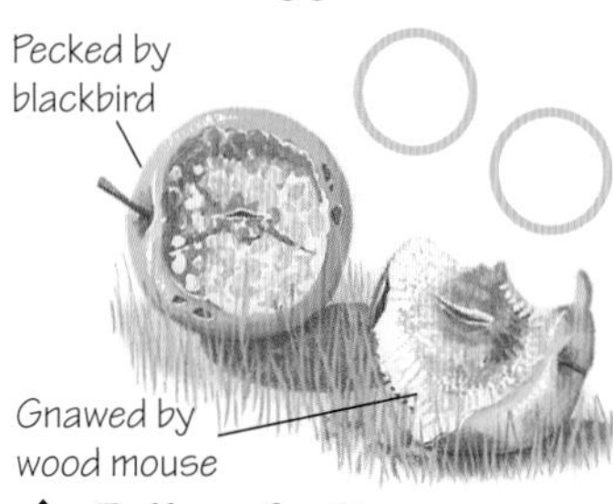

Fallen fruit

Look for teeth marks made by rodents near the edge of the skin. Birds leave peck marks in the flesh.

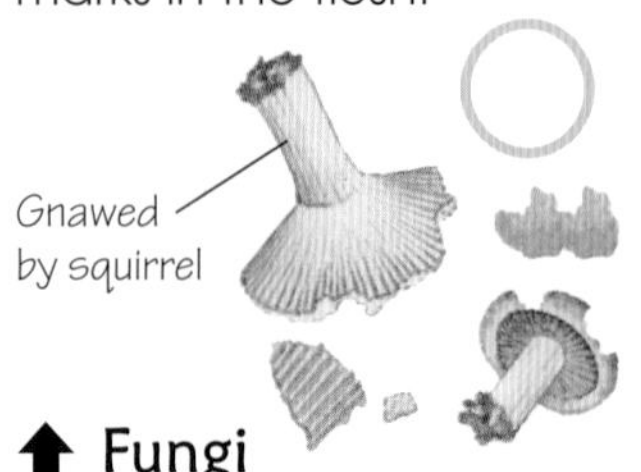

Fungi

Look on the flesh for teeth marks made by rodents. Slugs leave small, round holes on the surface.

Cones eaten by animals

Cones grow on conifer trees. They contain seeds, which are protected by tough scales. To get to the seeds, birds have to lift, tear or pull back the scales. Rodents gnaw at the cones, usually starting by chewing off the larger scales at the top.

Signs of squirrels

Scales are removed, leaving a rough stem.

Pine cone gnawed by squirrel

Signs of crossbills

Scales are either pushed out or split.

Pine cone pecked by crossbill

Signs of wood mice

Scales are gnawed off close to the stem.

Pine cone nibbled by wood mouse

Signs of woodpeckers

Scales are pecked, giving them a messy appearance.

Pine cone pecked by woodpecker

Nuts eaten by animals

In autumn, look under trees and bushes that produce nuts, such as hazel bushes, and chestnut, walnut and beech trees. If you find nut shells, look for teeth or beak marks, and notice the shape and edge of the hole made by the animal. Each type of animal has its own particular way of eating a nut.

⬇ Signs of rats and squirrels

Shells are split and gnawed.

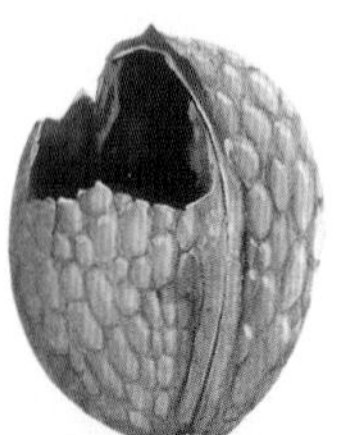

Walnut chewed by rat

Hazelnut split and nibbled by grey squirrel

⬇ Signs of hawfinches

Stones cracked open, usually split in half.

Cherry stones

⬇ Signs of woodpeckers

Nuts usually found wedged into cracks in bark. Shattered with several blows of the bird's beak.

Almond

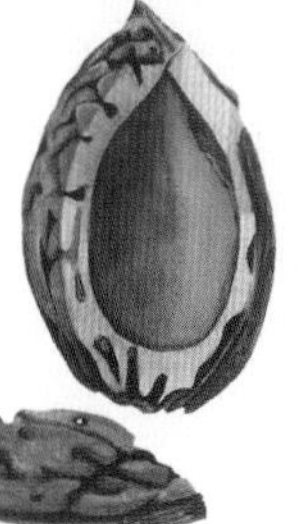

Beechnut

Hazelnut

Signs of rabbits

Long front teeth leave scrape marks.

Sweet chestnut

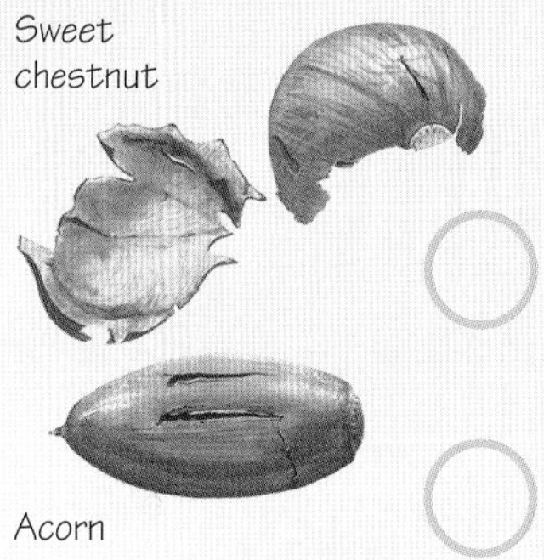

Acorn

Signs of tits

Jagged holes where the birds have chipped away at the shells.

Walnut pecked at by blue tit

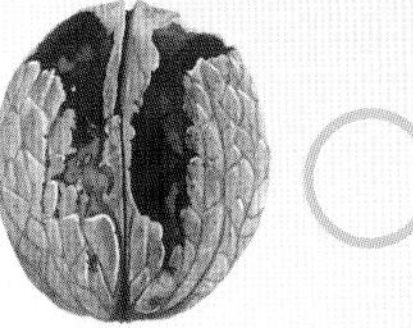

Walnut eaten by great tit

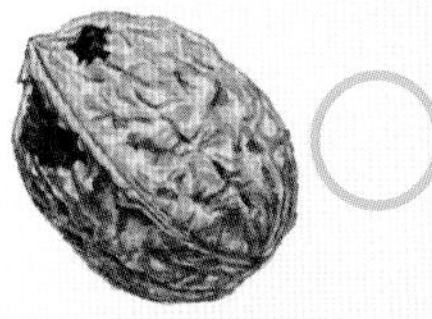

Hazelnut chipped by great tit

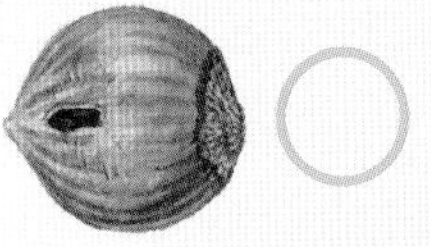

Signs of wood mice

Look for teeth marks around the hole.

Hazelnut

Cherry stone

Beechnut

Acorn

Almond kernel

Signs of voles and dormice

Leave smooth-edged holes, usually in base of nut.

Hazelnut eaten by dormouse

Hazelnut gnawed by bank vole

Mammal droppings

Droppings are mostly made of parts of food that an animal can't digest, such as bones, tough seeds, plant fibres, and hard parts of insects. Meat-eaters leave sausage-shaped droppings with pointed ends; plant-eaters usually leave small, round droppings. Remember never to touch the droppings you might find.

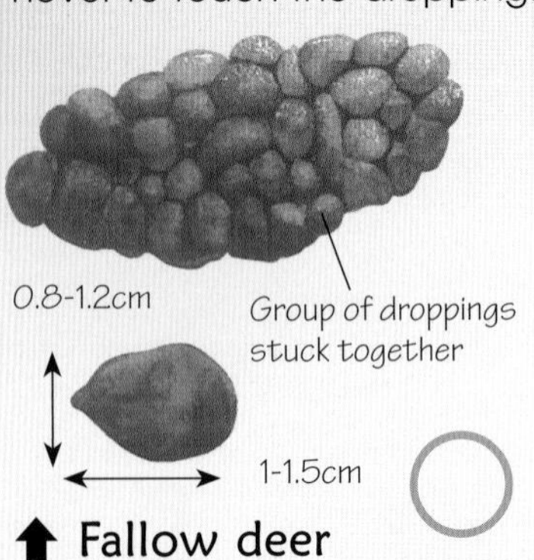

Fallow deer

Made up of plant fibres. In summer, often soft and may stick together.

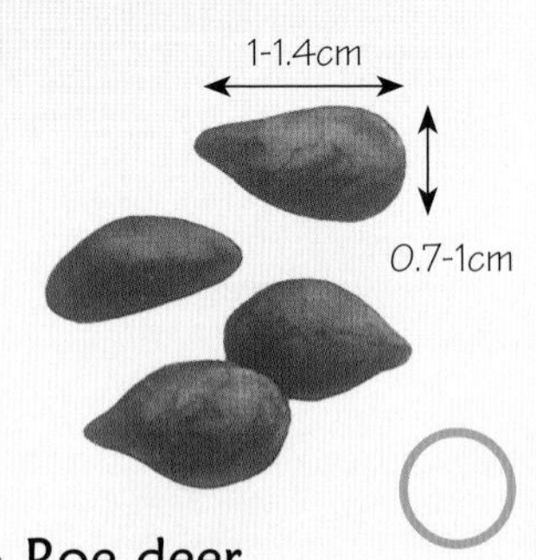

Roe deer

May be found singly or in heaps, sometimes stuck together. Very round in winter.

Rabbit

Used to mark territory. Usually in piles, often near burrows, sometimes on heaps of earth, clumps of grass, ant hills or tree stumps.

Hare

Pale brown in winter, dark brown in summer. Flatter than rabbit droppings. Left where the hare has been feeding or near its home.

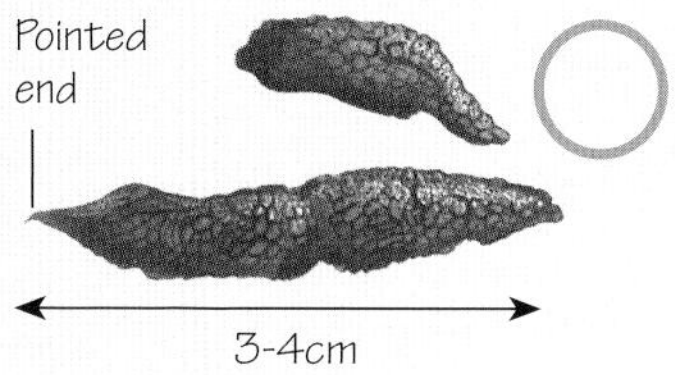

Pointed end
3-4cm

↑ Hedgehog

Often contains hard parts of insects, such as fragments of beetle wings. Can also be made up of fur, bones, feathers and berries.

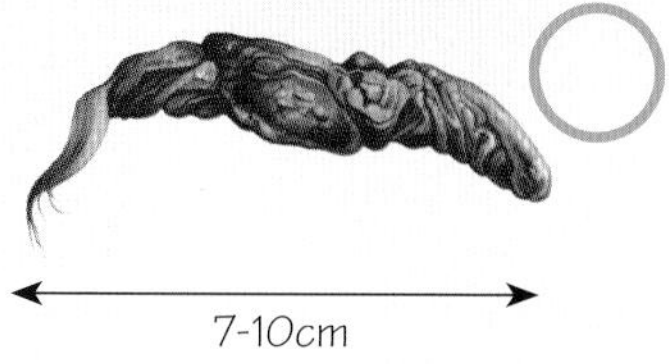

7-10cm

↑ Fox

Left outside the den, or on rocks or clumps of grass. Twisted at one end. Might contain bits of mice, birds, insects, fruit, seeds or berries.

May be oval-shaped or semi-liquid.
10cm

↑ Badger

Left in specially dug holes, about 10cm deep. Unlike cats, badgers don't cover their droppings.

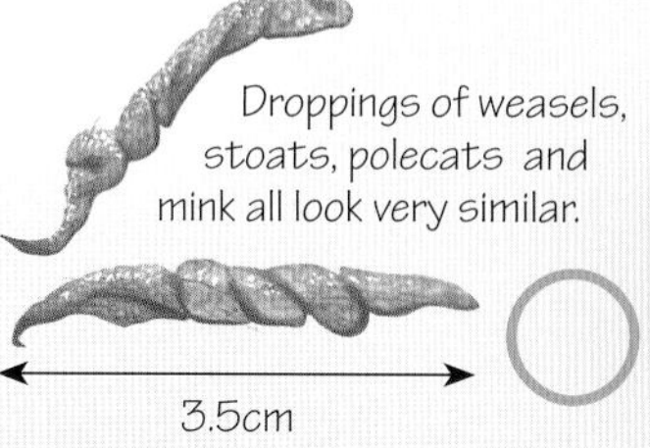

Droppings of weasels, stoats, polecats and mink all look very similar.
3.5cm

↑ Weasel

Narrow and twisted. Often left on rocks or clumps of grass. May contain fur, bones and feathers.

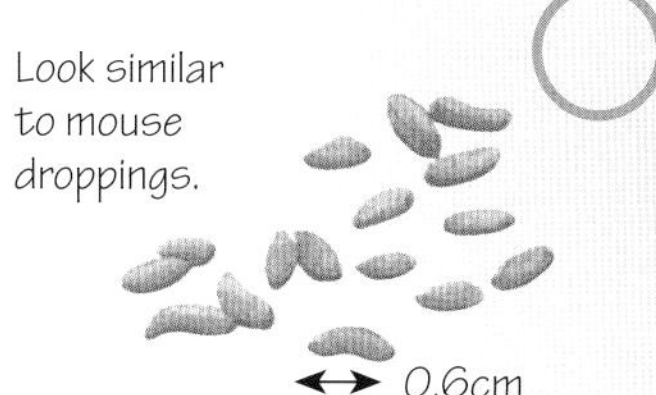

Look similar to mouse droppings.
0.6cm

↑ Field vole

Greenish or brown with a smooth edge. Made up of plant remains.

Droppings of black rat are shorter and thinner than brown rat droppings.

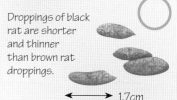

1.7cm

↑ Brown rat

Left singly or in piles. Made up of plant remains. Usually dark brown or black.

Bird pellets and droppings

Pellets

Some birds swallow their food whole, then cough up pellets of the parts they can't digest. These parcels can be made up of fur, bones, feathers or insect parts. Look for them in places where birds feed, roost and nest, but remember never to touch pellets with your bare hands.

Gull pellets

Loose pellets often made up of fish bones and plant remains. Look near water.

3.5-6cm

Crow pellets

Found in fields and other feeding places. Often made up of grit and plant remains.

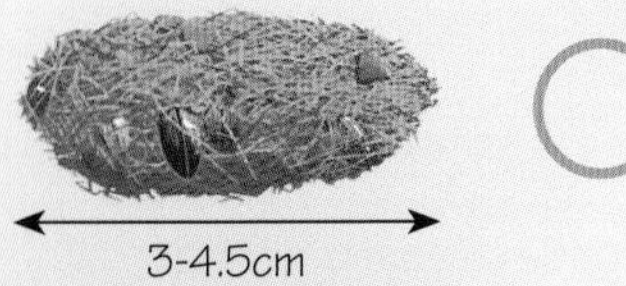

3-4.5cm

Rook pellets

May contain grit and plant remains. Look under nests.

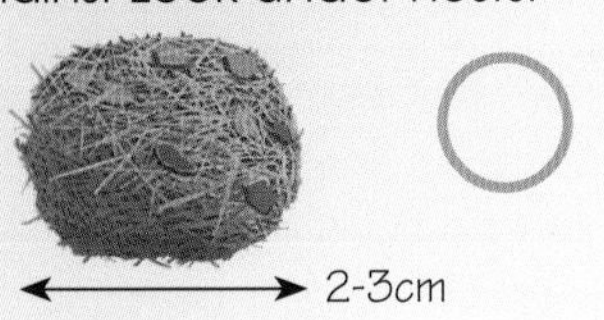

2-3cm

Birds of prey pellets

Can be found under perching spots, such as fences, tree stumps or tall trees. The birds don't swallow bones, so they are not present in their pellets.

Kestrel pellet showing mammal fur

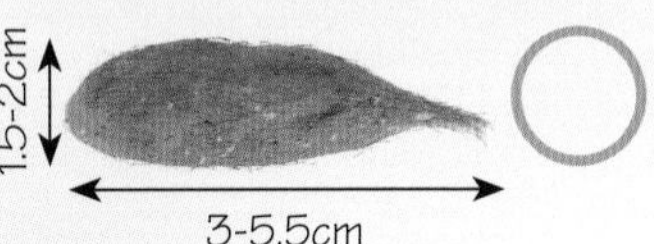

1.5-2cm

3-5.5cm

Sparrowhawk pellet showing bird feathers

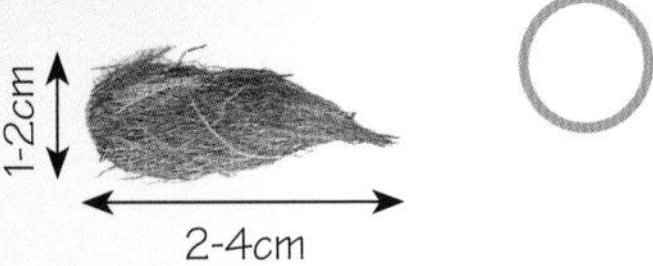

1-2cm

2-4cm

Common buzzard pellet showing mammal fur

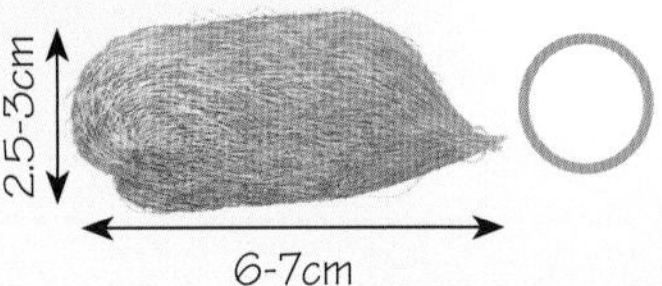

2.5-3cm

6-7cm

⬇ Owl pellets

Can be found under owls' perching or nesting spots such as posts, branches, barns and holes in trees.

Short-eared owl pellet showing bird feathers and bones

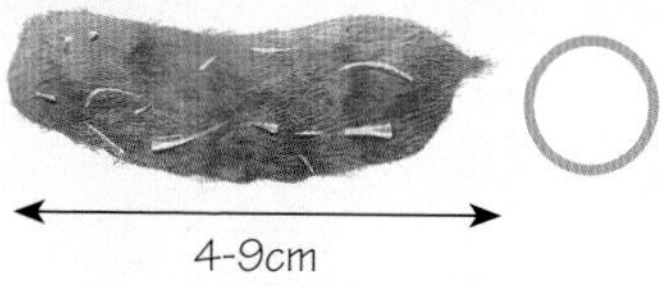

Little owl pellet showing bird bones and feathers, and insect remains

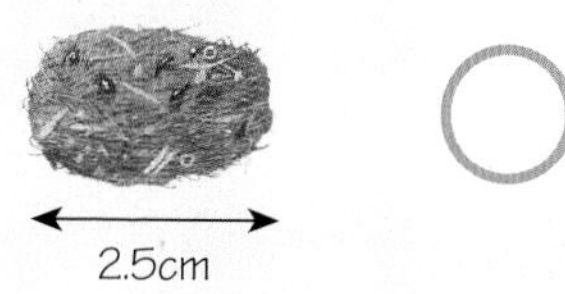

Tawny owl pellet showing bird feathers and bones

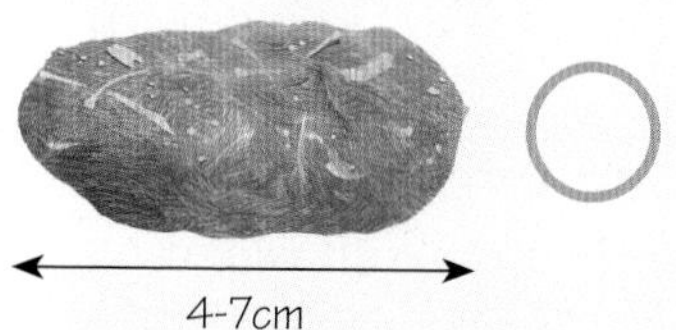

Barn owl pellet showing mammal fur and bones, and bird bones

Droppings

Birds that don't produce pellets get rid of any food they can't digest, such as seeds and berries, in droppings. Droppings come in three types: liquid, semi-firm and round, and firm and long.

⬆ Starling droppings

White liquid. Can be found at feeding and roosting sites, and under nests.

⬆ Pheasant droppings

Colour varies, but usually has white urine at one end. Semi-firm. 2cm long.

⬆ Goose droppings

Green or grey-brown. Made up of plant material. Firm. 5-8cm long.

Mammal homes

Below ground

Outside the entrance to its burrow, an animal might leave signs, such as droppings or tracks. The size of the entrance might also tell you what kind of animal lives inside. Spider webs across a hole tells you that the burrow is not being used.

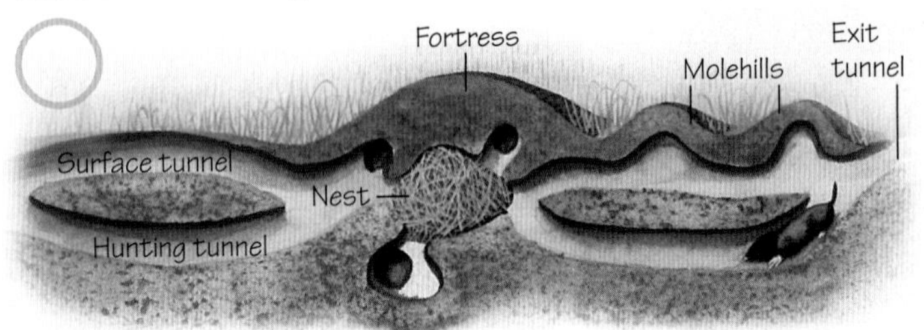

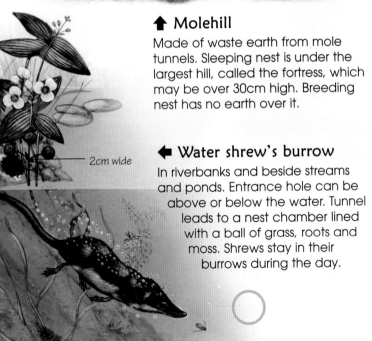

⬆ Molehill

Made of waste earth from mole tunnels. Sleeping nest is under the largest hill, called the fortress, which may be over 30cm high. Breeding nest has no earth over it.

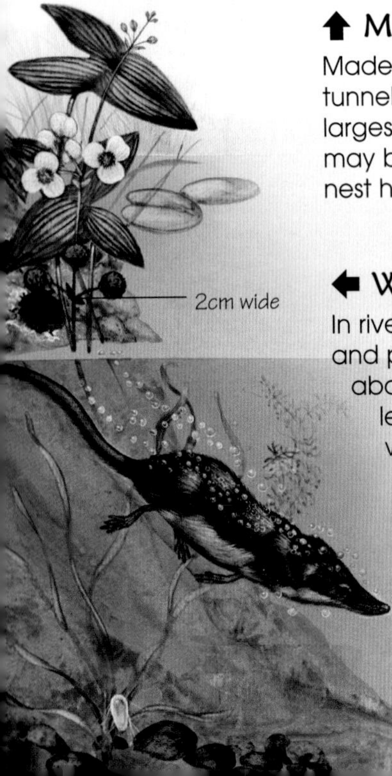

2cm wide

⬅ Water shrew's burrow

In riverbanks and beside streams and ponds. Entrance hole can be above or below the water. Tunnel leads to a nest chamber lined with a ball of grass, roots and moss. Shrews stay in their burrows during the day.

⬆ Rabbit warren

Lots of entrance holes and many tunnels. Rabbits live together in groups. Holes dug from the outside have piles of earth outside them. Can be shallow hollows nearby and droppings near the holes.

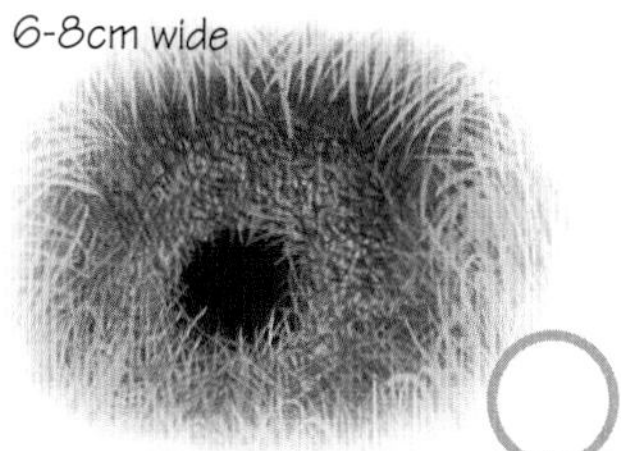

⬅ Water vole's burrow

Entrance hole just above water in the soft banks of rivers and streams. Voles usually eat the plants around the hole.

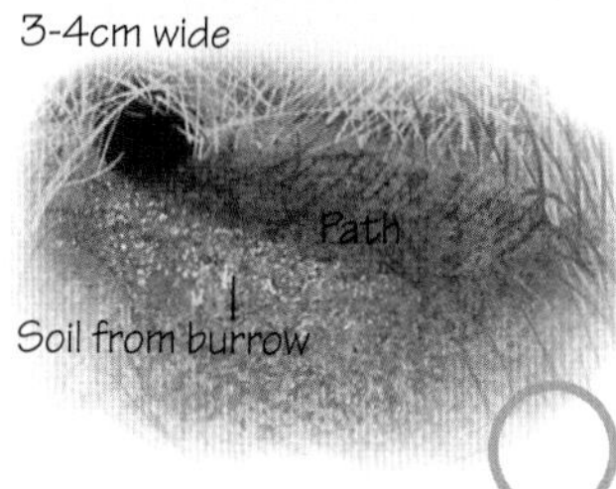

⬅ Wood mouse's burrow

In woods and hedgerows. Look for a well-trodden path and a mound of soil outside the entrance. Wood mice spend their days in their burrows.

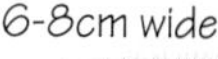

⬅ Rat's burrow

Rats can burrow in almost any soil or compost heaps. Each burrow has two holes – one main entrance and one emergency exit.

Mammal homes

Above ground

Some mammals, such as deer, don't have fixed homes, but sleep on bare patches of ground. Others build nests. You might see the nests in winter, when trees are bare and grasses have died away. It's important never to disturb a nest, otherwise the animal might abandon it.

20-50cm wide

➡ Grey squirrel's drey

Made of twigs, lined with moss, grass, feathers and fur. Looks like a round bird's nest in the fork of a tree or on a side branch.

8-10cm wide

⬅ Harvest mouse's summer nest

Made of grass leaves woven around long grass or reed stems, high off the ground, sometimes in bushes.

➡ Dormouse's winter nest

Made of plant material, mainly strips of bark. Found in undergrowth, often close to the ground, or in bushes and bird nesting boxes.

8cm wide

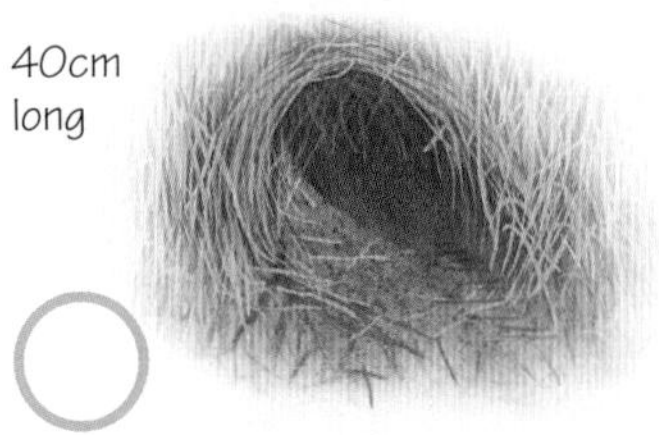

40cm long

⬅ Hare's form

A shallow hollow scraped away in earth, grass or snow, usually protected at the side by a clump of grass or a stone. Hare sits with its hindquarters in the form.

Bird nests

Birds usually build nests in spring and summer in places that are well hidden or difficult to reach – high up in trees, on water, or in a hole. You can look for nests in winter, when there is less cover. Nests must never be touched – even ones that look abandoned could be used again the next year. In many countries, it's illegal to disturb a bird's nest.

Lesser black-backed gull nest

Shallow hole in ground lined with plant material. On cliffs, stony beaches or moors. Eggs camouflaged to blend in with rocky surroundings. May to June.

Woodpecker nest

Bird makes hole in tree and builds nest inside. Hole about 38cm deep. You may see wood chips underneath. April to May.

Swallow nest

High off the ground, stuck to a surface, usually on a wall. Made of mud and bits of plants, lined with feathers. May to June.

Wren nest

Oval nest made of feathers, grass and moss. Well hidden in undergrowth, under leaves, or in holes in trees, banks or walls. April to June.

Bird nests

➡ Long-tailed tit nest

Large, egg-shaped nest well hidden in scrub, hedges, brambles or gorse. Occasionally in trees. Made of moss and lichen woven with hairs and spiders' webs. Lined with feathers. March to April.

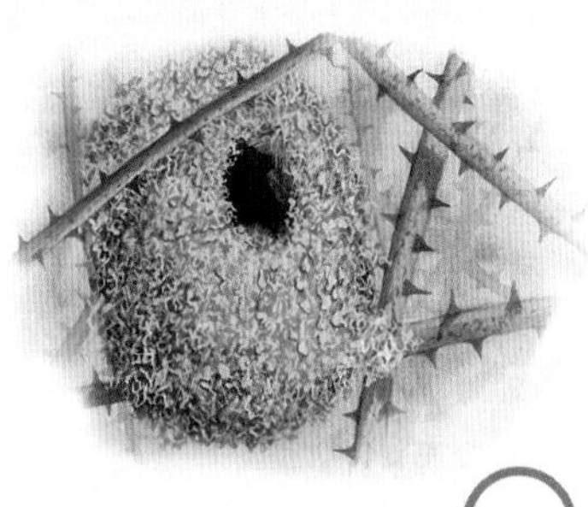

⬅ Rook nest

Rooks breed in colonies called rookeries. Nest built in tree tops, and made of sticks and earth. Lined with bits of plants, wool and hair. Same nest may be used year after year. Can be used for roosting. March to May.

➡ Song thrush nest

Nest is 1.5-3.5m off the ground, hidden in hedges, shrubs or trees, usually close to the trunk. Made of twigs, roots, grass, lichen and dead leaves. Lined with mud. March to June.

⬅ Coot nest

Built among water plants in or near water on lakes, ponds and streams. Made of stems of water plants and dead leaves. March to April.

Spider webs

➡ Garden spider / cross spider

Spins circular web with threads in a spiral pattern. Hangs, head down, in centre of web. Waits motionless for insects to become caught in the sticky threads.

9-14mm

⬅ House spider

Spins untidy, sheet web in corners of houses and sheds. Web has a funnel-shaped part in which the spider hides.

➡ Money spider

Has horizontal sheet web, attached to long grass or twigs by tangled strands. Insects fly into the strands and drop onto the sheet. Spider then runs underneath the sheet, and bites the prey through the web.

2mm

⬅ Wall spider

Makes tube-like web in cracks in walls, then hides underneath. Webs have tripwire threads sticking out. When an insect touches a tripwire thread, the web trembles and the spider dashes out to grab its prey.

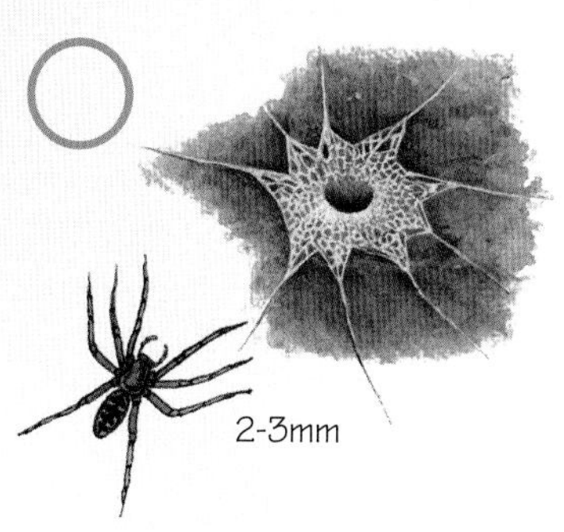

Scorecard

When you start spotting, you'll soon find that some plants or animals are rarer than others. To give you a rough idea of how likely you are to see them, all the plants, insects, birds, mammals, fungi and animal signs in the book are listed here with a score next to each one.

Common species score 5 points; rare ones are worth 25. Species are listed alphabetically. Where this book gives an alternative name, look up the first name that appears.

If you want to, you can use the "Date spotted" boxes to record when you saw each species.

Species

Species	Score	Date spotted	Species	Score	Date spotted
14-spot ladybird	15		Aphid	5	
22-spot ladybird	10		Arctic fox	25	
Alder fly	5		Arctic tern	20	
Alder moth	20		Arrowhead	15	
Aleppo pine	25		Artist's bracket	10	
Alpine marmot	25		Aspen	15	
Alpine rock cress	20		Atlas cedar	10	
Alternate-leaved golden saxifrage	15		Avocet	20	
Amethyst deceiver	10		Badger	15	
Aniseed toadstool	10		Banded demoiselle	15	
Annual seablite	15		Bank vole	10	
Ant beetle	15		Barberry	15	
Ant-lion	25		Bark beetle	15	
Antrodia serialis	15		Barnacle goose	15	

Species	Score	Date spotted	Species	Score	Date spotted
Barn owl	20		Black-headed gull	5	
Bar-tailed godwit	15		Black Italian poplar	10	
Bats-in-the-belfry	15		Black mulberry	25	
Bay bolete	10		Black nightshade	10	
Bean aphid	5		Black rat / ship rat	25	
Bean goose	25		Black redstart	25	
Beautiful demoiselle	15		Black-tailed godwit	20	
Beaver	25		Black tern	25	
Bee beetle	20		Blackthorn	5	
Bee fly	10		Black woodpecker	25	
Beech marten	25		Bladder campion	5	
Beef steak fungus	15		Blister beetle	25	
Bell heather	15		Blood-red geranium	10	
Bewick's swan	20		Bloody-nosed beetle	15	
Bilberry	10		Bluebell	10	
Birch sawfly	10		Blue hare	15	
Bird cherry	10		Blue-headed wagtail	25	
Bird's foot trefoil	10		Blue horntail	15	
Bistort	10		Blue stain fungus	15	
Black and red froghopper	10		Blue-tailed damselfly	5	
Black and yellow cranefly	10		Blue tit	5	
Black ant	5		Blusher	10	
Blackberry	5		Bolbitius vitellinus	15	
Blackbird	5		Bombardier beetle	15	
Blackcap	15		Brambling	20	
Black grouse	20		Brent goose	20	

Species	Score	Date spotted	Species	Score	Date spotted
Brick-red cap	15		Chickweed	5	
Brimstone butterfly	10		Chiffchaff	10	
Broad-bodied chaser	10		Chile pine	10	
Broad-leaved pondweed	10		Chough	25	
Brooklime	10		Cinnabar moth	10	
Brown bear	25		Click beetle	15	
Brown birch bolete	15		Clifden nonpareil	25	
Brown hare	5		Clitocybe vibecina	10	
Brown lacewing	10		Cloudy funnel cap	15	
Brown roll-rim	10		Cluster fungus	15	
Buckshorn plantain	5		Coal tit	10	
Bugle	10		Coast redwood	20	
Bullfinch	15		Cockchafer	5	
Buzzard	15		Collared dove	5	
Caddis fly	10		Collared earthstar	20	
Canada goose	5		Colorado beetle	25	
Canadian pondweed	10		Common alder	5	
Candle snuff	15		Common ash	5	
Capercaillie	25		Common beech	5	
Cardinal beetle	10		Common bird's nest	20	
Carpenter ant	25		Common blue butterfly	5	
Carrion crow	5		Common centaury	10	
Cedar of Lebanon	10		Common cockroach	5	
Chaffinch	5		Common dog violet	10	
Chamois	25		Common dormouse	20	
Chanterelle	15		Common earthball	10	

Species	Score	Date spotted	Species	Score	Date spotted
Common earwig	5		Corn bunting	15	
Common forget-me-not	10		Corncrake	25	
Common fumitory	10		Cornflower	25	
Common gnat	5		Corn spurrey	10	
Common gull	15		Corsican pine	10	
Common ink cap	10		Cow parsley	5	
Common lime	10		Cowslip	10	
Common meadow rue	15		Coypu	20	
Common monkshood	20		Crab apple	10	
Common olive	25		Crack willow	10	
Common orache	5		Creeping buttercup	5	
Common pear	20		Creeping cinquefoil	5	
Common puffball	15		Creeping Jenny	15	
Common rat	5		Crested lark	25	
Common redpoll	25		Crested tit	20	
Common St. John's wort	10		Crimson wax cap	10	
Common sandpiper	15		Crossbill	20	
Common seal	10		Cuckoo	10	
Common shrew	10		Curlew	15	
Common speedwell	10		Cypress spurge	15	
Common tern	15		Daisy	5	
Common walnut	15		Dandelion	5	
Coot	10		Dark green fritillary butterfly	10	
Cork oak	25		Daubenton's bat / water bat	15	
Corky-fruited water dropwort	25		Dawn redwood	25	
Cormorant	10		Dead man's finger	15	

Species	Score	Date spotted
Death cap	15	
Death's-head hawk moth	25	
Death watch beetle	25	
Deodar cedar	5	
Deptford pink	25	
Destroying angel	20	
Devil's bit scabious	10	
Devil's coach horse	10	
Dipper	15	
Dog rose	15	
Dog's mercury	10	
Domestic cat	5	
Domestic cow	5	
Domestic dog	5	
Domestic goat	10	
Domestic pig	5	
Domestic sheep	5	
Dor beetle	10	
Douglas fir	10	
Downy emerald dragonfly	20	
Drone fly	10	
Dryad's saddle	10	
Dung fly	5	
Dung roundhead	10	
Dunlin	10	
Dunnock	5	

Species	Score	Date spotted
Dusky cockroach	15	
Eared leafhopper	20	
Early purple orchid	15	
Edible dormouse	20	
Eider	15	
Elephant hawk moth	15	
Elk / moose	25	
Emperor dragonfly	10	
Emperor moth	15	
English elm	15	
English oak	5	
Entoloma sinuatum	15	
European fan palm	25	
European hamster	25	
European larch	10	
European mink	15	
European silver fir	15	
Exmoor pony	10	
Eyed hawk moth	10	
Eyed ladybird	20	
Fairy ring champignon	10	
Fallow deer	10	
False acacia	10	
False champignon	10	
False chanterelle	10	
False death cap	15	

Species	Score	Date spotted	Species	Score	Date spotted
False morel	20		German cockroach	10	
Fever fly	5		German wasp	5	
Field blewit	15		Ghost moth	10	
Field cricket	25		Giant cranefly	10	
Fieldfare	10		Giant funnel	20	
Field maple	15		Giant lacewing	15	
Field mouse-ear chickweed	15		Giant polypore	15	
Field mushroom	10		Giant puffball	20	
Field scabious	10		Giant wood wasp	20	
Firecrest	25		Glistening ink cap	10	
Flea	5		Glow-worm	25	
Fleecy milk cap	15		Goat moth	20	
Floating water plantain	15		Goat willow	5	
Fly agaric	15		Goldcrest	10	
Forest bug	10		Golden eagle	25	
Forester moth	20		Goldeneye	15	
Foxglove	10		Golden oriole	15	
Fritillary	20		Golden plover	25	
Frogbit	15		Golden-ringed dragonfly	10	
Fulmar	10		Golden rod	10	
Furze	10		Golden samphire	10	
Gannet	15		Goldfinch	10	
Garden dormouse	25		Good King Henry	5	
Garden tiger moth	10		Goosander	20	
Garden warbler	15		Goosegrass	5	
Gatekeeper butterfly	10		Goshawk	25	

Species	Score	Date spotted	Species	Score	Date spotted
Grand fir	15		Grey flesh fly	5	
Great black-backed gull	15		Grey heron	10	
Great crested grebe	10		Greylag goose	10	
Great diving beetle	10		Grey partridge	10	
Greater bindweed	10		Grey seal	15	
Greater plantain	5		Grey squirrel	5	
Greater stitchwort	5		Grey wagtail	15	
Great green bush cricket	15		Guillemot	15	
Great grey shrike	25		Harvest mouse	20	
Great horseshoe bat	20		Hawthorn	5	
Great silver water beetle	20		Heath assassin bug	10	
Great spotted woodpecker	10		Heather	5	
Great tit	5		Hedgehog	10	
Greek fir	20		Hedge parsley	15	
Greenbottle fly	5		Hemp agrimony	10	
Green-cracked brittlegill	15		Herald moth	10	
Greenfinch	20		Herb Bennet	10	
Green lacewing	10		Herb Robert	10	
Green leafhopper	10		Herring gull	5	
Greenshank	15		Hoary plantain	5	
Green shieldbug	10		Hobby	20	
Green tiger beetle	10		Hogweed	10	
Green tortoise beetle	10		Holly	5	
Green-veined white butterfly	5		Holm oak	10	
Green woodpecker	10		Honey buzzard	25	
Grey alder	15		Honey fungus	10	

Species	Score	Date spotted	Species	Score	Date spotted
Hooded crow	10		Jay	10	
Hoopoe	25		Jelly ear	5	
Hornbeam	10		Juniper	15	
Horned dung beetle	15		Kestrel	10	
Horned treehopper	15		King Alfred's cakes	10	
Hornet	20		Kingfisher	15	
Horn of plenty	15		Knapweed	10	
Horse chestnut	5		Knot	15	
Horse fly	15		Knotgrass	5	
Horse mushroom	10		Laburnum	5	
House cricket	15		Lappet moth	15	
Houseleek	15		Lapwing	10	
House martin	10		Large green ground beetle	20	
House mouse	5		Large marsh grasshopper	20	
House sparrow	5		Larkspur	15	
Hover fly	10		Lawson cypress	5	
Hummingbird hawk moth	15		Leaf-cutter bee	15	
Ibex / wild goat	25		Lesser black-backed gull	10	
Ichneumon wasp	10		Lesser celandine	5	
Inocybe erubescens	15		Lesser duckweed	5	
Italian cypress	20		Lesser earwig	15	
Ivy-leaved toadflax	5		Lesser glow-worm	25	
Jack-by-the-hedge	5		Lesser periwinkle	15	
Jackdaw	10		Lesser redpoll	20	
Japanese larch	15		Lesser spotted woodpecker	20	
Japanese red cedar	15		Lesser water boatman	5	

Species	Score	Date spotted	Species	Score	Date spotted
Leyland cypress	5		Maritime pine	15	
Lilac oysterling	10		Marram grass	10	
Lilac thickfoot	15		Marsh tit	15	
Lily-of-the-valley	15		Mayfly	10	
Lime hawk moth	10		Meadow brown butterfly	5	
Linnet	10		Meadow clary	20	
Little fan	15		Meadow pipit	10	
Little grebe	15		Meadow saxifrage	20	
Little owl	15		Meadowsweet	10	
Little ringed plover	20		Meadow wax cap	15	
Little tern	20		Merveille-du-jour moth	15	
Lobster moth	15		Millet's shrew	25	
Lombardy poplar	10		Mistle thrush	10	
London plane	5		Mole	10	
Long-eared bat	15		Mole cricket	25	
Long-eared owl	25		Monterey cypress	15	
Long-headed poppy	5		Monterey pine	15	
Long-tailed tit	10		Moorhen	5	
Lynx	25		Morel	25	
Magnolia	15		Mosaic puffball	15	
Magpie	5		Mother Shipton moth	10	
Magpie ink cap	15		Mouflon / wild sheep	25	
Maidenhair tree	20		Muntjac	20	
Mallard	5		Musk beetle	15	
Manna ash	20		Muskrat	25	
Mare's tail	15		Mute swan	5	

Species	Score	Date spotted	Species	Score	Date spotted
Nettle	10		Parasol	10	
New Forest cicada	25		Pasque flower	25	
Nightingale	15		Peach blossom moth	10	
Nightjar	20		Peacock butterfly	10	
Noble fir	10		Pellitory-of-the-wall	15	
Noctule bat	10		Penny bun	15	
Nootka cypress	20		Peregrine	20	
Norway lemming	25		Peziza badia	20	
Norway maple	5		Pheasant	5	
Norway spruce	5		Pheasant's eye	25	
Nuthatch	15		Pied flycatcher	20	
Nut weevil	5		Pied shieldbug	10	
Oak apple gall-wasp	5		Pied wagtail	10	
Oak eggar moth	15		Pigweed	10	
Oak marble gall-wasp	5		Pine marten	10	
Ochre brittlegill	15		Pink-footed goose	20	
Oil beetle	15		Pintail	20	
Old man of the woods	15		Pipistrelle bat	10	
Orange peel fungus	15		Pluteus cervinus	15	
Osprey	20		Pochard	15	
Otter	20		Polecat	20	
Ox-eye daisy	10		Policeman's helmet	15	
Oystercatcher	15		Pond skater	5	
Oyster mushroom	15		Poplar hawk moth	10	
Painted lady butterfly	15		Poppy	10	
Panther cap	5		Potter wasp	15	

Species	Score	Date spotted	Species	Score	Date spotted
Praying mantis	25		Red fox	10	
Primrose	10		Red grouse	15	
Privet hawk moth	15		Red helleborine	25	
Psathyrella multipedata	20		Red kite	20	
Ptarmigan	20		Red-legged partridge	10	
Puffin	20		Red milk cap	10	
Purple brittlegill	10		Red oak	10	
Purslane	15		Redshank	10	
Puss moth	10		Red squirrel	15	
Pygmy owl	25		Redstart	15	
Pygmy shrew	15		Red-tailed bumblebee	5	
Rabbit	5		Red underwing moth	15	
Ragged Robin	15		Redwing	10	
Ramsons	15		Reed bunting	15	
Rape	5		Reed warbler	15	
Raven	15		Reindeer	15	
Razorbill	15		Ribwort plantain	5	
Razor strop	5		Ringed plover	15	
Red admiral butterfly	10		Ringlet butterfly	10	
Red and black burying beetle	10		Ring ouzel	20	
Red ant	10		Robber fly	15	
Red-backed shrike	25		Robin	5	
Red-breasted merganser	20		Rock dove	25	
Red campion	10		Roe deer	15	
Red-cracked bolete	10		Rook	10	
Red deer	15		Rose aphid	5	

Species	Score	Date spotted	Species	Score	Date spotted
Rosebay willowherb	5		Sea holly	15	
Rose chafer	15		Sea kale	20	
Rove beetle	5		Sea lavender	10	
Rowan	5		Sea mayweed	10	
Ruby-tailed wasp	10		Sea milkwort	10	
Ruddy darter	10		Sea purslane	10	
Ruff	20		Sea sandwort	10	
Saffron milk cap	15		Sea wormwood	10	
Saint George's mushroom	15		Sedge warbler	15	
Sanderling	20		Sessile oak	10	
Sand martin	15		Seven-spot ladybird	5	
Sand spurrey	10		Shag	15	
Sand wasp	10		Shaggy ink cap	5	
Saucer bug	10		Shaggy parasol	10	
Scaly tooth	15		Shaggy pholiota	15	
Scaly wood mushroom	15		Sheep's sorrel	15	
Scarlet elf cup	15		Shelduck	15	
Scarlet pimpernel	10		Shepherd's purse	5	
Scarlet-tipped flower beetle	10		Shore pine	10	
Scops owl	25		Short-eared owl	20	
Scorpion fly	10		Short-tailed vole / field vole	5	
Scots pine	5		Shoveler	15	
Sea arrowgrass	10		Sickener	10	
Sea aster	10		Sika deer	15	
Sea bindweed	4		Silver birch	5	
Sea campion	5		Silver lime	20	

Species	Score	Date spotted	Species	Score	Date spotted
Silverweed	10		Starling	5	
Silver Y moth	5		Starry saxifrage	15	
Siskin	15		Stereum hirsutum	5	
Sitka spruce	10		Stick insect	25	
Six-spot burnet moth	10		Stinkhorn	15	
Skylark	10		Stoat	15	
Slimy spike cap	15		Stock dove	15	
Small heath butterfly	5		Stonechat	15	
Small tortoiseshell butterfly	5		Stonecrop	10	
Small white butterfly	5		Stonefly	10	
Snake fly	15		Stone pine	25	
Snapdragon	5		Stonewort	20	
Snipe	15		Suillus granulatus	15	
Snowdrop	15		Sulphur tuft	10	
Snowy ink cap	15		Summer pheasant's eye	25	
Soapwort	20		Summer truffle	25	
Song thrush	10		Swallow	10	
Sorrel	5		Swallow-tailed moth	10	
Southern beech	20		Swamp cypress	25	
Southern cicada	25		Sweet chestnut	10	
Spanish fir	20		Sweet William	20	
Sparrowhawk	10		Swift	10	
Speckled bush cricket	10		Swiss stone pine	25	
Spiked water milfoil	10		Sycamore	5	
Spotted flycatcher	15		Tamarisk	15	
Stag beetle	20		Tawny grisette	10	

Species	Score	Date spotted	Species	Score	Date spotted
Tawny owl	15		Variable brittlegill	15	
Teal	15		Velvet ant	15	
Tengmalm's owl	25		Velvet shank	10	
Termites	20		Violet ground beetle	5	
Thrift	5		Viper's bugloss	10	
Thrips	5		Volvariella gloiocephala	15	
Tinder fungus	20		Wall brown butterfly	15	
Touch-me-not balsam	25		Wart-biter	25	
Town pigeon	5		Wasp beetle	10	
Treecreeper	15		Water beetle	10	
Tree of Heaven	20		Water boatman	5	
Tree pipit	20		Water cricket	15	
Tree sparrow	20		Water crowfoot	10	
Tree wasp	10		Water forget-me-not	5	
Triangular-stalked garlic	20		Water measurer	10	
Tufted duck	10		Water rail	20	
Tufted vetch	10		Water scorpion	10	
Tulip tree	20		Water shrew	15	
Turkey oak	10		Water soldier	25	
Turkey tail	5		Water springtail	15	
Turnstone	15		Water starwort	10	
Turtle dove	15		Water stick insect	15	
Two-spot ladybird	5		Water violet	20	
Tylopilus felleus	15		Water vole	15	
Ugly milk cap	15		Waxwing	20	
Vapourer moth	10		Weasel	15	

Species	Score	Date spotted	Species	Score	Date spotted
Wellingtonia	10		Wild cat	20	
Western balsam poplar	10		Wild chamomile	15	
Western hemlock	10		Wild cherry	5	
Western red cedar	10		Wild pansy	10	
Wheatear	15		Wild pea	20	
Whimbrel	20		Wild strawberry	15	
Whinchat	15		Willow grouse	25	
Whirligig beetle	5		Willow warbler	10	
Whiskered bat	15		Witch's butter	15	
Whitebeam	10		Woad	20	
White bryony	15		Wolf	25	
White campion	10		Wood anemone	10	
White clover	5		Wood ant	10	
White dead-nettle	5		Wood blewit	15	
White-fronted goose	20		Woodcock	20	
White poplar	10		Wood cricket	15	
White saddle cap	20		Wood groundsel	15	
White stork	25		Wood hedgehog	15	
Whitethroat	15		Wood mouse	10	
White wagtail	25		Woodpigeon	5	
White water-lily	15		Wood sorrel	5	
White willow	5		Wood tiger moth	15	
Whooper swan	20		Wood warbler	20	
Wigeon	15		Wood woundwort	10	
Wild boar	25		Woolly milk cap	10	
Wild carrot	10		Wren	5	

Species	Score	Date spotted	Species	Score	Date spotted
Wych elm	15		Yellow-necked field mouse	15	
Yarrow	5		Yellow pimpernel	10	
Yellow archangel	10		Yellow stainer	15	
Yellowbrain	10		Yellow-tail moth	5	
Yellow-cracked bolete	10		Yellow wagtail	15	
Yellowhammer	10		Yellow water-lily	10	
Yellow horned poppy	15		Yew	5	
Yellow meadow ant	5				

Animal signs

Species	Score	Date spotted	Species	Score	Date spotted
Bird beaks	20		Mammal droppings	5	
Bird droppings	5		Mammal homes above ground	20	
Bird nests	10		Mammal homes below ground	10	
Bird pellets	20		Mammal skulls	20	
Cones eaten by animals	15		Meal remains of plant-eaters	15	
Feathers	5		Meal remains of predators	25	
Fur	5		Nuts eaten by animals	15	
Galls	5		Spider webs	5	

Useful words

These pages explain some specialist words you might come across when reading about flowers, trees, birds, insects, fungi, and animal tracks. Words that are written in *italic* text are defined separately.

abdomen – the rear section of an insect, attached to the *thorax*

air bladders – pockets filled with air, which help some water plants to float

algae – tiny water plants

annual ring – a ring of dark and light wood in the cross-section of a *trunk* or branch that shows one year's growth

antenna (plural: **antennae**) – a pair of feelers on an insect's head used for feeling and smelling

anther – the top part of the *stamen*. It produces *pollen*.

antlers – bony extensions that grow from the head of members of the deer family

bank – sloping land beside a lake, river or stream

bar – a natural mark across a feather or group of feathers

bark – a tough outer layer that protects a tree's insides

belly – part of a bird's body between its *breast* and tail

bill – another word for beak

bird of prey – a bird such as an eagle which hunts other animals for food

blossom – flowers

bract – (1) a leaf-like structure at the base of a *flower* or stalk (2) a leaf-like part of a *cone* supporting the seed

breast – part of a bird's body between its throat and *belly*

breed – (1) a variety of animal within a *species* that has ancestors and distinguishing characteristics in common, for example Jersey cows (2) to produce young

breeding season – the time of year when a pair of birds builds a nest, mates, lays eggs and looks after its young. In Britain this is usually spring.

broadleaved tree (**broadleaf**) – a tree that has wide, flat leaves. Most broadleaved trees are *deciduous*.

bud – an undeveloped *shoot*, leaf or *flower*

bud scale scar – a ring-shaped mark around a twig, left when the *scales* of the *terminal bud* fall off

bulb – a mass of thick, fleshy leaves which store food for a plant under the ground

burrow – a hole in the ground made by an animal for shelter

calyx – a name for all the *sepals* together

cambium – a thin layer that produces new *inner bark* and *sapwood* in a tree *trunk*

camouflage – when an animal's colour makes it difficult to see against certain backgrounds

cap fungus – umbrella-shaped fungus. Its *spore body* is made of a stem and a cap with *gills, pores* or *spines.*

carnivores – animals that feed on other animals

carpel – the female part of the *flower.* It consists of the *stigma, style* and *ovary.*

carrion – the flesh of a dead animal

castes – different physical forms in *colonies* which have different functions

catkin – an often sausage-shaped cluster of tiny *flowers,* all of the same sex, growing on one stalk

chlorophyll – a green chemical found in leaves that absorbs sunlight to help make food for the plant

chrysalis – see *pupa*

cloven hoof – a *hoof* split between two toes

coat – a growth of hair, wool or fur covering an animal's body

cocoon – a case which protects an insect *pupa,* made by the *larva* before it pupates

colony – a group of birds, insects or other animals of the same *species* that live close together

compound eye – an eye made up of many lenses

compound leaf – a type of leaf made up of smaller *leaflets*

cones – the fruits of *conifers*

conifer – a tree with needle-like or scaly leaves, which bears *cones* with their *seeds* inside. Most are *evergreen.*

copse – a small, low woodland

corolla – all a *flower's petals*

cover – anywhere that animals hide themselves, for example hedges, bushes or thick grass

crest – a showy growth of feathers on a bird's head

crown – (1) the collective name given to a tree's branches, twigs and leaves (2) the top part of a bird's head

cutting – a part of a tree, such as a *shoot* or *root,* cut off and used to grow a new tree

deciduous – losing its leaves over a few weeks, usually in autumn

display – courtship behaviour to attract and keep a mate

domesticated – kept by people

drone – male *social insect*

droppings – bird or animal poo

entire leaf – a leaf that has a smooth edge

entomology – the study of insects

estuary – the place where a large river meets the sea; a river mouth. Fresh water is mixed with sea water and at low tide large areas of mud are exposed.

evergreen – losing its leaves throughout the year, so the plant is always green

excrete – to get rid of waste from the body

eyrie – the nest of a bird of prey. The term is generally used for the large nests of eagles.

fawn – a young deer

fern – a flowerless plant that has fronds instead of *leaves* and spores instead of *seeds*

fertilization – the joining of an *ovule* with *pollen* to make a *seed*

filament – the stalk of the *stamen*. It supports the *anther*.

fleshy – plump, thick (used to describe leaves)

flock – a group of birds of the same *species* feeding or travelling together

flower – the part of a plant where new *seeds* are made

flowerhead – a cluster of small *flowers*. It often looks like a single flower.

foliage – all the leaves of a tree

food plant – a plant that an insect *species* feeds on

fore foot – the front foot of a four-legged animal

fruit – the part of a plant that hold its *seeds*

fungus (plural: **fungi**) – a simple, plant-like living thing that typically feeds off dead or living animals and plants

gall – a swelling of plant tissue caused by insects feeding

game bird – a bird such as a pheasant of partridge that is hunted by humans for food or sport

germinate – when a *seed* or *spore* sprouts and begins to grow

gills – the ribs on the underside of a fungus cap or bracket

habitat – the place where a plant or animal *species* lives

heartwood – old wood at the core of the *trunk* that has grown too solid to carry water

herbivores – animals that feed on plants

herd – a group of *mammals* that live together

hibernation – a sleepy state in which some animals survive winter

hind foot – the back foot of a four-legged animal

honeydew – a sweet liquid *excreted* by some insects

hoof – the hard, horny casing covering the toes or lower part of the foot of certain *mammals*

host – a plant or animal that is attacked by a *parasite*

hover – when a bird or insect stays in one place in the air by flapping its wings very fast

humidity – the amount of dampness in the air

hyphae (singular: hypha) – the tiny threads that make up *fungus mycelium* and *spore bodies*

immature – a young bird which has grown out of its juvenile *plumage* but is not yet in adult plumage

inner bark – a layer beneath the outer layer of *bark* that grows every year

intermediate gill – a *gill* that does not run all the way from the edge of the cap to the stem

irruptions – irregular journeys from the usual pattern of *migration*

juvenile – a young bird that does not yet have full, adult *plumage*

larva (plural: **larvae**) – the young stage of an insect which is very different from the adult insect

leaf – flat, thin growth from a plant's *stem*. Leaves make food for the plant.

leaflets – leaf-like sections that make up a *compound leaf*

leaf scar – mark left on a twig where a leaf has fallen off

leaf skeleton – the dried-up remainder of a leaf

lek – an area where the male birds of some *species* gather to perform a courtship *display* to females

lichen – *algae* and *fungi* growing together

lobed leaf – a type of leaf or *leaflet*, partly divided into sections called lobes

local – plants and animals that are found only in certain areas

mammal – a warm-blooded animal that has hair and feeds its young with milk

mandibles – the biting, piercing and cutting mouthparts of an insect

marsh – an area of low-lying land which gets flooded either by a river or the sea

metamorphosis – the process of changing from an egg to an adult, via a *larva* and (often) a *pupa*

migrant – a bird that breeds in one area, then moves to another for the winter, returning again the following spring

migration – a regular movement of birds from one place to another, from the breeding area to the area where they spend the winter. Migrating birds are called *migrants* or visitors.

mimicry – when an animal's shape or colour copies that of another *species*, sometimes of a different *order*, often to put off predators

mixed wood – a woodland that has both broadleaved and coniferous trees

moor – an open area of land that is wet and windy

moult – (1) the shedding of an insect's skin to allow growth (2) when birds lose their old feathers and grow new ones. All birds do this at least once a year.

mushroom – popularly used as a general name for edible *cap fungi*

muzzle – the pointed part of the head of some *mammals*, including the nose and jaw

mycelium – the mass of *hyphae* that a *fungus* is made from, and from which *spore bodies* form

mycology – the study of *fungi*

nape – the back of a bird's neck

native – originally coming from

nectar – a sweet, sticky liquid produced by some plants to attract insects

nocturnal – active at night

nutrients – the goodness in soil on which *fungi* feed

nymph – a young insect which looks like a miniature adult, and acquires wings during growth

offshore – out at sea, some way from a shore

omnivores – creatures that feed on plants and animals

order – one of the scientific divisions of animals

ovary – a female part of a *flower* that contains *ovules*

ovipositor – a female insect's egg-laying organ

ovule – a plant "egg"

pad – the fleshy cushion-like underside of an animal's toes

parasite – a living thing that feeds off another plant or animal without killing it

partial migrant – when some members of a *species* are migrant while others are resident

pasture – a grassland used to provide food for farm animals

pellet – a small parcel of undigested food that has been coughed up by a bird

perch – (1) when a bird stands on a branch or other resting place by gripping with its toes (2) the place where a bird perches

petal – a segment of the *corolla*, usually brightly coloured

plumage – all the feathers on a bird

pollen – a powder made by the flower's male parts for transfer to the female parts to make *seeds*

pollination – when *pollen* reaches the *stigma*

pores – tube openings from which *spores* emerge, on the underside of some *fungi's* caps

predator – an animal that kills and eats other animals

prey – an animal that is hunted by another animal for food

primaries – a bird's large, outer wing feathers

proboscis – a long, tube-like tongue of some insects

pupa (plural: **pupae**) – the stage after the *larval* stage, during which the adult insect develops

queen – a female *social insect* which lays eggs

resident – a bird that can be seen throughout the year

ring – the remains of the *veil* left on the stem of a *cap fungus*

rodent – a small *mammal* that has two pairs of constantly growing teeth used for gnawing

roost – (1) when a bird sleeps (2) a place where birds sleep

rootlet – the smallest of a plant's *roots*

roots – parts of a plant that grow into the ground, absorbing water and goodness from the soil and anchoring the plant

rostrum – the long, tube-like stabbing mouthpart of bugs and weevils

rump – the area of a bird's body above its tail

runner – a stem that grows along the ground

saltmarsh – a marsh which gets flooded by sea water

sand dunes – a mound or ridge of loose sand formed by the wind

sap – a liquid that carries sugars (food made in the leaves) around a plant

sapwood – the outer area of wood in a tree *trunk* that carries water up from the roots to the rest of the tree

scales – (1) the tough, woody parts of a *cone* (2) a *bud's* outer layers

scavenger – an animal that feeds on waste and dead matter

scrub – an area of land covered with grasses, herbs and low shrubs

secondaries – a bird's inner wing feathers

secrete – when an animal's body produces and gives off a chemical from a gland

seed – grows from a fertilized *ovule*, and may eventually form a new plant

seedling – a very young plant that has grown from a *seed*

sepals – leaf or *petal*-like growths which protect the flower *bud* and support the *flower* once it opens

shingle – (1) pebbles that have been rounded and worn to roughly the same small size by the sea (2) a beach which is made up of these pebbles

shoot – a young stem or twig bearing leaves

simple leaf – a type of leaf that is all in one piece

social insects – insects that live in *colonies* and are organized so that each of the *castes* has different duties to keep the colony running smoothly

solitary – living alone

species – a group of plants or animals that all look alike, behave in the same way and can breed together

spine – (1) a stiff, sharp-pointed outgrowth on a plant or animal, or under the cap or bracket of some *fungi* (2) a prickle

spore – a tiny grain from which the *fungus mycelium* will grow

spore body – the part of the *fungus* that can be seen above the surface. It produces *spores* and only grows at certain times of the year - usually autumn.

spur – a tube formed by the *petals* of some flowers. It often contains *nectar*.

stalk – a slender *stem* that supports a *leaf* and attaches it to a larger stem of a plant

stamen – the male part of a *flower*, where *pollen* is made. Each stamen is made up of an *anther* and a *filament*.

stem – the part of a plant that supports the *leaves* and *flowers*, and carries water and food around the plant

stigma – the top part of the *carpel*. It receives the *pollen* when the flower is *pollinated*.

stoop – a Peregrine's dramatic dive at its prey

style – part of the *carpel* which joins the *stigma* to the *ovary*

tendril – a thin stem or leaf that helps a plant to climb

terminal bud – a *bud* at the tip of a *shoot* or twig

territory – the area defended by an animal, or a pair of animals, for breeding

thorax – the middle section of an insect to which the legs and wings are attached

timber – wood, especially when harvested

toadstool – a general term for *cap fungi*, popularly used to refer to a poisonous *fungus*

toothed leaf – a leaf or *leaflet* with jagged edges

track – an animal's footprint

trail – a series of *tracks* made by a moving animal

trunk – the main woody stem of the tree that holds it upright

tuber – a large, underground stem

tundra – a frozen, treeless area in which only small shrubs, mosses and *lichens* can grow

undergrowth – small trees, bushes and plants growing beneath taller trees in a wood or forest

urine – bird or animal wee

variegated – a type of leaf that has two or more colours

veins – tiny tubes inside a leaf that carry water to all parts of the leaf and carry food away from it

veil – the outer "skin" of a young *spore body* that splits to reveal the *gills*

volva – the remains of the *veil* at the base of the stem

wader – one of a group of long-legged birds that live near water and often wade in search of food

waterfowl – birds that spend a lot of time on water

web – a net-like structure of sticky silk threads made by a spider for catching insects

webbing – flaps of skin connecting the toes of some water birds and mammals

weed – a plant that grows on waste or cultivated land, often getting in the way of other plants

worker – female *social insect* that cannot breed. These insects work for the *colony*.

Index

My nature notes

Trees

Holly
page 146

Wild flowers

Creeping Jenny
page 47

Bugs & insects

Rose chafer
page 221

Butterflies & moths

Small heath
page 198

Birds

Tawny owl
page 172

Mammals

Edible dormouse
page 309

Mushrooms & fungi

Chanterelle
page 278